Misinformation Nation

Misinformation Nation

Foreign News and the Politics of Truth
in Revolutionary America

JORDAN E. TAYLOR

Johns Hopkins University Press
Baltimore

© 2022 Johns Hopkins University Press
All rights reserved. Published 2022
Printed in the United States of America on acid-free paper

2   4   6   8   9   7   5   3   1

Johns Hopkins University Press
2715 North Charles Street
Baltimore, Maryland 21218-4363
www.press.jhu.edu

Library of Congress Cataloging-in-Publication Data is available.

ISBN 978-1-4214-4449-9 (hardcover)
ISBN 978-1-4214-4450-5 (ebook)

A catalog record for this book is available from the British Library.

*Special discounts are available for bulk purchases of this book. For more information,
please contact Special Sales at specialsales@jh.edu.*

So convenient a thing is it to be a *reasonable creature*, since it enables one to find or make a reason for everything one has a mind to do.
—Benjamin Franklin, *The Autobiography of Benjamin Franklin*

CONTENTS

ACKNOWLEDGMENTS

This book explores the ways that we are all informed by far-reaching networks of exchange. It is a product of such networks of friends, family, institutions, colleagues, and animals. I am pleased to acknowledge them.

My family made enormous sacrifices to pay for my undergraduate education. Perhaps most significantly, they trusted me to study what I cared about, a form of support that deserving students too seldom receive. Thank you to my parents, grandparents, and sister for teaching me to experience the world with the curiosity and empathy that sustain historical investigation.

As an undergraduate student at the University of Dayton, I benefited from dedicated teachers and mentors. This project grew out of an offhand comment from Michael Carter as I was trying to find a senior thesis topic: that someone should look into anti-Catholicism in the American response to the French Revolution. This isn't that book, but investigating the United States in the 1790s for my undergraduate thesis set me on the path to it.

This book is based on research for my doctoral dissertation, which was completed at Indiana University. I was lucky to have Sarah Knott as my graduate advisor. She guided the project from inception to completion while providing a model of scholarly generosity and precision. Her patient counsel and high expectations helped me to find my strengths as a researcher, writer, and thinker. Likewise, Konstantin Dierks always pushed me to think capaciously and ambitiously. This book would be far less interesting without his unanswerable questions. Additionally, Rebecca Spang, Ben Irvin, and Christina Snyder provided valuable feedback at crucial moments. Thanks to Ed Linenthal, Steve Andrews, and colleagues at the *Journal of American History* for keeping things light.

Thank you to Bloomington friends, including Adrienne Chudzinski, Mark Durbetaki, Dave Eacker, Justin Ellison, Jenn Haylett, Hannah Craddock Mossman, Fielder Valone, Jon Warner, and Bobby Wells. The Lilly Fellows, especially Laura Carlson, Lauren Eriks Cline, Jessica Criales, Josh Hasler, Karen Kovaka, and Stephen Margheim, sustained me during research trips and conferences and from afar. Thanks to Northampton comrades, including Vanessa Adel, Susanna Ferguson, Matt Ghazarian, Bona Kang, Rachel Newman, Javier Puente, Dan Vahaba, and Stefanie Wang, for helping us to make it through the pandemic.

While writing this book, I benefited from workshops, conversations, fellowships, conferences, Twitter exchanges, and reviewers too numerous to mention. Indeed, this book about falsehood would contain many more inaccuracies without the assistance of a larger community of scholars, editors, and public historians. Unlike my historical subjects, I take full responsibility for the errors that remain. Thank you especially to the participants in the Omohundro Institute Scholars' Workshop for two weeks of sparkling conversation. Thank you to the University of Dayton, Indiana University, Smith College, the Massachusetts Historical Society, the Library Company of Philadelphia, the Omohundro Institute of Early American History and Culture, and the National Society of the Colonial Dames of America for providing resources that supported this project. Thanks to Ben Carp and Mark Schmeller for their thoughtful comments and suggestions. Thanks to Laura Davulis and everyone at Johns Hopkins University Press for their help and advice. Thank you to my copyeditor, Merryl A. Sloane, for polishing my prose and sparing many future blushes.

I cannot live without dogs. Thank you to my beagles (and writing companions), Dustin and Charlie.

Thank you to my students at Indiana University–Bloomington, Indiana State University, Indiana University–Southeast, Purdue University–Northwest, and Smith College for challenging me to become a better communicator. Special thanks to Portia Caruso, Eli Cronin, Lena Miller, Elizabeth Sacktor, and Madi Spina for helping me to close the book on Northampton.

But even as I salute the people and institutions that made this book possible, it is worth acknowledging that creating this book has been a difficult journey. Unlike many professional historians, I did not write it as a tenure-track professor, or out of hope that I would one day earn a tenure-track position. Instead, I researched and wrote as a contingent faculty member teaching at several institutions and as an editor working outside of academia. I wrote this book on screens shared with anxious cover letters, sloppy resumes, and a dwindling list of teaching opportunities. A global pandemic didn't help. This book is undoubtedly a product of these contexts.

Ongoing institutional investment would have allowed this research project to blossom in ways that I try not to think about. Unfortunately, US society no longer values higher education or the humanities. Many great historians, including some of my close friends, will never publish their important research because of this shortsightedness. It is a great loss to our shared knowledge of ourselves. That this book has been published, while theirs may never be, is both an accomplishment and a tragedy, a testament more to stubbornness than talent.

One person has made it possible for me to overcome the obstacles of the past few years. My final thanks go to my partner, my wife, my beagle coparent, and my favorite historian, Paula Tarankow. As long as we have been together, she has been my strongest advocate. She used her considerable talents as a listener, thinker, and editor to improve every page of this work. She also understood it years before I did, which was handy. This book—and all that is to come—are for her.

Misinformation Nation

"any thing but the age of Reason"

The crowds roared, but the distance muted them. The banners unfurled, but the horizon swallowed them. In the late eighteenth century, revolutions bloomed across the Atlantic world in beaming colors and booming noises. The global sagas of the French, Haitian, and American Revolutions, as well as lesser-known revolutionary events in places such as Poland, Ireland, and Peru, captivated millions of North Americans. They cared deeply about these revolutions abroad, celebrating the heroes, cursing the villains, and praying for the victims. As revolutions came and went, people adopted new fashions, practiced new politics, and molded new identities. They remade themselves again and again in the image of the era.

Yet despite their absorption, few actually witnessed those heady moments when discontent boiled into revolt or when violence announced itself as re-generation. Instead, those at a distance pieced the era's revolutions together from whispered rumors, printed words, and scribbled letters, from a thousand tiny crumbs of information. Fragile chains of communication allowed North Americans to envision the faraway events that became a part of their realities. By hearing and reading about these events, they imagined them into being. Indeed, for the observers who devoted themselves to unraveling these occurrences, the news may have felt more urgent, more real, than the tedium of their daily lives. Just as it is today, information was indistinguishable from experience.

North Americans had long concerned themselves with news from the world, but the revolutions of the late eighteenth century intensified this interest. For some, news became an object of obsession. When forced by a surplus to omit some foreign news in a 1796 issue of the *Federal Mirror*, New Hampshire printers Elijah Russell and Moses Davis anticipated their readers' impatience and chided them like schoolteachers in a fidgety classroom, "Don't murmur, *patient* readers, you shall have it by and by." Atlantic revolutions, as I explore in this book, were the most important topics for American observers in the late eighteenth century. While some of this news included the spectacular events that historians continue to tell and retell—the destruction of slavery, the decapitation of an ancient dynasty, or new constitutions—still more of it might seem mundane to modern eyes. Newspapers overflowed with granular details about routine troop movements, speeches, legislation, and the comings and goings of foreign monarchs. Whether momentous or minor, all news offered at least the possibility of significance. The great events of the era, observers knew, were composed of many small details, any of which might later seem critical. To lose track of the news even temporarily, then, might mean missing something important. The issue of the *Federal Mirror* that Russell and Davis published a week after their apologetic notice devoted nearly three of its four pages to foreign news and featured almost no domestic information. They shared column after column about revolutionary France and European warfare from "French, London, and Hamburg papers." The most important news concerned the ratification of a treaty between France and Spain, but their pages also recounted a few minor battles and tracked the movements of armies and their leaders. Apparently impressed with this haul, Russell and Davis boasted, "Our readers will find, in this day's paper, much Important Intelligence relative to Foreign Affairs—We hope our News-Mongers will not *grumble* (this week) for want of News."[1]

Readers often had more reason to grumble about an excess, rather than a dearth, of foreign news. The growth of an extensive periodical press across the seventeenth- and eighteenth-century Atlantic world accelerated the production and distribution of news. The sheer volume of information originating from across the early modern world overwhelmed many observers, particularly as much of it proved to be contradictory. A surfeit of news required people to reconcile multiple, competing accounts of the world. Had the Duke of York been captured in battle? Was an account of emancipation in Saint Domingue fabricated? Whereas some contradictory accounts could be resolved in a clear, binary manner, others were subject to more dispute. When would the Irish revolt? How had the queen of France behaved during her execution?

Unfortunately, early North Americans were not very good at dispassionately answering these kinds of questions. While judges relied on rules of evidence in their courtrooms, newsmongers obeyed no rules. Instead, they trusted their intuitions. Treating truth as a commodity, observers sought out and shared the news that reinforced their preferred narratives of the world. The revolutionary events of the era seemed to be a triumph of liberty over despotism for many, while others saw them as conflicts between anarchism and order. Protestant Christians saw signs of a new millennium, while radicals expected an end to imperialism or slavery. With an unending supply of varied raw information, advocates for a particular interpretation of events had no trouble collecting evidence to support their perspective. Like pale mirrors, their letters and newspapers reflected their identities back to them.

Multiple representations of reality destabilized North American politics. As anyone on social media today knows, it is impossible to have a meaningful political discussion with someone who does not share your fundamental understanding of the world. Instead of proceeding along the tidy path of reason and persuasion, the information politics of revolutionary America became bogged in the mud of mutual mistrust and misunderstanding. Foreign news and politics, fact and friction, collided according to a predictable pattern. Encountering multiple renderings of reality, mediators made politicized choices about what foreign information to share with others. This created a context for political action within the continent as people made decisions about which political factions to join, which petitions to sign, and which arguments to pursue based in part on their imperfect understanding of the larger world. They also formed political factions that sustained themselves by molding the truth while accusing their rivals of doing the same. Convinced that their vision of reality was essentially truer than that of their opponents, parties circulated and validated congenial accounts while questioning news that they disliked.

This disordered and politicized distribution of news, so familiar in the twenty-first century, contributed to a polarized, confused, irrational, and ultimately revolutionary political climate. The politics of revolutionary America took shape through innumerable minor disputes about information and its mediation. During the 1770s, for example, even as Patriots and Loyalists disagreed about Parliament's right to tax the colonies, they also disputed the basic details of what was happening in Parliament. During the 1790s, the Republican and Federalist Parties debated the ideas raised in the works of Thomas Paine and Edmund Burke as well as the success of French armies in the Caribbean and Europe. Awash in contradictory, mistaken, and sometimes-fabricated news, people often made important political decisions without truly understanding the world around them. Such disagreements guided Americans' revolutionary politics from the first rumblings of the imperial crisis through the early years of the United States. The late eighteenth-century Age of Revolutions witnessed the birth of not only modern democratic politics but also modern information politics.

It started with rags. Used to clean up kitchen messes, wash windows, or wipe the corners of a child's mouth, rags were an intimate textile, soiled with family labors. Once an old rag reached the end of its usefulness, households sold it to paper mills, where it was boiled, pulped, and recast into the paper that printing offices made into newspapers. Newspapers were not just vessels for information. They were material objects that readers grasped between their fingers, shared with their neighbors, and usually crumpled up to throw away. They were goods that took time, labor, and resources to create and distribute. Their painted fibers were mingled with the sweat of many households. Something of their clotted past remains in the character of early American newspapers. They feel heavy and granular, almost coarse, compared to today's newsprint. Indeed, because they were printed on such durable stock, the newspapers of the eighteenth century that were not immediately discarded will probably outlast many more recent newspapers.[2]

Modern readers might be confused by the chaotic maze of columns and headings in eighteenth-century American newspapers. Their content was not broken into thematic sections nor laid out according to significance, as later newspapers would be. To decode these papers, we must understand the processes that created them. Early newspapers were made up of a series of components that printers and compositors assembled into a whole, like a puzzle. The first and most essential unit was the type, each piece smaller than a newborn's fingernail. A segment of type carried a letter, number, or symbol, which compositors heaped into words, sentences, and paragraphs. The paragraph was the key unit of printed news, the bricks that compositors stacked to build columns, pages, issues, and volumes.[3]

A typical issue of an early American newspaper devoted far more of its paragraphs to news reprinted from distant lands than to any other kind of content. Indeed, many offered little more than a reproduction of news composed in London. Printer Benjamin Franklin explained this preference for the foreign in a 1739 poem about his *Pennsylvania Gazette*:

If Home-Occurrences, that are well known,
And which concern but Few, are let alone:

The Printer sure deserves no Blame for this,
While in the foreign News he's not remiss;
And what important ever happens here
He carefully collects, and renders clear.[4]

While most modern newspapers focus largely on local reporting, in eighteenth-century America there was no point in publishing local news, because it could spread easily through word of mouth before a printer could even think about setting it into type. Early newspapers could go months without publishing any meaningful information about their own city or region. In March 1795, a "Scarcity of News," probably caused by shipping slowdowns during winter weather, led one satirist to joke that the printers should hire someone to investigate the personal lives of politicians or visit prisons and write about their inmates.[5] A few decades later, this sort of reporting was everywhere, but in the small, intimate eighteenth-century communities of North America, the idea of printing such content seemed laughable.

Early newspapers had no reporters. Instead, printers shared whatever they happened to come across, whether that was a rumor in the streets, a letter from an acquaintance, or a report snipped from another newspaper. They swapped copies of their papers for those of distant printing offices, hoping to find something fresh for their readers. This exchange system was just about the only way that a newspaper printer could gather four pages of material each week. Examining a newspaper filled with little more than reprints from other papers, it would be easy to conclude, as at least one irritated Philadelphian did, that the newspaper printer worked as little more than a "copyist."[6] Some of the first histories of the American press echoed this view, telling a story of printers emerging from the inferior status of mechanically providing a "mere statement of *facts*" to eventually taking on more sophisticated and "more important" forms of journalism.[7] Subsequent scholars have generally agreed, characterizing the practice of filling up columns with reprints from abroad as "passive" news-gathering, at best, and "regurgitated journalism," at worst.[8]

But these authors have not looked closely enough. Printers did not simply share a random assortment of news, even if they sometimes claimed to do so. They curated materials that they believed to be newsworthy or to express essential truths about the world. Brick by brick, paragraph by paragraph, they carefully constructed a reality for their readers to inhabit.

Assembling, printing, and distributing an eighteenth-century newspaper required a mix of hard labor and subtle skills. Most newspapers were printed on both sides of one large sheet of paper, which was folded in half to form four pages. Printing offices usually laid out advertisements, essays, older news, and other material that was not time sensitive on the side of the paper that, when folded, would become the front and back pages. A team of journeymen and apprentices then performed the back-aching labor of pressing ink onto that side of the paper hundreds of times. As they waited for the ink to dry on these pages, the printer and his workers put together the interior of the issue, which usually included the latest news.

Most of this news was arranged into sections according to the city where it was first published. Printers typically arrayed these geographic segments roughly according to how distant the place of origin was from themselves. The farthest news appeared earliest, so that a printer in Philadelphia would place news reprinted from Calcutta before Paris, Paris before Kingston, and Kingston before New York. This layout allowed printers to ensure that distant news was included as it arrived in the print shop, leaving room for regional or local news only if space allowed. The local section, which was headed with the name of the newspaper's city of publication and usually appeared on the third page, was one of the last sections to be typeset. It often lacked any local news. Instead, printers regularly used the local section to describe various rumors floating around the city as well as to summarize any news from abroad that had arrived too late to be shared at greater length elsewhere.

When newspaper printers reproduced something from another newspaper, they usually placed it under a heading, also called a head. If paragraphs were bricks, headings held them together like mortar. Unlike modern headlines, which provide an attention-grabbing summary of a news item's contents, eighteenth-century news headings functioned more like citations. Most simply provided the city where the news had originally appeared and the date of its publication. A heading such as "Dublin, Jan. 25" told readers that the material in succeeding paragraphs had been taken from a Dublin newspaper published on January 25.[9] Other headings provided more citational detail. "From the Dublin Journal, Jan. 25" told readers exactly which issue of which newspaper the material had come from.[10] Others described not just the source but also the material context and labor involved in conveying the news across the ocean. A typical heading in a 1795 Philadelphia newspaper cited "Latest London Accounts, by an Arrival at Charleston and the Ship Young Eagle, Pride, Arrived at New-York, from Dublin."[11] This heading informed readers that this bit of news had moved from London, where it was originally printed, to Dublin to Charleston (aboard the ship *Young Eagle*, led by Captain Pride) to New York and finally to Philadelphia, where it was republished. Of course, while news under such a heading was first printed in London, its actual contents may have had nothing to do with that city. A paragraph under a London heading might contain parliamentary debates or a summary of a Dutch newspaper or, as in this case, a report about political ferment in Eastern Europe.

Scholars have paid little attention to the foreign news that made up the bulk of early American newspapers, but they have completely ignored the citational headings that introduced this news. This makes sense: citations are boring little things, easily ignored and forgotten. Many readers of this book will likely skip its endnotes, because citations are usually understood to be subordinate to a larger narrative. Yet when read carefully, citations can tell us how that narrative came into being. Indeed, newspaper headings tell an important story of their own. Through their ubiquity, they show that Americans cared about knowing the places, people, and media through which they derived their news.[12] Moreover, the format and character of these citations transformed during the eighteenth century in ways that help us to understand North Americans' changing cultures of information. By citing the "London (or Lying) Gazette" or the "Courier du Bas Rhine, a Paper to Which Considerable Authority Has Always Been Attached," mediators expressed their evolving views of how information ought to flow.[13]

Citational headings tell us even more when examined in the aggregate. While historical sources are often most notable for their scarcity or brevity, the sheer abundance of newspaper headings made them difficult for previous historians to analyze. Digging through traditional archives to collect enough headings for a clear picture of information flows in the eighteenth century would have once been the work of a lifetime. The digitization of massive newspaper collections, though, has provided access to hundreds of thousands of headings at once. I have accumulated and analyzed tens of thousands of headings that cited a specific newspaper source in order to understand changing patterns of information flows, as I discuss in more detail in the appendix. Though rather dull on the surface, these newspaper headings disclose a dynamic world in which war, politics, diplomacy, commerce, and mediators' preferences shaped how information moved into and within North America. They tell us, in their way, the story of how revolutionary Americans came to know the world around them.

Uncovering this story requires looking beyond the traditional terrain of revolutionary America. In the final year of the eighteenth century, printer David Carlisle of the Walpole, New Hampshire, *Farmer's Weekly Museum* affixed a short poem above his summaries of the week's news. It promised: "We travel and expatiate, as the bee / From flower to flower, so we from land to land." From these "travels," they "suck intelligence in every clime / And spread the honey of our deep research, / At our return, a rich repast for you."[14] Carlisle understood his job as gathering and digesting news from around the world. Focusing solely on the history of news within revolutionary America, then, would be like telling a story of pollinators without pollen. It would ignore the ways that complex international and continental exchanges shaped national politics. Thus, while I primarily explore the history of the settler population of British North America and the United States, this is neither a fully national nor an entirely transnational story.

Instead, I engage with early America as one set of nodes in a vast global web of information exchange. Information networks took shape through pressures exerted by the environment, Atlantic trade, and the needs of localities, nations, and empires.[15] Comparing the United States with its neighboring colonial territories of Canada and Louisiana, as I do in the book's second half, illuminates how national and imperial boundaries restricted certain kinds of information exchanges as well as the ways that political actors evaded those limitations. The slow, fitful globalization of the early modern world ensured that all knowledge about events abroad was tenuous and uncertain. It was never inevitable that American observers would experience global news as they did. Rather, their image of the world, an image through which they defined themselves, came into form with the tides and currents of Atlantic history.

Many people are familiar with the truism "knowledge is power," but we too seldom recognize the inverse point: power can create knowledge. Something false may be acknowledged as true because the most powerful members of a society can convince or compel others to accept it. Dominant groups seek to define one account of reality, while aspirants project an alternative vision. For that reason, in popular systems of government, politics and truth are always entangled.[16] So it was during the American Revolution. The era's newspapers, pamphlets, and letters reveal a dramatic but largely unknown story about how contests for truth became central to American politics.

During the seventeenth century, information about events abroad spread mostly through letters and conversations. Anyone could share a rumor, and those who disliked such loose talk, including government administrators and religious leaders, found it almost impossible to contain. Over time, new information systems, including newspapers, allowed British colonial adminis-trators to exercise some control over the flow of news. As I show in chapter 1, a "mediation revolution" during the eighteenth century enabled a small num-ber of elite men to seize greater power in interpreting and defining truth. If someone wanted to share news that put the British empire, monarchy, or gov-ernment in a negative light, for example, colonial officials could declare it false and thereby limit the spread of the printed materials conveying that in-formation. Subject to the will of colonial administrators, newspaper printers generally abided by these restrictions. They even perpetuated the useful my-thology that they were not actual mediators of news, but rather "meer me-chanics," passing along the news as it came to them.[17]

In the 1760s, many British colonists began to question colonial officials' trustworthiness as information mediators. In chapter 2, I explore how pro-testing settlers critiqued what they called the "misrepresentations" of colonial leaders, who apparently exaggerated news from the colonies for their own purposes. Rather than accepting administrators' authority as brokers of news, colonists sought to define the truth about the world for themselves and to hold their leaders accountable for any departures from that truth. During the 1760s and 1770s, the angry settlers calling themselves Patriots began to shift the responsibility for determining the truthfulness of foreign news from co-lonial officials to a larger political community. Patriot newspaper printers took up prominent roles in this process, as I argue in chapter 3. They began to think of themselves not as conduits through which information passed, but rather as purposeful curators of truthfulness in a sea of contradiction and falsehood. Their methods for determining what was true, which involved scrutinizing news produced by the British ministry while largely accepting the testimony of opposition sources, turned out to be ineffective. By embracing several cru-cial misperceptions, they helped to catalyze the American Revolution.

Postrevolutionary Americans decided to take charge of how foreign infor-mation would flow through the new US republic. After complaining for years about British news sources during the imperial crisis and revolutionary war, as I show in chapter 4, powerful US mediators sought out alternative news flows from Europe. Because of commercial limitations, this process had begun slowly until the French revolutionary wars temporarily scrambled the cir-cuits of Atlantic information streams. Creating and protecting a steady flow of truthful reporting became urgent as Americans thought more carefully about the relationship between news and revolution. In chapter 5, I examine how American observers during the 1780s and 1790s articulated what I call the "information script" of revolution, which claimed that news of successful revolutionary change could spark imitative uprisings among oppressed peoples. They tied revolutionary events in Ireland, the Netherlands, Peru, France, Poland, and elsewhere to the example of the American Revolution. In the mid-1790s, as I document in chapter 6, revolutionary activists across North America unsuccessfully attempted to use this script to incite a continental revolt against despotism in British Canada and Spanish Louisiana. Abiding by a similar set of assumptions, colonial leaders in Canada and Louisiana fought to contain such information, with more success.

The American revolutionaries' rejection of the British government's authority to mediate news from abroad left unanswered many questions about who would decide what news was true. While Patriot control over most of the continent's presses had left little doubt about who held epistemic authority in the 1770s, during the 1780s and 1790s many groups vied to mediate foreign news. Under the new federal government created by the US Constitution, the Federalist and Republican Parties, as I show in chapter 7, waged a partisan information war about the French Revolution. Compared to Canada, where a steady stream of Francophobic news arrived from Britain, US observers contended with an enormous number of contradictory accounts about the revolution coming from France, Britain, and elsewhere in Europe. This was never the case, though, for the revolutions of the Caribbean in the 1790s. In chapter 8, I describe how a different assortment of media, more commercial in nature than news about revolutionary France, promoted a dehumanized and depoliticized version of Black-led revolutions in Saint Domingue, Grenada, Saint Vincent, and elsewhere.

Since the 1760s, many Americans had come to believe that ordinary people should be able to interpret foreign news and define truth for themselves. But only if they got it right. Even the most optimistic Patriots in the 1770s were unwilling to accept a fully democratic system of truth. By the 1790s, though, a freewheeling and cacophonous culture of news had developed. This openness, especially as the United States drifted toward war with France, worried the nation's Federalist leaders. Allowing an unrestrained flow of news, they believed, would invite malicious French deceivers to lure the people into embracing revolutionary radicalism. Fueled by an apparent crisis of false news, as I describe in chapter 9, they attempted to reverse this democratization of news mediation and regain some control over how information moved. These efforts ultimately backfired. A consensus coalesced around the idea that gov-

ernments should avoid regulating or mediating the news. This libertarian notion has proven to be remarkably resilient. Indeed, Americans still inhabit the
permissive news culture inspired by the Federalists' failures.

Americans in the late eighteenth century witnessed a series of massive
political transformations. There was not one decisive American Revolution,
but several revolutionary changes: from monarchy to republic, from colonists
to colonizers, from Anglophobes to Francophobes, and eventually from elite-
driven Federalist rule to the more populist leadership of the Republican Party.
When a revolution overturns established truths about government, it often
seems like the arrival of new information: the king, it turns out, is not as just
as we once thought. The constitution does not work as well as we believed.
The American Revolution and the various political changes of the late eighteenth century happened not only because of new ideas, but also because new
evidence arrived that seemed to support drastic action. A political revolution
is an accumulation of small truths that add up to something bigger. As people encounter new information, the premises that once supported older political arrangements fall away. In that sense, every revolution is an information
revolution.

I track several historical changes across the following chapters: a diversifica-
tion of foreign information sources, a politicization of news, and a narrowing
of mediation. Together, these changes caused misinformation to metastasize
in the late eighteenth century, steering many Americans into powerful misperceptions. During the 1760s and 1770s, for example, Patriot observers came
to believe that the British ministry was conspiring to deprive them of their
liberties, that the ministry was vulnerable to its rivals, and that Patriot mobilization might topple it. During the Reign of Terror in revolutionary France,
many believed that accounts of French violence and radicalism were exaggerated. By the mid- to late 1790s, even as France veered toward a more moderate
and stable government, a substantial number of Americans credited reports
suggesting that the French, led by a secret society called the Illuminati, were
nefarious villains bent on world domination. White Americans also generally
regarded the several revolutionary movements in the Caribbean during the
1790s as apolitical slave revolts. These beliefs and many more were, at their
core, inaccurate. Not everyone believed them, but each of these misperceptions attracted enough attention to powerfully affect the era's politics.

Early Americans assumed that the falsehoods rampaging through their society were the result of willful deception. Lacking a nuanced model of causality, they usually attributed errors to human intentions. Enemies seemed to lurk everywhere, confusing and cozening the innocent.[18] Quite correctly, some blamed falsehoods on the politicization of foreign and domestic news-gathering institutions. Others blamed the wiles of foreign agents and diplomats. Some also feared that financial speculators were manipulating commerce and earning undeserved profits through deception.[19] Error always reduced to self-interest.

Historians have long acknowledged that revolutionary Americans' understanding of the world often misaligned with reality, to put it nicely. They have not agreed, though, on the reasons. In the first half of the twentieth century, fearful of the manipulation of public opinion that helped to mobilize the world wars, a group of so-called Progressive historians, including John C. Miller and Philip Davidson, argued that a small number of Patriot elites during the American Revolution intentionally spread untruthful propaganda to mobilize the people.[20] Cold War–era "consensus" historians, such as Bernard Bailyn and Gordon S. Wood, rejected this interpretation and instead claimed that the revolutionary generation embraced falsehoods because their sincere attachment to deep-seated ideologies had caused them to become prone to conspiratorial "paranoia."[21]

While there is evidence to support each of these interpretations, getting caught up in these dramas of propaganda and paranoia, dupes and deceivers, can lead us to miss the duller, more ordinary ways that false information spread around the early modern world. I suggest that the American revolutionary generation constructed its misshapen view of the world primarily through well-intentioned but misguided efforts to interpret Atlantic information sources.[22] While deceitfulness can produce misperceptions, it is not necessary for them because errors are an inevitable consequence of communication. Humans are not very good at relaying complicated information to one another. While the most effective information systems encourage dispassionate and patient verification to minimize mistakes, the inefficient and unstable tools used in the early modern world often magnified them. American observers learned that printing presses allowed for a remarkably efficient replication of errors, ranging from misspellings (which I have left uncorrected in the quotations throughout this book) to major misunderstandings about the world.

Alongside the material constraints of early news-gathering, another fundamental reason that Americans embraced false news was because they experienced information socially. When people cannot fully investigate the premises behind a particular account of the world, which is quite often, they rely on those whom they most trust and identify with. Americans often evaluated news by discounting anything produced by nations, parties, governments, or groups that they distrusted. While this skepticism was sometimes well justified, it meant that they often listened only to sources they were likely to agree with and dismissed the rest. Though some people deliberately skewed the news for their own benefit, even those with the best intentions struggled to identify and share only truthful news. Much of the foreign news that American observers encountered did not need the help of malign mediators to be false any more than it required a fantastic imagination to seem outrageous. As truth became politicized, misinformation was unavoidable.

At stake in this story, though, is more than just the origins of particular false beliefs. In this book, I also address a more fundamental question about the origins of revolutionary politics, which observers have been debating since the late eighteenth century. Everyone agrees that the era of the American Revolution included significant political changes, but there is much less agreement as to why and how it happened. Why do revolutions happen at all? What turns political conviction into action? Why does anyone ever bother to argue with their neighbors, organize petitions, enforce boycotts, fight wars, and create new institutions? These questions might also be framed in psychological terms. What compels a person to do something so irrational and dangerous as to attempt to dethrone the most powerful people in their society?

Looking back on the revolutionary era in an 1805 letter, the American politician John Adams insisted that it should not be remembered as a time of wisdom, deliberation, and reason. Instead, he preferred to think of it as an "Age of Frivolity," though he "would not object if You had named it the Age of Folly, Vice, Frenzy Fury, Brutality, Daemons, Buonaparte, Tom Paine, or the Age of The burning Brand from the bottomless Pitt: or any thing but the age of Reason."[23] Adams's suggestions did not stick. Instead of emphasizing the folly of the era, many of those who lived through it and most of those looking back on it defined it according to the circulation of new theories about self-government, liberty, and equality, which originated in humanity's capacity for reason and self-reflection. Popular interpreters of the American Revolution, especially, often attribute revolutionaries' actions primarily to their devotion to vague, lofty principles, which also happen to accord with modern concepts of justice.

The question of how these revolutions happened continues to engage scholars. One group has proposed that revolutionary politics, broadly speaking, resulted from changing social, cultural, and economic conditions. This view builds in part on the insights of the German theorist Jürgen Habermas, who found that the early modern era witnessed the rise of a new "public sphere," which existed outside the realms of the state and the family. The public sphere took shape over time through networks forged in shared spaces, such as salons, coffeehouses, and newspapers. The existence of such public spaces allowed middling, bourgeois individuals to articulate shared interests and deliberate their way toward actions that would serve those interests.[24] For most of Habermas's acolytes, then, revolution emerged indirectly from the burgeoning public sphere to serve those who took upon themselves the mantle of the "public."[25] A second body of interpretation places early American politics within a larger realm of political thought stretching back to the Renaissance, the Reformation, the English Civil War, and the Enlightenment. According to these scholars, deep intellectual currents propelled the American revolutionaries into action.[26] For Bernard Bailyn, in particular, strongly held principles and ideologies provided revolutionaries with the "apparatus by which the world was perceived," defining how political actors experienced the world and responded to it.[27]

I offer a different though not incompatible interpretation. To understand how the revolutionaries' worldview led them to resist imperial rule, take up arms, and create a new nation, we must carefully reconstruct not only their social and intellectual worlds, but also their informational worlds. The news that they consumed, though often inaccurate, was an essential foundation for their political action. This is not to say, of course, that false accounts of reality on their own can propel such mobilization nor that information flows alone determined the shape of early American politics. Though inadequate by themselves, misperceptions were often necessary premises for political mobilization.

People throw themselves into the political fray for all kinds of reasons, but there is no route to meaningful political action that does not involve the conjoined perceptions, or misperceptions, that something significant is wrong with the world and that one's actions might help to set it right. This observation is perhaps so obvious that it has largely gone without notice. Of course people act according to their perceptions of the world. From where else would their actions derive? Yet because perceptions are to a significant degree built on news, and because early modern news could be easily manipulated and misunderstood, the perceptions that drove politics were often divorced from historical realities. Political viewpoints fundamentally arise from disagreements either about perceptions or about the significance and implications of those perceptions. Politics is not only a way of thinking and acting; it is also a way of seeing, hearing, and knowing.

Whether they are popular or scholarly works, histories of the American Revolution that center ideology and principled resistance provide a durable foundation for American national identity. Focusing on the late eighteenth century as a clear-minded moment of rupture between monarchy and republicanism, despotism and liberty, and aristocracy and democracy legitimizes and sanitizes revolutionary politics. The notion that high-minded ideals about liberty propelled the American revolutionaries is the sort of stuff to launch a Fourth of July parade. Acknowledging that misperception was essential to the founding of the United States paints a far less glamorous portrait of national beginnings. Adams's characterization of the Age of Revolutions as "any thing but the age of Reason" is not the sort of quotation that schoolchildren are likely to be quizzed on.

And yet even Adams's contemporary ideological rival Thomas Paine, who was far less cynical about the promise of revolutionary change and who remains an icon for those who view the American Revolution and the Age of Revolutions as a contest of principles, understood this era not only in terms of the revolutionary ideas he espoused, but also through the news he experienced. In a passage tucked away near the conclusion of his 1791 pamphlet, *Rights of Man*, Paine coined the term "Age of Revolutions." Reflecting on the tumultuous world around him, he wrote, "From what we now see, nothing of reform in the political world ought to be held improbable. It is an age of Revolutions, in which every thing may be looked for."[28] Though Paine's work is rightly remembered for its radical ideas, his description of the era referred neither to rights nor reason nor democracy nor the shredding of empires. He did not describe the period according to the outcome of events, which remained uncertain. Instead, at the moment of its first articulation, Paine identified the Age of Revolutions through the language of news. It was a time of *looking* at extraordinary events and *seeing* old things in new ways. Eventfulness, anticipation, and possibility defined how people experienced this moment. It was an age of observation, full of echoes and fog. It was anyone's guess what would come next.

CHAPTER ONE

Foreign Advices and False Friends

The Mediation Revolution in British America

British Americans felt deeply their global irrelevance. When they reached for their newspapers or listened to the latest reports at their taverns, they often sought news from abroad. Even to those who lived there, North America's settlements seemed like a dull backwater next to the metropolis of London, the great canals of Venice, the minarets of Constantinople, or the bustle of Mexico City. Did the people of those great cities care what happened in Charleston or Quebec? Most North Americans would have had to admit that they did not. Local events mattered, of course. Crime, business, gossip, and scandal never failed to garner interest among neighbors. Yet when eighteenth-century North Americans looked for the day's great events, the news that would reshape their world, their gaze fell not on themselves but on the harbors and post roads where news arrived from far away.

A nineteenth-century Parisian newspaper editor was once quoted as claiming that for his readers, "an attic fire in the Latin Quarter is more important than a revolution in Madrid."[1] For early American observers, though, something nearly the reverse was true. Foreign news, and especially news of revolutions abroad toward the century's end, attracted extraordinary interest. Indeed, the priority of the foreign was visible in the mastheads of many early North American newspapers, where the most common newspaper motto promised readers the "Freshest Advices, Foreign and Domestick."

In the inaugural issue of the Peacham, Vermont, *Green Mountain Patriot*, printers Amos Farley and Samuel Goss announced that they had been encouraged to produce their paper by "the ardent thirst for novelty—the general cry of 'What's the news abroad.'" In that 1798 issue, they met this demand with columns of reprinted news from Paris, Venice, and London. If these reprints were not enough, their readers would have found that much of the news under American headings was American printers' summaries of events in Europe and the Caribbean. Under the Charleston heading, for example, readers learned about Spanish reports of French pirates. Beneath "Baltimore" was news from Barbados and France. There were reports from Portugal under "Norfolk," Louisiana under "Pittsburg," and Austria, Louisiana, and France under "New York." If that still wasn't enough, under the Peacham heading Farley and Goss provided short descriptions of news from Paris, Milan, Sardinia, Naples, Barbados, and Saint Vincent.[2] For one week, at least, the cry had been answered, the thirst slaked.

Farley and Goss's emphasis on the public's need for foreign news was, to be sure, self-serving. Asking newspaper printers to assess their readers' appetite for any sort of news is like asking a hound if he needs a treat. An honest accounting is unlikely. Perhaps the most powerful testimony to North Americans' hunger for foreign news, then, was not printers' assertions but the actual content of their newspapers. More than two-thirds of a typical issue related to events abroad, which usually originated from Europe or the Caribbean.[3] Many issues were assembled by heaping together excerpts from British papers, with perhaps a column or two from a Dutch or French press. When a newspaper had not received fresh foreign news in a few weeks, readers would complain, leaving printers to plead for future ship arrivals to "relieve us from our present state of anxiety."[4] When he experienced a "dearth of news" in 1782, Philadelphia printer Eleazer Oswald apologized to readers for presenting a variety of uninteresting material "with not even one solitary column of useful, foreign information."[5]

How did North Americans gather this news from abroad? This simple question has some complicated answers, which historians have generally neglected.[6] In the eighteenth century, the amount of foreign news available in British North America grew unmanageable. To be intelligible, the continent's letters, newspapers, and rumors needed to be organized, summarized, filtered, and restrained. Foreign news, in short, needed to be mediated. This mediation revolution allowed a small group of elites to interpret massive quantities of news for observers more efficiently than in the past. The process heightened existing social inequalities and set the stage for decades of arguments about whether news mediators could be trusted. In the years to come, popular fears of misinformation were often rooted in concerns about unfaithful mediation.

Those empowered by the mediation revolution were not especially skilled nor even particularly interested in identifying and limiting the spread of falsehoods. That was never their priority. Indifferent to truth, they focused on maintaining profits and power. Even if they had decided to devote themselves to combating falsehoods, they lacked the tools and resources to do so effectively. To their credit, early mediators recognized their own limitations and accepted their role as curators of information rather than of truth. That attitude, though, did not last for long. By the end of the eighteenth century, a growing demand for truth pushed mediators to generate more errors than ever before.

British Americans rarely encountered the word "network." When they did, it often referred to fishing nets or ornamental lace, as when a newspaper advertised "Silk Clogs, Gloves, Silk and Thred Network."[7] The idea of a "communications network" would have meant nothing to them. Yet this early, more material sense of the term is worth considering alongside our modern understanding. In eighteenth-century printed sources, the word was often hyphenated as "net-work," a rendering that emphasizes the "work" involved, like "needlework" or "woodworking." This is appropriate for our purposes because communications networks *were* work. They did not come into being on their own, but resulted from the labor of thousands of writers, correspondents, printers, apprentices, journeymen, post riders, readers, ship captains, sailors, travelers, and speakers around the world.

Much of the work that allowed people to exchange information across oceans was commercial in nature. Early modern Atlantic information networks did not stand alone but latched on to more vibrant and powerful commercial networks. Some historians have asked us to think of the Atlantic Ocean as a "highway" of exchange, rather than a barrier.[8] While this metaphor might apply to many forms of mobility and trade, it can only partially describe the movement of information across the ocean. If news traveled on an Atlantic highway, it was neither as a driver nor as a passenger, but rather as a hitchhiker. Its movement was uncertain and subject to the will of others. It traveled only as quickly as its carrier and could be steered off course or lost entirely at the discretion of those who cared little about its eventual destination.

Most information media arrived in British America aboard commercial vessels, carried by captains, sailors, and passengers. Before he embarked on a journey, a ship captain generally collected any letters intended for his destination. He and his crew also inevitably imbibed local reports and rumors along with whatever else they imbibed before their departure. Upon a ship's arrival, the letters it carried would often be taken to a public space and distributed to the intended recipients. Oral reports from the ship's travelers and sailors circulated in taverns, churches, and coffeehouses.[9] These material and commercial exchanges, the work of networks, allowed information to move through space in the early modern world.

But in seventeenth-century British America, detailed information about the broader world remained quite scarce. Transatlantic passages were less routine than they would later become, and so long-distance communication was challenging to sustain.[10] As Virginia planter William Byrd wrote to his cousin in 1690, "Wee are here att the end of the World, & Europe may bee turned topsy turvy ere wee can hear a Word of itt." The scarcity of news made it easy for engaged settlers to absorb all the significant foreign occurrences circulating within their community. When the news did arrive, Byrd continued, "wee have itt by whole Sale, very often much more then truth."[11] As one settler put it in 1669, we are "longing for news."[12]

Letters were valuable channels of information, but transatlantic correspondences were fountains of frustration. Someone in North America could expect to wait three to four months for a response to a letter sent to Europe. An epistolary relationship might be halted indefinitely if, as often happened, a letter went astray. Much could go wrong during months of travel, and letters were often damaged, lost, discarded, or forgotten on their journey. Only the most persistent correspondents could maintain ongoing transatlantic letter exchanges. Because letters traveled along the lines of existing personal, professional, and political relationships, the most well-connected members of a society tended to send and receive the most letters.

Conversation was a more accessible and democratic communications medium than letters. Not everyone could read news or maintain personal channels of communication overseas, but anyone with an ounce of curiosity could overhear and share rumors, chatter on the streets, or interrogate a traveler for information. Rumor was not an ideal information medium because it so often blossomed into exaggeration and error, but it was highly decentralized. There could be no rigid hierarchies in an information economy built around interpersonal communication because no single person could direct how rumors flowed. For that reason, compared to later systems for gathering news, rumor-based information economies empowered women, enslaved people, and non-elites. This egalitarian news medium was a problem for some. Male leaders chastised women who exercised their voices as being scolds and gossips.[13] White enslavers feared that unheard whispers among enslaved people might stir revolt.[14] Uncontrolled rumors seemed to be dangerous to the public order. In 1685, Virginia governor Francis Howard complained that people's "vain imaginations and conceit" were "esteemed as news," which he believed had caused all of the "sedition and faction" in the colony.[15]

Seeking greater control over speech and news in the second half of the seventeenth century, elites in many British colonies, including Connecticut, Maryland, Massachusetts, New York, North Carolina, Pennsylvania, South Carolina, and Virginia, passed laws barring the spread of "false news."[16] By the 1690s, according to historian Larry Eldridge, prosecutions for spreading false news made up around 15 percent of British American colonial court cases.[17] Governments declared almost any destabilizing speech to be false. Many early prosecutions focused on libels against individual officeholders, but by the late seventeenth century, they increasingly targeted people for spreading rumors about faraway events. Despite these prosecutions, as well as many declarations debunking particular rumors, government officials and other mediators could not control the spontaneous diffusion of "false" foreign rumors.[18]

Truth was often the most dangerous news. When William of Orange and Mary Stuart swept into power in England during the Glorious Revolution of 1688, the Boston allies of the deposed King James tried to keep the news quiet. A passenger from England, John Winslow, recalled purchasing a copy of a declaration written by William so that he could carry it across the ocean to inform the people of New England that they should expect a "speedy deliverance . . . from arbitrary power." Edmund Andros, governor of the Dominion of New England, tried to confiscate the printed account that Winslow had brought. When Winslow refused to turn it over, Andros imprisoned him for "bringing *traitorous and treasonable libels* and papers of news."[19] It made little difference. Unable to contain this information, Andros's government soon fell to an uprising of Bostonians.[20] While a government could try to contain printed news, rumors were unstoppable, as relentless as fate.

As the settler population of the British American colonies expanded during the seventeenth and early eighteenth centuries due to a prodigious birthrate and large-scale migration, greater numbers of ships crossed the Atlantic to import and export commodities. One by-product of this trade was the arrival of more news reports. By the eighteenth century, news was no longer as scarce as it had once been. Rather, as observers' capacity to sort through the news became inadequate to its extent, they took up innovative uses of existing information media. Not quite a "media revolution" in the way that the term is sometimes applied to technological advances in print, broadcast, or digital communication, this was more precisely a mediation revolution.

From the late seventeenth century well into the eighteenth century, Americans saw the processes of transatlantic communication become more formal, centralized, and hierarchical. Managing a growing quantity of news required colonists and officials to develop two new, interdependent information systems in the early eighteenth century: a postal network and newspapers. Notably, these new information systems did not rely on any significant technological advances.[21] Between the inventions of the printing press in the fifteenth century and the telegraph in the mid-nineteenth century, Western communications technology remained remarkably stagnant. While they relied on communication tools that differed little from those in use three centuries before, the people of the eighteenth-century Atlantic world found new ways to harness them to manage a glut of news.

An increasingly efficient eighteenth-century postal system allowed handwritten as well as printed news to travel more predictably across space.[22] Early colonists' letters had moved around the Anglo-American world largely "by chance opportunity and personal favor," which meant that distant correspondences were difficult and uncertain.[23] In the early eighteenth century, the British government sought to remedy this problem with legislation to rationalize and mediate the transatlantic movement of letters. Slowly, the British empire established post offices, built post roads, and appointed local postmasters, who hired post riders to carry news between offices. Some entrepreneurial individuals also experimented with transatlantic packet ships, which carried mail and passengers on designated routes at scheduled times, though it was not until the 1750s that a successful packet service finally began.[24] Decades of gradual improvement and the creation of a specialized class of professional mediators allowed letters to travel with more certainty and efficiency. This also, though, placed epistolary communications under the watchful eye of British authorities, who inspected letters and withheld newspapers at will.[25]

Additionally, the British Atlantic experienced an explosion of newspapers during the eighteenth century. In earlier decades, news had sometimes traveled through the Anglophone world in printed broadsides or handwritten newsletters. In 1665, the British government began publishing the *London Gazette*, which remained the only legally sanctioned newspaper in the British realm for decades. Copies of the *Gazette* circulated in North America, and printers sometimes shared important extracts as broadsides. Thirty years later, everything changed when nothing happened. In 1695, Parliament failed to renew the Licensing Act, which had limited the production of newspapers in Britain and its dependencies.[26] In consequence, dozens of papers sprang up throughout the British realm. In London and in provincial Britain, a rich variety of newspapers and magazines competed for a growing transatlantic readership.

It took some time for British North America to develop its own newspaper culture. Fearing that newspapers would bring disobedience, colonial governors discouraged them. Only slowly did some governors realize that they could use newspapers to advance their own agendas. A decade after the lapse of the Licensing Act, just one very careful newspaper was printed in the colonies. But even without the threat of regulation, there was hardly enough news in seventeenth- and early eighteenth-century British America to bother printing it. Newspapers thrived in information-rich environments with relevant and interesting news arriving at regular intervals.[27] The proliferation of European newspapers in the late seventeenth and early eighteenth centuries, the creation of a reliable postal system, and growing transatlantic commerce were therefore necessary precursors for the emergence of American newspapers. As a result, the periodical press expanded only gradually in British America for most of the eighteenth century. A single paper was being published in 1710, 7 in 1730, and 14 in 1750. The American Revolution and the global Age of Revolutions, though, accelerated their growth by generating greater demand for news. By 1770, more than 30 papers were published in British America, and the number of newspapers printed in the United States swelled after the American Revolution: 106 by 1790 and 260 by 1800.[28]

As newspapers gained popularity, new exchange practices developed. Much as they collected letters, ship captains began gathering local papers before they departed a port and offering them to local officials or printers once they disembarked. Moreover, the recipients of interesting letters, who had long shared their contents with others, began funneling them to newspaper printers for extraction and publication. While foreign news had once spread organically from person to person, during the eighteenth century it was increasingly directed to printing and post offices, where a small number of government-aligned mediators sorted and distributed it.

Printers also exchanged information with each other. In an era before stringent rules about intellectual property, it was normal and indeed expected for newspaper printers to share materials that appeared in other papers. By pooling their news resources across cities and continents, printers could benefit from anything interesting that one of them happened to encounter. This was necessary because like any physical artifact, newspapers moved in unpredictable ways. A printer could never anticipate what a particular ship or post rider would bring: sometimes exciting letters and newspapers, sometimes nothing at all. Printers often received papers that had been published earlier than previously received accounts from the same place, making them nearly worthless. Who wanted to read about an army's march toward the enemy after they had already learned the result of the battle? Some printers could not conceal their irritation at this: "Capt. Lark brings nothing new—altho' he is the latest arrival."[29] As with people, some ships just weren't very interesting.

It would have been ideal for ships to arrive regularly from a variety of ports, allowing observers to gather a predictable stream of intelligence from around the world. But because packet boats only provided a small fraction of Atlantic traffic, the whims of commercial calculation guided the movement of news. That might mean seven ship arrivals in one month and none during the following month. When they arrived en masse, some ships inevitably conveyed little or no new information. In 1745 printer Benjamin Franklin rejoiced that the arrival of several ships had ended a "Dearth of News." But he was frustrated to have "a Series of Newspapers come to hand in a Lump together" after "months without having a Syllable." On such occasions, he explained, printers "crowd all the latest Events into our First Paper, and are obliged to fill up the Succeeding Ones with Articles of prior Date, or else omit them intirely, as being anticipated and stale."[30] Unable to find interesting intelligence from local sources, printers piled together the latest and most exciting news from abroad, whether it was true or not.

Newspapers were a mixed blessing. They allowed settlers to engage with far more foreign news than ever before. But they were not neutral. They promoted certain kinds of news at the expense of others and transformed news to fit their own needs. Both as material objects and as genres of expression, newspapers placed powerful limitations on Americans' efforts to observe the world during the eighteenth century.

Early settlers' letters and conversations had provided a rich context for interpreting foreign news. Using those media, an observer could evaluate the identity and reputation of a newsbearer while gleaning additional information from tone or handwriting. A person sharing news through letters or conversation could frame it appropriately for the audience and draw on shared knowledge and experiences. An observer could ask questions, probe for more detail, and determine their interlocutor's motives for sharing the news. In addition to the formal content of news, epistolary and oral communications provided several meaningful layers of context.

Newspapers collapsed much of that context. Their republication strategies, including letter excerpts and descriptions of oral reports, usually removed the signals that observers relied on to evaluate news. Valuing raw intelligence over contextualized news, printers and other mediators freely disassembled and shared information in new forms. Someone reading a letter excerpted in a newspaper could digest its contents but could do little to judge its truthfulness. Printers often plucked the juiciest paragraphs from letters and in the process lost the context offered by the full document as well as the larger epistolary relationship. They also usually redacted the names of informants and letter writers, replacing them with vague references to a "respectable gentleman" or something similar. Printers' descriptions of local oral reports likewise ripped news out of the environment of its articulation. A taverngoer listening to a half-drunken sailor describe news from abroad might have had reason to be suspicious of his more expansive claims, for example, but a reader encountering the same report in print would have fewer grounds for skepticism. As reports moved promiscuously back and forth between different media forms, they lost context with every leap. The anonymous, decontextualized nature of most printed news made it impossible for readers to evaluate the reputation of a source. Instead, readers could generally only judge the truthfulness of printed news according to its content or their attitude toward its publisher.

Reprints from other newspapers also introduced uncertainties. Printers and writers formulated their news paragraphs for readers who were encountering them within a particular issue, space, and time. They made assumptions about their audiences' knowledge and experiences, which did not travel well across long distances. In 1795, for example, Philadelphia printer Benjamin Franklin Bache reprinted an item from a New York paper pointing out that a ship captain's report had confirmed an account of the French fleet's movement discussed in a "preceding paragraph." But Bache had not included that paragraph, which left his readers to search in vain for more information under the New York heading or just scratch their heads.[31]

In some instances, reprinting produced downright incoherence. For example, in 1792 printer Francis Childs shared a report in his New York *Daily Advertiser* about the *journée* of August 10 in Paris, when revolutionaries stormed the Tuileries Palace and hastened the fall of the French monarchy. Childs took this report from a copy of the London *Star* that had been published on August 16. The *Star*'s report began, "As the passions of men begin to subside, we are enabled to collect more accurately the particulars of the late tumult." This would have made sense to the *Star*'s London audience, who had read an extended account of the affair in the previous day's issue.[32] But this prior report had not been published in New York. In fact, these details about the uprising were the first that New York City's readers would have seen. Childs had probably received the August 16 issue from an arriving ship that did not bring the previous number. The garnish had been served without the steak. More useful was a series of letters later published in American papers, which were attuned to an international audience and narrated the events of August 10 from beginning to end.[33]

The growth of newspapers also tied information exchange more firmly to commercial networks. Mercantilist regulations funneled newspapers between metropoles and colonies. While mercantilism was always more of an imperial aspiration than a reality on the ground, it significantly limited the amount of printed news arriving in the British American colonies from outside the British empire. Indeed, when British and French colonies existed alongside one another in North America in the early eighteenth century, news sometimes moved more quickly from Europe and back than between the two colonies. In 1755, for example, the *Boston News-Letter* published some news accompanied under the heading "The following Paragraphs dated at Quebeck, were taken from the last London Print."[34] This information had likely traveled from Quebec to France to London to Boston, moving more than a dozen times the distance of the relatively short trip from Quebec to Boston. As chapter 4 shows, the events of the late eighteenth century, especially American independence and the French revolutionary wars, disrupted the relationship between information and imperial commerce, allowing news from many nations to flow more easily into North America.

Some media obeyed imperial restrictions more than others did. Letters had a defined destination, and if trade ships were not moving between sender and receiver, letter writers could contrive to have them forwarded to their eventual destination. In 1789, for example, the postmaster of Montreal noted in a newspaper advertisement: "Letters for any part of the *Continent of Europe*, must be sent under cover to a correspondent in England, otherwise they cannot be forwarded from hence."[35] Imperial limitations meant that if someone in Montreal wished to contact a friend in France (no longer the colony's metropole by 1789), they would have to enclose that letter within a message to a contact in England, asking them to forward the letter to France. Indeed, correspondents often wrote complicated instructions about forwarding their letters.[36] While inconvenient, this method allowed letter writers to swim against the tides of Atlantic commerce and mercantilism. Newspapers, though, typically lacked a particular destination and just floated along with maritime trade patterns into the hands of whatever printer or mediator was in a vessel's port of disembarkation.

Because printers abided by a regular schedule that was indifferent to the comings and goings of ships or post riders, newspapers rarely provided the most recent information. If a printer published his paper on Wednesdays, but a ship left that locale on Tuesday, it would carry nearly week-old printed news to its destination. For similar reasons, once important news arrived in North America, people rarely learned about it for the first time in print. Letters and conversations usually provided the latest news. Correspondents often delayed writing their letters until they heard that a ship was preparing to depart or that a post rider would soon leave town. Letter writers often apologized for their haste, noting that they were rushing to get the letter out. One merchant noted, for example, "I am but just informed of this Opportunity which sails an hour or two hence."[37] As a result, the letters that a ship carried usually contained more up-to-date information than the newspapers on board.

The early periodical press had many weaknesses as an information medium. Printed newspapers provided little context, rarely trespassed imperial boundaries, and seldom carried the latest important news. Moreover, by including so much confusing and contradictory information, newspapers allowed readers to be misled and deceived. Yet for all these limitations, newspapers offered an extraordinary level of depth that conversations and letters could not provide. Memories faded, hands cramped. Travelers' recollections dimmed during months-long journeys across the Atlantic, leaving behind only the headlines. Likewise, when a news story required more than a few sentences of explanation, letter writers sometimes encouraged their correspondents to look to other media. In the seventeenth century, correspondents sometimes explained, "For news I must refer you to the passengers" of the ship that carried the letter.[38] By the eighteenth century, correspondents looked to newspapers to alleviate the burden of minutely describing global events. "The papers will show you our public proceedings," offered one London-based letter writer in 1775.[39] Others paired their letters with enclosed newspapers, such as when a couple of merchants wrote to their partners in New York, "The

Newspapers handed you by this mail will give you the particulars of the important news from Europe."[40]

Newspapers were useful because they collected the sort of information that was too complicated or dull to spread spontaneously through letters and conversations. News about ship departures, long speeches in legislative bodies, or reports about remote places could only spread through print. Newspapers were the most efficient medium for providing evidence, details, quotations, or carefully sequenced narratives. For many decades, this sort of news only appealed to a small segment of society that benefited from such precision. Indeed, the first American newspapers primarily targeted an audience of merchants, who used them to try to predict changing economic conditions. By the late eighteenth century, though, as revolutions roared, many other people became fascinated by even the pettiest trivialities about events abroad. As chapter 4 discusses, observers during the Age of Revolutions pursued every morsel of information, hoping to understand the destabilizing events unfolding abroad and perhaps even to look ahead to the future. For all their flaws, readers sought out newspapers because they offered a level of depth and specificity beyond the capacity of any other medium.

The new information systems of the eighteenth century allowed British Americans to manage an increasingly abundant stream of news. Whereas colonists had once relied primarily on a diffuse network of personal relationships to spread news, the growing volume of Atlantic information now required specialized workers in printing and post offices. A small number of people were charged with collecting, distributing, and mediating foreign news. But who could be trusted with this responsibility?

The British Americans who exercised the greatest power in shaping Atlantic communications, at least initially, were those closest to colonial administrators. Governors maintained correspondences with the ministry and its various officers in London, which lent them prestige and standing as mediators.[41] Moreover, governors' relationships with merchants and other elites provided them with yet more intelligence. If anyone in a colony was up to date on important events abroad, it was arguably the governor and his circle. The mediation revolution strengthened this position. More centralized information systems allowed colonial leaders to regulate communications in ways that had previously been impossible for them. Exercising leverage over information exchange, British leaders enhanced their standing in their colonial communities. Moreover, by filtering out seditious materials, they helped to promote British identity and loyalty.[42]

Presses that were open to all opinions and news were a threat to these goals. In 1690 when Benjamin Harris published *Publick Occurrences*, the first North American newspaper, he found that colonial leaders distrusted unsanctioned forms of news mediation. They may have been unable to halt the spread of rumors, but printed news could be more easily controlled. In Harris's first and, as it turned out, only issue, he promised to help curtail "that Spirit of Lying, which prevails among us," a point that may have been included to appease colonial regulators. But the issue also contained a salacious story about the king of France and some criticisms of Britain's Haudenosaunee allies. Massachusetts governor Simon Bradstreet immediately shut down the operation and prohibited all unlicensed publications.[43]

Some fourteen years later, with the Licensing Act lapsed, one of Bradstreet's successors, Joseph Dudley, permitted the creation of the continent's first long-running newspaper, the *Boston News-Letter*, published by the town's obsequious postmaster, John Campbell. Though not a printer himself (he outsourced the newspaper's production to printers Bartholomew Green and John Allen), Campbell's status as postmaster placed him at the nexus of the emerging information systems that tied the British American colonies to the broader British Atlantic. Just as important, Campbell's role as postmaster rendered him especially dependent on the governor's pleasure. Trespassing on the government's good graces could result not only in the proscription of his newspaper, but also the loss of his postmaster job. While he hoped to "give a true Account of all Foreign and Domestick Occurrences," Campbell did not undertake to cull out falsehood himself.[44] He left that to the governor's office, where he submitted his news copy for review before publication.[45] At the moment of its emergence in North America, the newspaper offered colonial governments a means to mediate and control the otherwise ungovernable flow of foreign news.

While not all subsequent newspaper printers were as dependent on the government as Campbell was, many found that independence could be dangerous. A printer who challenged the government was unlikely to be awarded its lucrative printing contracts and might be met with repression. When printer James Franklin shared a report in his *New-England Courant* about piracy that was gently critical of the Massachusetts colonial government, he landed in prison for a month.[46] When John Peter Zenger published more overt criticism of the New York government in his *New-York Weekly Journal* in 1734, he faced charges of seditious libel. After months in prison, he was famously acquitted by a jury on the grounds that his accusations were true. But this loss did not deter government leaders, who continued to prosecute people on similar charges for decades afterward.[47] To publish news that reflected poorly on the government was therefore to take a great risk. Even though he was vindicated in the end, Zenger had lost months of his life to the controversy. Unwilling to accept such risks, most colonial printers aligned their news mediation with the government's demands.[48]

While there were no partisan newspapers in British America during the early eighteenth century since colonists could not vote in parliamentary elections, the continent's printers nevertheless needed to navigate Britain's partisan press. They knew that it could be dangerous to reprint the wrong sort of news.[49] This meant avoiding material that questioned the legitimacy of the empire, the monarchy, colonial leaders, or parliamentary leaders.[50] For prudent printers, it also meant allying themselves with whatever party controlled the levers of power in London. Newspaper printers quickly learned that they could avoid any hint of controversy in their mediative practices by relying on the ministry's official organ, the *London Gazette*. No matter who held power in London and therefore controlled appointments to many colonial leadership roles, this publication followed the ministry's line. Indeed, anyone familiar with London prints would have detected the influence of the *Gazette* on nearly every aspect of the continent's newspapers. Campbell's *Boston News-Letter* imitated the formatting, tone, and structure of the *London Gazette*. He even borrowed its masthead's assurance that the paper had been "Published by Authority."[51] Clones of the *London Gazette*, often using the name "Gazette," proliferated across Britain's colonies, including Canada and the Caribbean.

Colonial printers' embrace of the *London Gazette* went beyond the aesthetic. As ministries rose and fell and as British newspapers flipped allegiances, the *Gazette*'s imperial orthodoxy lent stability to colonial reprinting practices. As a result, in the first two-thirds of the eighteenth century, about a third of all North American citations of newspapers abroad referred to the *London Gazette*. And citations of the *Gazette* increased over time. In the decade preceding the Stamp Act of 1765, for example, North American printers cited the *Gazette* about half of the time that they cited newspapers abroad (see appendix). This is particularly striking given that the number of newspapers printed abroad, and therefore the number of possible sources for colonial printers, grew significantly during the first half of the eighteenth century. Even as more news sources became available, colonial printers hewed more closely to the imperial line.

While the replication of news from the ministry's news organ was deeply political, it was also uncontroversial. For many colonists in the first half of the eighteenth century, reliance on the *London Gazette* seemed to express loyalty to the empire rather than to a political party. Few readers would have questioned the veracity of material printed in the *London Gazette*. Because this publication expressed the administration's views, the presence of a piece of information in the *Gazette* endowed it with a sort of functional truth within the boundaries of the British empire regardless of its actual correspondence to reality.

The periodical press has often been viewed as a democratic medium, a voice for the people against arbitrary power. But with the mediation revolution, news-gathering became more specialized, institutional, and susceptible to government regulation. Compared to the letter-writing and oral cultures that preceded them, newspapers were more likely to obey the whims of the mighty. Like the Enlightenment it unfolded in parallel with, the mediation revolution empowered elites to exercise greater leverage over political communications.

The surplus of news managed and created by the mediation revolution reached colonists unevenly, intensifying existing inequities. Members of professions adjacent to commerce, government, or public spaces, such as preachers, merchants, magistrates, tavern keepers, and mariners, functioned as informal conduits and gatherers of oral, printed, and epistolary news.[52] Those who occupied these roles usually belonged to the most privileged and powerful segments of society. Intersectional matrices of power provided foreign news to affluent white men and urban dwellers, but withheld it from women, enslaved people, working-class laborers, and rural denizens. It would be easy to divide the population of early North America into categories of the information elite and the information poor, or between news consumers and producers. Yet these would be false dichotomies. In the early modern world, news consumption was rarely separate from its production. When newspaper printers decided which news account to extract, they were both consuming and producing news. When someone received a letter from abroad, they consumed its news but also created a new version of it when sharing the information with an extended audience.

Rather than simple binaries, we might more helpfully conceive of colonists as existing in a multidirectional lattice of information exchange. When news arrived in North America, some individuals were in an upstream position, which allowed them to affect how and whether others experienced it. When newspaper printers, for example, collected and shared news, they stood upstream of their readers. Their decisions shaped how readers experienced the news while readers' responses to the news were less likely to affect how a printer engaged with it. These positions were relative. For parliamentary news, a Boston printer might be upstream of a farmer in New Hampshire, but that printer might stand downstream of a merchant in London. If a piece of news somehow originated in New Hampshire, the roles might be reversed. Yet one's place in this web of information exchange depended on much more than geography. In a single city, a ship captain might be upstream of a printer, who was upstream of a subscriber, who was upstream of a servant. At each point of mediation, someone could withhold, reshape, misremember, or intentionally transform the news. News usually degraded as it moved downstream, losing clarity, context, accuracy, and detail. Being in an upstream position, then, meant shaping how other people experienced the world.

In this book I generally use the term "mediator" to refer to people in relatively upstream positions and "observer" for those downstream. The distinction between these roles, though, was muddled and situational. Throughout a given day, a person could slip easily between moments of observation and mediation, learning and sharing. Only a few people could consistently mediate the news in ways that affected many others. An individual's place in this web of communication depended to a significant degree on their profession, geographic position, race, gender, and class. While women of all races, rural residents, men of color, and non-elites often had access to news from abroad (sometimes with difficulty), they were usually in a downstream position, unlikely to shape how large numbers of others would experience the news. There were some important exceptions to these tendencies: Black mariners and women printers sometimes played important roles in Atlantic communications.[53] In general, though, early modern regimes of power mapped closely onto the mediation of information.

Enslaved and free people of color faced the steepest barriers to gathering and sharing foreign news, because enslavers and their allies actively enforced racial limitations on its spread. Fearful that news from abroad might encourage resistance, white Americans often attempted to cut off people of color from nonlocal news.[54] As historian Julius S. Scott has demonstrated, North

America's enslaved population gathered as much news as possible about topics such as the Haitian Revolution and the French National Assembly's decision to abolish slavery.[55] Likewise, throughout the 1790s, the Spanish colonial government of Louisiana repeatedly expelled talkative people of color for spreading news about the French and Haitian Revolutions (see chapter 6). Such obstacles and the necessity of secrecy prevented people of color from operating upstream of white colonists.

Nevertheless, in a world where free and enslaved people of color labored and lived in all sorts of public and private spaces, they inevitably encountered white observers' chatter about the news and shared it among themselves. Numerous enslaved people worked in early newspaper printing offices. Primus Fowle, Peter Fleet, Caesar Fleet, Pompey Fleet, and at least one person who worked for John Campbell (whose name, like many others, will never be identified) labored at the presses as woodcutters, compositors, pressmen, and distributors.[56] Their work provided them with access to the hum of information and conversation as well as, in some cases, the printed product. One white printer later remembered that in the early nineteenth century, a Charleston newspaper's enslaved workers printed 200 extra copies of the paper "unknown to their masters."[57] What did these enslaved workers do with them? Perhaps they sold some for their own profit, as did three young, enslaved newspaper carriers for the *Louisiana Courier* in 1816.[58] Or perhaps they shared some copies in the local free and enslaved Black community.

Over time, enslaved people developed an ongoing network of oral communication, known as the "grapevine," which often surprised white enslavers with its efficiency.[59] By necessity, enslaved people and free people of color communicated about foreign news in private. To do otherwise would have invited repression. As a result, their information exchanges are not as visible in the historical record as those of white North Americans. Yet these absences should not lead us to conclude that such networks did not exist. One reason we know that these exchanges happened is that white enslavers and government regulators prioritized restricting Black communication.

Class and labor further shaped the mediation of news. Military leaders, government officials, and elite merchants often maintained transatlantic correspondences, conversed with world travelers, and subscribed to expensive newspapers. Preachers, likewise, maintained many transatlantic correspondences, which provided ongoing and surprisingly ecumenical exchanges of news.[60] Even in small communities, where many undistinguished religious leaders resided, a town's preacher was likely to be among its most literate and well-connected members. A nineteenth-century memoirist recounted a local "doggrel song" from his youth in eastern New York during the late 1790s, which included these lines: "I wonder what the matter means, / A cutting of such capers, / The parson says the French are mad, / He reads it in the papers."[61] This odd bit of verse evokes a likely chain of mediation beginning with what would have almost certainly been British accounts of the French Revolution deposited in the United States from a commercial vessel, which were then reprinted in an urban seaport, shared again by Elihu Phinney in the *Otsego Herald*, dropped off by a post rider, read by the local parson, and interpreted by him to those who did not have regular access to the *Herald*.

A poor laborer or even a middling tradesman was much less likely to mediate information. For the bulk of the eighteenth century, the subscription base for most newspapers was composed largely of wealthy merchants. A yearly newspaper subscription was a luxury that not everyone could afford. One Boston blacksmith, for example, prefaced a letter to a local newspaper with the admission that he "would buy your News-Letter if Times were not so hard."[62] While newspaper subscription lists gradually expanded in the late eighteenth century, they continued to be built around a core of elites.

During the eighteenth century, a growing proportion of North Americans engaged in transatlantic correspondences for professional reasons. The European settlers who first arrived in North America in the seventeenth century had left behind family, business partners, friends, and acquaintances. Transatlantic communication had been essential to these early colonists' social worlds. Generations long removed from Europe, though, engaged in less transatlantic communication than had their ancestors. Merchants and religious leaders continued to exchange letters across the Atlantic, while fewer colonists did so for purely personal reasons. By the second half of the eighteenth century, North Americans faced an "epistolary divide" between rich and poor.[63] To be sure, recipients often shared the contents of an interesting letter, either by sending a copy to a local newspaper or reading it to others. But they could also decide to withhold inconvenient letters or share only partial excerpts.

Likewise, women were less likely than men to mediate information. Many of the spaces saturated with reports from abroad, such as taverns, docks, coffee shops, printing offices, and post offices, belonged mostly to men. Of course, when men received interesting news, whether it was in written or oral form, they often shared it with the members of their household, mediating the news for the home's other inhabitants. A Philadelphia newspaper poem, for example, promised subscribers that access to news would allow them to "charm" their servants by providing them with "tales" of their "native land."[64] Dispersing news allowed a newspaper subscriber to accumulate power in their household. A woman who labored as a servant might be, at least partly, dependent on her employer for regular access to foreign news. Misbehavior could, in turn, lead the head of a household to deny their dependents access to news and newspapers.

Elite women often benefited from their proximity to well-informed men. In 1794 Susanna Dillwyn wrote a letter to her father, a wealthy Quaker merchant in London, to update him on the condition of her cousin Richard, who lived in Otsego, New York. She explained that Richard had plenty of comforts at home, among them "an account of what goes forward in the world from the Albany news papers." Along with a few other amenities, according to Susanna, access to news of the world provided Richard with the "sum of human happiness."[65] A few years earlier, while staying with an uncle in Burlington, New Jersey, Susanna had reported to her father that his home looked like the "apartment of a Batchelor," because "we were sometimes obliged to sit upon the bed every chair being loaded with newspapers, books and pamphlets, which are on no account to be displaced."[66] There is a certain detached amusement in her observations. For Susanna, these men were faintly ridiculous in their fascination with obtaining information. Yet she benefited from her family's obsessive news-gathering practices. She wrote often about the global news, including the "dreadful commotions" in France during the 1790s.[67]

In addition to social distinctions, geographic advantages usually placed urban dwellers upstream of the continent's rural majority. News clustered in port cities where travelers, commercial vessels, packet ships, and letters arrived, but in the eighteenth century the vast majority of North American settlers lived outside of cities. The 1790 US Census, for example, found that only about 5 percent of the country's population lived in urban areas.[68] With few opportunities to get swept up in the buzz of the streets, rural folk fed on a comparatively limited media diet. A politician named Levi Beardsley remembered running "through the woods over a hill (often before breakfast)" as a boy to get his family's copy of the local newspaper a mile away and reading it before he got home.[69] Such distances inhibited detailed foreign news from spreading spontaneously, which made printed news more essential for inhabitants of the countryside.[70]

Taking advantage of the special value of print for rural consumers, some printers published a separate "country gazette," which packaged the week's news into an affordable paper uncluttered with city advertisements.[71] In the late eighteenth century, newspapers also expanded well beyond urban sea-ports and into the continental interior. Yet only a small proportion of the rural population probably encountered newspapers on a regular basis. As a Maryland printer named James Cowan noted in a 1789 newspaper prospec-tus, "public prints have by no means had a general circulation" among rural inhabitants. Instead, according to Cowan, outside of cities only "The few" subscribed.[72] Even those rural dwellers who managed to keep up with Atlan-tic news remained downstream of urban mediators. Newspaper printers who lived outside of cities gathered almost all their foreign news from major pa-pers published in urban seaports. This reprinted news, in turn, shaped the conversation and information exchange among country dwellers.

It was unusual, but not impossible, for downstream information consumers and producers to affect the mediative choices of those upstream from them. Letter writers could ask their interlocutors pointed questions or demand up-dates on matters relating to their interests, but they often waited long months for the answers. Because they paid the printer's bills, newspaper subscribers could request that a printer share particular accounts or provide further cover-age on a topic. In 1791, for example, Samuel Neilson, the printer of the *Quebec Gazette*, offered a quick précis of news taken from the "London and Glasgow Papers," including information about Russia, France, and a riot in Birming-ham, England. This news had arrived too late to be fully included in the latest issue, but Neilson announced that he would decide whether to publish a sup-plement based on the "degree of anxiety the public may testify." Readers ap-parently clamored for it because Neilson published the supplement two days later.[73] In these ways, downstream observers could affect how the news came to them. But such opportunities were rare.

The mediation revolution of eighteenth-century North America provided elite, white, urban men with more consistent access to news while also allow-ing them to frame the production of news for large audiences. Newspaper printers, transnational correspondents, ship captains, and others who gen-erally stood upstream of North American communications made decisions about what news mattered, what mattered less, what was true, and what was false. While some of these decisions resulted from conscious reflection, others likely formed at the edges of thought, instinctual and unspoken. For example, how did so many upstream information mediators conclude, as succeeding chapters show, that a 1795 Black-led insurrection in Grenada would not be called a "revolution," while less radical events years earlier in Ireland had earned that distinction? How did they determine which news items would be reprinted in full and which would be briefly summarized? And how did they decide which news sources deserved their trust? As they made these choices, informed in ways they might not have fully realized by their status, race, gender, and politics, they foreclosed some interpretive possibilities for the people downstream from them. Like any other revolution, the mediation revolution had winners and losers.

By empowering a small group of people to interpret and distribute news, the mediation revolution created an ongoing problem of legitimacy. Why should a privileged few decide what news others would encounter? While imperial officials, including governors and postmasters, could rely on their government appointment as a sanction for their power to regulate communications, newspaper printers had no good answers to this question. And so, instead of justifying their power to shape the flow of news, early newspaper printers perpetuated the polite fiction that they were not engaged in the business of mediation at all.

When John Campbell found that he had accidentally shared some false news in 1705, for example, he resisted taking responsibility for it. Pointedly declining to apologize, he asked his readers if they "have themselves now & then told a Story that needed a further Elucidation."[74] Campbell did not draw a distinction between his readers' relationship with news and his own, positioning himself not as a mediator of news but as an observer just like them. No concept of "journalism" created professional obligations for news producers. Instead, Campbell viewed his decision to share an unfounded piece of information as being akin to a reader's choice to whisper a piece of juicy gossip to a neighbor. What was the difference? Campbell did not relish spreading falsehoods, but he also did not mind doing so. No one could accuse him of intentionally deceiving others because he offered no guarantee that his news was true.

Scholars have long known that colonial American printers avoided taking sides in political controversies.[75] Because they relied on a small subscription base, few printers would consider alienating half their audience by engaging in partisan advocacy. Moreover, much of that subscription base was merchants, who cared more about commerce than politics. It made financial sense for printers to remain neutral. This principle also extended to the potentially political act of news-gathering. Imagining their newspapers more like bulletin boards than publications, printers gathered a variety of accounts of the world without offering much comment on what could be trusted.

Over time, this timidity toward truth developed into a more coherent set of ideas. After *Pennsylvania Gazette* printer Benjamin Franklin published an advertisement that some of his patrons found objectionable in 1731, he wrote a lengthy "Apology for Printers" that expounded on a printer's duty to remain studiously oblivious of the truth. His policy, he explained, was to share a "great variety of things opposite and contradictory" and expect that "when Truth and Error have fair Play, the former is always an overmatch for the latter."[76] Franklin imagined a dialectical battle in which truth always possessed the advantage. To an extent he did not acknowledge, however, this optimistic vision of news distribution depended on qualities of rationality, fair-mindedness, patience, and detachment that his readers simply did not possess. Still, no one ever lost customers by flattering them.

The open press approach was not merely a cynical attempt to evade responsibility for printing choices, but also a prudent recognition of printers' limitations. Who could expect newspaper printers to verify everything that they republished from abroad? The information systems of the era did not permit rigorous efforts at verification, especially across great distances. It was impossible to track down the original sources for most reports from abroad. If a hard-bitten, objectivity-idealizing reporter from a mid-twentieth-century newsroom were somehow transplanted into an eighteenth-century printing office, they would struggle in vain to produce any authenticated foreign news each week. If newspaper printers of the time had excluded all unverified news, they would quickly have found themselves with empty columns and angry subscribers.

Unwilling to take responsibility for their mediation, printers published as much news as possible. Campbell was so committed to sharing nearly everything he encountered that his papers often ran several weeks or months behind the latest ship arrivals.[77] Despite the fact that he was drawing from several newspapers printed in Britain and the Caribbean, which meant that he must have discarded most of their paragraphs, he boasted that readers "will find no one piece of material News that is in them, omitted in ours."[78] If his press shared everything, Campbell would have argued, he could not be accused of filtering out news. Yet a truly open press was never possible. His claim to only publish "material News" and his promise to "prevent a great many false reports" suggest that he was engaging in some process of discernment.[79]

Because printers could not verify news before publishing it, false information spread easily. Without the benefit of omniscience, it is difficult to say what proportion of the news in eighteenth-century newspapers was false. But printers, who had little incentive to emphasize the falseness of their reports, accepted that they were frequent purveyors of untruths.

Lewis Timothy, printer of the *South Carolina Gazette*, complained in 1737 that a reader in Georgia had written to correct a report he had published a month earlier about a violent confrontation between nearby Creeks and settlers. The report had ended by claiming that after murdering the Natives, the settlers brought their horses to Savannah. After conducting a "strict Enquiry," Timothy sarcastically wrote, he would now admit that the horses had actually been brought to a plantation "about 6 Miles from the Town of Savannah." This fatuous fact-check irritated Timothy, who spent five paragraphs pointing out that such a small discrepancy was absurdly trivial compared to the mountains of muck that he and other newspaper printers shoveled on a regular basis: "How often was King *Theodore* [of Corsica] dethroned, and reinstated in his Dominions, before he thought fit to abdicate them himself. . . . How often hath *Tuscany* been upon the very point of being evacuated in the News-Papers, as well as Fort Kehl and Philipsburg of being deliver'd up to the Emperor [during the War of the Polish Succession]?" Because Savannah was near Charleston, his reader could easily verify the details of a local story through some inquiries. But Timothy could only detect falsehoods in Atlantic communications through an accumulation of reports. He knew that a king is not usually repeatedly dethroned any more than a city is repeatedly seized, and so at least one of those reports must have been false. But who could say which one was untrue in the moment? To defend himself, Timothy evenly noted that because his readers were "*eager* after *News*," he might as well fill the paper "with something or other of this kind," since they were "as much pleased with *false* News as *true*." Since such news came to him "ready prepared," he argued, there was "no harm" in sharing false stories in the absence of "real Facts" as long as he and other printers promised to contradict them once "convinced of their Error."[80]

Readers, in turn, understood that newspaper printers' selections were unverified. In 1747, a writer in the *New-York Evening Post* who signed their name "A, B." explained that when something appeared in print, it is "not beleived, because said or published." Rather, sharing news allowed only that "every one may judge for himself, whether these Facts are true, or not." As the word itself suggested, the act of *public*ation simply submitted information to the public, and readers could then decide what to do with it. In this way, "A, B." argued, "Truth will always prevail over Falshood."[81] The expectation that readers would sort out error from authenticity freed printers from that responsibility.

Indeed, printers often announced that they would "leave to our Readers to Judge" a report from abroad.[82] This was, of course, enormously ineffective. Most readers lacked even the printers' meager contacts and resources. By abdicating any responsibility for verification, newspapers displaced the burden of evaluating news onto those who were least prepared for that task. In so doing, they amplified false rumors and accelerated their spread.

The mediation revolution of the eighteenth century allowed for a more efficient distribution of news, but not necessarily of truth. Indeed, the communication structures of early America were built around mediators' indifference to truth. The only filters for falsehoods were those created by the colonial administrators, who defined truth selfishly. As a result, false news proliferated. Some people deliberately spread lies, of course, but the information systems of eighteenth-century America made even inadvertent errors unavoidable. With thousands of miles between themselves and the events that they sought to understand, observers could be misled by a false friend as easily as by an enemy.

For most of the seventeenth and early eighteenth centuries, British America's social and cultural expectations about news developed in ways that recognized the fundamental limitations of Atlantic communications. Unable to take responsibility for the news that they shared, early American printers could offer their readers little more than a slightly refined portion of the raw intelligence that they received. In a way, this was a form of humility. They knew better than to make expansive claims about their capacity for discernment.

In the late eighteenth century, as I demonstrate in subsequent chapters, social expectations about news began to change. Instead of viewing false news as harmless and inevitable, British colonists came to see it as dangerous and preventable. Observers began to anxiously search for truthful streams of news. Benjamin Franklin Bache, for example, complained in 1793 that "the many contradictory reports which are continually flitting through America, point out the importance of authentic information: It were much to be wished that some means could be devised of procuring intelligence which could be relied on, frequently and regularly from Europe."[83] Printers such as Bache began to abandon the open press pretense and assert themselves as mediators who would only share what they understood to be truthful news. While they were no better at discerning truth than the practitioners of the open press had been, readers could now hold them responsible for their errors. Printers began to expect regular accusations that they had intentionally manipulated the news.

Even as observers demanded and mediators provided more assurances about the veracity of the news, the work of determining what was true became more difficult. By the late eighteenth century, American observers encountered more news, less context, and more incoherence than ever before. In 1795, a correspondent of Philadelphia printer Mathew Carey described some rumors about an arriving French fleet but qualified them by admitting, "there are so many contradictory stories daily circulated here as well as among you, that a man has a just right to be very susceptible in these times."[84] Indeed, the tides of contradiction flowed so steadily that readers could ignore gloomy news and instead await a contrary report. In 1793, for example, printer Charles Peirce of the New Hampshire *Oracle of the Day* greeted unhappy news from London with the qualification "we anticipate a contradiction."[85] An abundance of unverifiable and clashing reports allowed observers to select the news that they preferred and discard the rest. As a result, news often circulated not because it was true but because it suited the aspirations and worldview of its mediators.

In their inaugural 1786 issue, printers John Scull and Joseph Hall of the *Pittsburgh Gazette* asked:

> Who would not give half a guinea to know, exactly as he does his own calf pasture, what is going on every day when he rises, at Smyrna and Amsterdam, and count as easily as he can the stripes of his waistcoat, the armies that are on foot in Europe . . . to be able to look up with the tail of his eye as far as Russia, and down again with the same glance to the islands of the West Indies, and to see all the intermediate space swarming with men and things?[86]

Scull and Hall framed a grand vista that promised to allow readers to become cosmopolitan world travelers without ever leaving the questionable comfort of western Pennsylvania. Their offer to mix the exotic with the quotidian, comparing the sight of Smyrna and Amsterdam with that of a pasture and waistcoat, would have been compelling to those readers who sought newspapers not just to be informed but also for diversion from the sameness of everyday life. Foreign news was exciting because it allowed readers to collect experiences of a world beyond their home. To mediate information was to transform and extend the world that others inhabited.

This was the way that newspaper printers spoke prospectively. But such promises rarely came to fruition. Instead of seeing the world as clearly as the "stripes of his waistcoat," the average newspaper reader muddled through a confusing morass of contradiction, confusion, and error. During the American revolutionary war, for example, a Grenada merchant named John Hunt passed along to another merchant a local report that George Washington had deserted the Continental army and complained, "I cannot embark on Politicks with any kind of satisfaction there being very little confidence reposed in the reports propagated here—they assert a circumstance in one paper and contradict it in the next."[87] For Hunt, false and uncertain news made it impossible to meaningfully engage in politics. If information preceded deliberation, then contradictory and confusing accounts could paralyze political action.

This disjuncture between an idealized world of news, as articulated by Scull and Hall, and the lived experiences of those, such as Hunt, who could not trust that they understood the world around them, proved to be a powerful element in the politics of revolutionary America. Observers dreamed of being able to see foreign shores as clearly as they saw their own homes, but a haze of uncertainty and falsehoods too often obscured the view. Anxiety ensued. Understanding that they derived their politics, in part, from their mediated experiences of foreign events, American observers worried that the manipulation of news could destabilize their political identities. Growing dissatisfied with mediators who shared information that might be false, news consumers began to demand more certainty and less humility. Protecting the integrity of global communications came to seem essential, even if that meant beginning anew.

CHAPTER TWO

Taxation with Misrepresentation

Fears of Deception in the Anglo-American Imperial Crisis

So much depended on an old, weathered barrel. What was in the barrel? Who put it there? Why would someone lie about a barrel? In the early 1770s, a single wooden barrel, whose content remains unknown today, improbably earned the attention of many people in Britain and America. It mattered to them because it seemed to offer a key for understanding why the British empire was falling apart.

During the economic depression that followed the end of the Seven Years' War (1756–1763), Britain's Parliament passed laws that raised taxes on colonists and restricted their commerce. Thrashed by economic decline, Boston became an epicenter of resistance to imperial reform. By the late 1760s, tensions were high.

As the city's inhabitants distinguished themselves through their defiance of the British empire, Massachusetts governor Francis Bernard asked his superiors to send imperial troops to maintain order. Their arrival in late 1768 outraged many Bostonians, who whispered that even more troops were due to arrive soon from Halifax and Ireland. Rumors floated around the city that some colonists had organized to prevent the troops from disembarking in Boston harbor. At about this time, someone stealthily deposited a barrel in a visible, elevated position near the harbor. Lieutenant Governor Thomas Hutchinson believed that the angry colonists planned to burn the barrel, which he thought to be full of tar, to signal for a mob to gather to oppose the British troops as they landed. He even wrote a letter to his superiors in London sharing these fears.[1]

But no one lit the barrel. The city government removed it, and everyone forgot about the matter. It was such a trivial affair at the time that the city's newspapers didn't even mention it. A few months after the barrel had been removed, though, rumors spread that someone had informed British leaders that a "beacon was erected" and that the people of Boston were prepared to attack arriving troops. The *Boston Gazette*, a newspaper aligned with the co-lonial protests, concluded that Britain's confrontational attitude toward the colonies was "wholly grounded upon the Misinformation, and false Repre-sentations" of colonial officials, such as this barrel rumor.[2]

About five years after the barrel incident, Massachusetts colonists obtained a collection of Hutchinson's letters to London. Among them was a letter dated October 4, 1768, which used the barrel anecdote to illustrate the "agitated" state of Bostonians. According to Hutchinson, the city had been quaking with "riots," "disorders," and public "distemper." Indeed, "all the authority of gov-ernment was not strong enough to remove" the barrel. Taken at face value, Hutchinson's story indicated that the empire's control over Boston was tenu-ous and that British leaders should send more assistance. Hutchinson cer-tainly had reason to question the colonists' temperament. Three years before he wrote the letter, a mob had violently attacked his Boston home while his family was eating dinner.[3]

Whether or not its contents were accurate, Hutchinson's incendiary letter enraged many colonists on its publication in 1773. Many of them viewed the barrel story as a blatant falsehood, including Boston shopkeeper Harbottle Dorr, who scrawled in his copy's margins "A Lie!" and "A Vile Lie!"[4] A town committee retrospectively investigated the matter. Its members collected de-positions from the sheriff who had ordered the barrel to be removed, from the workman who had removed it, and from those who happened to see the removal. Witnesses argued about whether anyone had tried to intimidate workmen from removing the barrel and about the barrel's contents. While Hutchinson had insisted it was a tar barrel, witnesses thought it was either an empty nail barrel or a container for turpentine. As pedantic as it seems, the contents mattered. A tar barrel would have provided a durable beacon for a mob to gather around whereas an empty barrel would have been incinerated too quickly, making for a lousy signal. A town meeting published a refutation of Hutchinson's letters, which asserted that it was an "empty nail barrel . . . ill suited for a signal to be fired in the night."[5]

To the angry colonists, this barrel evoked something essential about their relationship with the homeland. They believed that their communications with imperial authorities in London had become systematically skewed against them. Hutchinson's effort to smear the colonists, as they saw it, with his story of a tar barrel beacon seemed to be one example of a larger problem with imperial information exchange. The ways that government leaders in London gathered news about the colonies empowered a small group of officials at the expense of the colonists themselves. When officials and settlers disagreed about events in the colonies, as was happening in Boston, protesting settlers cried that they were being misrepresented. They went to great efforts to discredit Hutchinson's story because they believed that exposing the emptiness of the barrel would expose the emptiness of officials' assertions about them.

Bostonians were not alone in this argument. Throughout the late eighteenth century, colonial subjects across the New World regularly sought to expose what they considered to be untrustworthy news mediators. They imagined that officials were engaging in all kinds of mischief and misrepresentation. In the early 1780s, for example, Andean peasants rebelled against local rulers, believing that they were thwarting the will of Spanish king Charles III.[6] Shortly after, enslaved people rebelled in Cuba amid whispers that the Spanish king had granted them land and freedom but that local officials were hiding this news from them. Seeking independent sources of information, the rebels even sent an agent to Spain.[7] In colonial Saint Domingue, enslaved people exchanged similar rumors about the French king shortly before they rebelled.[8] Indeed, versions of this rumor persisted well into the nineteenth century.[9] The vastness of imperial distances allowed colonists, colonized people, and enslaved people alike to blame their woes on the wiles of self-interested intermediaries.

This trope was especially resonant in monarchies, where colonists often venerated the king without trusting his advisors or legislative bodies. "Evil counsellors" and "evil ministers" figured prominently in early modern French and British politics and literature. Advisors, such as George Villiers, Thomas Cromwell, Georges de la Trémoille, and Cardinal Richelieu, attracted popular scorn for seeming to use their influence over a monarch for their personal advantage.[10] This familiar archetype allowed angry subjects to mobilize against a tyrannical administration without necessarily striking at the institution of the monarchy itself. Protesting subjects hoped that if powerful ministers, advisors, and courtiers were replaced, the monarchs would correct whatever injustices were being enacted in their name. And yet in a society that believed kings possessed the sanction of the divine, and thus shared some of God's omniscience, it was destabilizing to imagine an ignorant king.[11] Colonists' accusations of misrepresentation delegitimized the image of the monarch as God's agent on earth. What need did anyone have for a fallible sovereign?

While angry American colonists' cries of misrepresentation echoed long-standing concerns about imperial and monarchical mediators, they also marked a transition into a new kind of critique. Instead of attacking evil ministers, American colonists went after the evils of mediation itself. No longer trusting hierarchical arrangements of epistemological power, many colonists argued that the public voice of the people, made audible through petitions, newspapers, pamphlets, town meetings, and local representatives, should reach across the Atlantic unfiltered. The American Revolution centered around not only the question of who should have the power to tax and legislate, but also the more fundamental question of who should have the power to decide what was factual.

In 1769, for example, a writer in the *Boston Gazette* questioned why the British government trusted the accounts of colonial officials, such as Francis Bernard, rather than those of the colonists themselves. Why should the "bare affirmation of a Gentleman, unsupported by any Evidence" be "deem'd sufficient to blast the Reputation of a Province"? Although Bernard was the "highest authority," this writer argued, that did not mean that he was "the best" authority.[12] This was an extraordinary statement. To this colonist, Bernard represented imperial and elite authority, which meant that he should be obeyed. But just because he should be obeyed, that did not mean that he should be trusted. The colonists were increasingly splitting the British government's political authority to rule from its epistemic authority to discern, define, and diffuse truth. And yet a political system that derived part of its legitimacy from the consent of the governed, from the fiction that the few could know the will of the many, could tolerate little separation between colonial officials' authenticity and their authority. Through their dissent about misrepresentation, colonial agitators suggested that the many knew more than the few.

In the late 1760s and early 1770s, protesting British North Americans complained about misrepresentation so frequently that it became a central piece of their shared vocabulary of resistance. Yet for all of its ubiquity, historians have paid relatively little attention to this discourse. It fits awkwardly into most narratives of the imperial crisis and revolution. Instead of suggesting, like many twentieth-century historians, that principled responses to British policy drove colonial resistance, this aspect of settlers' defiance indicates that Patriot politics arose out of their response to perceived error.[13] Likewise, because many of those who fought against misrepresentation were elites, this story does not serve social historians' attempts to reclaim the revolution for ordinary people. Finally, this narrative undercuts popular histories that divide revolutionary actors into heroes, victims, and villains. There's nothing particularly impressive or nefarious, after all, in a misunderstanding. Historian Pauline Maier, who does note the significance of the theory of misrepresentation, provides a telling exception. She describes the idea of misrepresentation as the American colonists' "entire explanation of British policy" for several years. But in recounting their grievances, she echoes the Patriots' rhetoric and affirms their belief that colonial officials had indeed "distorted daily events" in exchange for "influence in London."[14] In her account, the dissenting colonists emerge as heroes for overcoming imperial villains, such as Hutchinson.

Was there tar, turpentine, or nothing at all in the Boston barrel? Were the colonists truly misrepresented? It is impossible to know with any certainty. For historians, the barrel functions as a black box—impossible to understand except by its effect on the world. Indeed, it is often the case that the evidence we have inherited from the past does not allow us to determine the truth of a contemporary's assertion. For our purposes, the actual contents of the barrel or the veracity of the news matter less than the rhetoric of misrepresentation that they helped to inspire during the late 1760s and early 1770s. As a result of this discourse, many North Americans began to think more skeptically about the flow of news. Instead of accepting that information moved according to inevitable and immutable patterns, they began to see more clearly that its motion was the imperfect product of human will, inaugurating decades of political struggles over foreign news.

While these angry cries escalated the tensions between a vocal segment of North American colonists and certain institutions of the British empire, they did not immediately push the colonists toward revolution or independence. In fact, the long-standing search for the origins of the American Revolution has led scholars to deemphasize the aspects of the imperial crisis that mitigated escalation. The protests about misrepresentation raise questions beyond the causes of the revolution. They might lead us to consider, for example, why it took eleven years, from the Stamp Act crisis to the Declaration of Independence, for Patriots' hopes for reconciliation to expire. Eleven years is a long time. If their cherished principles had left them no option but separation, why delay? One reason is that many colonists experienced the conflict with Britain not as a matter of structural incompatibilities or constitutional differences, but simply as the bitter fruit of miscommunication. The truth, they believed, would soon win out if they waited patiently.

Communications were one of the central challenges of imperial governance in the early modern world. Weeks, even months, of travel time separated London from its North American colonies. The British leadership, including the secretary of state, the Board of Trade, and lower-level officials, could not govern at such a distance. If colonists needed to wait three or four months for every decision to be made, nothing would ever get done. Instead, for most matters the empire trusted local officials, including governors and their subordinates, to improvise based on their local knowledge and to transmit back "an exact and faithful Account of all Occurrences."[15] Additionally, colonial agents offered a complementary institution for communications. Usually appointed by a colonial assembly, agents functioned in London as the voice of the settlers. They presented petitions, forwarded news, and lobbied for the colonists' interests. Agents represented the colonists to London while governors represented London to the colonists.[16]

Britain governed its colonies largely through this hierarchical system of communication, trusting only a few chosen gentlemen to convey truths. If a group of colonists, including a local assembly, wanted to make something known to London, they could ask either their agent or their governor to pass it along to the secretary of state or the ministry. London officials did not implicitly trust these representatives, but they generally preferred their word to most other sources. Governors, especially those in royal colonies, wrote regularly to London leaders. In an era with few other forms of regular information exchange between the colonies and the metropole, this regular contact with London was an important source of colonial officials' power.[17] The mediation revolution also gave them great leverage over the distribution of news, because printers and postmasters prudently recognized that colonial leaders could choose to reward or punish them based on their allegiances.

This system began to break down, though, with the conclusion of the Seven Years' War. In 1764 and 1765, the British Parliament began to enact taxes on the colonies to pay down the empire's massive wartime debt. The most controversial of these taxes was a stamp duty. When Parliament began to debate the proposed stamp tax in 1765, Connecticut's agent Jared Ingersoll was taking notes in the gallery. Parliament did not produce records of its deliberations at the time, making Ingersoll's one of the only available accounts of the debate.

According to his version, discussions initially centered on the issue of representation. Were the North American colonies truly represented in Parliament, given that this body had, as one member pointed out, an "almost total unacquaintedness" with them?[18] The ministry might communicate with its representatives in the colonies, but members of Parliament could go their whole careers without giving much thought to the lives and affairs of the colonists. The act's opponents argued that Parliament could only justly represent those with whom it could directly communicate.

At this point, Colonel Isaac Barré, one of the few members who had spent a considerable amount of time in North America, rose to speak. Born in Ireland, Barré had served in the British army with distinction in the North American theater of the Seven Years' War. According to Ingersoll's account, Barré challenged MP Charles Townshend's argument that Britain had "indulged" the colonies: "as soon as you began to care about Em, that care was Exercised in sending persons to rule over Em . . . sent to Spy out their Lyberty, to misrepresent their Actions & to prey upon Em." The problem, Barré argued, was that most members of Parliament knew nothing about the colonies and were therefore "acting very much in the dark."[19] The occasional letter from colonial governors, he suggested, could not provide Parliament with the information needed to rule effectively. Nor could it provide a full accounting of colonial affairs. For Barré, misrepresentation begat misrule.

According to Ingersoll, Barré eloquently rose above the scrum of debate to defend the colonies. While an MP named Nathaniel Ryder recorded a much less dramatic version of the speech in his private notebook, Ingersoll's account spread widely.[20] After he sent it home to Connecticut, it appeared in newspapers and pamphlets in Rhode Island, Massachusetts, and Canada.[21] A Boston town assembly sent him a message of thanks.[22] While the speech is mostly remembered today, if at all, for Barré's description of the colonists as the "Sons of Liberty," which a radical group of colonists adopted for themselves, the speech's focus on communication and misrepresentation had a more immediate impact. His argument helped to spark a broader debate among the settlers about how information should flow between the colonies and London. Crucially, Barré's speech connected the issue of representation with concerns about misrepresentation. For many colonists, these topics were indistinguishable. To the extent that they worried about taxation and representation, they were worried about consent.[23] Drawing on the ideas of John Locke and others, they believed that any deprivation of property without consent, including taxation, was tyranny—or even slavery. Representation allowed them to express or withhold that consent.[24]

As Barré's speech indicates, many Britons held an expansive vision of what it meant to be represented. They recognized the importance not only of formal, institutional representation through election and deliberation, but also of representations through communication and persuasion.[25] As early modern Britons increasingly came to believe that constituents had the right to advise their elected representatives, formal and informal modes of representation blurred together.[26] According to these emerging views, a constituent could consent to the government not only at the ballot box, but also by expressing their sentiments through petitions, instructions, and other ongoing communications. Prime Minister George Grenville and others had a different interpretation that was similar in its implications. He suggested that all colonists, like non-voting Britons, were "virtually represented in Parliament" because its members served the entire empire's interests regardless of who elected them.[27] Whether Parliament's legitimacy depended on its responsiveness to the people's will or to their needs, these models of representation depended on British subjects' ability to communicate effectively with their leaders. This was much easier, though, for someone in Hampshire than someone in New Hampshire.

Barré's rallying cry pushed colonists to reconsider the stakes of imperial communications. Simultaneously, the failure of his protest created new opportunities for a different kind of information exchange. The passage of the Stamp Act, as historian Joseph Adelman has shown, would have ruined the businesses of many colonial printers. Formerly allied with colonial administrators, printers quickly mobilized against the tax and the ministry that had passed it.[28] They helped to open an alternative model of imperial communications. Instead of information flowing privately among the trusted few, newspapers and other publications allowed colonists to represent themselves to London through popular channels. While imperial officials argued that private communications allowed them to be candid, colonists believed that it left them unaccountable for spreading falsehoods. By collecting and publishing the testimony of their fellow settlers after inflammatory events, colonists asserted the priority of public forms of communication.

Jealously protecting their centrality in imperial communications, governors and other leaders viewed these new forms of Atlantic information exchange as illegitimate. They disparaged popular media, including newspapers, as the "common fame" and emphasized that their own reports were far more reliable.[29] When colonists attempted to sidestep this hierarchical system of information exchange, governors such as Bernard chided them that it was "irregular and unconstitutional" for an assembly to speak directly to the king "except thro' the Mediation of his Representative."[30] He believed that colonists who sent letters to the king and his ministers were "deficient in Duty, Respect and even common Civility."[31] There were good reasons, he believed, that ordinary people did not communicate publicly with London leaders. Worthy hands and privacy protected the integrity of information exchange. Harrumph.

Protesting colonists, in contrast, viewed public representations to be necessary correctives to private misrepresentations. They hoped that their publications would correct the ministry's unjustified credulity toward imperial officers. What made their testimony more trustworthy than those of the people? A Bostonian lamented that the government had "disregarded the fair and honest representations" of the people while giving "full credit" to the "misrepresentations of *self-interested* and designing men."[32] A Maryland newspaper writer with the pseudonym "Atticus" argued strenuously that the "humble and dutiful petitions and remonstrances of all the colonies, and the cries of four millions of loyal subjects" deserved "greater weight" than the "infamous arts and misrepresentations of a few men in office."[33] An essayist in a New York paper marveled that Britons trusted observations from Hutchinson, a "solitary trumpeter of his own popularity and praise," more than information from the "people themselves."[34]

Perhaps, some argued, those in positions of power were uniquely ill suited to determining the truth. A letter supposedly written by a British officer in Boston, published in a Virginia newspaper, explained, "It is impossible you should gather any thing but misinformation from the men who, I find, surround head quarters."[35] Patriot leader Charles Lee likewise complained to British Whig leader Edmund Burke that Hutchinson's successor, Thomas Gage, "took all possible means of shutting up the avenues of truth" by speaking only to those already within the orbit of the British government. Lee contended that if Gage had attempted to "listen to the representations of the town at large," then the entire conflict could have been avoided.[36]

This epistemological reorientation, from trusting the testimony of powerful gentlemen to trusting ordinary people in the aggregate, grew out of temporary exigencies. Elite colonists did not stop believing that their word counted more than those of ordinary working people. Nor did they delegate the task of communicating and challenging misrepresentation to non-elites. But they called upon an amorphous, unitary "public," which they claimed to convene and speak for, to challenge imperial leaders. Historian Mark Schmeller has shown that elite North American revolutionaries initially resisted the rhetoric and logic of "public opinion" as a foundation for self-government.[37] As a voice arguing for future courses of action, for what *ought* to happen, elites found "public opinion" to be too democratic and destabilizing at this point. It was more convenient and less dangerous for elites to call upon the testimony of the people about what had *already* happened. By claiming to speak for a broad public, Patriot political elites suggested that they—rather than imperial administrators—were the proper mediators of truth.

Throughout the late 1760s and early 1770s, angry colonists repeatedly attempted to defeat the misrepresentations of government officials and replace them with their own narratives of events. Battered by the collapsing economy, Boston led much of this resistance.[38] Additional taxes and tighter enforcement of trade regulations made matters worse. The city was tense, which made villains handy.

Many colonists blamed Governors Bernard and Hutchinson, as well as other British officials, for the city's pain. Their exaggerations, it seemed, had invited the empire's repressive and economically punitive policies. Indeed, colonists so often accused Bernard of misrepresenting them to his superiors that by the summer of 1768, he could dismiss the allegations being lobbed at him by referring to a fresh one as being "in the old Strain, complaining that they have been misrepresented." He imagined himself as a martyr to public mania, "sure to be made obnoxious to the Madness of the People, by the Testimony I am obliged to bear against it."[39]

One of the earliest incidents to provoke Bostonians' cries of misrepresentation had involved a merchant named Daniel Malcolm. In 1766, customs officials asked Malcolm to open his cellar, where they suspected he stored smuggled wine. Malcolm refused, and a crowd gathered to intimidate the officials. After a tense standoff, the customs officers left, and Malcolm treated the spectators to buckets of wine.[40] Wary colonists quickly recognized that London officials could use this anecdote to bolster the rapidly coalescing narrative that the settlers were unruly and defiant. When they learned that Bernard had ordered that depositions be taken about the incident, they worried that he would exaggerate the story.[41] Colonists organized a town meeting to preemptively denounce Bernard's account, stating, "There is a set of men in America who are continually transmitting to the mother country odious and false accounts of the collonys" to excite "a groundless Jealousy" in Britain. They also expressed fear that Bernard's "partial account" could "be made the grounds of further misrepresentations." They sent to London their own depositions, which minimized the drama of the confrontation and instead complained at length about Bernard's efforts to inflame tensions.[42]

As the London ministry grew increasingly hostile to them, angry Massachusetts colonists continued to blame Bernard. After a squabble in 1767 between Bernard and the Massachusetts House of Representatives about appointments to the colony's council, Lord Shelburne, then serving as secretary of state for the colonies, sent a letter supporting Bernard's position.[43] This raised some questions. What did Shelburne know about the individuals in question? How could he evaluate the fitness of men, the House of Representatives asked, "whom he *never saw*, and in all likelihood, *never heard of* before"?[44] The answer seemed obvious. Bernard must have misrepresented the men to Shelburne. Colonists interpreted the actions of Lord Hillsborough, Shelburne's successor, in much the same way. After Hillsborough sent a letter to the Massachusetts House of Representatives demanding that it rescind an "inflammatory" circular letter, the body responded by remarking that Bernard must have provided Hillsborough with "some very aggravated Representations" to create such an extraordinary demand.[45]

The most serious allegations against Bernard related to the arrival of imperial troops in Boston. When soldiers disembarked in 1768, the Massachusetts Council blamed the lies of "some illminded persons" for their arrival.[46] Propagandist Samuel Adams began a regular newspaper series called "Journal of Occurrences," which denounced the "interested and false mediums" deceiving London about the colonies. Ominously, he argued that "those persons whose misrepresentations have procured troops to be quartered among us" had also led the troops to seek confrontation.[47] Adams's cousin John later remembered the arrival of these troops as a low point: "every thing We could do, was misrepresent[ed] and Nothing We could say was credited."[48]

Amid this environment of suspicion, a group of colonists gathered and published a collection of letters directed to London officials from Bernard, a few customs commissioners, and two British military commanders, Commodore Samuel Hood and General Thomas Gage. Published as a pamphlet with the unimaginative title *Letters to the Ministry from Governor Bernard, General Gage, and Commodore Hood*, these letters caused a massive scandal. Yet in many ways, they were quite benign—dull, even. A few passages, nevertheless, aroused indignation. Bernard's suggestion that the Massachusetts charter be altered to weaken the council and strengthen the office of the governor led to widespread condemnation.[49] The customs commissioners' suggestion that "two or three Regiments" would be necessary to "restore and support Government" in Boston also sparked outrage.[50] Here, it seemed, was hard evidence that a group of officials was conspiring to intentionally exaggerate the disorder in Massachusetts and bring troops into Boston. Angry colonists reacted with newspaper essays and protests. A grand jury indicted Bernard. The assembly demanded his recall.[51] Before things could get out of control, Bernard returned to England, leaving Lieutenant Governor Thomas Hutchinson in charge of the colony.

Much as they had done after the incident involving Daniel Malcolm, Bostonians convened a town meeting to address these letters. They directed a committee led by Samuel Adams to publish a refutation. Its text focused mostly on batting down specific details in the letters, but Adams and his fellow writers also threaded throughout the pamphlet a critique of how the empire's leaders gathered information about the colonies. They claimed that Bernard's sources were unreliable and mocked him for relying on "pimps [i.e., informers] and parasites," the "dependents and expectants" of customs officers, and even, in one case, the "vague and idle reports" of a supposedly hysterical woman. Eighteenth-century British elites, they knew, would have distrusted intelligence derived from "dependent sources," that is, individuals who offered information in exchange for pay or patronage. An unstable woman might have seemed even worse.[52] Moreover, the pamphlet blasted Bernard for passing along unverified rumors. In one letter to the secretary of state describing an incident of disorder, Bernard had explained that he did not "relate these accounts as certain facts."[53] If they were not facts, the pamphlet writers responded, "To what purpose then did he relate them at all!"[54] The point was clear. Bernard—and perhaps colonial officials more generally—could not reliably mediate between the colonies and London.

Concern over misrepresentation rose to a new pitch in 1770. On March 5, the British troops that Bernard had invited to Boston engaged in a bloody confrontation with a crowd of colonists. Colonial propagandists quickly labeled this event the Boston Massacre, a name that has stuck through the centuries. As before, colonists worried that the violent events would be misrepresented abroad. A town meeting appointed a committee to produce a "full and Just representation" of the events for British readers. The report's authors framed it as the unanimous voice of the city in contrast to the governor's partial account. In addition to a litany of charges about misrepresentation, the colonists claimed that the violence in Boston would never have happened if Bernard's earlier lies had not brought the troops to the city in the first place. In this sense, misrepresentation was a "a blameable cause" of the massacre.[55] Colonial leaders' lies, it seemed, had finally resulted in violence and death. The stakes of miscommunication had mounted.

Several years later, another round of secret communications appeared in print. In 1773, colonists published a volume of letters that Thomas Hutchinson, Lieutenant Governor Andrew Oliver, and customs officer Charles Paxton had sent to England. In these letters was Hutchinson's account of the barrel controversy and a passage about the abridgment of the colonists' liberties. Hutchinson claimed that he was predicting, rather than prescribing, that those liberties might eventually be limited.[56] While this seems to be true in context, angry colonists did not read the letter generously. Additionally, Paxton begged the ministry to immediately send "two or three regiments" or else "Boston *will be in open rebellion.*"[57] Printers widely shared the letters in their newspapers, and the pamphlet *Representations of Governor Hutchinson and Others* went through ten editions. With the title's first word, the compilers reminded readers that these accounts were the foremost way that the colonists were being represented in England.

Perhaps the most dramatic example of Patriots' use of newspapers to drive opinion in Britain occurred after the Battles of Lexington and Concord in April 1775. Knowing that imperial officers would send their own account of the confrontations to London, the Patriot colonists' local Committee of Safety quickly gathered depositions and published them in friendly newspapers. Hearing that the British army's version of the battles would soon be sent aboard a brig called the *Sukey*, the Patriots secretly dispatched a quicker schooner, the *Quero*, loaded with copies of their newspapers.[58] The *Quero* whizzed across the ocean, delivering the Patriots' account, which denounced the "Cruelty" of the "brutal" British soldiers, well before their enemies' story. It was rushed to the presses of America's sympathizers in London. Even according to British secretary of state Lord George Sackville, the news "occasioned a great stir."[59] The ministry had no answer for two weeks. In the interim, the *London Gazette* instructed its readers to wait patiently.[60]

Patriot colonists understood that readers abroad followed their accounts closely. "Every dispatch from America changes the plan of Government," one London reprint claimed. It seemed that the "hue of the Ministry changes, like the cameleon, with the objects that approach it."[61] Patriots hoped that their public representations would correct the record about events in the colonies. Concerns about misrepresentation had led them to believe that if they did not provide news for British audiences, false rumors would occupy the vacuum. They were somewhat successful. Because Patriots controlled most of the political newspapers on the continent, they flooded Britain with information that affirmed their cause.[62] Reprints from Patriot newspapers led at least one Tory printer in London to grumble that the British papers were "daily filled with the grossest Falsities," which had been "copied from one another all over this King's Dominions."[63]

Colonial newspapers regularly printed any indication that London was taking notice of them. In 1774, the *Newport Herald* published the "Substance of the American papers read before the House of Commons."[64] The next year, a handbill published in New York breathlessly indicated the stakes of colonial printing: "The ministry are alarmed at every opposition, and lifted up again at every thing which appears the least in their favour. . . . every paper from hence are read by them."[65] Some Patriot printers took great satisfaction when they saw that their accounts were republished in England. In 1773, Patriot printer Isaiah Thomas shared that a Boston town meeting's pamphlet in response to the Tea Act had appeared in a London newspaper. Pleased that the Boston account had been "so well approved of by our friends on the other side of the water," he returned the favor by sharing the London printer's lengthy introduction. In it, this printer had argued that while the ministry had "suppressed" the "true state of affairs" in the colonies, the Bostonians' account offered an antidote, more credible for being the "unanimous act of a large American city" rather than the "production of a private writer."[66] Thomas did not share this introduction for its novelty. His readers had encountered these arguments before. Rather, he reprinted it because it indicated to his Patriot readers that their efforts to challenge misrepresentation were successfully reaching their desired transatlantic audience.

While historians sometimes view Patriots' publications as "propaganda" intended to mobilize Americans, the audience for these pamphlets was not only other colonists, but also, and in some cases primarily, metropolitan Britons.[67] The Boston town meeting's pamphlet about the Bernard letters, for example, was titled *An Appeal to the World*. Similarly, the town meeting convened in response to the Boston Massacre ordered a pamphlet to be printed but distributed only in Britain to avoid prejudicing potential jurors. Such texts spread widely around the British Atlantic and met a receptive audience. Claims of misrepresentation meshed well with the British radical movement led by

John Wilkes, which was pushing for parliamentary reform based on the premise that Britain's political institutions were not representative of the people.[68] Though they only spoke for a small portion of the British population, Wilkes's followers amplified colonists' complaints about misrepresentation.

Readers of Patriot newspapers would have regularly come across evidence that some Britons agreed with their complaints about misrepresentation. An item reprinted in a Boston newspaper, for example, claimed that one of the "popular and prevailing toasts" in England was "May the unrepresented Americans be no longer misrepresented."[69] A New York paper likewise shared a petition signed by Bristol merchants suggesting that the colonists' "disposition" was "by no means so unfavorable as many persons, from passion or misinformation, may possibly suggest."[70] Another London account reprinted in a Patriot paper explained, "Much has been said of a *virtual representation*, which the Colonies are supposed to have here; but we know what kind of *actual representation*, or rather *misrepresentation*, is continually made of them by those from whom Administration chiefly have their information." After summarizing the colonists' complaints about false accounts, the article asked, "Thus REPRESENTED, how can it be otherwise but the governing people in Britain should conceive the most unfavourable idea of Americans?"[71] To the protesting colonists reading these words, it must have appeared as if their arguments were beginning to resonate among the British public.

Moreover, protests against misrepresentation spread to colonists outside of Massachusetts. Many British Americans worried that falsehoods about Massachusetts could harm their own colonies' relationship to the metropole. A group of New Jersey merchants, a Philadelphia town meeting, a committee of Philadelphia merchants, and the South Carolina House of Representatives all denounced the misrepresentations of imperial mediators in Massachusetts.[72]

Bostonians' well-publicized accusations of misrepresentation inspired other British Americans to guard against the possibility that their own colonial officials were lying and exaggerating about local conditions. In 1766, a group of Pennsylvanians accused stamp tax officer John Hughes of writing several letters to London, which they printed in a Philadelphia newspaper. One of those letters claimed that "unless my hands are strengthened *it will never be in my power to put the act in execution.*" In response, Hughes denied that he had written the letters and threatened legal action against the printers who published them.[73]

The publication of the Bernard and Hutchinson letters in 1769 and 1773 encouraged people in other colonies to be vigilant toward their own governors' correspondence. In 1776 Patriot leaders came across a series of letters between London authorities and Maryland's royal governor, Robert Eden. The Continental Congress ordered Eden and his papers seized. After he was ultimately exonerated from accusations that he had misrepresented the colonists, the Congress asked him to leave the colonies in the hope that he would favorably "represent the temper and principles of the people of Maryland."[74]

Virginians, too, feared that their governor, the Earl of Dunmore, was misrepresenting them to leaders in London. In June 1775, in the aftermath of violent conflicts in the colony that had caused Dunmore to flee to a British warship in the York River, the House of Burgesses took note of a pair of letters from Dunmore to Lord Dartmouth, secretary of state for the colonies, from the previous year. In the first letter, Dunmore had expressed alarm at a resolution from the House of Burgesses urging Virginians to publicly fast and pray because he believed it was intended to "prepare the minds of the people" for more violent measures.[75] In response, the House of Burgesses explained that this expectation was misplaced and that suspicion did not "justify direct and positive Accusation."[76] The House saved its most acerbic words, though, for Dunmore's claim that boycotts were leading the colony's gentry to hoard supplies. Perhaps because the House of Burgesses primarily represented the gentry, the members objected that this was exaggerated and added that in the event of a scarcity, "the middling and poorer sort will fare much better than those of Fortune, who have large numbers of Slaves to provide for." In sum, they believed that "our Conduct should be fairly and impartially represented to our Sovereign." Though they civilly declined to accuse Dunmore of intentionally misrepresenting facts, they suggested instead that "you too easily give Credit to some designing Persons" who "possess much too large a share of your Confidence."[77]

One did not need to be a colonial governor or officer to arouse suspicions of engaging in misrepresentation. A number of colonists accused their neighbors of sharing false news with British contacts. In late 1775, for example, Patriot newspapers reported that passengers aboard a ship from Philadelphia to London had discovered that a person named Christopher Carter carried letters full of "the most infamous lies . . . to spirit up the ministry against this city and province" and to encourage Britain to send troops.[78] A year earlier, Connecticut colonists had intercepted letters from an Anglican preacher named Samuel Peters, which seemed bound to "incense the government at home." In response, according to newspaper accounts, a mob of 300 men went to Peters's home and intimidated him into showing them his correspondence.[79]

Not long after, colonists intercepted another incriminating letter from Peters, and he left for England.[80] Despite protesting his innocence, Peters would eventually knowingly spread a batch of misrepresentations about the colonists. His hatred of the Patriots led him to compose a history of Connecticut that fabricated absurd colonial "Blue Laws" and mocked Puritans. Perhaps knowing that his former interrogators would read it, he explained in the preface that any errors in the book owed to his "having been deprived of papers," presumably by the Patriot mob that had seized his letters in 1774.[81] Peters's misrepresentations repaid earlier accusations of misrepresentation.

In Tidewater Virginia, a committee of Patriots charged a schoolteacher named David Wardrobe with authoring a series of misrepresentations in 1775. Under pressure to confess, he admitted to composing a "false, scandalous" letter that had appeared in a Glasgow newspaper concerning a crowd's protests. The committee affected disappointment about the "fatal consequences" that could result for the colonies. The members decided to disallow his use of a building for his school, to warn the area's children about him, and to require him to write a letter of apology for the newspapers. They also arranged for further criminal charges.[82] Not all Virginia Patriots, however, were so confident in attacking misrepresenters. That same year, someone signing as "Censor" wrote an essay in the *Virginia Gazette* to an unnamed villain who, they claimed, exerted "every quality of the head, and passion of the heart, to misrepresent and magnify" incidents of Patriot overzealousness.[83]

Early modern epistolary culture designated some letters as public, available for communal readings or to be excerpted in newspapers, and others as private, whose contents were to remain inviolate. Indeed, the Hutchinson letters circulated among Patriot leaders for quite a while before anyone dared to make them public, contrary to their author's intentions.[84] An intercepted letter thus held a position of particular interest in early modern communications. Taking private materials to the public seemed to lift the veil of a secret underworld of elite exchange, to which ordinary people otherwise had little access. Drawing on long-standing symbolic links between secrecy, corruption, and conspiracy, it seemed as if legitimate communications should occur in public.[85] Even the most unremarkable findings could seem outrageous if ripped from beneath a veil of secrecy. As a result, many of the Patriots' efforts to detect misrepresentation, including the events surrounding the Bernard and Hutchinson letters, were often more sensational than substantive.[86]

While Patriots worried about private communications misrepresenting them, Loyalists worried that the Patriots would misrepresent them publicly.

Patriot leaders succeeded in taking control of the levers of communication to such an extent that some Loyalists feared Patriot mediation. New Jersey's Loyalist governor, William Franklin, for example, worried that some Pennsylvanians were aiming to "intercept many of my letters from England, in hopes of finding something of which they may take advantage."[87] Likewise, Samuel Curwen, a Loyalist merchant who had fled to London, explained to a North American correspondent that he was reluctant to discuss politics in his letters in case they should "get into the hands of the provincials," who could take "the most innocent expressions" and twist them "into a sense entirely foreign to one's intention."[88]

Indeed, the Patriots' strategy of uncovering misrepresenters and flooding Britain with their own media served to silence and sideline Loyalists. Their reports ignored the existence of dissenting Loyalists. After the Boston Massacre, the pamphlet that the colonists created featured a title page that identified it as "Printed by Order of the Town of BOSTON."[89] The pamphlet took no questions, but its readers might have reasonably asked a few: How many Bostonians were involved in creating this publication? How many agreed with it? How many would dispute it? How many were totally indifferent? In 1768, Bernard protested to leaders in London that the Massachusetts House of Representatives, which charged that he was "misrepresenting the Generality of the People," was itself a falsehood. That body, he insisted, only "pretends to be the Voice of the People," but was in fact the "Voice of a Faction."[90] He was largely correct. Historians now agree that the Patriots spoke for only a minority of the colonial population.[91] In their zeal to challenge misrepresentations, they had misrepresented themselves as the voice of a public consensus.

If the American Patriots believed that pamphlets and newspapers could defeat misrepresentation by speaking for a vague "public," petitions provided actual evidence of the existence of such a public. Patriots coordinated dozens of petitions in the late 1760s and early 1770s.[92] Petitions seemed to allow for direct communication between the people of Britain and of North America, bypassing the layers of mediation that produced misrepresentation. As a convention of Massachusetts citizens wrote in a petition in 1768, "Nothing, we apprehend, is wanting to restore a much desired harmony, but for his Majesty's subjects, on both sides the atlantic, fully to explain themselves to each other."[93] In their bid to speak for a broad public, petitions often counterposed the open voice of the "people" against the private words of a small group of officials. In 1769 a Boston town meeting sent a petition to Isaac Barré to be presented to the king, complaining that the monarch had received "greatly exaggerated" accounts of Boston. They wished that the town, "having a clear and precise understanding of such matters," be allowed to defend itself from these charges, but the Bostonians were instead "kept in total ignorance of such representations as have been made against them, even until they have felt their unhappy effects."[94] Private communications, they protested, were immune to corrections.

Petitioners insisted that their efforts were necessary to elude untrustworthy mediators. In a 1774 petition to King George, for example, the Continental Congress attacked the "designing and dangerous men . . . daringly interposing themselves between your royal person and your faithful subjects." They grumbled, "So greatly have we been misrepresented, that a necessity has been alleged of taking our property from us, without our consent" when they would have gladly (or so they claimed) paid taxes for the support of the king's government.[95] In July 1775, the Continental Congress issued its famous "olive branch" petition in a final effort to reconcile the colonies with Britain. The petition blamed the conflict largely on the "irksome . . . artifices" and "delusive pretences" of "your Majesty's Ministers."[96] Like most complaints about misrepresentation, this petition allowed colonists to protest imperial actions without disowning the Crown, in hopes of bringing about a reconciliation.

These hopes proved futile, however, as petitions rarely reached their intended audience. Parliament and the king often ignored petitions, believing that direct communications of this sort were inappropriate.[97] Many petitioners feared that the very intermediaries whom they were attempting to skirt prevented their message from reaching the homeland's leaders. One frustrated colonist asked, "What can the Subjects do, if the King's Minister, by whom our Petitions are to be presented to the Royal Ear, flings them under the Table?"[98] What kind of system was it, a Philadelphia town meeting asked, that suppressed the "cries and petitions" of subjects, while the "grossest misrepresentations" of "ministerial tools" were "listened to with attention"?[99] Yet petitioning continued, particularly in the early 1770s, as colonists hoped that one of their pleas would make it through the mediators separating them from the king and the ministry. A Boston town meeting in 1773, for example, had optimistically concluded, "we yet perswade ourselves that could the Petitions of his much aggrieved Subjects be transmitted to his Majesty, through the hands of an honest impartial Minister, we should not fail of ample Redress."[100]

Patriot agitators hoped that their voices would reach several audiences abroad: the British people, Parliament, the ministry, and the king. Navigating the rapidly shifting needs and expectations of each group, though, was very difficult from afar. The Patriot leaders often needed to rely on colonial agents to challenge misrepresentations and thereby shift the balance of transatlantic communications. By the 1760s and 1770s, agents who had once focused on lobbying for colonial interests increasingly worked to represent colonial bodies to British audiences. As one Massachusetts town put it, agents now needed to "counteract and defeat, the Devices and Intrigues of our Enemies, and to keep us duly informed of their Machinations against us."[101] Among many others, Connecticut's agent William Samuel Johnson dedicated himself to countering the "flattering, fallacious representations" of the ministry's "interested, wretched sycophants."[102]

Agents also actively gathered information to combat misrepresentations. Dennys De Berdt, a London merchant who served as an agent for Delaware and the Massachusetts House of Representatives, wrote a 1766 letter to Massachusetts Patriot leader James Otis reporting that rumors about colonists speaking ungratefully about the repeal of the Stamp Act were circulating through London. Recognizing that this could damage the colonists' cause, he asked for materials that would put it "in my power to contradict it."[103] Similarly, in 1767 Rhode Island's agent Joseph Sherwood asked his colony's governor for "a true State of the Real Facts" so that he could "Contradict and Falsify" the "highly Coloured and aggrevated" information arriving in London.[104] In sharing Patriot accounts, agents often aimed to reach public audiences. On one occasion, after he determined that Parliament would not receive a Connecticut petition in the "official way," Johnson promised to bring it to the people so that it would be "sufficiently known, both within and without doors."[105]

Yet because colonial agents better understood the political dynamics and conventions of London, they sometimes chose to temper the colonists' instinct to make public all their communications. While angry colonists sought to unclog Atlantic communications by speaking directly to the people of Britain, agents knew that this would sometimes backfire. Public communications, after all, irritated imperial officials who felt that news should properly travel through mediators such as themselves. De Berdt took care to use private communications when appropriate. When addressing Lord Dartmouth, then serving on the Board of Trade, De Berdt conceded that "Popular Representations," like newspapers, were "often fallacious . . . but Letters from one Friend to another without any View but that of Representing naked Truth may be relied on." To that end, he enclosed a letter from an American merchant that contained the man's "Native Sentiments without Disguise."[106] Whether or not De Berdt truly distrusted popular sources of news, he presented evidence that he expected to satisfy a leading London official.

Johnson, likewise, advised the colonists to avoid publishing "extracts of letters from agents and others residing" in London because these actions had already caused "very great offence." Some news sources were too candid for public airing. He also explained to Connecticut's governor that the colony should hide the fact that it had paid off its debts because any information about "our internal circumstances" could be "liable to much misconstruction." By hiding the truth from British officials, he hoped to "meet Ministerial art with American prudence."[107] Compared to earlier hopeful efforts to clear the air, this was a more cynical approach to defeating misrepresentation. Instead of direct communication bringing two peoples together, as many protesting North Americans had once imagined, the agents aimed to strategically represent the colonists in order to defeat misrepresentation.

Benjamin Franklin, who spent nearly the entire imperial crisis in London, served as a colonial agent at various moments for Massachusetts, Pennsylvania, Georgia, and New Jersey. Even someone with Franklin's extensive connections, though, struggled to break through the barriers erected by colonial officials. In a 1769 letter to Noble Wimberly Jones, the speaker of Georgia's lower house, Franklin explained that he had presented an address from the Georgia legislature to Lord Hillsborough to be submitted to King George. Yet Hillsborough dismissed the petition and sent his answer not to the assembly, but to Georgia's governor, determining that "all applications from the Colonies to Government here ought to be thro' the hands of the Respective Governors."[108]

With official channels blocked, Franklin used his gifts as a writer to shape public opinion in Britain. The next year, he wrote an essay for the *London Chronicle* titled "The Rise and Present State of Our Misunderstanding." Franklin insisted that the colonists should not be punished "at the instance of *angry Governors, discarded Agents, or rash indiscreet Officers of the Customs*, who, having quarrelled with them, are their enemies, and are daily irritating Government here against them, by misrepresentations of their actions." The colonists were innocent but misunderstood. He explained that by refusing to accept petitions from them, "the ancient well contrived channel of communication between the head and members of this great Empire, thro' which the notice of grievances could be received that remedies might be applied, hath been cut off." With their petitions ignored, the American colonists had con-cluded, according to Franklin, "We are too remote from Britain to have our complaints regarded by the Parliament there. . . . They will not hear us, but perhaps they will hear their own people, their Merchants and Manufactur-ers."[109] This was the logic behind the colonists' boycotts. It was a way of mak-ing themselves difficult to ignore. For Franklin, the early stages of the Amer-ican Revolution were a contest between the colonists' desire to be heard and imperial officials' desire to silence and misrepresent them. Through advocacy in public venues, such as the *London Chronicle*, Franklin and his allies hoped to communicate their way out of the crisis.

Through their discourse of misrepresentation, colonists rejected the long-standing belief that government officials were the colonies' proper mediators of Atlantic information. In earlier decades, newspaper printers and other me-diators had feared that sharing news that contradicted the government could land them in jail. But the support of a mobilized faction allowed popular mediators in the 1760s and 1770s to vocally challenge the government's arbi-tration of truth without a serious threat of reprisal. If anyone had reason to be worried, it was officials such as Bernard, Hutchinson, Eden, William Frank-lin, and Dunmore. The violence and anger of colonial protests excited the anxieties of colonial officials, who worried about sharing news of which the colonists might disapprove. Colonial protestors did not reverse the mediation revolution of previous decades as much as they replaced it with their own.

Yet for all this resistance, colonists conceived of their concerns about mis-representation as fundamentally a loyal action. A 1768 letter published in the Patriot *Boston Gazette* suggested that if "*misrepresentation* has been the chief cause of *Distraction*," then a "*removal* of the cause of distraction may be the means of *reconciliation*."[110] By reforming the eastward flow of imperial infor-mation, colonists hoped to dispel "this Mist . . . from [Britain's] eyes."[111] The belief that misrepresentation stood at the core of the crisis of the British em-pire, and the conviction that it could be fixed, allowed the crisis to stretch through a decade of futile protests.

But British leaders were not the deluded victims of artifice that some col-onists imagined them to be. They did not solely rely on official correspon-dence for news about British America. They read the colonists' newspapers, pamphlets, and petitions. They heard from their agents. They even began to intercept and screen letters from North America to uncover the colonists' true sentiments.[112] From all of these sources, they understood that the Patriots disagreed with the versions of events presented by official mediators. They just didn't particularly care. No petition or pamphlet would change that. If imperial leaders erred, it was in overestimating the strength of colonial loyalty. Perhaps they sensed that this endless talk about removing the sources of misrepresentation indicated that even the Patriot colonists simply wanted a reconciliation.

This was not to be, of course. By the mid-1770s, colonists' hopes for restoring honorable channels of communication gradually began to wilt. In late 1774, members of the Massachusetts Provincial Congress told their constituents that they no longer believed there was any "reasonable expectation that the truth of facts would be made known in England."[113] It seemed as if the truths cultivated by popular mediators in the colonies could not be reconciled with the truths held by British officials. Complaints about misrepresentation and hopes for reconciliation could only be sustained for so long. After exhausting every effort to correct the flow of information, some colonists began to ask if perhaps misrepresentation was not the only problem but was symptomatic of larger problems.

Thomas Paine's 1776 pamphlet, *Common Sense*, helped to push protesting colonists from focusing on reconciliation to imagining independence. One of the ways Paine accomplished this was by drawing on and extending existing conversations about misrepresentation. Rather than blaming individuals for their lies, as Patriots had long done, Paine attacked a system that enabled them to share such lies. The fact that misrepresentations had misled the king may not have been the fault of the king himself, he argued, but it *was* the fault of monarchy. In one famous formulation, Paine wrote that there is "something exceedingly ridiculous in the composition of monarchy; it first excludes a man from the means of information, yet empowers him to act in cases where the highest judgment is required." Similarly, Paine envisioned the distance between Britain and North America not as something that could be overcome with improved information exchange, but as a "strong and natural proof" that British authority over the American colonies "was never the design of Heaven." He concluded that the time for petitioning was over. Britons would remain "very ignorant of us," no matter how many times the colonists petitioned them. "To be always running three or four thousand miles with a tale or a petition, waiting four or five months for an answer, which when obtained requires five or six more to explain it" was absurd.[114]

For Paine, massive empires could never sustain meaningful, truthful communication. Misrepresentation was an inevitable feature of an imbalanced imperial relationship and an irrational monarchical government. There could be no honest communication within a fundamentally corrupt system. The imperial crisis could not be solved through protests, petitions, or representations. Reconciliation was impossible.

CHAPTER THREE

The Lying Gazettes

News from London in Revolutionary Politics

Hugh Palliser was losing patience. As governor of Newfoundland, he faced the challenging task of protecting the sparsely populated British colony's fishing economy while also keeping peace with the region's Indigenous people. He had recently agreed to a peace deal with a local Inuit leader, but their relationship remained fragile. The boisterous New Englanders to the south were no help. In 1764, according to Palliser, a group of Massachusetts fishermen, who had begun "Robbing, Plundering & otherways Ill treating on the Coast of Labrador, took away five [Native people], who they either murther'd or carry'd home to make Slaves of." A year later, a Boston schooner stole a Native community's furs instead of trading for them. In a letter to a colonial official in London, Palliser did not mince words. Describing numerous specific atrocities, he called the New England fishermen "Barbarous, Savage, Lawless Banditti," "a disgrace to human Nature," and "a Scandal to the Country to which they belong."[1]

In August 1766, Palliser wrote to the governor of Massachusetts, Francis Bernard, asking him to try to end these practices by placing printed notices in whaling towns warning against such violence. Bernard seems to have quickly done so without even bothering to respond to Palliser.[2] Perhaps he was distracted by escalating protests against British authority in Massachusetts. Or perhaps that resistance helped to confirm Palliser's allegations for Bernard. In any case, Bernard ensured that Palliser's proclamation, which forbade violence against Newfoundland Natives and attacked New Englanders for their "cruel Conduct," was published in the *Massachusetts Gazette and Bos-*

ton News-Letter. At the top of this notice, Bernard appended an explanation that he was publishing it at Palliser's request.[3]

By passing along Palliser's proclamation, Bernard was acting according to prevailing expectations about how information should move around the Atlantic world. Through decades of experience, Britons had learned that it wasn't practical for individuals to verify every piece of information before sharing it with others. If communication were restricted to verified facts, they knew, there would be very little communication at all. According to this standard, Bernard did not need to confirm Palliser's charges in order to share them. But the political ferment of the 1760s led some British colonists in North America to question this long-standing consensus. Fears that they were being misrepresented to the British government led some colonists to reconsider the dangers of unverified streams of news flowing within and into the continent.

When the members of the anti-imperial Massachusetts House of Representatives saw Palliser's proclamation republished by Bernard, they admonished their governor, fearing that these "heinous charges" would harm the colony's reputation in the eyes of London authorities. But more significantly, they were shocked that Bernard would publish Palliser's accusations without having seen any evidence to support them. Unless he had the "most plenary proof of the allegations," they told Bernard, he should not have shared Palliser's proclamation.[4]

In his typical elevated and unapologetic tone, Bernard responded that he did not "make himself answerable for the truth of the facts mentioned therein" when he shared another governor's proclamation. As he understood it, he was simply making his subjects aware of a proclamation that could affect them. Unsurprisingly, the House of Representatives understood this differently. What mattered to them was not the newsworthiness of the proclamation but its truthfulness. They explained that Bernard could not simply hide behind another governor's word because "all men are in some degree answerable to the world for the truth of facts alledged not only in their own publications, but in re-publishing the works of others."[5] Despite their claim to be drawing on a long-standing set of expectations, this was new. Printers, who engaged in the work of republication more than any other group, had long exempted themselves from the burden of verification, leaving it to readers to decide what was true and what was false. But this new doctrine—that falsehoods could and should be both identified and suppressed, rather than republished—began to guide colonial protests during the 1760s and 1770s.

The problem was that early modern news mediators were not exactly up to the task of verification. As I describe in chapter 1, it was nearly impossible to tell which news stories were true if they originated from thousands of miles away. The era lacked the wire services, reporters, and shared standards of evidence that would eventually allow journalism to develop as a profession in the nineteenth century. Mediators only had a few tools for assessing the truthfulness of a piece of news. Some observers, for example, compared the contents and dates of a questionable account with what they considered to be more trustworthy news from the same region. Others judged news according to the social status of its bearer. Frustratingly, though, the best method available for assessing the quality of a piece of news was to simply wait. With enough time, further news would confirm truthful accounts and expose false-hoods. For newspaper printers who promised their readers the "Freshest Advices," though, this last strategy was unattractive.

Instead, in the late eighteenth century, mediators such as newspaper printers began to use a shortcut. When a politically charged piece of news arrived, Americans judged its truthfulness not according to its content or its context but based on the apparent political motives of its source. Today we know this analytical lens as "bias." As the world of politics grew angrier and more dichotomous, colonists began to disregard news that originated from their ideological opponents. For Patriots, this meant discarding most information from publications affiliated with the British ministry, whereas Loyalists tossed away paragraphs from the London opposition press.

Unsurprisingly, this impoverished approach to information literacy caused problems. By the mid-1770s, most North Americans had divided themselves not only into political camps, but also into epistemic camps. Believing that their adversaries in London were busily concocting news to deceive a credulous public, Loyalists and Patriots primarily read the news that served their interests. In fact, neither side was entirely wrong to be skeptical of their rivals' news sources. Both the British ministry, which pursued harsh measures against the colonists, and its more sympathetic opposition supported newspapers that slanted information toward their own ends. In this way, Britain's political culture in the late eighteenth century supported the creation of transatlantic information bubbles, in which aspiration and observation reinforced one another.

Looking back on the revolution in 1790, the Patriot propagandist Samuel Adams recalled of the British ministry, "We feared their Arts more than their Arms." He had worried that the ministry's "Finess, Tricks, and Stratagems" could fool Americans into giving up their liberty.[6] The contest over truth and information formed an underexamined but crucial front in the American war for independence. While historians have closely tracked the ways that the American Revolution politicized North American print and society, they have not appreciated the extent to which revolutionary politics reshaped American colonists' attitudes toward their news.[7]

This is perhaps because colonists deployed the squishy language of "truth" to justify and legitimize their campaign to control information flows. The word "truth" evokes much: claims both prescriptive and descriptive, statements both normative and falsifiable. Revolutionary texts that appealed to "truth" as their justification and lodestar evoke the elegant prose of the American Declaration of Independence's preamble: "We hold these truths to be self-evident . . ." But the declaration devoted far more space to factual assertions than it did to statements of principles. The American revolutionaries fought not only for self-evident truths, but also to make their convoluted, often unjustified description of reality into a "truth" that others would need to acknowledge and abide by. By monopolizing information mediation and relentlessly attacking the legitimacy of contrary news sources, they succeeded. The result was the beginning of the United States, a nation conceived in the seemingly permanent truths of equality and liberty, as well as the momentary, more questionable truths of British weakness and American victimhood.

In late 1767, the Scottish Loyalist printers John Mein and John Fleeming published the first issue of their *Boston Chronicle*. It contained a lengthy account reprinted from a London newspaper about the comings and goings of the British nobility and parliamentary leadership. Toward its conclusion, this section featured a paragraph disparaging the Whig leader and former prime minister William Pitt, the Earl of Chatham, whom American Patriots revered. It accused Pitt of feigning illness, deceiving the people, and being "a miserable monument of wrecked ambition."[8] A writer using the pseudonym "Americus" responded to this article's republication in the Patriot *Boston Gazette* published by Benjamin Edes and John Gill. Instead of providing "impartial Accounts concerning Affairs at Home," Americus charged, Mein and Fleeming had fabricated the report and shared it "under Cloke of being taken from the London Papers."[9]

Only hours after Edes and Gill published this letter, an agitated Mein arrived at the *Boston Gazette*'s print shop. According to a description of the scene that Edes published later, Mein said, "I suppose you know what I am come about." When Edes expressed confusion, Mein explained that he had come "to demand the author of the piece you printed against me." If Edes withheld the real name of Americus, Mein declared that he "should look upon us [Edes and Gill] as the author" before vaguely threatening his rivals with violence.[10] Citing long-standing practice, Edes refused to divulge the name. A few days later, seeking to recover his honor, Mein attacked Gill on the street with a cane.[11] The claim that Mein had manufactured a London newspaper account was apparently too serious an insult to be left unanswered. This violent incident, well known to historians of the American Revolution, exhibits the growing stakes of reprinted news in the 1760s and 1770s. Americus had been so disgusted by a piece of news ostensibly reprinted from London that he accused Mein and Fleeming of inventing it. Mein attacked Gill to defend his honor and, therefore, the credibility of his newspaper.[12] Aside from the violence, this was a typical example of the sorts of disputes about the London press that became common in subsequent years.

Angry colonists' concerns about falsehoods from abroad assumed an even greater urgency in 1770 when a confrontational Tory ministry led by Prime Minister Frederick North rose to power in London. The new government's defense of parliamentary power earned the colonists' ire during its lengthy tenure. As numerous historians have shown, protesting colonists came to believe that a "plot" or a "cabal" of ministers was aiming to "enslave" the Americans.[13] A crucial premise of this conspiracy was the idea that North and his allies had initiated a devious campaign of deception. During the 1770s, colonists began to accept that the North ministry was intentionally misinforming both the British public and the colonists in North America about all manner of events. Of all the colonists' conspiratorial ideas, this was among the most well founded. Throughout the eighteenth century, the British government had invested in shaping public perceptions by spending thousands of pounds each year subsidizing friendly papers and silencing opponents.[14] The ministry also directly controlled the *London Gazette*, allowing Undersecretary of State William Knox to choose what its readers would learn about the American controversy.[15]

The notion of a ministerial conspiracy of deception was, in some ways, an inversion of the misrepresentation narrative, which led many colonists to blame local officials, such as Francis Bernard and Thomas Hutchinson, for deceiving London leaders (see chapter 2). For most critics, however, these accounts were entirely compatible. Hutchinson, Bernard, and other colonial officials in North America melded easily into the broader gallery of ministerial villains. In a newspaper annotation, Boston shopkeeper Harbottle Dorr explained that Hutchinson "is a Tool to L[ord] Hillsborough, Lord Hillsborough is a Tool to [Tory leader John Stuart, Earl of] Bute, and the Earl of Bute [is] a Tool to the Devil!"[16] Likewise, Edes and Gill reprinted an essay from the London *Public Ledger* claiming that both the "Ministry at home, as well as the friends of that Ministry abroad" aimed to destroy the colonies' liberties. The anonymous British author blamed "all the troubles" in America on the "traitorous misrepresentations of the King's ministers in that country."[17] Referring to Hutchinson, Bernard, and others as "ministers," a word not typically used for colonial officials, blurred the line between the government in London and its representatives in the colonies.

In this new political cosmology, colonists initially exempted King George from condemnation.[18] At worst, George appeared to be a credulous victim of this campaign of deception rather than its abettor. Colonists had regularly complained that the ministry was keeping their protests and petitions from the sovereign's eyes. Indeed, according to some Patriot newspapers from the 1770s, King George seemed to be the only man in London unaware of the colonists' innocence. As one London opposition newspaper, which was reprinted in Pennsylvania, put it, " 'Tis difficult for a Prince to know the Truth."[19]

The Tory ministry controlled many of Britain's newspapers during the 1770s, but so did the Whig Party. Opposition presses stoked fears of ministerial deception. The London *Morning Post*, for example, complained that the North ministry's payments to the press served to "deceive both Parliament and the world."[20] The article did not mention that opposition money helped to fund the *Morning Post*. Another opposition account, reprinted in New York, dramatically attacked the writers of ministry newspapers as "the basest tools of the most abandoned scum."[21] A London letter writer likewise informed an American correspondent that "Six hundred pounds per annum" had been paid to "writers of false intelligence" so that the ministry could "intimidate you and deceive you" and give "a false turn and coloring to every thing."[22] Another observer estimated the ministry had spent 50,000 guineas "on hirelings employed to tell lies in pamphlets and in the news-papers in Europe and America."[23] Why engage in this kind of deception? Several theories circulated. Some thought that the ministry hoped to retain its power by deceiving the electorate.[24] Others felt that the ministry's deception was aimed at scaring the rebellious colonists. Through "propagated chimeras and falshoods," one observer wrote, the ministry hoped to "frighten and to divide us."[25] According to one London writer, the ministry was attempting to "conquer you by art rather than by force."[26]

Some Patriots also extended the conspiracy theory of ministerial deception to the vocal minority of colonial newspaper printers who opposed the Patriots' protests. If the government could subsidize and support massive London newspaper operations, it seemed, it could surely buy off a few small Loyalist newspapers in the colonies. Patriots regularly accused Loyalist writers and printers of being "ministerial hireling scriblers" who took "bribes" from London in exchange for their service in raising "doubts and divisions."[27] One writer in London evocatively described American printing presses as "fettered by golden chains sent over by the Ministry."[28] Patriots seemed to enjoy mocking the venality of Loyalist printers. One satirical advertisement, for example, invented a Loyalist printer named "Hugo Lucre," who promised that his print shop would supply visitors with "False Intelligence for hard money" but would offer "Truth upon no terms whatsoever."[29]

Loyalist printers Hugh Gaine (who supported the Patriots until 1776) and James Rivington both published newspapers in New York City during the British occupation of that city. They felt the brunt of this criticism. At a 1774 public meeting in Newark, New Jersey, colonists accused Rivington of boosting his status from bankruptcy to wealthy independence in the course of a few years by working as a "ministerial hireling."[30] One gathering of New Jersey Patriots even hanged Rivington in effigy.[31] For some, the fact that Rivington, "the greatest liar upon earth," regularly republished material from the ministry's papers was proof enough of his corruption.[32] A Boston critic mockingly noted in 1780 that "all the hums, puffs, wonders, and extravagant lies fabricated by the ministerialists in the London papers" had been "faithfully reprinted by Rivington in New-York."[33] Patriot writer Thomas Paine likewise mocked Gaine in his essay series *The American Crisis* by noting that "we can tell by Hugh Gaine's New-York paper what the complexion of the *London Gazette* is."[34] While ample evidence suggests that the ministry supported friendly London newspapers, there is little to corroborate the idea that it directly subsidized Loyalist presses in North America. Since there were no parliamentary seats to be gained in the colonies, the opposition and the ministry had long neglected the colonial press.

Despite an absence of evidence, the Patriot leadership became more concerned over time about Loyalists' participation in the ministerial campaign of deception. In early 1776, members of the Continental Congress spoke of "honest and well-meaning, but uninformed" people "being deceived and drawn into erroneous opinions" by "the art and address of ministerial agents." The members blamed the North ministry for beguiling Loyalists about the controversies between London and the colonies. To address this problem, the Congress proposed that Loyalists be reeducated about the "origin, nature and extent" of the conflict and shown, among other things, the many petitions that colonists had sent to the king. If the ministry's falsehoods could deceive some colonists, they seemed to suggest, then exposure to the truth could redeem them. But those "unworthy Americans" who had "taken part with our oppressors" by "misrepresenting and traducing the conduct and principles of the friends of American liberty" would be treated differently. The Congress recommended that they be disarmed and arrested.[35] Deceitful mediators seemed far more dangerous than deluded victims.

The onset of war enlarged these concerns. By May 1777, a committee of the Continental Congress prepared an address warning colonists of the "Danger" of British agents, who "invent and propagate false and injurious Reports" that "magnify the Power, Number, and Resources of the Enemy," while minimizing Patriots' strength. Shortly afterward, members of the Congress expressed concern that these agents were aiming to "intimidate the people by false news."[36] Some former colonies, like North Carolina, also threatened treason prosecutions against anyone who "knowingly spread false and dispiriting news."[37] It was essential to the Patriot leadership that they maintain a monopoly on the power to determine which news was true and which was false.

Loyalists were generally more cautious about sharing news than Patriots' inflated rhetoric suggested. Though Loyalists sometimes accused their Patriot rivals of lying or exaggerating, they often maintained the same posture of indifference toward truth that colonial printers had long relied upon. Taking pains to portray himself as impartial, Rivington adopted the motto "Printed at His Ever Open and Uninfluenced Press" for his newspaper in the spring of 1774. Indeed, at least early on, Rivington did print material from multiple sources and points of view.[38] Yet even this effort to maintain neutrality could not protect him. Only a few months after affixing that motto to his masthead, Rivington faced a backlash from a group of Baltimore subscribers who alleged that he had printed materials that were "very unfriendly, in our opinion, to the common cause of American Liberty." They specifically addressed what they saw as the hypocrisy of Rivington's claims to be open and uninfluenced: "The motto to your paper beguiled us, and induced us to suppose you, really, an impartial printer." In response, Rivington claimed that he was only doing his "duty as a Printer" by offering the "Liberty of the Press" to a range of voices.[39] On another occasion, Rivington wrote that his newspaper was "impartial" and that he did not "arrogantly set himself up as a judge" of what he published but simply presented news to the public "to have their merits tried, as they ought to be, by the public voice."[40]

Likewise, during the imperial crisis a Boston Loyalist printer named Richard Draper steadfastly refused to make determinations about the veracity of his reports. In 1770, for example, he left it to "our Readers to judge, as they have a right, which of the London Intelligences are most to be depended upon." A few years later, after a reader asked Draper to clarify a rumor that the British government had corrupted the New England clergy, Draper refused to answer. He asked to be "excused from meddling in the above Affair" because his goal was to "impartially" collect information "without being too officious, especially in the Affairs of Government."[41] In Quebec, Loyalist printer William Brown shared material from all kinds of newspapers, including the *London Gazette*, New York Loyalist papers, and even Patriot papers under headings such as "From a Rebel Paper."[42] Indeed, he made a point of printing items that he doubted or disagreed with to "evince the impartiality of our Paper."[43] While in previous decades these attitudes were common, during the imperial crisis and revolutionary war they set Loyalist printers apart.[44]

Indeed, opponents of the British ministry began to assert that news mediators, especially printers, should be weeding out falsehoods. In the spring of 1770, for example, a New York Patriot named Isaac Low argued that anyone approving a "Piece before it went to the Press" was equally the "Author and Publisher" as the person who "actually wrote" it.[45] Having apparently experienced a campaign of deception led by ministerial and Loyalist agents, some printers saw the dangers of a press that was indifferent to truth. No longer reluctant mediators, many of them embraced their role as active participants in boosting truthfulness and excluding falsehood. In 1770, printer John Holt, who would become a vociferous supporter of the Patriot cause, noted that he had been inclined to "publish Things on all Sides" in the past, including items that he thought were false, but he now felt that the "Freedom of the press" should be "subservient to . . . the public Good." Truth, as he defined it, seemed to matter more than his inclination toward balance. Five years later, as tensions escalated, he was even more direct. He explained that the ministry's and Loyalists' intentions to "deceive and impose upon the ignorant" had led him to print only pieces that "support . . . the cause of truth and justice."[46] Other Patriot newspaper printers, such as William and Thomas Bradford, also believed that the "present unhappy controversy between G.B. and these colonies" left them no choice but to reserve a "right to judge" what they would print.[47] Their judgment, though, was quite fallible.

Aiming to avoid falsehoods without possessing the tools to discern what was truthful, Patriot mediators simply excised news that originated from what they considered to be untrustworthy sources. According to newspaper citations from the 1770s and early 1780s, the continent's printers shared very different news from Britain depending on their politics. In the early 1770s, Patriot and Loyalist printers republished a similar amount of material from ministry papers, such as the *London Gazette*, the *London Chronicle*, and the *Morning Herald*. But compared to their Loyalist counterparts, Patriot printers published more than twice as much news from opposition papers, such as the *Public Ledger*, the *Whitehall Evening Post*, and the *Morning Chronicle*, during the first half of the 1770s.[48] These differences widened as war broke out. During the war for independence, the *London Gazette* supplied nearly half of the news that Loyalist printers published from abroad, whereas news from the *Gazette* made up between one-quarter and one-third of external citations in Patriot papers.[49] Patriot papers reprinted news from opposition papers, including the formerly impartial *St. James's Chronicle*, *Morning Chronicle*, and *Public Advertiser*, at twice the rate of Loyalist papers during the late 1770s and at three times their rate during the early 1780s.[50] Patriot papers, in turn, cited radical opposition papers three to four times as often as Loyalist papers did.[51] Throughout the crisis and war, Patriot and Loyalist mediators sought out and amplified congenial news sources while limiting their readers' engagement with unfriendly newspapers.

Indeed, Patriots rarely placed much value on the ministry's news. On the rare occasions when Patriot printers uncritically accepted ministry newspaper accounts, it was often because they conceded facts that ran counter to the British government's interests. In 1780, for example, *Maryland Journal* printer Mary Katherine Goddard listed among many reasons to believe that Britain's power was waning that "the London Gazette gives a melancholy Picture of conquering America!"[52] If the ministry's own mouthpiece was expressing doubts about its prospects in the war, she suggested, then the Patriots could take heart. More often, though, printers republished and cited news from opposing papers to dismiss it. Perhaps adapted from the jibes of the London opposition press, some Patriot printers embraced the epithet "Lying Gazette" to mock the *London Gazette*. Philadelphia Patriot printer John Dunlap, for example, passed along an account of troop movements with the heading "From the London (*or Lying*) Gazette of May 3."[53]

When they republished material from Tory papers, Patriot newspapers regularly pinned the term "ministerial" to their headings. When Patriot printer

Isaiah Thomas shared a report about the Americans' "impoverished state," he identified it as coming from the "Morning-Post, a British Ministerial News-Paper." But he went further. Just below this reprint, Thomas also republished a report from the opposition *London Courant* that mocked the *Morning Post* by conjuring a dramatic scene of "American refugees appointed to manufacture such letters and advices, as may any ways tend to amuse the King of Great-Britain with a hope of subjugating America."[54] Some Patriot printers also attacked American Loyalist papers with such paratextual put-downs. Benjamin Edes and John Gill echoed the popular attacks on the *London Gazette* by mockingly citing "James Rivington's Loyal, Royal, Lying, (what do ye call it) Gazette."[55]

This aversion to ministry sources became central to Patriot information literacy. It provided a pathway to rejecting any unhappy news. In the summer of 1776, a rumor circulated around Britain and North America that the ailing William Pitt, Earl of Chatham, had renounced his formerly conciliatory view toward the colonies and had taken up a more confrontational posture. This would have been devastating news for Patriots, who regarded Pitt as a hero. Some Patriot newspapers shared what was "said to be a genuine extract of a letter from the Earl of Chatham" that expressed disdain for the colonists, but more newspapers republished a notice from the opposition *St. James's Chronicle* calling this account "totally without foundation, and in every respect a gross and scandalous imposition on the world."[56] Newport Patriot printer Solomon Southwick commented on Pitt's supposed conversion account, "[*The letter referred to above is wrote in a true ministerial language.*]"[57] Southwick's bracketed response implied that he had unmasked a piece of government propaganda, but in fact the letter had originated in the opposition *London Packet*. Yet because the article ran against Patriot interests, Southwick and others assumed that it must have been the product of the ministry. And if it was created by the ministry, according to many Patriots, it was false. In this way, any negative news could be quickly dismissed as an invention of the enemy.

Distrustful of ministry sources, Patriot mediators turned to Britain's radical and opposition newspapers. Patriots often shared the opposition's claims about the ministry's various "acts of Despotism and Tyranny," its conspiracy against English liberties, and the notion that a "double cabinet" of "secret advisors" was manipulating and controlling North.[58] Both radicals, such as John Wilkes, and more mainstream Whig dissenters, such as Edmund Burke, stoked fears of an oppressive ministry.[59] By importing so much material from opposition presses, Patriot printers effectively extended the overheated politics of London across the ocean.

Having fled from Massachusetts to England, Loyalist merchant Samuel Curwen complained in the spring of 1779 that "our newspaper fabricators" in England "have so many purposes to serve quite distinct from truth and the good of society" that he read them only for "amusement," rather than for "facts." A few months later, frustrated that "of fifty reports five only will be founded in fact," he wrote that newspaper reports "present only the party complexion of the relator." As he saw it, newspapers offered politics disguised as news. The problem was that "all the world" had become "divided into American and anti-American, ministerial and anti-ministerial."[60] News mediators' aversion to unfriendly news sources had polarized the flow of information through Britain and its American colonies.

Aside from London, the media polarization of the 1770s was perhaps most visible in New York City. In most other cities, Patriot mobs ensured that Loyalist newspapers seldom lasted for longer than a year or two. But the British occupation of New York City, which lasted for most of the war, sustained Gaine and Rivington. Simultaneously, John Holt's *New-York Journal* fiercely defended Patriot politics. As a result, throughout the 1770s and early 1780s, it was easier to read both Loyalist and Patriot newspapers in New York City than anywhere else on the continent. Perhaps for this reason, a controversy erupted in the city in the middle of the decade over how its printers were collecting news from abroad.

The initial salvo in this debate came from a Loyalist using the name "Mercator" in *Rivington's New-York Gazetteer*. This correspondent attacked Holt for his choices in selecting foreign news from abroad. "With respect to foreign intelligence," Mercator wrote, Holt unfailingly chose material that disparaged "the Ministry and the Parliament, and tend[ed] to widen the breach between Great Britain and the Colonies. . . . This partiality is so glaring, that a Boy of ten Years old cannot fail observing it."[61]

Holt responded angrily in his own newspaper. He insisted that he had never inserted anything in his paper "from any unworthy Motives," but instead had "published such Pieces, as in my judgment had the greatest Tendency to promote the Interest and Happiness of the whole British Nation, as well in Europe as America." Denying the charge that he was "misrepresenting . . . the Ministry and Parliament," he boasted that his aim was to "expose them in their true Characters." Perhaps the most notable feature of Holt's defense, though, was what he failed to say. He did not claim, as generations of news mediators before him had done, that he was simply providing a balanced digest of available news. Rather, he admitted to his political purposes. Instead of providing balance, Holt suggested that printers should serve the public good. The fact that not everyone agreed about what news would "promote the Interest and Happiness" of the British nation was left unsaid. Nevertheless, Holt's response seems to have resonated with his readers. One contributor to the *Journal* penned a poem addressed to Mercator, mocking the complaint that Holt, "misled by motives sinister, / Will publish nothing for the minister."[62]

In early 1775, "An Observer" wrote a letter to Holt's paper that inverted Mercator's claims by arguing that Loyalists, not Patriots, had manipulated the news and produced a series of "Twistifications." The author accused Rivington of "publishing such parts of letters from London, and elsewhere, as can be made to suit their purpose, and suppressing the rest." As evidence, "An Observer" noted a pair of letters from London reporting on the 1774 parliamentary elections in Britain, which had appeared in Rivington's paper. The writer pointed out that other newspapers had printed more complete versions of these letters. By comparing these versions, "An Observer" correctly noted that Rivington had removed several negative comments about the ministry.[63] In one letter, Rivington had deleted the correspondent's claim that the ministry's success would cause Americans to "wear our chains for another seven years" and the recommendation that Americans "not depend on the hypocrisy of our Ministry." From another letter, Rivington had apparently removed a comment claiming that the 1774 elections would result in an equally "venal" and "arbitrary" Parliament as before.[64] These deletions seemed to provide evidence that a gang of subversives led by Rivington was limiting the flow of information for their own political ends. Rivington half-responded to these and other accusations by asserting that he was an "impartial" printer who did not "arrogantly" judge the material he published.[65] "An Observer" answered by alleging that Rivington reprinted materials derived from Loyalist papers but ignored news from Patriot presses. When asked about this, according to the anonymous author, Rivington had implausibly explained that the Patriot papers "were blown out of the printing office window."[66]

As this exchange between "An Observer" and Rivington was unfolding, a Massachusetts Loyalist using the name "Plainheart" wrote an essay for the *Boston News-Letter* lecturing the Patriots about their reliance on misinformation. "You have no notion how grossly you are imposed upon," Plainheart argued. Their "implicit credulity" toward news that aligned with their own beliefs, according to the writer, had built a "baseless fabrick" of grievances. Instead of hearing from "both sides," Plainheart claimed, the Patriots simply dropped their subscriptions to Loyalist papers and "listen[ed] with greediness to one side only." When they encountered essays and news that had been written by Loyalists, Patriots "read them with a prejudice which has blinded your judgments."[67] According to Plainheart, the Patriots' unbalanced consumption of news had led them astray. Cordoned off from unfriendly information, Patriots were developing a misguided and dangerous political culture. If the Patriots simply considered a broader range of news, Plainheart suggested, this might be prevented. Yet Plainheart probably did not expect this essay to persuade anyone. Although addressed to wayward Patriots and haranguing them directly—"You have been persuaded," "You have no notion," "you have been told"—Plainheart's essay appeared in the Loyalist *Boston News-Letter*. Even while chiding the Patriots for addressing an echo chamber, Plainheart was shouting into another.

Were these accusations correct? Did printers share materials that supported their cause while excluding everything else? In the cases of Rivington and Holt, at least, these criticisms were generally accurate. On the same day that Rivington published Mercator's essay, Holt published an issue containing an astounding thirteen columns of news derived from London sources. This included a petition signed by Americans in London appealing to Parliament, an account of a duke wishing the Americans well in Parliament, an elliptical reference to the ministry having received "very alarming" news from Boston, a report from a French gentleman claiming that war would soon break out between France and Britain, dissent in the House of Lords over the ministry's treatment of Massachusetts, and an account of a petition opposing the Quebec Act that was marked "[*ministerial*]," probably because it suggested that the Canadians were not yet "contaminated" with American ideas.[68]

In Rivington's issue published that day, almost none of this intelligence appeared. Instead, Rivington's London news included a paragraph assuring readers that the "ministry are determined to stand their own ground with respect to the Americans," a story about Boston Patriot leaders evading arrest, a refutation of the idea that Britons generally supported the American Patriots, an account of the king taking careful notice of the "disorders in America," a claim that the British ministry was "firmly fixed," and a claim that Natives in North America would soon attack Virginia.[69] The only reports shared by both Rivington's and Holt's papers related to parliamentary debate. To read Holt's newspaper was to learn of a distressed ministry and an emboldened opposition in London. Rivington's issue, though a bit more balanced, suggested nearly the opposite. From the distance of centuries, it is impossible to verify or disprove most of these news stories, but none of them is implausible. Despite critics' allegations and Rivington's questionable record, it is unlikely that either printer fabricated these accounts. Rather, in an environment that supplied printers with an enormous surplus of information, both men directed readers' attention to news that aligned with their politics and discarded the rest.

Rivington, Mercator, and Plainheart each claimed that the politicization of news had led their Patriot rivals to become misinformed about events abroad. They were quite correct. In the mid-1770s, Patriot leaders were internalizing several significant misperceptions. The news accounts that they consumed were coalescing into an improbable narrative of how the imperial crisis might unfold: an unpopular and unstable ministry would be destroyed by a nonimportation scheme, allowing Patriots to reconcile with the metropole on their own terms. This vision of London politics guided Patriots' decision-making, allowing them to stubbornly refuse the terms of reconciliation offered by the ministry.

Patriot news mediators insisted that Britons broadly, even unanimously, sympathized with their cause. The radical *Boston Gazette* claimed in early 1775 that letters from England demonstrated that "the people" were "extremely enraged at the measures pursuing against America."[70] A few weeks later, a writer in the same paper summarized the prevailing notion that "thousands of letters from persons of good intelligence" and "the general strain of publications in public papers, pamphlets, and magazines" all indicated that most Britons "are friends to America, and wish us success in our struggles against the claims of parliament and administration."[71] Patriots reprinted material from the radical London *Evening Post* claiming that Britons "despised" the "Cabinet Junto" as much as the Americans did and that the people would soon rise up against "ministerial tyranny."[72] Over the course of a single month in 1774, for example, three different reports in Connecticut Patriot newspapers claimed that "two out of three," "three quarters," and "ninety-nine in an hundred" Britons sympathized with colonial protests.[73] Based on such information, Patriots overestimated their support in Britain.

In an essay responding to prominent Loyalist writer Daniel Leonard in late 1774, a Patriot with the pseudonym "A Son of New England" explained that the colonists would defeat the ministry because, according to "undoubted authority," the people of Great Britain were "generally for us" and would not allow an "infatuated Ministry to continue a War with the Americans."[74] In response, a third party with the confusingly similar pseudonym "A Friend to New-England" disagreed, noting that "Letters from the highest authority" said quite the opposite and that the British public was "absolutely determined" to see the colonists "submit to the supreme authority of the state."[75] What happened when the "highest authority" disputed the account of an "undoubted authority"? Very little. Both Patriots and Loyalists reading this exchange probably assumed either that their rivals were the dupes of malevolent deceivers or that they were actively sowing deception. Both sources might have had an earnest intent, even as they shared conflicting accounts.

For years, American colonists vacillated between disappointment and hope. Expectations continually rose for an imminent revolution in Britain, whether through violence or voting. But this salvation never came. As late as the spring of 1776 the London opposition paper *St. James's Chronicle* speculated that if a "national poll" asked Britons to choose sides in the "present Contest between the Ministry at home, and the Congress at Philadelphia," the ministry would lose.[76] This was pure speculation. There was not yet any sort of organized polling, and Patriots could only guess at their level of support, using fuzzy terms such as "most" or "the people" to characterize it. A person living in Britain could only draw conclusions about the state of public opinion by tallying up public demonstrations, petitions, printed comments, and conversations within their personal networks. Such an unscientific process would be unlikely to do anything more than reproduce a person's own point of view. Someone thousands of miles away faced even greater challenges in assessing British public opinion. They could only make guesses based on letters, oral reports, and newspapers that made their way across the ocean. But the London newspapers that Americans relied on overrepresented radical, opposition, and elite voices relative to the population, making them imperfect measures of popular sentiment.[77] Indeed, the city of London, which provided the colonists with most of their news, was anomalously pro-American compared to the rest of Britain. Moreover, Patriot printers like Holt, who outnumbered Loyalist printers, generally filtered out news of the ministry's popularity. Patriots' assessment of British public support, as mediated through this information, proved to be painfully inaccurate. Historians have shown that pro-American sentiment in Britain was never as robust as the Patriots hoped, and it largely dissolved with the escalation of colonial resistance in the mid-1770s.[78]

Additionally, building on the notion that the British public supported them, many North Americans mistakenly believed that Frederick North's government stood "on slippery ground" and that it might fall from power at any moment.[79] London opposition publications often suggested that particular members of the ministry were squabbling with others and would soon face removal.[80] Patriot newspapers eagerly shared these rumors in the early 1770s.[81] In May 1771, the *Pennsylvania Gazette* included a typical item from an opposition paper that claimed the ministry "stand[s] at present" on a "*hairbreadth*" and that a change was imminent.[82] Another report insisted that if the American "patriotic party" continued its opposition, they would see a "total change in the Ministry."[83] These accounts were ultimately misleading. While the North ministry's continued strength was not inevitable, its support in Parliament proved durable, and an election in 1774 strengthened its position. North remained in power from 1770 through 1782, the longest ministry in decades.

Finally, Patriot colonists overestimated the impact of their boycotts on the British government. In response to the Stamp Act in 1765, in a series of uneven protests in the late 1760s and early 1770s to protest the Townshend Acts, and in a well-organized 1774 boycott called the Continental Association, Patriots tried to leverage their economic power against the ministry. The repeal of the Stamp Act and partial repeal of the Townshend Acts encouraged Patriots to view nonimportation and nonconsumption agreements as being among their most powerful weapons. Friendly correspondents in London also encouraged the colonists to be sanguine about their economic power.[84] One piece published in the opposition London *Public Advertiser* and reprinted in the Patriot *Pennsylvania Journal*, for example, described how "our trade was distressed" during the boycotts of the late 1760s and that "it was impossible for us to have held out much longer against the demands of the Americans."[85]

As they prepared for boycotts in 1774, Patriot printers cited "London papers, letters, &c." indicating that the ministry and London's merchants were "alarmed" at the possible "tumults and riots" that American boycotts could stir up.[86] Edes and Gill of the *Boston Gazette* claimed that news from London indicated that if the 1774 boycotts went into effect, "the present Ministry must go out, and their late measures be all reversed."[87] Other Patriot printers shared materials from London opposition papers expressing Britons' worries about the economic impact of the boycotts.[88] One letter from London went so far as to say that a one-year boycott would "establish American freedom, for this country cannot support itself without the colonies."[89] Arthur Lee and William Lee, two Virginians living in London, wrote to their many correspondents in North America that adherence to the boycott would "produce a Revolution" in Britain.[90] Yet historians now agree that the boycotts did not have the consequences that the colonists hoped for. Many merchants remained supportive of the ministry. Some found alternative markets. Those who did protest to the ministry about the Patriots' economic pressure were neither as influential nor as vocal as the Patriots hoped.[91]

While each of these misconceptions partly resulted from misinformation, Patriot colonists also had access to contrary reports. London correspondents sometimes acknowledged that most Britons still supported the government. One message from Patriot allies in the House of Commons in 1774 took pains to point out that "the people" approved of the ministry's actions, emphasizing "it is not all owing to the junto of a ministry. . . . It is the people at large, whom I am sorry to say, are misled."[92] Loyalist mediators also published accounts questioning the ministry's imminent demise. In 1773 the Loyalist *Boston Post-Boy* concluded that the ministry gathered "Strength every Day."[93]

But when Patriots encountered such narratives, they often found ways to dismiss them. One Virginia observer, for example, shrugged off a London petition supporting the government's recent actions because they regarded it as an invention of the ministry.[94] London printer William Strahan, who initially sympathized with the colonists but became more supportive of the ministry over time, maintained a regular correspondence with David Hall, who printed the Patriot *Pennsylvania Gazette*. Strahan regularly admonished Hall that "hardly a Paragraph" of North American newspaper reports about London was true. He affirmed that the ministry was "gather[ing] strength," that there was "No Change in the Ministry so much as thought of," and that reports of such a change were "absolutely without Foundation." Strahan even claimed that the ministry maintained a "good disposition . . . towards you."[95] While Hall regularly shared extracts from letters in his newspaper, as did all printers, he did not publish extracts from Strahan's letters.

Likewise, Britons regularly warned Patriots that boycotts would not solve their problems. In the Loyalist *Boston News-Letter*, Plainheart explained during the height of the Continental Association that "whatever you may be told, there is not the least probability, that Great Britain will be intimidated by your threats, by your non-importation schemes, or by your parade of war."[96] Such reports rarely appeared in Patriot media, but when Patriot observers encountered them, they did their best to sow doubts. In 1770, for example, a Charleston Patriot paper shared two sets of claims about nonimportation actions. The first, which cited information from "Ministerial Writers (who thereby discover their base views, as well as their ignorance)," asserted that the boycotts had caused "no sort of inconvenience" to British merchants. The second, based on "private letters" from "eminent merchants and manufacturers," "flatly contradicted" the previous statements.[97] By framing the latter information as coming from an eminent source and the former as the work of ignorance, this printer left no doubt about which they recommended. Indeed, several Patriot writers suggested that the ministry's "scribblers" were raising "doubts and divisions throughout the colonies" about the efficacy of nonimportation.[98] Long-standing fears of ministerial deception and the belief that the British government funded Loyalist printers allowed Patriots to dismiss such intelligence.

In his August 1775 proclamation declaring the colonies to be in rebellion, King George III blamed "traitorous Correspondence" from Britain for encouraging the rebels. He insisted that the rebellion had taken place because the colonists had been "misled by dangerous and ill-designing men," and he ordered his subjects to report anyone maintaining such communications with the insurgents.[99] George believed that the colonists had been seduced into disobedience by false reports from Britain.

While many factors contributed to Patriot resistance, this theory is worth consideration. Fundamentally, Patriot misperceptions resulted from a misunderstanding of London's complex information politics. The decentralized and confusing nature of early modern Atlantic communications rendered London's culture of print and politics unintelligible to colonists living thousands of miles away. As a result, Patriots underestimated the opportunism of the opposition press and overestimated the North government's deceptiveness. While Patriots correctly recognized that ministry-aligned information sources were not always trustworthy, they did not scrutinize sources that aligned with their resistance. In 1775, printer Hugh Gaine published a letter from London claiming that Patriot misperceptions came from "false friends" who "conveyed from hence, wrong Accounts of the situation of Affairs here, which made the Americans view them through a false Medium: Local politics influenced some, others oppose Government on any Principles, and care not if America was deluged in Blood, if their private Purposes were answered."[100] While this explanation was itself no doubt exaggerated, the letter's author was not wrong to suggest that the opposition's "private Purposes" shaped the choices they made about sharing information.

The commonly held belief that the ministry was conspiring against the colonists built on the London opposition press's misleading portrayals of the

North government. As scholars have long understood, Patriots' beliefs about the ministry's evil intentions and its efforts to "enslave" the colonists were plainly improbable to anyone not immersed in the political world of revolutionary America. If these "persecutory delusions" can be traced in part to ideological predispositions, as historians have long contended, they also clearly grew out of the disordered, bifurcated, and politicized nature of Atlantic information flows.[101] In that sense, the political origins of the American Revolution lay not only in the dissenting tradition of radical Whig politics from previous decades, as Bernard Bailyn and his acolytes have argued, but also in the Whig opposition media of their present.[102]

While a reader in London might have known to approach the opposition's claims with skepticism, an ordinary North American reader lacked some of that context. Letters from London contributed to this misperception. As historian Paul Langford has shown, Patriot newspapers regularly reprinted letters from colonial agents, friendly merchants, colonists living abroad, radicals, and dissenters in London. These individuals, because of either their own cognitive blind spots or a desire to challenge the ministry, fed Anglo-American colonists with exaggerated information that encouraged resistance.[103]

Perhaps Patriot colonists should have noticed that their information sources were conveniently partial. But ordinary newspaper readers could not always know which claims came from their allies. The reprinting process usually stripped away context about the identity and masked the motives of news mediators. In part because of an absence of context, these exaggerated letters and reprints from opposition newspapers formed an essential foundation for Patriot news-gathering—and indeed for Patriot resistance more broadly.

As scholars have shown, newspapers mobilized Patriot action against the British empire in all kinds of ways. Political essays taught readers about the justice of Patriot protests, while reports of atrocities committed by British soldiers and their allies convinced readers of the dangers of British rule.[104] Yet arguably the Patriot printers' most important impact was to collect, organize, and present a coherent version of the world in which resistance seemed worthwhile. No amount of rhetoric or outrage could convince hundreds of thousands of people to take risks and make sacrifices for a hopeless cause. Patriot printers' optimistic news-gathering about the political conditions in London, then, was a necessary precondition for the escalation of resistance. While it is impossible to know if the conflict would have surged during the 1770s without these politicized perceptions, it seems unlikely. The recurrent discrepancy between Patriots' expectations and the ministry's actions was founded in exaggerations, outright falsehoods, and an abundance of contradictory information.

So much contradiction and misinformation created a demand for truth. During the 1770s, Patriot newspaper printers finally asserted themselves as experts who identified facts and not just retailers of raw intelligence. But this was much harder than it seemed. Even the most well-intentioned colonial fact-checker would have been defeated by the vast distances that separated them from Britain. Like the colonial leaders whom they displaced, Patriot printers and their political communities pushed others to acknowledge and abide by their accounts of reality. That these mediators were successful in convincing so many of their contemporaries of their truths, however, does not mean that their inheritors must accept them. Americans ought to question and not just valorize the perceptions of their predecessors. The search for truth, after all, is not something that is settled in the heat of a revolutionary moment; it carries on and on until some truths are confirmed, some truths recede, and some become myth.

CHAPTER FOUR

An Ocean of News

Independence, War, and Atlantic Information Exchange

Once Americans earned their independence, it seemed possible, for just a moment, that they would never again think of Europe. The war was over. The peace was won. The nation belonged to them. Who cared about old King George or his Parliament? Who needed a weekly digest of the affairs of Europe? Since they were no longer members of the British empire, who would still direct their gaze eastward for their news? Despite his Irish ancestry, the Philadelphia printer Mathew Carey argued in 1785, "Europe no longer affords the inexhaustible fund of intelligence" that it once did. Printers, he added, could no longer simply copy "London and other European news in America."[1] It seemed unlikely that European news "can be very essential, or even entertaining to us now."[2] With independence, some expected that an "American reader" would find "trifling observations" about the English royal family quite dull.[3]

If no one cared about Europe, though, what would newspapers report on? The conclusion of the war brought an end to the thrilling news that had led many Americans to subscribe to newspapers for the first time. The serialized drama of armies, fleets, and diplomats maneuvering for advantage across a vast terrain had stretched across years but was now over. Some complained that the "News-Papers are less entertaining, than they were some months ago."[4]

A poetic address written for the *Connecticut Courant*'s subscribers in 1784 pointed out that the end of the war had left a vacuum: "Peace comes hard at all adventures / On Merchants, Heroes, and News-printers." While admitting that the "folks, who live by news" had "lost the news you crave," the writer came to the same conclusion as Carey, suggesting that printers would "make the best of what we have," sharing news and commentary on local politics, "town-resolves," and "Congress and Assemblies."[5] Perhaps Barzillai Hudson and George Goodwin, the printers of the *Courant*, hoped to stimulate demand for their paper by making the case for American news as an object of interest. If this was their plan, they dropped it quickly. The next year, the *Courant's* address to its subscribers described an altogether different set of public appetites: "Though war at home has ceas'd to rage, / Yet foreign news your minds engage." The writer went on to boast that the *Courant* had offered news about events in Britain, Ireland, the Holy Roman Empire, Holland, Spain, France, India, and North Africa.[6] After experimenting with local and national news, Hudson and Goodwin had found that their readers still craved news from abroad.

They were not alone. Other writers and printers in the 1780s found little local or national news to fill their columns. For much of that decade, national politics were not a theater of great political intrigue. The American colonies had agreed to the Articles of Confederation, which created a weak central government that invited apathy rather than engagement. Moreover, local news tended to stay local. In the small cities of revolutionary America, printers had little incentive to publish information that their readers would learn through conversation before they received their weekly issue. Because newspaper printers shared little news about their town or region, other printers had little to draw on. In late 1788, for example, printer George Jerry Osborne explained in his *New-Hampshire Spy* that his paper contained so little "American news" because "there is none to publish." He sarcastically asked why it was that "on a continent so extensive . . . so little intelligence should occur."[7] As Osborne knew, it was not that nothing happened in North America but rather that other papers didn't record what did happen.

As a result, foreign news continued to dominate the pages of postrevolutionary newspapers. Given the choice, most printers opted for a piece of foreign news ahead of a political essay. In a 1790 issue of his *Federal Gazette*, for example, printer Andrew Brown explained that he was delaying the publication of various letters and essays from correspondents because he was "obliged to devote the Gazette chiefly to foreign news, a few days longer."[8] Likewise, in late 1787, even as Americans were debating the ratification of the proposed US Constitution, printer Isaiah Thomas previewed the contents of a new magazine by emphasizing the importance of foreign news, with domestic news only as an aside:

By the foreign news inserted in this Magazine, our readers will perceive that there are great commotions amongst the European Nations; these commotions, although at such a distance, will in some degree affect us—this, together with the important period we have now arrived at, of settling a National Government, will undoubtedly, for months to come, furnish our Readers with as great a variety of truly momentous and interesting matters, as ever did, or perhaps ever will, come under their consideration.[9]

When they sought to attract subscribers in the 1780s and 1790s, printers often emphasized that their newspaper would concentrate on foreign news and particularly on revolutionary events abroad. A Boston newspaper prospectus in 1794, for example, noted, "In the present convulsed situation . . . when revolutions are taking place, and when Empires, which have lasted for ages, and whose adamantine pillars mocked the force of time, now totter to their basis . . . no person will, surely, question the utility of a periodical publication."[10]

American independence began a decades-long process of negotiating the relationship between long-standing British habits and a nascent American national identity. Many historians have demonstrated that the end of the revolutionary war caused colonists to reconsider the place of British culture, commerce, and politics in the new nation.[11] These scholars, though, have left unexplored postrevolutionary Americans' concerns with foreign and especially British news. Could the denizens of the new United States be truly American if their view of the world continued to be that of a British colony? Relying on British news sources, some feared, would weaken the new nation's independence. Others worried that their nation's transition away from British information was too gradual, and they looked for ways to accelerate it by translating and circulating alternative news sources. By seeking fresh information sources after they achieved independence, Americans hoped to reimagine their relationship to the world.

Even as Americans negotiated the impact of independence on their news-gathering practices, the meanings and material contexts of that news were in flux. The global revolutions and wars of the late eighteenth century disrupted epistolary communications while also creating more demand for lengthy, detailed reports. Since newspapers provided more detailed accounts of events than letters or conversations could ever hope to do, Americans began to rely more on printed news sources to understand their world. Moreover, as US commerce expanded beyond the British empire in the aftermath of independence, Americans could engage with a more diverse international print culture. A greater variety of news offered competing narratives and explanations, which created more confusion and division. As news became more plural, so did Americans' experience of it and their application of it to their politics. The expansion of Americans' news sources created a world of many possibilities and few certainties.

While independence did little to affect Americans' interest in foreign news, it led them to reconsider where they were getting that news. As previous chapters demonstrated, the politics of misrepresentation and London news sources during the American Revolution drew observers' attention to the artificial pathways along which information traveled around the British world. But while they had once interpreted news sources from abroad according to their politics, American observers after the war began to judge them based more on their place of publication. A London newspaper was no longer identified as an "opposition" or "ministerial" print but rather as primarily a *British* paper.

It grated on some Americans that their nation remained so dependent on Britain for global news years after they had declared independence. As long as US newspapers practiced an "indiscriminate publication . . . of English articles of news and politics," one printer commented, they were behaving as if the revolution had never happened.[12] Americans' continued reliance on British news sources was obvious even in London, where a correspondent shared his "disappointment and disgust" at seeing so many US newspaper printers engaging in a "servile copying" from British papers: "A stranger here, who had heard nothing of the American revolution, would, I am confident, from the greater part of your American Newspapers, suppose you were English colonies still."[13] In 1795, a group of Philadelphians echoed these sentiments. They suggested that if someone could read US newspapers without knowing where they had been published, they would naturally conclude that they were from "the meridian of London."[14]

For many Americans, London papers' apparent lies during the imperial crisis and war for independence disqualified them as legitimate news sources. Printer Nicholas Power of the *Poughkeepsie Journal*, for example, dismissed a series of "extracts from English papers" in 1793 on the basis of those papers' "former impositions during our own war with them."[15] Likewise, an anonymous writer in a 1793 issue of the Boston *Independent Chronicle* compared those who attacked revolutionary France to Thomas Hutchinson's supposed misrepresentations during the Anglo-American imperial crisis. The essayist implored Americans to ignore British accounts of events in France and wait instead for news that came directly from the French. To drive the point home, the writer implored Americans to "remember that there were formerly *corrupted channels* through which every vile insinuation was forwarded to Britain. Should we look over the British papers printed during the late [American revolutionary] war, we should find the same abuse of our patriots, and the same reflections on our public measures, as are now so liberally bestowed on our Gallic Friends."[16] For these observers, the American Revolution had exposed the corruption of all British newspapers, regardless of political affiliation.

During the 1780s and 1790s, American observers continued to detect incongruities between realities in the United States, as they perceived them, and British papers' reporting. Seeing that "British news-papers teem with abuse of America," some people imagined that Britain's campaign of deception and misrepresentation was continuing apace.[17] These self-appointed experts about the state of America judged the accuracy of the London press by comparing their own experiences with the ways that London newspapers described the United States. When these diverged, they decried the London presses' deceit. This commonsense, empiricist approach to evaluating news has long been the practice of news consumers. "What better criterion does the man at the breakfast table possess," asked writer Walter Lippmann in 1922, "than that the newspaper version checks up with his own opinion?"[18]

American printers regularly shared London papers' derisive descriptions of the United States.[19] Francis Childs noted that British papers were "filled with reproaches, invectives, and indignities" about the United States and suggested, "Let us be no longer indebted for our intelligence to channels so corrupt."[20] Some readers posited that the British government was spreading lies about US instability in order to prevent a massive postrevolutionary wave of migration to the new nation.[21] Printer Daniel Fowle wrote in his *New Hampshire Gazette*, "By the late London papers we find, that, in order to discourage Britons from emigrating to America, they descend to the same low cunning . . . which they so much practiced in vain before the late war, of painting the characters of the Americans in the blackest colours."[22] Of course, the United States did experience a series of crises and disputes during the 1780s that both worried American elites and delighted the Britons who felt that the Americans had been unprepared for self-government. Their "reproaches" were not entirely unearned.

Another reason that American observers distrusted London newspapers is that they seldom reprinted from American papers. Instead, much as angry colonists had accused the ministry of doing during the imperial crisis, they seemed to gather reports about the United States from letters, travelers, and diplomatic sources, or they summarized and paraphrased American newspapers' reports. As one Briton wrote, "news printers cannot be prevailed on to copy any thing from your papers."[23] The result was a trade imbalance between British and American newspapers. A Portland, Massachusetts, writer noted that British newspaper editors "carefully avoid publishing any extracts from our papers but such as are calculated to shew the whole world that we are starving with famine, or torn to pieces by factions. In return for these insults and neglects, we copy every event that happens in Great-Britain, as if we were still dependent upon them."[24] Some felt that Britons' reluctance to reprint US newspapers' reports resulted from their perceptions of American inferiority. One anecdote circulated in American newspapers in 1788 about an American captain offering a British merchant a copy of a newspaper so that he could read the new US Constitution. But the merchant "could not condescend to read an American newspaper, saying he should soon have an opportunity of seeing it in the English papers."[25]

Seeing apparent misrepresentations about North America printed in London, US observers became increasingly distrustful of British reports about the broader world. If they were willing to lie about North America, why not Europe or the Caribbean or Asia? Unimpressed with some news that arrived from Britain in late 1785, the printer of the *State Gazette of South-Carolina*, Ann Timothy, shared a summary of this information with the heading "Lies Collected from British News-Papers." This collection included a bit of news about the United States, which claimed that the country was in a "pitiful condition" and its people "half scalped by the Indians." But as she dismissed these accounts about America, Timothy also tossed aside several reports about events in Europe and Canada about which she had less direct knowledge.[26] London newspapers seemed so unreliable that almost anything they reported was suspect.

The revolutionary events that broke out in Europe at this time heightened American observers' concerns about their continued reliance on British news sources. Boston printer Nathaniel Willis dismissed accounts coming from Britain about Irish resistance in 1780 as being "on the ministerial side."[27] British newspapers' reports about the Dutch Patriot Revolt, an uprising in the Netherlands during the 1780s, seemed equally suspect. In a letter published in US newspapers in 1788, an Amsterdam merchant warned that English accounts of events in the Netherlands were "as much beyond the truth as what they quote of the Americans."[28] Despite "contradictory articles," London newspapers largely took the side of Stadtholder William V against the Dutch rebels.[29]

American observers' distrust of British news sources sometimes guided them into misperception. Printers who sympathized with the Dutch Patriot cause, for example, largely discounted British reports of Prussia's successful invasion of the Netherlands in 1787. Rejecting news from London that appeared to exaggerate the size of the Prussian force, New York printer Thomas Greenleaf chose instead a few paragraphs that "seem to have been written with a degree of impartiality."[30] Benjamin Russell of the *Massachusetts Centinel* likewise suggested that the "partiality of the English in favour of the Stadtholderan party, in Holland, induces very unfavourable representations respecting the Dutch patriots." He clucked that the accounts from Britain "are copied into the American papers much to the prejudice of the latter." But, he assured his readers, he could inform them based on a "better authority than that of the British news-writers" that the Dutch would stand firm against foreign encroachments.[31] When it became clear that the Prussian invasion had in fact succeeded in dispersing the Patriots, Russell admitted that "the London papers . . . like the greatest liars, tell the truth for once."[32]

The French Revolution particularly intensified Americans' distrust of British newspapers. Writers regularly pointed out the absurdity of relying on Britain, France's ancient enemy, "whose inhabitants have been educated with a determined hatred against France," for news about that country.[33] Some observers only trusted London newspapers' accounts when they ran contrary to the ministry's wishes. Printers Francis Childs and John Swaine commented in 1791, for example, that "France (even by the English accounts) is going on quietly."[34] Boston editor Paul Joseph Guérard de Nancrède drew on this distrust to promote a Francophone newspaper. In a 1789 prospectus, he wrote that his aim was to free Americans from the "moral slavery in which they now moan, by means of the public English newspapers. . . . The American lacking all other means of Information, searches his papers, reads [British papers] and very often gives credence to them; it is in this way that they become, without wanting it, the partisan of a rival nation." In contrast, Nancrède promised, the *Courier de Boston* would rely on direct correspondence with "all parties in Europe" to receive continental papers.[35] This scheme did not pan out, and Nancrède's paper lasted only a few months. Instead of translating material from other papers and corresponding with foreigners, it remained far easier for printers to continue reproducing material from the British prints that arrived at the harbor.

As reprints from British papers continued to dominate American papers, observers might have hoped to receive a more varied selection of news from other media. While newspapers generally trailed behind the movement of commerce, letters and oral reports followed their own paths. Correspondents knew how to navigate the limitations of commercial movement by sending letters under cover and having them forwarded to their ultimate destination. It is difficult to precisely determine where North Americans received letters from, but one suggestive measure can be found in the letters from abroad published in North American newspapers. While their points of origin varied considerably, only about two-fifths of extracted letters came from the British empire during the eighteenth century.[36] The spread of oral news is even more difficult to track, but it was probably as diffuse in origin as letters were. Sailors, traders, soldiers, and other travelers crossed imperial boundaries regularly, dispersing news as they went. While newspapers seemed stuck in an imperial past, letters and oral reports arrived in the United States from all over.

The Age of Revolutions, though, changed the availability and meanings of these forms of media. Even as wars and revolutions created news, they disrupted epistolary communications. Wartime pressures caused correspondences to wither, leading North Americans to gather less of their transatlantic news from letters. The American war for independence limited communications between Americans and Britons by reducing the number of direct commercial passages between the territories. Even Benjamin Franklin, with his diplomatic and commercial connections, struggled to maintain a transatlantic correspondence with his sister Jane Mecom during the war.[37] Knowing that some of her letters to him "fell in to the hands of the Enemie," Mecom could do little but hope that when peace came, "we may at least have the comfort of Each others leters."[38]

During the war for independence, newspapers published considerably fewer letters from London. The citational headings of eight long-running American papers reveal that while they published one letter from London every three issues in the early 1770s, they published such a letter every twenty-three issues from 1776 through 1781, when the war was at its height. From 1782 through

1789, as normalcy returned, these papers published a letter from London every eleven issues. This pattern held true for both Loyalist and Patriot newspapers, suggesting that this resulted more from structural conditions than from political calculation.[39] While this transition probably owed something to the scene of action transferring from Parliament to North American battlefields, it also likely resulted from a declining number of publishable letters from London.

The French revolutionary wars had a similar impact during the 1790s. The US government declared itself neutral in the conflict, but this neutrality was vulnerable to exploitation. Hoping to cut off American food supplies from their rivals, both Britain and France sought to define US neutrality on their own terms. In March 1793 Britain declared neutral trade with the French Caribbean to be illegal. France retaliated by temporarily ordering the seizure of neutral ships heading to enemy ports. In June, Britain's navy began to seize ships carrying food to French ports. Fearing that commodities necessary to its war effort were being exported to Britain, France laid an embargo on neutral ships at Bordeaux from September 1793 through March 1794. In April 1795, facing significant food shortages, the British admiralty extended Britain's blockade, calling for its ships to seize provisions on all ships entering French ports or that "Commanders . . . have reason to believe are proceeding to France."[40] While Americans believed that their neutrality allowed them to trade with both belligerent nations, France and Britain effectively defined neutral trade as only taking place on neutral ships traveling between two neutral ports.[41]

As a result, American captains had every reason to deceive any belligerent ships that they encountered in the Atlantic about their destination. If set upon by a British vessel, a US ship that had left Philadelphia for Bordeaux, for example, might claim to be bound for a neutral port, such as Hamburg. If the British believed this, or if they simply could not prove otherwise, the ship might be allowed to go untouched.[42] Ships that seemed to be bound for France or its allies would be towed to a British port and its contents unloaded there. In this fluid world of maritime trade, it was often difficult to pin down a ship's identity and movement. Just as American sailors began to use paper documents to verify their citizenship and avoid naval impressment, belligerent cruisers began to use confiscated letters to identify a ship's point of origin and destination, providing a pretext for ship seizures.[43] Indeed, British sailors regularly searched American vessels for incriminating letters addressed to someone in France. The British admiralty directed its officers to not be "over nice or scrupulous respecting the nature of the papers of those ships, as we know the greatest deceptions are attempted to be put into practice."[44]

These directives were largely unknown to North Americans, although some heard rumors about such searches from each other and from stories printed in newspapers.[45] But questions remained. When a ship captain reported on a 1793 seizure order, his fellow merchants and a newspaper editor questioned the story, noting that "no such proclamation . . . has ever been published in the London Gazette."[46] Indeed, British government decrees calling for naval seizures were not publicized. One 1795 edict was unknown until historians discovered it in the twentieth century.[47] North American ships sailed the Atlantic uncertainly during the mid-1790s, not knowing what meanings the letters they carried might bear.

These new challenges made it far more difficult for North Americans to correspond across the Atlantic. Massachusetts merchant Samuel Cary, who relied on letter writing both for business and to keep in touch with his geographically dispersed family, grew frustrated at the challenge of getting a letter across the ocean. He complained to a business associate in 1795, "Captains will not tell where they are going nor take any thing that looks like either French or English as both sides stop them."[48] He asked his son to share communications with a business partner since "it is not unlikely but that some of my letters may miscarry." He explained, "Vessels will not take any thing looks as if they where bound to any particular port, not knowing what they may meet with on their passage."[49] Cary aimed to increase his chances of getting messages through by sending multiple copies on different ships.[50] Some captains accepted letters but tossed them overboard at the first sight of a naval vessel to avoid providing incriminating evidence of their destination. Cary wrote to his wife to relay news that an English man-of-war had captured a ship that held several letters intended for his family. He expected it would be "some time before you get the Letters . . . if they should not be thrown into the sea."[51] Likewise, a gentleman named Henry Corbieres despaired about a letter intended for his mother. "As fresh letters are often thrown over board," he wrote, "I doubt whether she will receive my letter."[52] Because of expectations of reciprocity in the exchange of letters, a single letter lost or tossed into the ocean could halt a correspondence indefinitely.

These disruptions starved US newspapers of epistolary intelligence. Indeed, printers and readers occasionally complained when ships arrived without any letters.[53] In my analysis of the citational headings of nine US newspapers, letters printed from Paris dropped considerably once war engulfed Europe beginning in 1793. While these papers had published a letter from Paris on average every twenty-two issues from 1790 through 1792, that rate slowed to once every fifty-nine issues from 1793 through 1799. The frequency of letters from London, though, changed relatively little during that time. Prior to the wars, these papers published one letter in seventeen issues on average. During the wars, this nearly held steady at a rate of once every twenty-one issues.[54] While the United States did not officially join in the French revolutionary wars, Americans found that the war damaged many of their transatlantic epistolary relationships.

Even as the violence of the Age of Revolutions constrained the flow of letters across the ocean, it also increased North Americans' appetite for foreign news. In the first issue of his Philadelphia newspaper, the *National Gazette*, poet and polemicist Philip Freneau penned a "Poetical Address" to his readers at the end of 1791. It had been a busy year. Readers would have learned about a rebellion in Saint Domingue, a new constitution in Poland, the reform of the Canadian government, an invasion in Liège, and a war in India. The most exciting bit of news, though, was the French royal family's flight to Varennes. With all this information to contend with, Freneau understood, his readers faced a challenge: "This age is so fertile of mighty events / That people complain, with some reason, no doubt; / Besides the time lost, and besides the expence, / With reading the papers they're fairly worn out." Adopting the metaphor of a theatrical production, Freneau joked that King Louis XVI and Marie Antoinette were at the "head of the play for the season." He offered to "enliven the scene" for his audience in exchange for a subscription fee as the price of admission: "For a peep at the farce a subscription he'll give; / Revolutions must happen—that Printers may live."[55] With this couplet, Freneau directly tied his livelihood as a printer with the public's ongoing interest in revolutionary events.

But why printers? Newspapers were not the only available news medium. For centuries, newspapers had competed for early modern people's attention with other information technologies, including letters, conversations, magazines, broadsides, and manuscript newsletters.[56] Much of the time, newspapers had lost these battles. Unless they received significant support from a government or party, most eighteenth-century newspapers failed to sustain a subscriber base and folded after only a few years. In towns where presses failed, news resumed its spread through the other forms of information exchange. Why, then, did Freneau connect revolutions to printers so explicitly?

Why didn't revolutions support others whose work enabled the spread of news, such as postmasters or tavern keepers?

Setting his reader adrift in a sea of information, Freneau provided an answer in his final stanza:

> Thus launch'd as we are on the ocean of NEWS,
> In hopes that your pleasure our pains will repay,
> All honest endeavours the author will use
> To furnish a feast for the grave and the gay;
>   At least he'll assay such a track to pursue
>   That the world shall approve—and his news shall be true.[57]

Unable to contain himself, Freneau had switched freely in the poem between metaphors of theater, sustenance, fertility, and the sea. No single metaphor could capture the complex experience of engaging with revolutionary events. But the poem drove toward an essential point: the Age of Revolutions had produced an "ocean of NEWS," which was impossible for ordinary observers to navigate on their own. To stay afloat, people needed the help of mediators, such as Freneau, to help make sense of vast quantities of news.

Newspapers were particularly well suited for managing information about revolutionary events. The Age of Revolutions produced millions of little details, such as battles, legislative speeches, and election results. It also created a smaller number of big events that everyone heard about. But except for remote, rural spaces, newspapers were poor vehicles for sharing the latter. Because of publication schedules and the slowness of print production and distribution, newspapers could not keep pace with the spontaneous diffusion of important news through other media. Some newspapers would not even bother to announce major events, presuming that their readers had already encountered that news through other media.

While newspapers were inefficient at sharing major news items, they were very capable brokers of details. Letters and conversations could not match the length or detailed precision of newspaper reprints. Someone might hear of Louis XVI's beheading from friends and neighbors well before they read about it in a newspaper, but conversations or letters probably would not provide precise descriptions of the charges against him or the temper of the crowd at the execution. It was through such detailed accounts that readers made predictions about the future, built narratives about the past, and felt the texture of the era. These millions of details, rather than the dozens of major events, filled up Freneau's "ocean of NEWS."

Wartime pressures on epistolary channels and a growing demand for detailed foreign information helped to position newspapers as the essential tool for foreign news-gathering during the Age of Revolutions. In the 1780s and especially the 1790s, the number of newspapers published in North America exploded. US printers published about 38 newspapers in 1780, 106 by 1790, and 260 by 1800.[58] Likewise, only 5 newspapers had been founded in Canada prior to 1780, but at least 18 were established in the last two decades of the century. While historians of US print culture often attribute this postrevolutionary transformation to the ferment of the new nation's electoral politics, it was not confined to the United States.[59] Newspaper printing expanded globally in the 1780s and 1790s. Widespread interest in international revolutionary events drove this expansion alongside political developments that raised new questions about who should be allowed to speak, who could make things public, and who could access those materials. For many, addressing these questions resulted in the creation of newspapers.[60]

As part of this trend, some regions of the British empire, including the British Caribbean, began to host larger numbers of newspapers in the late eighteenth century. Whereas only about seventeen newspapers had been founded in the British Caribbean between 1718 and 1780, twenty-eight began over the next two decades.[61] Likewise, while no newspapers had been published in British India prior to 1780, twenty-five papers began in the century's final decades.[62] In 1789, Boston printer Benjamin Russell enthused about receiving one of these papers: "A gentleman who arrived with Capt. Roberts, from India, has favoured us with *The Madras Courier*, of Sept. 17, 1788, perhaps the first ever brought to this country."[63] By the 1790s, around 5 percent of US newspapers' citations to newspapers abroad referred to Indian prints.

Revolutionary politics also inspired a massive growth in the French empire's print infrastructure. In metropolitan France, the early stages of the French Revolution inspired a momentary embrace of the press as an instrument of political mobilization. While the French government had severely constrained the publication of newspapers for most of the eighteenth century, from 1789 through 1792 hundreds of newspapers sprang up around France.[64] Moreover, while the size of France's overseas empire had been significantly reduced by the 1790s, its Caribbean colonies of Martinique, Guadeloupe, Saint Lucia, and especially Saint Domingue all saw a burst of newspaper formation in the late 1780s and early 1790s. Only two newspapers were published in the French Caribbean prior to 1780, but twenty-six appeared between 1780 and 1800—twenty-one of them in Saint Domingue.[65] As the prospectus for one

Port-au-Prince paper commented, "Free peoples have lots of journals and gazettes."[66]

Many more newspapers also appeared across Europe, whether among "free peoples" or not. By the end of the eighteenth century, around 200 newspapers were being published in German-speaking lands. Across the Italian peninsula, small city-states and maritime republics supported newspapers, whether they served as government mouthpieces or as vessels for mercantile intelligence. Even Catherine the Great of Russia, whom many American observers regarded as the epitome of a despot, countenanced the publication of newspapers in St. Petersburg, Moscow, and elsewhere. Many of these newspapers were published in French, the international language of diplomacy, which allowed American mediators to understand and translate their contents.[67]

As the global periodical press expanded, American commerce reached out to meet it. The United States was the first settler nation in the New World that did not belong to a single empire's mercantilist sphere of influence. As a result, many Americans hoped that independence would bring extraordinary commercial benefits, allowing trade with any nation interested in such exchange. In the summer of 1784, for example, a ship arrived in Boston harbor from the Dutch colony at the Cape of Good Hope, which led a Boston writer to beam that "our commerce is freed from those shackles it used to be cramped with, and bids fair to extend to every part of the globe."[68] The US government signed commercial treaties with France, the Netherlands, Sweden, and Denmark, opening previously forbidden trade opportunities. Arrivals from new ports brought newspapers, letters, and conversations that printers shared with their readers. In a 1786 address written to the subscribers of a Charleston paper, Philip Freneau reflected on the relationship between newspapers and commerce:

> What e'er the barque of commerce brings,
> From sister states or foreign kings,
> No atom we conceal;
> All Europe's prints we hourly drain,
> All Asia's news our leaves contain,
> And round our world we deal.[69]

This optimism, though, was premature. New trading opportunities proved to be more elusive than expected. Franco-American trade, for example, surged during the war but declined with peace.[70] American merchants quickly returned to trading mostly with Britain.[71] Americans' participation in commercial exchanges outside of the British empire grew only gradually in the years following the end of the revolutionary war.

The French revolutionary wars accelerated this process. Warfare created a massive market for American grains in continental Europe. With armies to feed and farmers drafted into war, neutral American merchants hoped to export foodstuffs to both sides. Eyeing the mounting prices of provisions, Salem merchant William Gray Jr. licked his lips at the prospect of selling cargo "at the Isle of France at one hundred per cent profit."[72] Merchants reading US newspapers would have seen numerous letters remarking on the financial and political incentives for American grain ships to visit the ports of continental Europe. Huge European demand made wheat the most important US export during the 1790s, an often-forgotten interregnum between the reigns of tobacco and King Cotton.[73]

By the mid-1790s, the dream of bringing together commerce and news from across the world seemed to have been realized. While ship arrivals prior to the American war for independence predominantly listed British ports of departure, by the 1790s ships were arriving from all over the world. In the spring of 1764, for example, as ice floes receded and ships rushed into the harbor, Philadelphia newspapers noted the arrival of four vessels from London, which brought not only ribbons, gunpowder, and spices, but also news from the London papers.[74] Thirty years later, the spring thaw brought ships from Bordeaux, St. Petersburg, Martinique, Porto, Saint Barthélemy, Amsterdam, Sint Eustatius, and Bermuda. These ships carried wine, hemp, iron, and news from Russia, the Caribbean, and France.[75] Indeed, throughout the mid-1790s, ships arrived in the United States from numerous regions and empires, carrying newspapers, letters, and loquacious crowds of sailors, travelers, merchants, diplomats, and ship captains.

Americans had never consistently gathered news from French sources, even during their war for independence. Beginning in 1792, though, the massive wartime mobilization of French society created a huge demand for American shipping. This transformation opened a substantial, ongoing line of public communications between the United States and France for the first time. During the 1790s, Americans received more than eighty times as much of their news from France as they had three decades before. American reliance on French sources peaked near the middle of the decade. By 1795, US newspapers cited French newspapers more than seven times as often as they had done five years earlier (see the appendix). This rate of exchange gradually declined after the mid-1790s, as the demand for American crops waned and as a new commercial treaty with Britain and growing tensions with France led US merchants to reorient trade back toward a prerevolutionary equilibrium.

Commercial changes also allowed Americans to engage regularly with the print cultures of northern Europe. Wartime trade with Bremen and Hamburg during the 1790s provided Americans with regular access for the first time to the *Hamburgische Unpartheyische Correspondent*, one of the oldest and most reputable German-language publications and one of the most widely circulating newspapers in the world.[76] Though reprints from German-speaking lands never dominated the pages of US newspapers, they were a noticeable presence in the 1790s. It was not unusual for printers to comment, as one did in 1793, "The following is translated from the Hamburg Gazette, of the 21st of September; handed to the Editor of the Federal Gazette by a merchant of Philadelphia."[77] As this citation indicates, the availability of German news depended on the growth of commerce between American and German merchants. In the second half of the decade, about 6 percent of all citations in US newspapers referred to German newspapers.

Irish-American trade also accelerated in the early 1780s. The Irish had won concessions from the British government during the American revolutionary war, including the right to determine their own trade policy. Long restricted by imperial authority, the Irish set generous terms with the Americans, and trade between Ireland and the United States grew steadily.[78] This new commercial activity brought Irish newspapers into North America. Previously absent from the continent's newspapers, Irish print sources made up nearly 6 percent of North American printers' citations in the late 1780s and around 2 percent in the 1790s. In part, this greater rate of citation likely resulted from growing interest in the Irish Volunteer and United Irishmen movements (see chapter 5). However, it also reflected the growing commerce with Ireland and the increased availability of Irish newspapers.

Likewise, Americans accessed more information directly from the Netherlands during the late eighteenth century. As a result of a new commercial treaty, Dutch-American commerce grew after the revolution. North American readers and printers had long recognized that the Netherlands provided one of the few environments for free newspaper printing in Europe. As a result, they trusted Francophone Dutch newspapers, such as the *Courier du Bas-Rhin*, the *Brussels Gazette*, the *Gazette d'Amsterdam*, and especially *Nouvelles extraordinaires de divers endroits*—better known as the *Gazette de Leyde* or in the Anglophone world as the *Leyden Gazette*—for news about Europe.[79] North Americans praised the *Gazette de Leyde* as the "most authentic medium of intelligence," the "most authentic vehicle of European intelligence," and the "most correct paper, for political intelligence, published in Europe."[80] Newspapers such as the *Gazette de Leyde* allowed North American observers to read about the Dutch Patriot Revolt of the 1780s and the events unleashed by the French Revolution in the early 1790s through a trusted intermediary. In the 1780s, US newspapers cited Dutch prints at seven times the rate of the 1770s. This rate trebled again in the 1790s, making up nearly 7 percent of all citations.

With these changes, US newspaper printers drew on a wider variety of sources in the 1780s and 1790s than ever before. From the beginning of the century through the 1770s, only about 5 percent of British American newspapers' citations of newspapers abroad referred to sources outside of the British empire. But during the 1780s, this rate rose to a quarter of all citations. In the 1790s, around a third of citations pointed beyond the British empire. American papers were increasingly composed of reprints taken from France, the Netherlands, Ireland, Germany, India, and the British and French Caribbean. Yet while newspapers' reprints had broadened compared to previous decades, the available sources remained quite partial and limited on a global scale. Few reports originating in South America, Africa, East Asia, or elsewhere appeared in US newspapers. Americans' cosmopolitan interests extended only so far, and few complained about these omissions.

John Sevier kept a terse diary. Most entries were only a few lines long. On June 8, 1790, for example, he wrote, "Tarried in town, bought five yds callico, got a Round made cost 20 shillings. paid for Wine Expenses &c 4–."[81] A prominent Tennessee soldier and politician, Sevier usually recorded little more than details about the weather, his health, social visits, and other movements. Only occasionally did he provide any glimpse of an interior life. One such example is a diary entry recording a lengthy, vivid dream in January 1794.

Unusually, Sevier began by describing himself in the third person: "John Sevier Gen[era]l Dreamed he was in an unknown country Supposed from some immagination that it was france." In the dream, he encountered his son, who guided him up a hill toward a "large building which appeared to be built of either Diamond or Glass as I could see through the walls with doors & windows all round." As they continued to ascend through the building, they reached a "very great height," looked out, and saw "all the nations in the world." His son explained that "such a place was Russia, another . . . was Germany, then prussia England, Holland, Denmark Turky and as well as I can remember all the Countries in the known world." He was amazed by the building and astonished that he had never heard of it before. As he wondered why other nations had not also built this kind of structure, he woke up.[82]

Sevier dreamed of this diamond observatory about two years after the earliest publication of Tennessee's first newspaper, the *Knoxville Gazette*. Having lived for many years in rural Tennessee, Sevier might have had reason to feel isolated from the larger world. The arrival in late 1791 of the *Gazette*, which Sevier likely read, gave him a fresh vantage onto the "known world." The imagined location of Sevier's observatory in France was significant. For decades, North American newspapers and readers had depended on information routed through London. For most of the eighteenth century, the observatory through which North Americans saw the world would have been planted firmly in England. Toward the century's end, though, US independence and an explosion of global print sources allowed Americans to draw a greater quantity of news from outside Britain, especially from places such as Ireland, the Netherlands, and France.

Independence pushed mediators to think about the ways that information sources, like Sevier's diamond observatory, refracted even as they revealed. Having seen falsehoods flow like a mudslide during their revolution, Americans understood that media and news could tear down the United States as easily as they had built it up. There was strength in mediation. As Americans saw the current of revolution streaming through Ireland, the Netherlands, Peru, France, Poland, Saint Domingue, and elsewhere in the aftermath of American independence, many observers ascribed those events to the power of information. If shunning falsehoods could bring about the American Revolution, why couldn't it bring an end to tyranny the world over? News could do more than report about events. It could regenerate the world.

CHAPTER FIVE

The Genius of Information

Scripting an Age of Revolutions

How do revolutions happen? In the late eighteenth century, this was an urgent, if deceptively simple, question. Unlocking the pathology of revolution could allow one to control its transformative impact, whether that meant regenerating the world or enforcing the status quo. In the early 1790s, a French Canadian named Henri-Antoine Mézière thought that he had solved this puzzle. He worked in the print shop of the *Montreal Gazette*, and he described his theory in a March 1792 issue. Ideas did not cause revolutions, he explained: "It would be ridiculous to mention the writings of Voltaire as the sources of freedom. Even those of Locke will not adequately account for the wonderful revolution in the opinions of men with respect to government. Those authors were but little read, and still less understood." Rather, Mézière wrote, the "genius of information" had activated revolutionary fervor around the globe. The spread of news had brought enlightenment and liberty, he believed, to lands that had once been "in a deplorable state of ignorance."[1]

In another essay published a year later, Mézière pressed the point that ideas were not enough to bring about revolutionary change. In Canada, he explained, "the townspeople have all the philosophical works; and . . . they read them, the French gazettes, the Declaration of the Rights of Man with passionate attention." But the revolutionary ideas that they encountered could not bring about political change on their own. Instead, Mézière thought, news from France had done more to stimulate his countrymen to action: "I dare say that the French Revolution has electrified the Canadians and enlightened them more about their natural rights in a year than a century of reading would have been able to do." France's declaration of war against the British empire had not intimidated the Canadians, who publicly wished for France's success. "Every day," he recounted, "they assemble in the towns in small groups, tell each other about the latest news received, rejoice with each other when the news is favorable to the French and grieve (but not desperately) when it is unfavorable."[2] Mézière believed that the most effective way to generate revolutionary change was not to use lofty language and ideas to convince people that despotism was bad, but rather to demonstrate that despotism was vulnerable by providing examples of successful revolutions elsewhere. In this way, news from abroad could change the world. One revolution's example could be electrifying. That was the genius of information.

Mézière's essays offered a particularly crisp explanation of how revolutions worked, but his model was not an original one. Other North Americans had been articulating similar ideas for years. According to what might be called the "information script" of revolution, the flow of news about successful uprisings into a place beset by despotism and ignorance could provoke revolutionary ruptures.[3] Once they learned about revolutions abroad, oppressed people would recognize that they, too, could challenge the tyrants who ruled over them. Crucially, this model suggested that despotic governments sustained themselves with ignorance and misinformation. Lacking proper sources of news, an entire nation might be uninformed or misinformed about revolutionary events abroad. Mézière and others believed that intelligence about political uprisings did not reach everyone around the world because that was how despots preferred it.

The accumulation of revolutionary events around the world led Mézière and many of his contemporaries to conclude that they were connected, like links in a chain. What bound them, they believed, was the exchange of information. News of the American Revolution provided an example to inspire the French people into action, while the French Revolution inspired the Polish people, and so on. Revolutions seemed to fall into each other like dominoes. In this model, the news was not simply a chronicle of the past, but a force that created the future.

Yet the information script was only one of several discourses circulating around the Atlantic world about the origins of revolutions. For many, the "principles of liberty" were the motor of revolutionary change.[4] Those who relied on the information script did not reject the significance of ideas, but merely questioned their preeminence. In a 1795 Fourth of July oration delivered in Boston, George Blake suggested that abstractions were necessary, but insufficient, catalysts of revolution. Without the "example of America," which "roused the virtues of her people into action," he argued, France would have remained the "most enlightened, and yet most oppressed" nation in the world.[5] Ideas may have legitimized revolutionary change, but information produced action.

Unlike contemporary observers, historians have generally not seen the information script as a legitimate explanation for the Age of Revolutions. Many nineteenth- and twentieth-century historians, often engaged in nation-building projects, emphasized instead the importance of ideologies in sparking revolutions. Ideology, after all, offers sturdier bedrock for national identity than imitation does. Today, while scholars are increasingly interested in the ways that earlier revolutionaries inspired each other, they also recognize that an array of distinctive local, national, and imperial conditions ignited revolutionary movements.[6] But if Mézière underestimated the complexity and unpredictability of revolutionary change, he was right to acknowledge that people do not usually embrace lost causes. The example of successful revolutions elsewhere, even when they took place in wildly different circumstances, probably convinced many that change was possible.

Watching revolutionary events unfold in Ireland, Peru, the Netherlands, France, and Poland, the inheritors of the American Revolution traced the great events of the era back to their own example. For many Americans—although not for Mézière—the information script served to bolster an emerging sense of American national identity. As they saw it, the American Revolution had not merely liberated the colonies from Britain. It had catalyzed a chain reaction of information exchanges that promised to liberate the world.

The information script held that a well-informed people would inevitably resist despotism. "It is an axiom as certain as any in Euclid," a 1790 report in a New York newspaper explained, "that in every country where the people possess a free and uncorrupted source of information, there rational liberty will reside."[7] Once someone learned about effective revolutions elsewhere, it seemed, they would understand the fragility of the governments and social structures that they detested. Those who failed to challenge despotic structures, therefore, were unable to imagine the possibility of successful revolutionary change. They might be well versed in Enlightenment maxims, yet accept that oppressive rule was inevitable.

Crucially, tumult and strife alone were not enough to inspire imitation. A revolution needed to be successful to provide an example for others. "Our success," according to an American commentator in 1790, had "inspired" the

French to revolution.[8] From the perspective of the elite men whose narratives mediated the Age of Revolutions, the American Revolution seemed to be self-evidently successful and, therefore, self-evidently exemplary. One Boston assemblage drew on this presumption when they toasted in 1782, "May the success of the American revolution stimulate the oppressed throughout the world to like exertions."[9]

A revolution's failure could also provide a powerful example. A state founded on political experimentation needed to ensure the people's continued prosperity and safety in order to encourage further challenges to despotism. Why would an oppressed people rise against their oppressors if it would lead only to disorder or new forms of tyranny? Congregational preacher Joseph Lathrop argued in 1795 that if Americans "should disgrace our revolution, our example would damp the spirit and obstruct the progress of liberty in the nations, which have begun to cherish it." Yet if Americans "appear to be happy" with their government, then "many nations will partake with us in the felicity."[10] Another preacher, Thomas Fessenden, argued that the "eye of other nations" had been fixed on the United States since its revolution and that if Americans "prosper," other nations would "retreat . . . from despotism."[11] For Lathrop, Fessenden, and many others, appearances mattered. Revolutionary nations, such as the United States, were burdened with the ongoing task of demonstrating their triumphs to the world.

But even as they believed that some revolutions provided powerful examples, North Americans could not help but notice that uprisings were not breaking out everywhere. For every revolution, there was much more continuity. As he worked through reports of revolutionary events in 1793, printer Isaiah Thomas's mind kept wandering to "other European countries," where "tyranny has been supported by ancient establishment, by ambition, and by ignorance."[12] Ignorance was widely understood to be the "essential ingredient in monarchy," restraining millions around the world from understanding the benefits of revolutionary experimentation.[13] Why else would they abide their chains? In a 1795 oration, physician Phinehas Hedges remarked that humanity had existed since its beginning in a condition of "ignorance, stupidity, and bondage." Whenever any "faint, imperfect perceptions of liberty" threatened this system, they had been "extinguished by the industrious agency of tyrants."[14] Prior to their revolution, a Massachusetts newspaper essayist pointed out, the French people had been "kept in ignorance and darkness by the overbearing few."[15] The American writer and traveler Joel Barlow argued, "Unequal governments are necessarily founded in ignorance and they must be supported by ignorance." In his eyes, the "undisturbed ignorance of the people" was "the pillar of the state." To maintain their power, despots needed to prevent their subjects from "acquiring that ease and information" that would allow them to "discern the evil and apply the remedy."[16] A Philadelphia printer put it more baldly: "ignorance and slavery always go hand in hand."[17]

According to this model, ignorance always preceded, and usually prevented, revolution. The apparent ignorance of so many countries therefore seemed to promise the possibility of change in the future. Revolution marked the moment, according to Lathrop, when the "bright effulgence of truth . . . at last dissipated the heavy clouds of ignorance and superstition."[18] In his pamphlet *Rights of Man*, Thomas Paine was even more hopeful about the flimsiness of political ignorance. He believed that revolutions had "thrown a beam of light over the world," which could not be undone, and that once ignorance had been dispelled, "it is impossible to re-establish it."[19] Some observers reimagined the American Revolution as an emergence from a state of ignorance. A 1792 newspaper writer, for example, concluded that "light and information" had led British colonists to realize the need to challenge imperial authority.[20]

Likewise, many writers and leaders in the early republic argued that information was the best check against encroaching ignorance and despotism.[21] Hoping to encourage the spread of information among ordinary people, the US government passed a law in 1792 that set low postal rates for newspapers. "Wherever information is freely circulated, there slavery cannot exist," Congressman Elbridge Gerry explained in debate about the proposal. He noted that "the light of information has enabled the French to discover their rights," but in any nation this liberty "cannot long subsist, if the channels of information are stopped."[22] Unless guarded against, many believed, ignorance could bring the American Revolution to an unhappy end.[23]

The term "revolution" was only one of many that North Americans wielded to refer to popular political challenges to despotic regimes in the late eighteenth century. Indeed, the phrases "American Revolution" and "Age of Revolutions" only began to appear in public discourse in the last two decades of the century. Long imagined to imply a cyclical change, like a planet *revolving* around a star, many understood a "revolution" to be a modest change that left governmental and social structures intact, such as the death of a monarch. It was only in the 1780s and 1790s that "revolution" began to refer to broader structural ruptures.[24] Alongside the language of revolution, North Americans employed a bevy of metaphors and euphemisms. They spoke of political revolution in terms of seeds, flames, and infections. In this figurative language, like created like. Seeds begat more seeds, flames consumed and spread, and pathogens were transmitted between people. Revolutions reproduced themselves.

The most common trope that North Americans employed to refer to revolutionary change was the "flame of liberty." Used in thousands of essays, pamphlets, letters, and other writings in the late eighteenth century, this term referred to the spread of revolution across space. The imagery of a flame, which catches quickly and spreads indiscriminately, indicated spontaneity and impulse rather than measured deliberation. Writers often used the term to describe revolutionaries boldly fighting despotic rule, but rarely to describe a constitutional debate. It evoked action rather than reflection. Moreover, commentators almost always accompanied the phrase with a definite article—it was *the* flame of liberty, not *a* flame of liberty.[25] This usage suggests that American observers saw the flame as something shared, rather than as something independently produced in multiple places. Revolutions in Geneva and Cuzco might be quite distinct in many ways, but they seemed to be expressions of the same global impulse that had been generated first during the American Revolution. Instead of attending to each event's distinctive circumstances and complexity, the language surrounding revolutionary events encouraged observers to adhere to simple binaries: revolution or continuity, liberty or despotism, information or ignorance.

The flame of liberty trope also evoked diffusive imitation. In printed discourse, writers typically used it to connect two or more spaces: a source that offered an example of revolutionary change and a target where the flame had, or could, spread. When they wrote the phrase "flame of liberty," American commentators often paired it with the word "example." Referring to one event as an "example," commentators suggested that observers in other places would learn about and imitate it. Philadelphia printer Eleazer Oswald, for example, told readers that Ireland had caught the "glorious flame of liberty" after being "inspired by the noble example of America."[26] In a 1793 sermon, preacher Chandler Robbins wrote of the French Revolution that "the *other nations* of Europe ... from this example, will catch the flame of liberty."[27] Likewise, after describing the spread of the flame of liberty into Savoy, a report in a New York newspaper explained, "Wherever men feel themselves oppressed, they only want an example to assert their rights."[28] The flame of liberty spread when an oppressed group learned about the example of a successful revolution elsewhere.

Writers and speakers sometimes combined the flame of liberty trope with the language of education. They often referred to revolutionaries in one place teaching others how to successfully defeat despotism. Massachusetts printer William Butler, for example, described how the Irish had been "encouraged, and animated by our example and success" and by the "flame of liberty which burst out in America," while the French had avidly read "the story of the American Revolution."[29] Preacher John Lathrop similarly spoke of revolutionary examples as a kind of pedagogy. "Taught by your examples, and encouraged by your successes," he told a Boston audience, the "oppressed inhabitants of other nations" were fighting despotism.[30] Though it often went unsaid in discourses about revolution, news provided the crucial link between an example and its target. Information was kindling for the flame of liberty.

The earliest revolutionary event abroad to seize North Americans' attention was the Irish Volunteer movement. It was also the first "revolution" that American observers attributed to their own example. Historians of the Age of Revolutions have largely neglected this short-lived movement both because it was ultimately unsuccessful and, perhaps, because it was quickly overshadowed by the United Irishmen uprising of the late 1790s. Yet contemporary observers were deeply interested in it. At the height of the American war for independence, Americans initially avoided suggesting that the Irish were following their example. Once the war concluded, however, they began to surmise that an Irish revolution was unfolding according to the American model.

Although the American war for independence was important to Irish dissidents, it was useful first for providing an opportunity for mobilization and only secondarily as a source of inspiration. Irish Patriot politics had been simmering for decades before the outbreak of the American war offered an opening.[31] When the American war erupted, a series of militia groups calling themselves the Irish Volunteers organized across the island for the avowed purpose of protecting against foreign invasion. With the ministry distracted and the empire's resources drained by the war, they quickly realized that they could take advantage of the moment—with an implicit threat of violence—to demand greater autonomy. They abandoned the original purpose of the Volunteers and consolidated into a political movement. Their most important grievance was the empire's trade restrictions. Mercantilist policies had long forced the Irish to channel their commerce through Britain, which drained away their profits. Exerting pressure on Britain's political institutions, the Irish

Volunteers secured commercial concessions in 1779. Emboldened, the Volunteers' allies in Parliament pushed ahead, and in 1782 a group led by MP Henry Grattan forced Westminster to concede some legislative autonomy to Ireland.[32]

Initially, American Patriots observed the Volunteers through an imperial lens. They were interested in the unrest in Ireland mostly because of what its causes and consequences revealed about the instability of the British empire. Did the quick expansion from American to Irish resistance indicate that the empire was falling apart? As an American emissary in Paris in 1780, John Adams wrote to the Continental Congress claiming that the Irish movement indicated that "the British empire is crumbling to pieces like a rope of sand." He wondered if Scotland or India would be the next parts of the empire to revolt.[33] For the moment, most regarded Ireland's and America's resistance as indications of one empire's crisis, rather than a more general crisis of empires. Other Patriots also took a narrow view of the American Revolution's international impact. In a 1779 newspaper essay, a Boston writer could only imagine that the American Revolution would encourage European migration to the United States and that some governments would "relax the reins of power," particularly England's tight grasp on Ireland.[34] This anonymous essayist did not, or perhaps could not, consider the possibility that the American Revolution would provoke a wave of general revolution throughout Europe and the world.

Indeed, the idea of an emerging global awakening might have endangered the Patriot cause. Patriot leaders knew that a transnational flame of liberty would be unattractive to their European allies, who sought to contain anti-imperial movements and revolts in their own empires. When his diplomatic post switched to the United Provinces of the Netherlands, Adams tried to quash the idea that the sentiments of the American Revolution would spread outside of the British empire. He assured the Dutch that there was no truth in the "Supposition, propagated by the English to prevent other Nations from pursuing their true Interests, that other Colonies will follow the Example of the United States." His reasoning was that no other European power would follow the "Example of England" in suddenly adopting a cruel and oppressive government.[35] While the flame of liberty trope suggested that the American Revolution provided an example for oppressed people to emulate, Adams intimated that it would provide an example for rulers to avoid. Aiming to secure Dutch financing, Adams recognized that the geopolitical imperatives of the war required that its consequences be confined to the British empire for the moment.

Americans during the war eagerly sought out news about Ireland. Though they generally distrusted British newspapers, Patriots had no choice but to rely on them for accounts about Ireland. This created uncertainty. When Boston printer Nathaniel Willis passed along some London papers' reports about Ireland in 1780, for example, he admitted that they were "on the ministerial side."[36] Some Patriot mediators also took note of their Loyalist rivals' choice to ignore news from Ireland. Printer Isaiah Thomas, for example, mentioned that the "late papers from N. York," where Loyalists dominated the presses, "say nothing of the affairs in Ireland."[37] While he did not say so directly, Thomas implied that Loyalists were suppressing news about the Volunteer movement because it boded ill for their cause.

Once the American war for independence concluded, though, US newspapers gained access to new information sources. The Volunteers' success in lifting imperial trade restrictions allowed Irish-American commerce to flourish in the early 1780s. In 1783, Thomas Bradford of the *Pennsylvania Journal* trumpeted that a ship led by Captain Stephen Connick had arrived from Dublin, the "first vessel that sailed from Ireland with the manufactures of that country since they threw off their servile subjection to Britain. She is the first that cleared out for these United States, and is the first arrived directly from Ireland since our revolution has taken place." As the ship left port in Dublin, it had raised the American flag, which was "saluted soon after by a corps of the Irish Volunteers." Connick brought with him an Irish newspaper that carried information of events in Ireland, the Netherlands, Paris, and London.[38] He was not alone. As ships from Ireland piled into American ports in the early 1780s, they brought letters, personal accounts, and newspapers into the United States. As I indicated in the previous chapter, American newspapers began to cite Irish prints far more often in the 1780s and 1790s, offering a new vantage on the British Isles.

Irish sources framed the conflict on the Volunteers' terms: as a high-minded quest for liberty and freedom. A poem from the *Belfast Mercury*, for example, commanded readers to "rouse, rouse" to "gain a bright emancipation."[39] Other accounts glowingly announced that the "emancipation of Ireland" would come quickly, and the Irish would "soon triumph over the enemies of liberty."[40] Noting this change in perspective, an Albany printer pointed out in 1783, "Some late papers, received by the last vessels from Ireland are wholly filled with the most patriotic resolutions of the people."[41]

With greater access to Irish information sources and without the distraction of their own war, Americans' sympathy for the Irish Volunteers exploded from 1783 through 1785. Many US observers expected an Irish revolution to rival the American one. Several commentators anticipated that the Irish would imminently declare independence. A correspondent writing to the New York *Daily Advertiser* in 1785 noted that British accounts indicated that a "genuine revolution spirit is up in Ireland," and the author expected to "hear by the first vessel, that they had openly declared *Ireland* to be a free and independant nation."[42] The *New-Haven Gazette* predicted in 1784 that "it is probable that Ireland will recover her ancient Independence."[43]

It was in this postwar moment, in relation to Ireland, that Americans first imagined the American Revolution as a model for revolutionaries everywhere. Shortly after the end of the American war for independence, US observers began to insist that the Irish Volunteers had "learned the lesson from Americans," and they were "pursuing . . . the same course."[44] This observation depended on the premise that prior to the American Revolution, Ireland had been in a state of ignorance and had only emerged once the Americans demonstrated the possibility of revolution. In the *Boston Gazette*, an essayist using the name "Consideration" suggested that America "hath set Ireland free" by spreading "light and liberty" among the Irish.[45] A commentary in a New York newspaper claimed that after the Americans "nobly dared to set bounds to the inroads of despotism," the Irish had "caught a spark from the flame" and had begun to loosen their own "manacles."[46] It was self-evident to many American observers that the Irish Volunteers had been "inspired by the noble example of America."[47]

Although these self-congratulatory accounts exaggerated Americans' influence on Ireland, the Volunteers did take some inspiration from the American Revolution. In the most sustained scholarly study of the movement, historian Vincent Morley has concluded that while the Irish were "not inspired by American *thought*," they probably benefited from "the force of American *example*."[48] Indeed, American readers regularly encountered evidence from Ireland's newspapers that their example had galvanized the island's people. While several Irish newspapers supported the British government, US printers seem to have preferred to republish materials from newspapers sympathetic to the Volunteers, which sometimes invited readers to compare the American Revolution with the Volunteer movement. In a lengthy extract from a Dublin newspaper that printer Elizabeth Holt (John Holt's widow) shared in the *New-York Journal*, for example, an Irish writer warned that England's actions would soon be "rewarded with American gratitude."[49] An essay from a "late Irish Paper" reprinted in John Miller's *South Carolina Gazette* sought to rouse readers to action by asking, "Are not Irishmen as well prepared, as valiant, and as determined as Americans?"[50] Likewise, a speech from the *Dublin Evening Post*, reprinted in Philadelphia, attributed the Volunteer movement to Americans' shouts for liberty, which had "reverberated here."[51]

When Irish sources failed to draw these connections, American observers sometimes did so on their own. In 1784 William Warden and Benjamin Russell, the printers of the *Massachusetts Centinel*, summarized the contents of several Irish newspaper issues, noting the unanimity of the Irish people against Britain, the "outrages" committed by British troops, and the misgovernment of imperial officials. They concluded that "Ireland is now in the same state that America was in 1774," complaining of "accumulated wrongs" and preparing to act against the British government.[52] Indeed, reports directly from Ireland allowed US observers to imagine the conflict as a repeat of the American Revolution. When Francis Bailey of the Philadelphia *Freeman's Journal* heard some oral reports emanating from an "Irish Vessel now in our river" in 1784, he wrapped them up in an American cover. Describing some armed clashes between the Volunteers and the British, Bailey mockingly reported that the "*victorious conquerors of America*, now in Hibernia, 'advanced backwards' to their strong holds, with as much activity as they did nine years ago from the Plains of Lexington."[53] The script of the American Revolution seemed to be replaying itself in Ireland.

Concerned that the Volunteers were not making quick enough progress, a Pennsylvania newspaper essayist calling himself "An Old Man of Chester County" urged the Irish to follow the American model and seek their liberty more forcefully. They had engaged in enough "talk, printed resolves, mere parade and military ostentation," he believed, and the time had come for them to openly rebel. He asked, "What would the American war have ended in" if the Patriots had failed to act?[54] In response, an essayist signing as "A Volunteer" questioned the "source of information" that An Old Man had relied on. Perhaps A Volunteer suspected that An Old Man was getting his news from London prints. Contradicting his interlocutor, A Volunteer argued that the Irish rebels had "presented an object for the admiration of the world . . . an object which no nation has yet equalled." If the Irish revolution was slow, that did not mean that they had diverged from the example of the American Revolution, which had itself dragged on for quite a while.[55] While these two writers disagreed in their assessments of the Volunteer movement, they shared a conviction that the American Revolution provided the script that the Irish ought to follow.

Even as American excitement for the Irish Volunteers crested in the mid-1780s, though, the movement's prospects began to dim. The end of the American revolutionary war and the return of British soldiers restored the empire's authorities to a position of strength relative to the rebellious Irish. The British successfully resisted the demands of the Volunteers and Irish Patriots for legislative reforms in 1783 and 1784. Growing religious disunity among the Volunteers combined with greater British strength to stall the success of the movement. What had once looked like the beginning of an Irish revolution began to dissipate.[56]

One of the clearest signals of the imperial government's renewed strength over Ireland was its increased regulation of dissident print.[57] Mathew Carey, who was among the island's most prominent radical printers, aroused the British government's ire when he published several essays demanding Irish independence and attacking British officials. In response to Carey and other critical printers, the government passed a law to punish the "publication of traitorous, seditious, false and slanderous libels."[58] As a result, radical newspapers were silenced, and critical printers were jailed. Such repression outraged Americans.[59] The government briefly imprisoned Carey before he slipped away to Philadelphia to become, eventually, one of North America's most prominent printers.[60] Beginning in 1785 when he opened the *Pennsylvania Evening Herald*, Carey was particularly active in sharing news from Ireland about what one of his correspondents called "the extinction of every glimmering beam of political freedom."[61] Nevertheless, as Irish agitation decreased and as ships from Ireland carried fewer radical accounts to the United States, Americans' interest in Ireland declined. US newspapers reprinted more from Irish papers in the late 1780s than they had earlier in the decade, but American enthusiasm for the Volunteers died with their hopes.

Several other revolutionary events competed for Americans' attention in the 1780s, including in the United Provinces of the Netherlands. Dutch participation in the American revolutionary war, which also came to be known as the Fourth Anglo-Dutch War, proved disastrous for them. Blaming Stadtholder William V of Orange, a faction calling themselves the Patriots began to mobilize popular opposition to his rule. This tense standoff occupied Dutch politics for most of the 1780s. While the structural impact of the American revolutionary war probably contributed more to causing this revolt, as in Ireland, the Patriots occasionally ascribed their actions to the example of American action. During the American war for independence, for instance, a Dutch ally named J. D. van Der Capellen called for his people to fight against their own oppression: "Take up arms . . . and proceed with modesty and composure just like the people of America where not a single drop of blood was shed before the English attacked them."[62]

While the Dutch Patriot uprising did not cause as much comment as the Irish Volunteer movement, US newspapers provided a considerable amount of commentary and news material from Europe about events in the Netherlands.[63] Some Americans linked the Dutch Patriot cause to their own. The revolt came to a head in 1787 when a British-backed Prussian army invaded. This led one Boston writer to comment that the United States was "more deeply interested" in events in the Netherlands than "most people appear to have an idea of." If the invasion force succeeded, this writer explained, it would embolden Britain and the enemies of freedom around the world, who would eventually force the United States to defend its independence against a despotic force.[64]

Americans also learned of a series of revolts in Spanish South America in the early 1780s. Over the course of the eighteenth century, the Spanish imperial government had aimed to strengthen its ability to efficiently extract wealth from its New World colonies. In the Andes, this provoked a peasant revolt in November 1780 led by Túpac Amaru II, who claimed to have descended from the last Incan leader. He assembled an army of hundreds, which overpowered the initial wave of Spanish troops sent to contain his rebellion. After failing to capture Cuzco, though, Amaru's army lost momentum, and Spanish reinforcements dispersed his troops and killed him. At about the same time, another rebel leader, Túpac Katari, led a similarly ill-fated rebellion to the south.[65]

North Americans lacked a direct line of communication with the Andes, unlike Ireland and the Netherlands. Because no newspapers were printed in Spanish America at the time, observers learned about these Andean revolts primarily through mariners' reports and letters. In fact, much of the substantial intelligence that filtered into North America about Peru came from British military sources. During the revolts, Spain was at war with Britain, and the collision of their naval forces sometimes allowed for accidental information exchange. In 1780, after a British ship captured the Spanish vessel *Diligencia*, the sailors discovered a "box of letters" describing the revolts. These accounts, initially published in a Loyalist New York newspaper, seem to have been the first reports about the Andean revolts printed in North America.[66] Likewise, one of the most detailed accounts of the uprisings arrived in North

America after a British privateer captured a Spanish vessel that carried three letters from a colonial official addressed to the Spanish ministry.[67]

Perhaps because Spain was fighting against the British empire, many reports in London and Loyalist newspapers were quite sympathetic to the Andean rebels. One British officer who had been captured by Spanish forces and taken to South America reported in Loyalist printer Hugh Gaine's newspaper that Peru was "governed by Spanish Corregidors, who greatly oppress the Indians. . . . These oppressions have caused a revolution in Peru."[68] A rumor even circulated that England was preparing to send troops to aid the rebels, aiming to do "only as France and Spain have done towards England, and her possessions in America."[69] In contrast, when American Patriot newspapers shared material originating from their Spanish allies, it tended to be more critical. One account from Spain, purportedly based on "two boxes filled with papers, which contain[ed] the correspondence" of "Tupac Amaro," accused him of "seducing a weak and credulous people, and for exciting them to rise against the government."[70]

The Irish Volunteers, the Dutch Patriots, and the Amaru and Katari revolts in Peru were not the only revolutionary events of the 1780s. In June 1780, for example, London experienced significant street violence, motivated largely by anti-Catholicism. A short-lived "revolution" shook the city-state of Geneva in 1782. An insurrection at the end of the 1780s known as the Brabantine Revolution in the Austrian Netherlands (today's Belgium) saw rebels briefly declare independence before Austria restored its control. North Americans read about all of these events. For many observers, the various proto-revolutions, uprisings, and political movements reinforced the notion that political rupture was inevitable in spaces of ignorance.

Claims about the ignorance of a people were often tied up with American Protestants' long-standing anti-Catholic attitudes. In the words of a correspondent to a New York paper, "Priest-craft" had long combined with "King-craft" to keep the "human mind in fetters, and the world in the most slavish state of ignorance and bondage."[71] For many observers, revolutions seemed to promise the decline of Catholicism around the world. Indeed, some of the phrases that Americans used before they settled on the term "revolution," such as "reformation" and "glorious revolution," evoked the historical imagery of Protestant triumph over Catholic deception and ignorance. Anglo-Americans also made use of widespread Hispanophobic stereotypes to interpret some of these events. For centuries, Britons had justified their own colonial projects by exaggerating accounts of Spanish cruelty and oppression in the New World, which later became known as the "black legend."[72] Even after they partnered with Spain in their war for independence, Protestant Americans remained deeply suspicious of Catholic empires. Newspaper reports emphasized that the Spanish empire was "plunged in ignorance and slavish bigotry."[73]

The ignorance apparently enforced by despotic rule and by a "popish" religion seemed to promise future revolutionary upheaval. A New York essayist, for example, observed in 1784 that "the decay of the Papal influence that so long kept the world in stupid ignorance" had contributed to "the revolutions of Portugal, Holland and Switzerland." He urged the victims of Catholicism to "struggle thro' the mists of barbarous ignorance" to defeat the clouds of "slavish superstition."[74] The Andean revolts seemed to confirm this possibility. One Massachusetts writer concluded that they demonstrated that revolution was possible anywhere on the globe, "even in South America, where superstition and priestcraft had rivitted the fetters of tyranny."[75] By the late 1780s and early 1790s, as the rate of revolutionary change seemed to accelerate, North Americans persistently predicted that the flame of liberty would soon visit Spain. One account published in 1789 claimed that the Spanish people had discovered that their government was taking "pains . . . to prevent them being made acquainted with the causes & effects of the late revolution in France." If the Spanish people had not mounted a full revolution yet, this account alleged, they had at least "mustered up revolution enough to call for the heads of the Inquisitors."[76] Other reports that "foreign newspapers are now read by every one in Spain" suggested that the nation would soon yield to the momentum of global revolution.[77]

Indeed, for many observers, the events of the 1780s seemed to promise a transnational wave of revolution. In typical fashion, a 1784 newspaper report saw a clear trajectory between events in the United States and the Irish Volunteer movement, the rebellions in Peru, and the Dutch Patriot Revolt: "The enthusiasm for liberty, which has spread from North to South America, which has occasioned a revolution in Ireland . . . begins to rouse the cold minds of the Dutch."[78] These events encouraged some Americans to toast during celebrations to the hope that "the example of America, in the late revolution" would be "copied by enslaved people throughout the world."[79] Speaking to an audience about the treaty ending the American revolutionary war, Levi Frisbie cheerfully noted that the "struggles of America" had already roused "some nations, who formerly have but sparingly tasted the sweets of Liberty." He asked his audience to imagine whether "our example and our intercourse with foreign nations" would not "widely diffuse this sacred flame, and extend its happy influence thro' all the kingdoms of Europe, if not to the most distant quarters of the globe."[80]

Others, however, noticed that the revolutions of the 1780s had been largely unsuccessful. The Irish Volunteers had accomplished some things, but Britain had clawed back other gains. A Prussian army had smothered the Dutch Patriots. A Spanish invasion had dispersed the Andean revolts. The 1780s were as much an age of continuity as an age of revolutions.

The overall failure of these movements contributed to some Americans' fears about their ability to sustain their own revolution. In the debate over the ratification of the proposed US Constitution in 1787 and 1788, both those favoring and those opposing the document's adoption used the examples of these failed revolutions to their own ends. Those who supported the Constitution argued that the failure of the Patriot movements in Ireland and the Netherlands resulted from their military weakness and vulnerability to invasion. The proposed Constitution, they promised, would strengthen America's central government and equip it with the power to create a standing army to repel such invasions. James Madison argued that the Dutch confederacy's weakness, much like the decentralized American confederacy, had caused its recent "calamities." For Madison, this offered a "very emphatic lesson for the U. States."[81] In making this case, Madison reversed the typical direction of revolutionary discourse: instead of American success offering an example for others, rebels' failures abroad offered an example for the United States.

The Irish Volunteers' inability to enact lasting change also inspired some proratification writers. One humorous essay, purporting to be the work of a poorly educated man named Roderick Razor, who was opposed to ratification, undermined the antiratification position by pretending to misunderstand events in Ireland. Razor explained that the United States didn't need a standing army. If they needed military aid, "why I dare say the volunteers of Ireland, who took up arms, they say, for liberty and a fair and free trade, would come over to help us."[82] The author's joke was that the British had crushed the Irish Volunteers and that consequently the Irish would be unable to help the Americans. Madison and Razor both made the case that consolidation was necessary to protect revolutionary movements and that the United States might follow the path of Ireland and the Netherlands without the Constitution.

Yet others used the revolutionary events of the 1780s to argue against the Constitution. Some of those who questioned the proposed structure of the

US government believed that it would threaten hard-won liberty, just as European empires had stifled the revolutionary movements within their borders. During the Constitutional Convention, Massachusetts delegate Elbridge Gerry, who eventually refused to sign the document, compared the national government's power to regulate trade with Britain's domination of Irish commerce, which had sparked the Volunteer movement a decade earlier.[83] At the Virginia ratifying convention, the famed revolutionary orator Patrick Henry argued that the Constitution would place the American people under the same kind of tyranny that Britain held over Ireland.[84] For these thinkers, the revolutions of the 1780s were instructive because they demonstrated the dangers of coercive government power. If the United States accepted the proposed Constitution, they implied, it might create a new tyrannical government that would make another revolution necessary.

The events of the 1780s prepared Americans to observe and narrate the more spectacular revolutions of the succeeding decade. The French Revolution's outbreak in 1789 accelerated North Americans' belief that the American "example" had sparked a global wave of revolutionary change. US observers insisted that France had "catched the flame of liberty from these American shores."[85] American preachers especially warmed to the idea. Unitarian minister Richard Price told a Boston audience in 1790, "Behold, the light you have struck out, after setting America free, reflected to France, and there kindled into a blaze that lays despotism in ashes."[86] Preacher Benjamin Wadsworth exulted, "For America's sons the honor was reserved, to teach the world how to be free." He proposed that the French had "caught the fire" by learning from their American allies during the American war for independence.[87] The notion that the American Revolution's example had inspired the French people appeared in hundreds of sermons, newspaper essays, orations, and pamphlets printed in the United States during the early 1790s.[88]

If the revolutions of the 1780s, including the French Revolution, had resulted from the American example, then American observers expected the French Revolution to inform others around the world of the vulnerability of despotism and ignite a new wave of revolution. Writing in London in 1792, Joel Barlow claimed that the "example of America" had not led Europeans to overthrow their governments because North America was "too little known to the European reasoner, to be the subject of accurate investigation." According to Barlow, Europeans did not know, or perhaps did not care, enough about America for a revolution there to inform their behavior. Though it was possible to ignore the United States, France offered a "great . . . theater" that Europeans could not disregard.[89] Others concurred. A letter written by a traveler in Paris in 1789, which was reprinted in US newspapers, argued that while the "example of America" and the US Constitution had helped to transform France, the French Revolution ensured that "the other nations of Europe have now an example nearer home." This correspondent went on to predict, "It cannot be ten years before Germany, Spain and South-America will be free."[90] Given that the revolutions of the 1780s, which Americans had linked to their own example, had largely fizzled, the French Revolution offered a new chance to witness a global regeneration—which could be attributed ultimately to the American Revolution.

As the revolution progressed in France, some observers saw the flame of liberty spreading to the east. In 1791 Poland ratified a new constitution supported by King Stanisław August Poniatowski, which rolled back the power of the nobility and monarchy.[91] This new constitution excited some observers, including the conservative Philadelphia printer John Fenno, who saw a "great and important revolution in favor of the Rights of Man."[92] Others, including Fenno's radical rival Benjamin Franklin Bache, scoffed that the new constitution was "far from a regeneration" because the Polish government remained a "government over the people; not the choice of the governed, but a gift of the governors."[93] This ambivalence did not prevent some observers from attributing it to the American example. Another Philadelphia printer, David Claypoole, suggested that the "late revolution in Poland" was "another instance of the advantage derived to mankind from the independence of the United States."[94] Though the revolution in Poland was hardly as earth-shattering as other events, many Americans viewed it as a clear result of the American and French examples.

While some Americans questioned the revolutionary nature of Poland's new constitution, the nation's despotic neighbors did not. A combined Prussian and Russian force invaded Poland in 1792 and partitioned the country between 1793 and 1795. A series of popular uprisings erupted in 1794 and 1795, which temporarily sparked renewed American interest. Many observers focused on Tadeusz Kościuszko, who led an April 1794 revolt in Cracow. He won the attention of Americans in part because he had participated in the American war for independence. Just as many had suggested that the French army had carried the flame of liberty home from America, some described Kościuszko as having been "train'd in freedom's land" as the "pupil of Washington."[95] Ultimately, however, Kościuszko's rebellion failed to overturn the partition, and the "revolutions" of Poland whimpered to an end.

The information script led many North Americans to develop extravagant expectations that news of the American and French Revolutions would bring about a wave of global revolutionary change. They came to believe that news not only could reflect the world as it was, but also make the world anew. In the early 1790s, some North Americans decided to bring about this change themselves. As I relate in chapter 6, Mézière and numerous other North Americans sought to apply the information script to foment revolutions in Spanish Louisiana and British Canada. These hopes did not last for very long. The popular movements that followed the American Revolution, including those in France, the Netherlands, Peru, Poland, and Ireland, failed to provide attractive advertisements for revolution, since they stalled, descended into disorder, or fell to foreign invaders. Because the information script depended on the success of revolutionary politics, American observers eventually abandoned it.

Growing increasingly wary of revolutionary politics in the mid-1790s, Americans no longer viewed events abroad as affording meaningful examples for imitation. Instead, they began to parse out differences between the various challenges to authority. Was the French Revolution really an extension of the American Revolution? As uprisings failed or revealed themselves to be uncongenial to American ideals, observers in the United States retracted the once-obvious connections between their revolution and those abroad. In doing so, they came to regard the American Revolution less as an example for the world than as an inimitable, exceptional event. Though quite distinct, these successive understandings of the American Revolution, as exemplary or as exceptional, both flattered it. Whether its inheritors constructed a narrative of the American Revolution as the beginning of a global regeneration or as a unique event that defied patterns of revolutionary failure, they told a story that strengthened the development of a nascent American national identity.

But even as Americans in the 1790s began to question the relationship between their revolution and events abroad, they did not entirely give up the information script. Indeed, the protectors of the status quo in North America reflexively linked the flow of news with the spread of revolutionary action and sought to contain news that might inspire further change. By linking news with revolutionary politics, the information script raised the stakes of news-gathering. False news and ignorance, Americans understood, preserved arbitrary and despotic governments. So how could truth be protected? What sorts of news sources could be trusted? These were the questions that beset American politics in the aftermath of the revolutionary war. Unfortunately, Americans never reached a consensus, and few came to anything like a coherent answer. Even as they worried about avoiding public ignorance, their information-gathering practices ensured that much of the news circulating in the United States would be false. In the final years of the eighteenth century, arguments about news and truth became more prominent than ever before.

CHAPTER SIX

The American Constellation

Dreams of a Continental Revolution

There is little that is less interesting than hearing about someone else's dreams. Yet on Christmas Eve 1793, a Charleston, South Carolina, newspaper called the *Columbian Herald* devoted four columns to a lengthy description of an anonymous person's dream. The author, "Fiducialis," identified himself as a veteran of the American revolutionary war whose "bosom beats high in the cause of the *rights of man*." It was therefore impossible "in these times of wars & rumors of wars" for him to remain an "unaffected observer" while learning about the stirring of revolutions around the world. One evening at home, after reading troubling news of French military losses at Condé, Mainz, and Valenciennes, the author fell asleep and dreamed that the "guardian angel of America" offered him a vision of the future. The angel presented a pair of politically laden images: an eagle, representing "France just liberated from the despotism of ages," fighting off a pack of other birds, and a lamb torn apart by a Russian bear and a Prussian wolf, representing Poland's partition.[1]

After presenting these bleak visions, the angel guided Fiducialis on a tour through much of the rest of the world, including several other nations' animal avatars, before turning to a constellation of stars "illuminating yonder [Western] hemisphere." He pointed out that the "united light" of these stars together was as bright as the sun, but that even so, their brightness would continue to grow. "There is thy native land," the angel said. "There it is that my happy charge is placed—The reign of reason is there commencing, and liberty has fixed her abode, from thence to diffuse her divine influence through the globe." A few "clouds" might dim "for a *moment only* the brightness of the stars," but they were just the "daemons of despotism, of ignorance, and superstition," which sought to "bury in barbarous darkness forever, the entire light of reason and liberty." The angel reassured the dreamer that "Providence rules," and God would not allow liberty to be smothered by the world's tyrants.[2]

The account of Fiducialis's dream consumed nearly all of the *Columbian Herald* issue's second page. Just below it, running on to the facing page, appeared a discussion of Edmond-Charles Genêt's turbulent tenure as French ambassador to the United States. At that moment, Genêt was aiming to export revolutionary politics from the United States to the neighboring colonies of Louisiana and Canada. Having internalized the information script of revolution, Fiducialis and Genêt both saw "ignorance" and "superstition" as the principal obstacles to dispelling tyranny from North America. Indeed, Charleston, where Fiducialis's dream was published, was one of the epicenters of Genêt's schemes to revolutionize the continent.[3] Watching revolutions cascade globally during the 1780s and early 1790s, North Americans like Fiducialis could not help but think locally. In his dream, Europe was violent and unwieldy whereas North America granted ample room for the constellation of freedom to glow brightly. Unlike Europe with its resilient despots, the New World seemed ripe for revolutionary change.

Imperial conflicts in the middle of the eighteenth century had rearranged the colonial map of North America, which left many people of French descent residing in new and unfamiliar empires. France had ceded its claims on Canada to Britain and on Louisiana to Spain because of its losses in the Seven Years' War. Believing that European oppression and Catholic superstition kept the colonists of these lands ignorant of the broader world, many North Americans and Europeans hoped that news of revolutionary France's successes would provide an example that the French settlers could imitate. While historians have examined the contest for Louisiana and Canada in the 1790s as two separate stories, Fiducialis's account demonstrates that for revolutionary activists, they represented two theaters of a broader vision.[4] A variety of Americans, Louisianans, Canadians, and Frenchmen worked together to bring about a continental revolution through the circulation of news. Some, too, collaborated to prevent revolution.

Fiducialis's vision, replete with biblical allusions and obscure imagery, was probably not a faithful description of a single dream. Suggesting that "dreams are *sometimes* the medium of supernatural communications," the author likely crafted the story to evoke the Christian tradition of prophetic dreams. Indeed, the beliefs that tyranny would soon be extinct, that humanity had met the edge of history, and that progress was as irresistible as a waterfall shared much with the millennial eschatology popular in Protestant Christianity at this time.[5] Fiducialis hoped his readers would believe that this dream was a sign of things to come. Many would have. Guided by such prophecies, revolutionary activists hoped to call forth a flood of news that would cleanse the continent of despotism.

Canada and Louisiana were both immense territories, populated by a variety of Native peoples and a sparse collection of European settlers. To European empires, these colonies offered neither the lucrative monocrop agriculture of the Caribbean islands nor the commodity markets of the British colonies along the eastern seaboard nor the great silver and gold mines of Mexico and South America. Louisiana especially frustrated the Spanish government. Viewing the territory as a buffer zone between Anglo-American colonists to the east and its more valuable holdings in Mexico, the Spanish government had invested little in Louisiana. As a result, it provided lackluster commercial value and an unruly populace. Seeking to remedy the former problem, while perhaps exacerbating the latter, the Spanish royal government allowed Louisiana's residents to trade with France's Caribbean colonies beginning in 1782.[6] This policy, though, merely ratified existing patterns. Because most settlers lived near the mouth of the Mississippi River, Louisianans were already more closely tied to the Caribbean world than to the Spanish empire. Their loyalty to Spain was always tenuous.

Canada had a more stable relationship with Britain. Compared to Louisiana, only a small number of enslaved and free people of color lived in Canada, which meant that the risk of a slave revolt was minimal. Moreover, attitudes toward the British government were split across class, ethnicity, and region. Britons and thousands of Loyalists fleeing the American war had migrated into Upper Canada and the Atlantic colonies of New Brunswick and Nova Scotia. Lower Canada, which surrounded much of the St. Lawrence River, continued to be dominated by Francophones, but even there many French merchants and religious leaders worked closely with the British imperial government. Britain's Quebec Act of 1774 and the Constitutional Act of 1791 granted Canadians a significant degree of toleration and autonomy. Discontented Canadians generally channeled their discontent toward reform, rather than violence or revolution. Most did not think of themselves as conquered people, but as subjects of an enlightened empire.

US observers may not have grasped the intricacies of the internal politics in Canada and Louisiana, but they understood that the Seven Years' War had left behind a combustible legacy in North America. A revolutionary Louisiana would have been particularly exciting to them. While many American settlers had seized massive amounts of land from Natives to the west of the Appalachian Mountains after gaining independence, Spain's control of New Orleans allowed it to refuse use of the Mississippi River to Americans. Without the right to navigate the Mississippi, western farmers struggled to bring their goods to market.[7] Americans hoped that they would have access to the river if a friendly steward controlled the mouth of the Mississippi—whether that was France, an independent Louisiana, or a new territory of the United States. Likewise, many Louisiana colonists hoped for a regime change and periodically asked France to rescue them.[8] Spain stationed only a small garrison in the colony, and agitators believed that it could be easily overrun. US observers took note of any sign of discontent in Louisiana and wondered about the possibilities of an invasion.[9] A Boston newspaper, for example, reported in 1786 that some Americans in the West were confident that a force of "two thousand brave Americans" could quickly conquer Spain's possessions in North America.[10] All that was needed was a small push.

Similarly, many Americans fantasized about a revolution in Canada. During the American war for independence, the Continental Congress repeatedly invited Canadians to join the war against Britain. They also attempted to take advantage of discontent against British rule with an ill-fated invasion of Quebec.[11] Frederick Haldimand, a British military commander stationed in Quebec, wrote to his superior officer in 1782 that the Canadians were "in early Expectation of some Revolution from which they expect to derive Advantage," which was taking shape based on an "Intercourse . . . between them and the French." Haldimand suggested that rumors had led Canadians to believe that the French might invade and liberate them.[12] After the war, some still felt that a Canadian revolution was inevitable. A letter from Montreal printed in US newspapers in 1784, for example, predicted that Canada would join the United States in a few years: "It is impossible that half a century should elapse, or even twenty-five years, before the revolution of our re-union to the democracy of the new independents."[13] A Boston newspaper from the same year similarly printed an account "By a gentleman from Canada," which claimed that the people of Canada "most seriously meditate a revolt from their present usurped masters, and seem determined to add another star in the *American constellation*."[14] It appeared that the flame of liberty would soon arrive in Canada.

The French Revolution also led many observers to believe that revolutions in Louisiana and Canada were imminent. In 1790, a group of Francophone colonists in Louisiana sent a petition to the French National Assembly begging to be reannexed.[15] Three years later, 150 Louisiana colonists signed a petition asking France to rescue them, and a group of New Orleans merchants sent a deputation to the National Assembly with a gift. The most zealous Louisiana colonists even organized a Jacobin club.[16] Americans noticed that news of France's revolution seemed to be inciting the continent's French colonists into action. It had become possible to imagine, as a Welsh American preacher named Morgan John Rhees did, the formation of a "vast continent, from the gulph of St. Laurence to the gulph of Mexico, from the Pacific to the Atlantic, forming a grand republic of brethren."[17] Moreover, as Fiducialis had noted, France's struggles in Europe made a continental revolution more urgent. While Europe's ancient despotism strangled liberty in the Old World, North America offered it, according to Thomas Paine, "a place to stand upon."[18]

Some Europeans concurred. A 1791 issue of a Paris newspaper reprinted in New York City predicted that an "Empire of the West" would soon form in the Americas as the continent's people became better informed about the world around them: "Slavery and tyranny are at an immense distance when knowledge is disseminated alike to all."[19] The Marquis de Condorcet claimed that year that it was "almost impossible to doubt" that Canada would "follow the example of the neighboring colonies" in leaving the British empire.[20] People around the world looked expectantly to France's former colonies.

A continental revolution also seemed to offer an opportunity for huge profits. If Britain and Spain could be expelled from North America, the continent's western lands would instantly gain value. With this in mind, a hopeful group of American expatriate land speculators in Europe lobbied France to seize Louisiana. The writer Joel Barlow was among the leaders of these opportunists. He had taken a position as a land agent for the Scioto Company, which was one of many French companies that speculated in the Ohio Valley.[21] He sincerely believed in the information script, having invoked it repeatedly in his popular radical manifesto, *Advice to the Privileged Orders*.[22] In late 1792, Barlow wrote *A Letter Addressed to the People of Piedmont*, which advised Savoyards that they had been "fatally misinformed with respect to the nature of the French revolution." He explained that "your court and clergy wish to conceal" knowledge of the transformation of France, "lest you should follow the example."[23] His financial interests and belief in the information script led Barlow to eagerly participate in discussions about liberating Louisiana from the Spanish empire.

Only a month after Barlow penned his letter to the people of Piedmont, French leader Jacques-Pierre Brissot prepared a plan for an expedition against Spanish colonies. Brissot was among the leaders of the universalist Girondin faction, which held power in France from 1791 through the spring of 1793. The Girondins, and Brissot in particular, sought to export their revolution abroad. Brissot shared his friend Barlow's cosmopolitan vision and his interest in the North American West. Brissot wrote a 1791 pamphlet chronicling his travels through the United States three years earlier, which Barlow translated into English. Toward its conclusion, Brissot described how the "western inhabitants" of the United States were "determined to open" the navigation of the Mississippi "by good will or by force," and he predicted that the "slightest quarrel will be sufficient to throw them into a flame."[24]

Once he ascended to power in France, Brissot had no reason to believe that circumstances had changed. The French government received a letter dated October 1792 from another Paris-based land agent, James Cole Mountflorence, who offered to seize the territory by raising a "legion" of "American hunters, Canadians, and inhabitants of Illinois, all sworn enemies of Spanish despotism."[25] The French government formed the Committee for the Expedition against Louisiana, which included Barlow. Together with another American, Mark Leavenworth, Barlow submitted a plan to France's leadership advising them to form an invasion force. They argued that the liberation of Louisiana would provide a "great example to their neighbors in Mexico and Florida" and could lead the people of South America to "banish Spanish despotism" as well.[26]

Though the onset of a global war in 1792 limited France's ability to commit military resources to North America, Brissot did not give up hope. Within a few weeks of receiving Mountflorence's proposal, he used his influence to have Edmond-Charles Genêt appointed as minister to the United States.[27] The Girondin ministry's instructions for Genêt reflected its universalist vision: "liberate Spanish America, open the navigation of the Mississippi to the inhabitants of Kentucky, deliver our former brothers in Louisiana from the tyrannical yoke of Spain, and perhaps return the beautiful star of Canada to the American Constellation." This cosmological metaphor, with stars as states and a nation as a constellation, dated back at least to the Continental Congress's resolution that the new US flag design would include "Thirteen Stars, white in a Blue Field, representing a new Constellation."[28] It is a striking image. A constellation, after all, is a collection of stars arranged together not according to their inherent relation to each other but by an observer's subjective vantage. The Age of Revolutions had scrambled observers' field of view. What had once seemed a random and unconnected group of stars could, with a new perspective informed by a new worldview, look like a constellation.

Genêt's appointment and his instructions formed a part of a larger strategy of the Girondin leadership in France. Instead of expecting other empires to follow their example, France's leaders increasingly aimed to stimulate revolutions abroad. Unlike the American revolutionaries, who had distanced themselves from political convulsions abroad during their war in order to avoid alienating potential European allies, the early French revolutionary leaders aimed to weaken their enemies by arousing revolutionary discontent among their subjects. To do so, they would turn information into a weapon. In late 1792, France's National Assembly offered to grant "fraternity and help to all peoples who wish to regain their liberty" and instructed generals to share this decree with the peoples of occupied territories.[29] The members of the National Assembly hoped that this information would incite rebellions against Europe's despots, distracting their rivals or even turning enemies into allies.

In this context, Genêt's instructions to dislodge Louisiana and Canada from France's imperial enemies were quite logical. Though they gave Genêt few resources, the Girondin leaders expected that the combined strength of American westerners, French colonists, and Native people, some of whom they believed to have remained loyal to France, could overwhelm the continent's imperial defenses.[30] If Genêt could rally these groups for revolutionary France, he would not need a French army. Initially, these hopes seemed prophetic. Shortly after his ship docked in Charleston in April 1793, just as news arrived of France's declaration of war against Spain, Genêt found willing accomplices. Along with France's consul in Charleston, Michel-Ange-Bernard Mangourit, Genêt identified and recruited numerous potential invaders of Louisiana.[31]

Genêt also found allies willing to help him rouse Canadians to revolution. Henri-Antoine Mézière, the Montreal man who believed in the "genius of information" to provoke revolution, decided to seek out Genêt. After walking for three weeks, Mézière eventually reached Philadelphia and managed to arrange a meeting with the ambassador.[32] Genêt recognized Mézière's passion and offered him a job as one of his secretaries. For his part, Mézière helped to connect Genêt with radical and prorevolutionary circles in Lower Canada. Agreeing on a strategy based on the information script, they would seek to dislodge Canada from the British empire by spreading triumphant news of the French Revolution among the French Canadian population.

Though Genêt relied on advisors such as Mézière and Mangourit, he was an acute observer of North American politics. As an avid reader of US newspapers who maintained an extensive file of handwritten news abstracts culled from American papers, Genêt would have understood that more French news circulated through the United States than elsewhere in the continent (see chapter 7).[33] According to the information script, then, Genêt might be able to spark a continental revolution on the cheap if he could export the news from the United States across imperial boundaries. A report that Mézière wrote about the situation in Canada would have reinforced this conviction.[34] In it, he suggested that Genêt "spread an address through Canada" prior to any invasion. Though Mézière knew that Canadians were aware of the French Revolution, he believed that an address could assure them that the revolution was succeeding and would offer the French people greater liberty than the British empire did. If Canada were to be freed, Mézière believed, its people would need to know that France had already been freed.[35]

Based on Mézière's recommendation, Genêt composed two pamphlets, one addressed to Canadians and the other to the inhabitants of Louisiana.[36] Both expressed the presumptions of the information script. The address to Canadians, *Les français libres à leurs frères les canadiens* (The Free French to Their Canadian Brothers), described the triumphant progress of the French Revolution: "today we are free, we have regained our rights, our oppressors are punished . . . just as independent as our neighbors the Americans." Genêt then called for readers to "imitate their example and ours, the route is drawn." The Canadians merely needed to follow the path laid out by the French and Americans in order to leave the "abject state in which you are immersed." He urged his readers to "reprint on your brows" this fact. The instruction to *reprint* others' revolutionary actions suggested a focus on exemplarity and imitation. Moreover, the idea that people would carry these sentiments on their brows, on their skin, reflected how the information script melded abstraction with bodily action. Only through physical effort could someone imitate the examples that they experienced through disembodied text and speech. Genêt concluded the pamphlet by calling for Canadians to resist ignorance by awakening from the "lethargic sleep in which you are plunged."[37]

In the other pamphlet, Genêt urged his "brothers in Louisiana" to perform the information script. He suggested, "Compare with your situation that of your friends—the free Americans," whose land was prosperous and growing. Politely informing his audience of their ignorance, he suggested that they "tear off the veil" that shielded Louisianans from Spain's "abominable designs" against them. To dispel this ignorance, he again offered an accounting of the French Revolution: "The French people, irritated by the outrages and injustices to which they had been subjected, rose against their oppressors, who disappeared before them like dust before a rushing wind." France's "successes," he claimed, indicated that challenges to despotic powers could succeed. Louisianans should "profit by the great lesson which you have received," the "virtuous example" of the French Revolution, and rise against Spanish despotism.[38]

Genêt's rhetorical strategy was identical in both pamphlets. He explained to Canadians and Louisianans that their oppressors had kept them ignorant of the true state of the world, and he offered a narrative about the successes of revolutionary America and France that suggested these examples were worthy of imitation. He urged his readers to rise in rebellion against their feeble imperial masters. But while these pamphlets followed the information script quite precisely, Genêt and Mézière understood that two texts would be insufficient to accomplish their ends. More prorevolutionary information would be necessary to unsettle these vulnerable territories.

In the summer of 1793, Mézière hired an agent named Jacques Rous, a recent migrant from Canada to New York, to distribute several items throughout Lower Canada. Mézière provided Genêt with an inventory of these materials. Most prominently, he trusted Rous to distribute 350 copies of Genêt's address throughout Canada. It caused an immediate stir. One of Rous's allies, Jean-Baptiste Colombe, read the pamphlet aloud outside a Montreal church.[39] As if taking up Genêt's invitation to reprint his lessons on their brows, a St. Jean tinsmith named Auguste Lavau made copies of the pamphlet and recited it to illiterate Canadians. Distributors working with Rous acted furtively, sometimes throwing copies into open windows before riding away. One observer noted that Canadian small farmers were referring to Genêt's pamphlet as "le Catechisme" in 1794. But Rous and his acolytes did not limit themselves to distributing the pamphlet. Noting that the British government was raising a militia as a hedge against French aggression, they also encouraged Canadians to welcome the French invasion forces.[40]

Mézière's expense reports document that he also used Rous to funnel a few letters for correspondents in Montreal in which he "sought to convey all the warmth of the Republicanism which reigns in France today, giving them hope of an approaching liberation." Additionally, he sent "several American papers mentioning the repeated Successes of the Great Nation over its enemies." Mézière probably hoped that these newspapers, which provided friendlier accounts of the French Revolution than their Canadian counterparts did, would circulate around town or even make their way into print. He also provided Rous with "several leaves of the journal of Gorsas," referring to the Paris newspaper *Courrier des quatre-vingt-trois départements* published by the firebrand Antoine Joseph Gorsas. The *Courrier* and Gorsas were closely tied to the Girondins. While we do not know which issues of the *Courrier* Rous carried to Montreal, Mézière explained that they contained essays "in which the death of the Tyrant Capet is fully justified." Louis XVI's death was fresh news in North America and had alienated some Canadians, who had viewed him as a benign monarch. Material from France to counter that perception would have been valuable in changing attitudes.[41]

Mézière also gave Rous several pamphlets, including Thomas Paine's *Rights of Man*, which among other sentiments suggested that revolutionary France "holds out the example for the world."[42] He also provided a dozen copies of a Fourth of July sermon written by the New York Presbyterian minister Samuel Miller, which served their purposes well. Drawing on the information script, Miller referred to his hope that the French Revolution would kindle "a general flame, which shall illuminate the darkest and remotest corners of the earth." Coupling the cause of freedom with that of religion, he defended the French Revolution as a step on the road to universal liberty. Like many of his countrymen, he dismissed the "totally groundless" reports of France's "disorder, vice, and contempt of all sacred things."[43]

While Genêt and his allies harbored some doubts that a people "entirely plunged in the thick darkness of ignorance" could quickly recover their liberty, their intrigues seemed to bear fruit for a time. By the middle of the summer of 1793, Genêt wrote to France that he had "prepared the Revolution of New Orleans and Canada."[44] Revolution seemed afoot in Louisiana, where the former revolutionary war general George Rogers Clark enthusiastically helped France to gather equipment and men. It also appeared that France would support Genêt's efforts with the arrival of a naval force. As more pressing needs for the warships arose, though, Genêt was left to wait.

One unexpected lifeline came when a mutinous French fleet from Saint Domingue, led by the colony's former governor General François-Thomas Galbaud du Fort, arrived in New York City.[45] Genêt sent Mézière aboard this fleet as a political officer and translator with instructions to attack British holdings in Canada and also "spread among them [the Canadian people] our principles, our Constitution of June 24, 1793, our patriotic songs, the *Bulletin*, and revolutionary addresses that I have drawn up for the Canadians." The two schemers hoped that the arrival of a fleet would spur Canadians to enact the information script, which would then allow the ships to leave and "take possession of New Orleans." This was an ambitious, risky plan that depended on the cooperation of disloyal sailors. And so it failed. Once they set out to sea, the sailors decided to ignore Genêt's instructions and return to France. By the end of 1793, Mézière found himself accidentally in France and far from a potential liberation of Canada.[46] Needing to replace the eastward-bound Mézière, Genêt wrote to an ally that he was looking for another "sincere friend of liberty and independence" whose task would be "bringing to our former brothers of Canada news of their old fatherland."[47]

Having lost his most ardent supporter and his naval support in one blow, Genêt was forced to suspend his plans. This delay was crucial. Hearing reports of Genêt's intentions, officials in Louisiana and Canada prepared their defenses, tightened communication exchanges, and girded their populace for an attack. But none came.

Genêt never got the chance to put his plans in action. Even as he was strategizing, the political ground was shifting underneath him. His adventurousness angered the Washington administration, which sought to prevent a potential invasion of Louisiana. President George Washington complained to the French government, which was no longer led by Genêt's benefactor and ideological ally, Brissot. Instead, the Montagnard faction, which had begun to strengthen as Genêt was sailing to the United States, had ascended to power. The Montagnards (who would eventually execute Brissot, charging him with, among other things, alienating the United States through his expansionist schemes) were uninterested in universalism or in sparking a global revolution.[48] Instead, they worried about protecting the nation from "foreign plots" and the interference of outsiders.[49] In April 1793, the month that Genêt had first arrived in the United States, the Montagnards had passed a decree guaranteeing that France would not "interfere in any manner in the government of the other powers."[50] They halted their predecessors' universalist schemes. When Barlow's Committee for the Expedition against Louisiana submitted its report, the Montagnards tossed it aside.[51] Upon receiving word of Genêt's prorevolutionary actions, the Committee of Public Safety voted in October 1793 to recall and arrest him. Knowing that traveling back to Paris would result in his death, Genêt wisely sought, and received, asylum in the United States.[52]

Although Genêt's dismissal brought his continental schemes to a temporary halt, the dream of transforming North America did not end with his tenure as ambassador. The plans did change, though, in some significant ways.

French and American subversives increasingly looked at Canada and Louisiana as separate projects. Genêt's immediate replacement, a sulking, stubborn man named Jean Antoine Joseph Fauchet, remained intrigued by the geopolitical possibilities in North America. He arrived in the United States in February 1794. At about that time, a young man from Granville, New York, named Stephen Thorn wrote to Fauchet to discuss the possibility of inciting Canadian resistance to British rule. With Fauchet's blessing, Thorn set off on a fact-finding trip through Lower Canada for most of 1794. Probing Canadians' political attitudes and their knowledge of events in Europe, he came to believe that British officials were attempting to keep Canadians ignorant of France's military successes by suppressing the free flow of news.[53]

Thorn arrived at a fortuitous moment to witness Canadian discontent. The British government's efforts to raise a militia for a possible invasion sparked large-scale riots in May 1794. British officers heard rioters shouting, "How could we fight against our brothers?"[54] Descriptions of these riots and popular discontent made their way to the United States. An Albany report that circulated widely in American newspapers claimed, "The strongest symptoms of a revolutionary spirit are observable in the province of Lower-Canada. . . . We wish them a happy deliverance from tyrannic insolence and oppression."[55] A Vermont man reported that "a revolution is on foot in lower Canada. . . . The Canadians say they want nothing to carry their plan into complete effect, but persons of enterprise and perseverance to take the lead."[56] This sort of news reenergized Americans' interest in spreading revolution to their northern neighbors.

Having seen firsthand the people's violent anger with British rule, Thorn reported back to Fauchet about the unrest. But Fauchet's hands were tied. The Committee of Public Safety had instructed him to give up on Genêt's ambitions.[57] The Montagnards, who now led the government in Paris, were less concerned with spreading revolution abroad than with winning the European war. Fauchet decided to allow Thorn to travel to Paris to present a plan to attack Canada. Once there, Thorn submitted a proposal and made contact with the Committee of Public Safety, but before his plan could be considered, the Montagnards fell and a new government rose from their ashes.

The French Directory, a more moderate leadership, worked with Thorn and an ambitious Vermonter named Ira Allen, who had come to Paris for similar reasons. Unlike the high-minded Mézière, Allen aimed to provoke a revolution in Lower Canada to benefit his own business interests.[58] The Directory approved a plan to send 20,000 guns to Vermont, where Allen promised to lead an expedition into Lower Canada in 1797. The directors would support this effort by instructing their ambassador to send agents to prepare the people for an invasion while also dispatching a French fleet to the St. Lawrence.[59] The plan might have succeeded, but it ultimately came to nothing after a British naval vessel intercepted the disarmingly named ship the *Olive Branch*, which the schemers had commissioned to transport their weapons.[60]

In late 1794, as Fauchet's supporters fell from power in Paris, he was replaced as ambassador to the United States by Pierre-Auguste Adet. After months of waiting for naval protection to cross the violent wartime Atlantic, Adet arrived with the renewed intention of liberating Canada and Louisiana. He admired Genêt's plans and commented, "Never were we so close to success" as during Genêt's intrigues, and "if his orders had been executed this brilliant revolution would have doubtless taken place."[61] But Adet confronted a very different geopolitical challenge than his predecessors had, since a series of treaties in the mid-1790s had upended France's relationship with North America. First, the Jay Treaty between the United States and Britain, ratified in 1795, soured Franco-American relations. The French increasingly viewed the United States as a hostile power, effectively leagued with Britain against them. Another pair of treaties caused much of the impetus for an attack on Louisiana to dissipate. In 1795, the United States and Spain agreed to the Treaty of San Lorenzo, known in the United States as Pinckney's Treaty, which allowed Americans to navigate the Mississippi River. The next year, France and Spain signed the Treaty of San Ildefonso, agreeing to fight together against Britain. Neither France nor the United States would benefit any longer from a revolution in Louisiana.

As a result, with the approval of the French Directory, Adet's efforts shifted toward Canada.[62] France's objective seems to have included not only weakening Britain by seizing Canada, but also using Canada as leverage over the increasingly Anglophilic United States. With Spain now aligned with France, a revolutionized Canada would allow the French to encircle the United States and pressure it to return to friendly terms with France.[63] Having endorsed Ira Allen's and Stephen Thorn's plans to attack Canada, the Directory instructed Adet to prepare for an Atlantic invasion. He did not discover until 1797 that the seizure of the *Olive Branch* had caused French leaders to abandon those plans. As a result, he spent much of 1796 and 1797 earnestly encouraging Canadians, Frenchmen, and their allies to prepare for an attack that would never come.

Though Adet admired Genêt's efforts, his plans were more direct. He distributed an incendiary pamphlet throughout Canada, but it apparently did not make use of the information script. The text of this document has not survived, but if Lower Canada's zealous attorney general, James Monk, can be trusted, it claimed that France would soon "subdue Great Britain, and meant to begin with her colonies." Additionally, Adet sent several agents and spies into Canada. These men focused not on spreading news about France's revolution, as Genêt's confederates had done, but on convincing Canadians that an invasion would soon come.[64] One agent worked with Indigenous communities to plan an attack from the west to coincide with a French invasion.[65] British officials uncovered a few of Adet's other spies and agents who aimed, as one official put it, at "perverting the minds of the People."[66] But there is little evidence that they aimed to enact the information script.

In a 1794 circular titled "Warning against Revolution," Louisiana governor Francisco Luis Héctor, the Baron of Carondelet, asked his readers to dismiss the news that they were hearing about the French and Haitian Revolutions. "Will you let yourselves be deceived," he asked, "by the false hopes of a liberty" in France and the "ghost of liberty" in Saint Domingue? Carondelet insisted that accounts of the flourishing state of these revolutionary lands were false. Hoping to turn colonists away from revolutionary politics, he told them about exorbitant taxation, massacres, and universal conscription in France as well as looting, bloodletting, and property losses in Saint Domingue. If anyone doubted his account, he noted, "I shall be pleased to show him the incontestable proofs on which it is founded."[67] As governor, he had decided that he would not just administer the territory, but also mediate its news. He would decide which accounts were true, which were false, and, eventually, which news would be illegal.

Although Carondelet and other imperial administrators didn't agree with French radicals and their allies about much, both groups believed that information was a powerful tool for stoking the fires of revolutionary upheaval. Indeed, Carondelet's letter echoed Genêt's pamphlet for Louisianans, published the previous year, which had asked them to imitate the French and American Revolutions and free themselves from despotic ignorance.[68] The information script guided not only the actions of revolutionaries, but also those of reactionaries. With good reason, colonial officials feared that a French invasion would spark an uprising or that colonial militias would join the invaders. Neither Canada nor Louisiana possessed the fortifications or armies to repel even a small invasion force or a modest insurgency. Officials reasoned that the colonists would be more likely to fight for France if they believed that its revolution was a boon for humanity, instead of a bloody catastrophe. In this sense, prorevolutionary news from France seemed to be the vanguard of a conquering force.

Louisiana's government officials feared that their colonists were corresponding too freely with the French empire. Manuel Gayoso de Lemos, the district governor of Natchez, remarked that Louisianans "of French extraction . . . have communicated with France and with their possessions in America, and hear with the greatest pleasure of the revolution in that kingdom."[69] He particularly feared that news from the French Caribbean—and Saint Domingue in particular—could lead enslaved people to revolt. In 1792, he recommended that in order to remediate the "distrust of our inhabitants" toward the government, it should be made "more difficult for them to communicate with the French islands."[70] Likewise, Carondelet wrote to a Spanish official that the "close connection" between Louisiana and the French empire kept the territory "exposed to a revolution."[71] Fearing that enslaved people in Louisiana would emulate those in Saint Domingue, Carondelet worked to suppress news about the abolition of slavery in the French empire.[72]

During this time, a group of enslaved people in a rural Louisiana town called Pointe Coupée, about 150 miles north of New Orleans, began to hear rumors about the revolutionary events in France and Saint Domingue. They were eager listeners. Upon learning that France had abolished slavery, they hired a coachman traveling to New Orleans to gather news to verify or disprove it. News of emancipation in France and Saint Domingue encouraged them to coordinate a major rebellion in the spring of 1795. If they could overthrow their Spanish masters, perhaps they could make their way to French territory. But they never had the chance. After their uprising was suppressed, the Spanish gathered testimony suggesting that the example of the Haitian Revolution had inspired the rebels. A leader named Jean Baptiste apparently incited his fellow enslaved people by pointing out that "we could do the same here as at Le Cap," referring to the city in Saint Domingue. The example of the Haitian Revolution beckoned.[73]

Carondelet feared that outsiders spreading news from France and Saint Domingue could cause disaffection and rebellion. Louisiana's government aimed to stamp out French news by regulating both print and oral communication. There was no local newspaper printed in Louisiana until Carondelet spurred the creation of *Le moniteur de la Louisiane* in 1794. He intended the newspaper to provide more authoritative (progovernment) information and thereby challenge the flow of false (prorevolutionary) rumors. Yet, perhaps because it was heavily censored and government-subsidized, the paper failed to circulate widely or create the impact that Carondelet hoped.[74] Nevertheless, he tried to encourage its circulation with a proclamation urging government officials to subscribe in order to combat "false reports" with "authentic intelligence."[75]

With relatively little print material to regulate, it was more important for Louisiana's government to control oral communication. Knowing that enslaved people were one important vector of disruptive speech, Carondelet closed off Louisiana from slave trading with the French Caribbean in March 1792 and from the entire Atlantic slave trade in June 1795.[76] But free people of color and people of French descent proved to be more troublesome to Louisiana's colonial government. Informers helped to identify numerous people sharing news from and about the French empire. The legal foundation for Carondelet's regulations was a 1790 royal proclamation barring French people of color from entering the Spanish empire. Enforcement of this decree, though, had always been uneven. Louisiana officials did not attempt to deport all French people of color wholesale, but rather removed individuals who misbehaved, who were often those sharing news that colonial administrators deemed to be false.[77]

Carondelet and lower-level officials aggressively dispatched talkative Francophone migrants. A man named Beauré, who had arrived in Louisiana from Bordeaux in 1791, was arrested and banished for sharing news of the French National Assembly and its experiments in governance.[78] In 1792, Carondelet banished a man named Egron who, in the governor's words, "was convinced of the need to divulge publicly all sorts of dangerous rumors" among the people. He falsely claimed that Louisiana had been retroceded to France and that he was commissioned by France's National Convention to "take possession of it in the name of the Republic."[79] Another resident of New Orleans, called Girod, also drew Carondelet's ire for spreading the "doubtless apocryphal" rumor of the retrocession of Louisiana to France. Carondelet suspected that Girod's actions were the result of a scheme by a cabal of merchants in Bordeaux, who aimed to overthrow Spanish rule in Louisiana.[80] In 1794, Carondelet convicted a free man of color named Bailly of prorevolutionary actions. Bailly's tribunal noted that he had "asked a gentleman who had just arrived from Cap Francais if he had any information."[81] For every rumormonger expelled, though, more were waiting. In early 1795, Carondelet decided to make an "example" of "French troublemakers" starting with a Frenchman named

Bujac, whom he described as "the most fanatical of all the partisans of the revolution," a notable distinction in raucous Louisiana. What set Bujac apart, in the governor's eyes, was that he was "always on the lookout for dangerous news" and spread it "in the most public places." Upon arresting him, Spanish officials found a copy of the French Constitution among his possessions. They banished him with instructions that he not be allowed "paper or ink, until affairs in France become settled."[82]

Based on these incidents as well as other reports, Louisiana officials concluded that the unrestrained flow of information was a widespread problem. Just after he ordered Bujac's arrest, Carondelet issued a proclamation to prevent "aliens" from "spread[ing] rumors." He "absolutely prohibited" anyone to "peruse or read aloud in public writings, printed matter, or papers relating to the public affairs of France" under penalty of being banished to Havana, and anyone who found this order to be "too rigorous" should "withdraw from the colony."[83]

A few months later, Carondelet adopted an even more stringent measure. In a decree, he castigated "restless enthusiasts" for spreading a series of "injurious reports" that would lead Louisiana down the path that had "ruined the French colonies." To prevent the spread of this false information, he instituted a new regime of surveillance. For every three leagues of the territory, he decreed that there would be a low-level administrator called a syndic, who would act as an informer to keep the government apprised of the circulation of "seditious reports." Carondelet further decreed that all travelers with "news of importance" must first make it known to their local syndic, who would determine whether to "permit or forbid him to divulge it, according as it may effect the public good."[84] With this new layer of local supervision, Carondelet hoped to exert control over communication in the territory.

As in Louisiana, the British government in Canada worried about its colonists' information streams. The 1794 militia riots in particular led officials to worry about popular unrest. British official James Monk reported to the governor in June 1794 that the "Country round Montreal [is] in a state of Allmost Universal, and Alarming disaffection," especially among the French Canadians. He described an unknown "leading Character" in Montreal who "guides the Canadians to their disloyalty and defection, and is relied upon 'That the French are coming.'"[85] The riots led officials to conclude that sedition and false news were endangering the stability of their colony. Monk feared that falsehoods were beginning to "poison the minds and alienate the affections of His Majesty's subjects."[86] In a letter to the British ministry, Quebec governor Guy Carleton, Lord Dorchester, attributed various "seditious assemblages," which preceded the militia riots, to "false and absurd reports."[87]

Such fears led some Canadians to demand that their government act to stem the flow of French falsehoods. Hundreds of Canadians joined popular associations to express their loyalty to their government and to challenge false news. These groups were not the product of organic, grassroots activism, but rather the result of top-down organizing. Elites hoped that they would create the appearance of popular consent and support for restrictive measures. The groups were likely modeled after similar associations formed in Britain in the early 1790s.[88] A London group chaired by John Reeves was dedicated to protecting "Liberty and Property" against "Republicans and Levellers."[89] "Reeves associations," aiming to combat seditious speech and false information, sprang up around Britain and were heavily publicized in sympathetic newspapers. One such association suggested that "all sellers of newspapers, news carriers, [and] persons delivering handbills" be held accountable for the truthfulness of the print that they circulated. It also recommended that employers "use their best endeavours to undeceive and inform" their employees about the true state of the world.[90]

Beginning in 1794, James Monk encouraged the growth of similar loyal associations across Canada. They aimed to "foil the efforts" of those who sought to "create discontent, and through lies, to provoke infidelity" among the people.[91] As in Britain, the progovernment *Quebec Gazette* published pages upon pages of these associations' declarations along with the signatures of hundreds of Canadians attesting to their loyalty. These declarations were quite formulaic, usually expressing revulsion at "wicked and designing men" who circulated "false news" to provoke the king's subjects to disloyalty. They branded news that came from information channels other than those sanctioned by imperial officials as "sedition" or "falsehood."[92] The association for the town of William Henry asked its members to seek out all those who "attempt to disturb the peace and quiet" of the colony with "seditious Discourses or by propagating fals news."[93] Eventually, about 1,100 people joined seven antirevolutionary associations across Lower Canada. Based on their names, nearly three-quarters appeared to be of French descent.

While readers of the *Quebec Gazette* might have concluded that a broad consensus had spontaneously formed against sedition and "false news," this is only part of the story. It was very difficult, and often impossible, to muster popular enthusiasm for these associations. One resident of Trois-Rivières complained to Thomas Dunn, chair of the Quebec association, that his group was delaying the creation of an association because their numbers were "too small."[94] Another reported that "the people of Ecureuils are totally averse" to the association, and even the captain of the militia refused to sign on.[95] A resident of New Carlisle wrote to Dunn that while he had collected only 180 signatures, he hoped that "the others will be quiet as long as there appears no favorable opportunity to declare their sentiments."[96] If dissenters would simply remain silent, this observer seemed to suggest, the fictive consensus cultivated by the associations might remain intact.

Loyal Canadians often blamed popular disaffection on ordinary people's credulity toward false news. As the government's drive to encourage loyalty escalated, two Canadian towns that had recently experienced riots over militia conscription dispatched apologetic petitions to the government, which blamed the riots on the incapacity of ordinary people to separate truth from error. The declaration of "a number of inhabitants" of Beauport blamed their "transgression" on the "error created by the artifices and falsehood of crafty knaves, who by repeated crimes have brought the curse of Heaven upon *a certain country* [France]." The people's "credulity" had allowed "insidious and seditious characters" to turn them away from proper obedience. A similar declaration from Charlesbourg, an epicenter of the militia riots, echoed these sentiments and added that they had been trying to "remove the evils that wicked men for bad ends, have endeavoured to bring upon credulous minds."[97] The suggestion that Canadians could be easily duped made the task of surveilling and regulating information more urgent.

Such assertions told Canadian officials what they believed they already knew. Leaders sometimes haughtily mocked the credulousness and ignorance of the people of their territory. "Ignorance, profound Ignorance is surely the characteristick of the Canadians and certainly renders them liable to be imposed upon by the grossest assertions," remarked the jurist and legislator Jonathan Sewell in 1797.[98] Likewise, Guy Carleton complained about the "ignorance of the common people which lays them open to the influence of all intrigues."[99] It seemed to him that "nothing is too absurd for them to believe."[100] Whereas prorevolutionary activists, such as Genêt, called North Americans "ignorant" because they lacked knowledge about revolutionary events abroad, officials such as Carleton and Sewell saw Canadians' ignorance as a lack of judgment. A credulous and ignorant people could easily be misled by false news and therefore needed to be protected from it.

Canadian government leaders drew on English common-law precedents to punish false news. Historically, English common law had defined false stories about the kingdom's great men, known as scandalum magnatum, as a kind of sedition because they undermined the authority and stability of government.[101] Canadian leaders relied on these precedents to define French news as sedition. In August 1792, the *Quebec Gazette* reprinted King George III's proclamation identifying "seditious writings" and those who had entered "correspondences . . . with sundry persons in foreign parts" as dangerous to the realm. Once France and Britain fell into war, Canada's governor, Lord Dorchester, extended this prohibition to dangerous news from France, issuing a proclamation threatening those who "spread false News" and used "false Representations" to encourage discontent.[102]

At Monk's recommendation, the Lower Canadian legislature passed a law in 1794 that included a provision to punish those who "maliciously spread false news."[103] The government set to work gathering intelligence about those suspected of sharing prorevolutionary news. A deposition from an informer named Jean Vocel Belhumeur, for example, stated that his acquaintances had spoken "often and too often" about the "Success of the French." He also vaguely noted that they had possessed "Gazettes." Belhumeur accused a man called François Romain of corresponding with a Canadian in the United States and (equally vaguely) of owning "pamphlets."[104] Belhumeur may not have been able to identify which gazettes and pamphlets these men had, but in the context of his other accusations, simply possessing print materials seemed suspicious.

Even loyal printers fell under government suspicion. John Neilson, the younger brother of Samuel Neilson and now publisher of the *Quebec Gazette*, was supportive of British rule and published anti-French propaganda.[105] But in late 1794, fearing that Monk would arrest him, he fled Canada. When he returned, he explained that Monk had "threatened to have him punished for a bad translation, saying that if such a thing happened again he would put him & all about him in a Dungeon."[106] The nature of this "bad translation" is unclear. The *Quebec Gazette* was published in both French and English, and so nearly everything that it printed was translated. But for Monk to react so sternly (even if there's no evidence that he had a dungeon) suggests that the translated material might have been politically potent news from abroad.

Significant parts of Canada, though, lacked a print infrastructure. In 1793, Lieutenant Governor John Graves Simcoe established the *Upper Canada Gazette* as an official organ for the government. In a 1795 note, Simcoe's secretary instructed the *Gazette*'s editor that when the paper was choosing among a "variety of intelligence," Simcoe wished them to select the information, "if it appears to be true, which is most favourable to the British Government."[107] In other words, Simcoe's secretary directed the paper to avoid sharing contradictory and confusing news and to instead offer a view of the world that suited the government's preferences.

Officials in Canada lacked the royal sanction that Carondelet enjoyed to deport or surveil foreigners. But as in Louisiana, Canadian elites and officials viewed them as potential sources of dangerous news. In 1794, Lower Canada's government passed the Alien Act, based on a similar law in Britain. It called for foreigners to register with the government and to carry certificates indicating their status. It further required ship captains to provide a list of foreigners traveling with them and allowed the government to imprison or deport foreigners at any time. Government officials imprisoned between fifty and a hundred Francophone Canadians on suspicion of seditious activity and prevented many more Francophone people from entering Lower Canada.[108] The infiltration of French agents, Vermont-based agitators, and American radicals, led in part by France's ambassadors to the United States, likely contributed to fears of dangerous outsiders.

Canadian leaders also relied on the church to monitor rural tongues. By late 1794, Jean-François Hubert, the bishop of Quebec, had issued a circular to the priests of Canada, asking them to challenge the spread of "rumors." Hubert instructed the priests to inform their parishioners that revolutionary France was in a state of anarchy and irreligion, and he suggested that they read this information aloud from the pulpit as many times as necessary.[109] Over time, these measures seem to have met their aims. After 1794, Canadian discontent began to mellow, and no revolution came to the colony.

For those who trusted the information script, politics lay downstream from news. To reshape the flow of information in North America was to build or foreclose new political possibilities. While there was no continental revolution during the 1790s, North Americans witnessed a cross-border information war whose combatants hoped to control the news so that they could define the future. Years after their counterparts in Louisiana and Canada, the Federalist leaders of the United States joined this battle by developing similar policies to control the movement of news. The infamous Alien and Sedition Acts of 1798, in particular, helped to bring the United States in line with the tactics that North America's colonial leaders used to control information (see chapter 9).

In part because of these restrictions, dreams of a continental regeneration ran into the grim realities of global war. As it became clear that an invasion force, or even a naval attack, would never come, the hope for revolutions in Louisiana and Canada faded. Canada remained in the British empire for more than a century after the French Revolution, and it eventually attained independence through reform rather than revolution. A realignment of the center of North America likewise came not through revolution but through the will of empires and the force of settler colonialism. In 1803, having regained Louisiana from France, Napoleon Bonaparte sold it to the United States, and the Americans then purchased and invaded lands long held by numerous Native polities.[110]

Why did a popular revolution fail to take hold in Louisiana or Canada in the 1790s? A revolt was surely possible since both territories held discontented colonists who were openly hostile toward their imperial rulers. Revolutionary activists saw ideal conditions to defeat the callous mediation of colonial leaders and to overcome the people's enforced ignorance. The various schemers, though, encountered numerous reversals. Genêt's dismissal, the Washington administration's decision to maintain American neutrality, the mutinous Caribbean fleet's decision to sail for France instead of Canada, the seizure of the *Olive Branch*—all of these forestalled revolution until popular discontent had fizzled and the powerful example of France had waned. Even as revolutionary activists, such as Fauchet, Adet, Barlow, Leavenworth, Allen, and Thorn, gradually gave up on the information script, colonial officials, such as Carondelet, Gayoso de Lemos, Monk, and Carleton, aggressively limited the flow of news in their territories. Their worries about the capacity of information to provoke revolution outlasted revolutionaries' faith in its power. In the contest for North America's future, imperial leaders' ability to control the flow of news defeated information's potential liberatory power. The dream of a new American constellation was at an end.

Looking back several decades later on his childhood during the 1790s, a New York lawyer and politician named Levi Beardsley remembered his hope that the French Revolution would bring about a new world. Writing with hindsight of the revolution's eventual failures, he recalled:

> In the latter part of '89 or early part of '90, there was a remarkable exhibition of northern lights, which formed a beautiful crown over head, bright and nearly red, which my childish imagination turned into cart wheels, from its forming many circles resembling wheels. It was so brilliant, that my father went out and

read by its light. This exhibition was afterward remembered and talked about, and as the French revolution soon after broke out, which was ultimately attended with horrid cruelties, some who had seen this aurora borealis, superstitiously regarded it as the precursor of that bloody revolution.[111]

During the Age of Revolutions, the uncertain future of humanity seemed to be painted across the highest canvas. While many had hoped that the 1790s would witness the birth of a constellation of liberty in North America, Beardsley and others would remember only cosmological chaos. When they looked up, and when they read their newspapers, observers saw the very foundation of the universe coming apart.

CHAPTER SEVEN

Bentalou's Wager

The French Revolution and the Birth of American Partisanship

Seven hundred dollars was a small fortune in 1793. It might take several years for a well-paid laborer to earn that much. Even wealthy elites would have regarded it as a substantial amount of money.[1] But in September of that year, a Baltimore man named Paul Bentalou staked that sum on a dangerous game of chance—the news.

The world was focused on the war unfolding between revolutionary France and a coalition led by Great Britain, the Holy Roman Empire, and Spain. Over the previous month, North American newspapers, including those in Baltimore, had published conflicting accounts from Europe about the status of the antirevolutionary coalition's lengthy sieges of the French town of Valenciennes and the Holy Roman Empire city of Mainz. On September 9, the *Baltimore Daily Repository* reprinted an account claiming that "the Austrians have quitted Valenciennes, being obliged to raise the siege." This report had originated in a Paris newspaper whose publishers took pains to describe themselves as "sincere friends of Liberty." Several weeks later, on September 27, the *Repository* published a letter from France's ambassador to the United States, Edmond-Charles Genêt, to the French consul in Baltimore confirming the "Account of the Raising of the Siege of Valenciennes." Yet the very next day, it also published a report from the ship *Atlantic*, captained by James Tucker, which had just arrived from Liverpool, claiming that the monarchical armies had taken the two cities.[2]

Like the spin of a roulette wheel, these conflicting reports introduced uncertainty. Had France's enemies taken Valenciennes and Mainz, or had they given up the sieges? As a prominent merchant, Bentalou heard about Tucker's report before it went into print. Perhaps he overheard Tucker on the docks or in a nearby tavern. Knowing that the captain's report would make its way into the papers, Bentalou asked David Graham, the *Repository*'s printer, to insert two sentences just below it in both French and English: "A person offers to bet 700 dollars, that Valenciennes and Mayence [Mainz] are not taken. Any body inclined to take the bet, may find his man by applying to the printers thereof."[3] Born in France, Bentalou had become quite wealthy in the United States. The 1790 census recorded him as the head of a household of eighteen, including six enslaved people.[4] He was also a well-known supporter of the French Revolution in the city.[5] But even for an affluent merchant committed to the French cause, $700 was a substantial bet on the authenticity of a doubtful piece of news, particularly because he was wrong.

Bentalou's misplaced confidence did not come from a private source of intelligence but rather, as he explained in the *Repository* a few days later, from the "improbability of the truth of the details of captain Tucker."[6] Most likely, he had trusted the accounts from the French newspaper and the French ambassador more than Tucker's report from Liverpool. For many prorevolutionary observers, such as Bentalou, information about Europe that came directly from France was more credible than news that came from Britain or from ship captains' reports. Yet Tucker took exception to this choice, as he explained in the newspaper, because he had "told Mr. Bentalow, personally, that both Valenciennes and Mayence was taken." Merchants often sought out ship captains to bet on commodity prices before their news became generally known, and so it surprised Tucker that his account had been discarded. He fumed that if Bentalou had "not been content" at the time that he shared his news, "I would have given him such information as would have satisfied any reasonable man that was not stupidly bigoted to his own imagination."[7] During their discussion, Tucker might have discovered Bentalou's sympathy for revolutionary politics, or he could have known this from their previous encounters. While Tucker's own politics are unknown, his scorn for Bentalou's "imagination" suggests that he might have been skeptical of the information sources upon which the Frenchman relied.

The combined powers had, in fact, successfully taken Mainz and Valenciennes from France. Bentalou was lucky that, as he later clarified, no one agreed to his bet.[8] The two sieges turned out to be minor events in what would be a long war. But Bentalou and Tucker did not know that. Observers in North America experienced revolutionary events one at a time. They did not experience a single "French Revolution," but rather an infinity of small events, snatches of uncertain information, and the occasional bombshell. To find out what was happening at Valenciennes and Mainz, North Americans had to sort through a "great mass of matter" composed of claims, contradictions, and confusion.[9] While Tucker and Bentalou expressed no uncertainty about the news, many of their neighbors struggled to make sense of this muddle.

For many observers, the revolution in France was impossible to separate from the wars that it caused. The early stages of the French Revolution resembled, in many ways, a civil war between royalists and revolutionaries. The outbreak of war between France and most of the neighboring monarchies only extended this dualistic understanding of the conflict. Many saw the battles between the French and coalition armies as theaters of a broader contest between liberty and despotism, not unlike debates in the French National Assembly or clashes in the streets of Paris. For religious observers, the success or failure of French arms revealed God's will, while others believed it spoke to the virtues or weaknesses of revolution generally.[10] Through narratives like these, people assembled an otherwise impenetrably complex stream of news into a comprehensible narrative, which in turn shaped how they encountered future information. Perhaps Bentalou drew conclusions about Mainz and Valenciennes from his convictions about the ultimate outcome of revolutionary mobilization.

Bentalou's decision to gamble on news from France illustrates the complex connection between politics and observation during the era of the French Revolution. While they relied on Atlantic information exchange for news, North Americans also actively shaped how news flowed into and within the continent. They decided what news to share and what to discard largely based on their political commitments. Because Bentalou aligned himself with revolutionary France, he was more likely to trust information that came from France than to trust Tucker's information, which had originated in Liverpool. Another observer, though, might have been suspicious of accounts from self-interested French sources and decided that Tucker's account was the likelier. Such decision-making strengthened observers' preexisting convictions. Those who despised revolutionary France could find in Tucker's report evidence that France was weak and doomed, while the accounts from France could lead Bentalou and his allies to believe that the collapse of monarchical rule was imminent. The availability of geographically disparate, contradictory news resulting from changing commercial patterns allowed observers in the United States to select the news that they preferred. This stoked the flames of polarization and emerging partisanship in the new country. In contrast, the reports about France circulating in Canada were less ambiguous because they were primarily reproductions of British accounts. Canadians did not argue over the siege of Valenciennes. They only heard about its capture.[11]

The French Revolution was a singular event for North Americans. It consumed their attention and called forth new forms of politics. It made them rejoice and made them weep. The Canadian Henri-Antoine Mézière recalled the response when Montreal received reports of the early French Revolution: "more than once we watered [the newspapers] with our tears, more than once they were carried in triumph in the clubs and private societies in the bosom of which we sang the dawn of Liberty."[12] Historians have long recognized that the French Revolution provoked formative political discussions throughout North America. Yet because scholars usually examine this story through national, imperial, or local lenses, they have not appreciated the extent to which transnational communications shaped these conversations.[13] Placing the histories of the French Revolution in Canada and the United States alongside one another, as I do in this chapter, raises new questions. For example, why did Canadians broadly reject French revolutionary politics between 1792 and 1793 while Americans did not do so until around 1798? Social and cultural factors, such as religion, print culture, and ideologies, must have shaped this response. But as Bentalou's wager demonstrates, the asymmetric movement of politicized information across the Atlantic Ocean deeply informed how North Americans understood and responded to revolutionary France. While Canadians and Americans received relatively similar news about the early French Revolution, by the middle of the 1790s they might as well have been reading and talking about entirely different events. In North America, there was not one French Revolution, but many.

North Americans first learned about the seizure of the French prison known as the Bastille through newspapers and letters from England.[14] News of the major events in France during the next three years, including the abolition of feudal privileges, the flight of the royal family to Varennes, and many declarations of war, came to North America mostly from British sources aboard British vessels. There were few other options. At that stage, British sources offered a variety of perspectives. Some supported the revolution's direction and explained away moments of disorder, while others eyed Britain's ancient enemy warily. After Americans' experience with British newspapers during the American Revolution, they initially scorned those papers, but they nevertheless recognized distinctions among them.

Some British papers appeared to offer more credible intelligence about France than others did. A reader of the New York *Gazette of the United States*, "S. F. P.," complained in 1789 that many British newspapers "misrepresented" events in Paris and demanded that printer John Fenno and others "inspire some doubts" among readers about these accounts. This writer did not request that printers "translate French papers," perhaps knowing that they were unavailable, but insisted that Fenno and others "give *impartially* a copy of *all* the English papers in their possession." To encourage this, "S. F. P." enclosed a copy of the London *Evening Post*, which was friendlier to France than "*some other papers*." Just below this scolding letter, Fenno dutifully shared the *Evening Post*'s "Parisian Intelligence."[15] Americans such as this author took note of letters from Britain instructing recipients to question ministry newspapers, which "cry down the present government of France," and trust only opposition papers.[16]

In their early burst of enthusiasm for the French Revolution, some Canadians likewise disdained British papers' gloomy accounting of France. Fleury Mesplet, the acerbic prorevolutionary publisher of the *Montreal Gazette*, loved to sneer at British prints. In a 1790 French-language item headlined "Faux rapports" (False Reports), he printed fifteen paragraphs, each beginning with the phrase "Il n'est pas vrai que . . ." (It is not true that . . .) followed by a variety of pessimistic claims circulating about the French Revolution.[17] The essay's rhythmic repetition evoked concern about the regularity of antirevolutionary news reaching Montreal. Mesplet only published this item in the Francophone right-hand column of his newspaper, omitting it from the Anglophone left-hand column. Most of his material, however, appeared paired in translation, which suggests that he intended the "Faux rapports" as a critique of the British news reports that composed the bulk of his information sources. Perhaps, too, he hoped that the colony's Anglophone officials wouldn't notice it in the French column.

A few months later, Mesplet published a particularly biting piece of satire mocking the distortions he detected in British newspaper reports. Adopting the tone of the British papers he targeted, he announced a "bloody and terrible slaughter" in Paris on July 14, the first anniversary of the seizure of the Bastille. He described a conspiracy directing every corner of the French empire in a simultaneous "general massacre." The poor victims "cried aloud to heaven for a Counter Revolution," he wrote, but the bloodthirsty and "terrible Revolutioners" killed everyone. Only after describing these outrages at length did he slyly end the piece by noting that the violence had not been committed on traitors or counterrevolutionaries but on "oxen, the calves, sheep, Lambs, pigs, Geese, Poultry, Pigeons and all kinds of game."[18] Far from an early bit of vegan propaganda, Mesplet's parody implied that the French were innocently enjoying a celebratory feast while ill-disposed mediators were misrepresenting it as a massacre. Faced with the possibility of censorship or punishment from British colonial officials, Mesplet could only make his point obliquely, but his readers would have understood his meaning. Why should they trust British reports of events in France if those accounts might twist a joyful celebration into a feast of horrors?

Some prorevolutionary Canadians probably took pains to develop alternative information sources. Looking back on the early 1790s in later years, Mézière (who worked in Mesplet's print shop) recalled, "The revolutionary papers reached us then."[19] He did not explain exactly what he meant by "revolutionary papers," but he was likely referring either to French prints or to English newspapers that directly reprinted material from France. At that time, it would have been possible for Canadians who sympathized with the French Revolution to engage someone in England to forward copies of French papers to Canada through Halifax or New York packet ships.

The earliest British reports about revolutionary France were often uncertain and contradictory. Under the heading "The English Newspapers," Boston printer Benjamin Russell complained, "Amidst the great variety of accounts of the same transaction, it would puzzle an Oedipus, on this side the Atlantick, to find out the truth. The situation of France, in one set of Prints, is represented as deplorable and ruinous—in another set, as prosperous and auspicious."[20] Mesplet agreed, noting that he had received "various accounts of the same transactions [in France] . . . none of which perfectly agree."[21] The extent of these contradictions in British reports baffled many observers. In a 1791 newspaper article, a Philadelphia writer ridiculed the dissonance among the "latest accounts published from British papers." In the left column of a table, marked "Pro," appeared the good news received from Britain about revolutionary France, including the claim that the clergy were "warmly attached to the revolution." In the right-hand "Con" column was information casting revolutionary France in a negative light, including the statement that "the Bishops have remonstrated against the decrees of the National Assembly."[22] In this thicket of confusion, printers could only profess that they were trying to pick the "best accounts" from an "infinite variety of reports and hearsay."[23]

Observers across North America encountered a similar assortment of news about France in the early 1790s—usually a mix of British newspaper reprints as well as letters and travelers' accounts. Some reports were tinged with revolutionary optimism, whereas others indicated that France was tilting toward instability. By the middle of the decade, though, this began to change. The French revolutionary wars disrupted American observers' experience of global events, even as they affected Canadians' news sources very little (see chapter 4). Naval warfare endangered transatlantic correspondence, which caused letters to become less valuable sources of intelligence, while European wars stimulated demand for American grains, bringing more commerce and newspapers from continental Europe than in previous years. Greater access to such newspapers came just as war was transforming them. Beginning in 1792, leaders in the United Provinces of the Netherlands, Britain, and France all sought to align their news output with the needs of their governments and militaries. Because they relied so heavily on European newspapers in those years, state regulation significantly shaped Americans' view of the French Revolution.

Americans had long trusted Dutch newspapers, especially the *Gazette de Leyde*, because of the Netherlands' protection of press freedom. While Dutch printers initially enjoyed consistent, direct overland communications across the Austrian Netherlands for news from France, the outbreak of war between France and Austria in 1792 turned this region into an active battlefield. By 1795, the *Gazette de Leyde* gathered most of its news about French affairs secondhand from Parisian newspapers, such as the *Moniteur*. No longer able to provide timely and original reports about the revolution, the *Gazette* and other Dutch papers lost some of their preeminence among North Americans. Moreover, the war led to new limitations on the Netherlands' vaunted press freedom.[24] Philip Freneau, once the *Gazette de Leyde*'s greatest booster in North America, claimed in the summer of 1793, "There are no free papers now printed in Amsterdam or any part of Holland. Even the Leyden Gazette has become a corrupted source."[25] From 1792 to 1795, the rate at which US newspapers cited the *Gazette de Leyde* for news about revolutionary France declined precipitously.

Likewise, French print culture experienced a series of massive wartime changes. After a moment of relative freedom from 1789 to 1792, the ascendance of the Montagnard faction in 1792 and 1793 led to new restrictions. The new French leaders shuttered the presses associated with their Girondin rivals, which Atlantic observers had long relied on.[26] Surviving printers faced threats of censorship, intimidation, imprisonment, or even execution. A new official press sponsored by the Montagnard Committee of Public Safety filled this vacuum, but this era of repression was brief. The fall of the Montagnard leadership in late 1794 led to a renewed era of diversity and freedom for French print culture.[27]

US observers were not particularly bothered by the homogenized condition of the Montagnard press. While Americans protested that British newspapers were in the pay of the government, they did not express the same concern for French papers controlled by the state. One reason for this may have been that the Paris *Moniteur*, France's journal of record and an important source for American mediators, remained relatively unaffected by restrictions on press freedom. The *Moniteur*'s editor, Charles-Joseph Panckoucke, survived successive revolutionary governments by avoiding partisan reporting, ingratiating himself with each wave of leadership, and aping the neutral style of the *Gazette de Leyde*.[28] Americans, however, grew more critical of French print culture after the fall of the Montagnards allowed the return of a limited amount of press freedom. The orthodoxy enforced in France's news culture from 1793 to 1794 had produced the appearance of consensus to outsiders, while the end of that repressive atmosphere created a sense of gathering conflict.[29]

With the outbreak of war, the British government began seeking to drive public opinion against revolutionary France. The William Pitt ministry subsidized (some would have said "bribed") newspapers with as much as £5,000 per year. Subsidized newspapers, such as the *Sun*, poured a torrent of invective on revolutionary France.[30] Even opposition papers, such as the *Morning Chronicle*, gradually abandoned their sympathetic stance toward France and shifted toward antirevolutionary news and opinion.[31]

The turn to a more resolutely antirevolutionary British print culture affected Canadians more acutely than it did US observers. Even as more material from French newspapers was reprinted in the United States, less appeared in Canadian publications. Canadian officials had begun to police print materials more stridently after the beginning of the war. By 1793, no one dared to defend France in print. Whether persuaded by British sources or British threats, after the outbreak of war Mesplet's sympathy for revolutionary France dissipated like breath on a mirror. He denounced the revolutionaries as "monsters" and "wild beasts."[32] Indeed, when a French news item slipped into a Canadian newspaper, it could spark controversy. In 1793, after Quebec's government-friendly printer John Neilson unusually shared some news directly from a French source, a reader using the name "Philanthropos" admonished him. Worried that Neilson had "calculated to recommend," rather than "reprobate" the reprint, Philanthropos wrote that it was "indecent" for such material to "proceed from the Pen or Press of a British subject."[33] Canadians risked a reprimand if they dared to share news that came directly from France.

British news sources, though, were not always available. During winter months, when ice floes discouraged Atlantic commerce in colder climates, almost no news arrived in Canada from Britain. In the 1790s, Canadians began to depend during the winter on overland routes from New York for news, which allowed the comparatively diverse sources that Americans enjoyed yearlong to become seasonally available to Canadians.[34] But Canadian mediators had mixed feelings about these sources. While they relieved some readers of wintertime boredom, they irritated others. In 1794, when Neilson faced a "variety" of American accounts about the French Revolution, which "differ[ed] essentially in many respects," he decided against reprinting them, declaring that it was "better not to insert them, and to wait until proper intelligence shall be received upon the subject."[35] By altering Americans' relationship to global news, US independence had created new problems for the other empires of North America. News from America now seemed improper to this loyal Canadian. Perhaps it was even a bit dangerous.

As Canadian mediators shunned prorevolutionary news, growing Franco-American commerce in the mid-1790s allowed Americans to obtain more of their news directly from France. Beginning in late 1792, travelers moving between the two nations began to remark on the disparity between what they had witnessed in France and British reports in American newspapers. It seemed to many that "the affairs in France wear not so gloomy an aspect as is held forth by many of the British prints."[36] By the mid-1790s, American newspapers shared much more information from France than they had in the past. From 1793 through 1795, US papers cited French publications at more than three times the rate from 1790 through 1792. American readers saw approximately seven times as many reprints from France in the year 1795 as they encountered in 1790. This flood of French news invited Americans to view events from the perspective of France's most powerful mediators.

During this time the Montagnard government in France perpetrated thousands of politically driven executions, often in public. Drawing heavily on Montagnard-aligned French sources, which tended to explain rather than denounce such violence, American observers often dismissed accounts of unrestrained bloodshed and anarchic massacres in France as English disinformation. As a result, many experienced this period more as a train of error than a reign of terror. According to one Boston newspaper essayist, by spreading "doleful stories" of French violence, English and American mediators were displaying the same "rancorous disposition" that had guided Thomas Hutchinson and various British officials during the Anglo-American imperial crisis.[37] It seemed to some of the French Revolution's allies in the United States that the "ministerial writers in Great Britain" were "distort[ing] the conduct of the French patriots, and conjur[ing] up every phantom of horror and carnage to alienate the affections of Americans from them."[38] Others accepted that violent excesses had taken place, but saw them as necessary bumps on the road toward universal liberty.[39]

The growing commercial exchange with France raised questions about British accounts of Gallic violence. In late 1793, a merchant writing in the Boston *Independent Chronicle* recalled that after a journey through France, he discovered that British newspapers had provided US readers with "ridiculously false notions . . . respecting the actual situation of French affairs." He had arrived in France "with my head full of the accounts which are copied in America from English papers, of its distracted situation. I really thought the whole nation was doing nothing but standing on their heads, cutting one another's throats, and singing ca ira [the French revolutionary anthem]. But indeed I was agreeably disappointed." When the merchant sought out the "most impartial information" about the "massacres and assassinations" spreading throughout France, he had found "fresh proof how entirely ignorant" Americans were of events there. Parroting the Montagnards, he explained that violence was necessary to contain "the impending danger of some diabolical plot of their internal enemies."[40]

Additionally, French and British accounts portrayed the wars that began in 1792 very differently. As they followed the march of France's armies into the Austrian Netherlands, American readers in August 1792 may have noticed the use of first-person pronouns in an extract from the Paris *Gazette universelle*. The article described the combined armies as "the enemy" and France's actions as "our operations."[41] In contrast, London reports about the same campaign created distance between the observer and France. One reprint from "London Papers" not only relied on a third-person perspective to describe these events, but concluded, "the affairs of France are truly mysterious."[42] The differences between French and British news sources were not only rhetorical, but often substantive. During the same summer campaign, for example, reports surfaced of a battle involving General Lafayette's army, but its result was disputed in Philadelphia. A Paris paper that had arrived by the ship

Perseverance from Havre de Grace pronounced the French to be the victors, but a reprint "From London Papers" claimed to confirm "the disaster . . . of Fayette's army."[43]

While this particular engagement did little to decide the conflict's larger outcome, it was typical of the hundreds of questions about the authenticity of information concerning revolutionary France and its wars that arose over the next few years. France's admirers in North America dismissed war news that they disliked. When accounts of French losses arrived in New Hampshire in late 1793 from a British ship, for example, printer Charles Peirce wrote that considering the "channel through which this intelligence was communicated," his readers needed to make "allowance" for the "prejudices which commonly influence an enemy in rumours of this kind." Knowing that a French account would soon arrive, he pragmatically counseled them to be patient.[44] After the spigot of news from France opened, American observers were repeatedly forced to reconcile competing claims from British and French sources.

Asymmetric changes in Atlantic information exchange in the mid-1790s led Americans to encounter a range of contradictory news while Canadians faced a swelling antirevolutionary chorus. Given the immense quantities of both signal and noise crossing the Atlantic, the best way to obtain a textured illustration of the confluence of British and French information in North America is to zoom in on a single moment, a single month. According to newspaper shipping reports, in January 1794 twenty-one ships arrived in the ports of Philadelphia, Baltimore, Boston, and New York from France and Britain. Eleven came from France and ten from Britain—many of which brought sensational news.[45] None arrived in Canada, where winter ice blocked the movement of ships. In the autumn of 1793, republican forces in northeastern France had defeated the armies of the Duke of York and the prince of Saxe-Coburg, which forced the combined armies to lift their siege at Dunkirk and retreat for the winter. To the south, revolutionary armies had captured the rebellious city of Lyons but lost Toulon to their enemies. Meanwhile in Paris, the executions and violence that would be labeled the Reign of Terror were under way. Notable figures, such as Queen Marie Antoinette, the Duke of Orleans, and former revolutionary leader Jacques-Pierre Brissot, lost their lives at the guillotine.

Marie Antoinette's execution on October 16, 1793, provoked particular controversy across the Atlantic world. British newspapers generally expressed horror.[46] London accounts first arrived in North America on a ship called the

Eliza, which docked in New York City in early January 1794. British papers from the *Eliza* emphasized the injustice of Marie Antoinette's beheading, the grace of her comportment, and the inhumanity of her persecutors. One extract fulminated that this "once all powerful and beautiful" woman had been treated like the "meanest malefactor."[47] Likewise, a letter aboard the *Eliza* from a "gentleman in London" tersely noted his "regret" that the queen had "suffered" under the guillotine.[48] Printed accounts from Britain also surfaced in Boston aboard the ship *Hazard*, which had journeyed from London. These articles provided new details and claimed that the queen had "conducted herself with invincible fortitude."[49]

In Boston and Philadelphia, though, the first news of the queen's death came from ship captains arriving from France. Rather than emphasizing the violence of the event, they focused on the orderliness of the French crowds during the execution and the lewd charges against Marie Antoinette. In Boston, Captain Hallet of the *Peregrine* conveyed details of the beheading to printer Alexander Young of the *Massachusetts Mercury*. Under the heading "Important Intelligence! Direct from France," Young published the sensational accusations against the queen, adding that she had been "found guilty of the several charges, condemned and executed."[50] Instead of focusing on the moment of execution, Young's report lingered on the queen's crimes. Printers Thomas Adams and Isaac Larkin of the *Independent Chronicle* went further, claiming that Hallet had explained that "charges of the most heinous and infamous nature were proved against her."[51] In New York, Captain William Culver, who had arrived from Havre de Grace, claimed that "every thing in France was . . . going on well for the Republic," and the execution had been "conducted with the utmost order."[52]

News of French military victories in October and November 1793 had arrived in North America from both France and Britain. While these accounts sometimes differed in tone or detail, they generally agreed that France's armies had succeeded in a series of battles and sieges. At the same time, the status of the Duke of York and his armies excited considerable controversy. The most prominent British military commander in France, the Duke of York had gained some renown earlier in the year after successfully commanding the siege of Valenciennes. In late 1793, however, while leading the British force in Flanders, his army lost an engagement with French armies led by Generals Jean-Baptiste Jourdan and Jean Nicolas Houchard. The duke's forces quickly withdrew and escaped a French pursuit. Yet rumors abounded that he had been captured.

In North America, these rumors seem to have come from one or two sources. A letter from Havre de Grace received via the *Eliza* matter-of-factly informed a Philadelphia correspondent, "The Duke of York is made prisoner and has been conducted to Lisle." The writer added, "It has been proposed in the convention to expose him in Paris to public view in an iron cage." A second source of this news may have been through French diplomatic channels to French ambassador Edmond-Charles Genêt, who announced that he had received news via the *Eliza* that "the duke of york, with all his army, are taken."[53] Genêt had this announcement printed into handbills for public distribution.[54] His report did not identify a definite source for the news, though, causing printer John Buel of the *Columbian Gazetteer* to point out, "It is not certainly known from what particular documents this intelligence was derived," and while "some say" the news came from New York, it was "more probably" derived from "the verbal accounts received by the sloop [*Eliza*], and a letter from Havre."[55] Indeed, Genêt may have simply been repeating what everyone had already heard.

Despite thin documentation, the report spread quickly. One merchant in Philadelphia wrote to a friend that once he heard reports of the Duke of York's capture, he thought it "best to give you the rumour as we have it," though he couldn't find "any letters of much authority" to support the claim.[56] When Genêt's account of the Duke of York's capture reached Congress, it hastily adjourned "owing to the sensation" the story produced. Yet even as US observers and newspapers gleefully passed on rumors of the duke's capture, a number of reports arriving from Amsterdam, London, and elsewhere noted his escape.[57] These accounts eventually convinced New York printer Thomas Greenleaf, who admitted by mid-January that the duke had not been captured: "the rumours" that had been passed around Europe have "lately crossed the Atlantic in various directions, and caused us to be sharers in the general deception."[58] Because of its content and provenance, a single mistaken letter from Havre de Grace had sparked a minor sensation.

Just as some Francophile Americans amplified accounts about the Duke of York's capture, they also minimized hostile accounts of Marie Antoinette's execution. On January 10, 1794, the *Massachusetts Mercury* explained to readers that France's recent wartime successes dwarfed the queen's death in importance: "The execution of the Queen may perhaps throw a gloom over the minds of some, who warmly advocate the revolution; this melancholy impression will however be only the feeling of a humane moment; while the brilliant and unparalleled success of our illustrious Allies will be the eulogy of ages!"[59] More often, however, observers simply discounted reports that sympathized with her plight. Readers and printers of the *Philadelphia Gazette*, the *Vermont Gazette*, and the *Western Star* complained about what seemed to be obvious exaggerations in the printed accounts of Marie Antoinette's death. One writer using the name "Vive la Republique" accused the "daemons of monarchy and aristocracy" of feigning sympathy for the queen. They argued that these accounts exposed the fact that in the United States, "occurrences in France are almost without exception drawn thro' channels hostile to liberty and equality."[60]

Readers in Canada had an altogether different experience of these events. Relying on an overland route through Albany, New York, for news during colder months, Lower Canadians were exposed to American news-gathering practices for nearly half of the year. Mediators aligned with imperial interests recognized this availability as a problem. In February 1794 John Neilson of the *Quebec Gazette* received a copy of the New York *Daily Advertiser* that contained the *Eliza*'s reports from Liverpool about the queen's death.[61] But the *Montreal Gazette*'s printer (Mesplet had recently died, and his immediate successor's identity is unclear) could apparently only find the January 13 issue of John Barber and Solomon Southwick's *Albany Register*, a paper that generally sympathized with revolutionary France. The *Montreal Gazette*'s printer, however, must have decided that the *Albany Register*'s reports would be unacceptable to their audience because they fabricated several pieces of news and credited them to the *Register*.

In early February, the *Montreal Gazette* published a letter from New York dated January 8, 1794, and attributed it to the January 13 issue of the *Albany Register*. The letter relayed news from Liverpool about the French queen having "shared the same fate as her late unfortunate partner," suggested that her son had been killed, and noted a series of "the most horrid accounts of the massacre of thousands of men" at Lyons. But this letter had not appeared in the *Register*. Southwick and Barber had indeed printed a short extract of a letter from New York City dated January 8 describing news from Liverpool, but it had only blandly described the arrival of an "official account of the trial, condemnation, and execution of Antoinette." The letter did not call the execution of the king or queen "unfortunate" and had not alluded to the dauphin or a "massacre" at Lyons at all. Rather, a separate report had cheered the revolutionary armies' victory at Lyons against the "crowned robbers, and their servile minions." The *Register*'s reports were optimistic about France's prospects, whereas the accounts invented for the *Montreal Gazette* depicted the revolution as an unending string of tragedies.[62] In the next issue, the *Gazette* also declared that the "news lately circulated in this City with regard to the defeat of the armies commanded by the Duke of York and General Cobourg [Frederick Josias of Saxe-Coburg-Saalfeld] is absolutely false, as also the recapture of Toulon."[63]

Early 1794 was an unusually busy time in North America for news about revolutionary France, but the spatial, commercial, and governmental dynamics that created a dramatically different news landscape in Canada and in the United States were not unusual. Week after week, observers across the continent received news about France that differed according to where they lived and what they read. Yet while geography was powerful, it was not destiny. Some Canadians questioned the predominantly antirevolutionary accounts that they encountered. Americans, though, did more than question the news. They developed their disagreements about French revolutionary news into a key constituent of an emerging system of partisan politics.

In April 1793, a writer using the pseudonym "The Spirit of 1776" wrote a letter to Philadelphia's *National Gazette* protesting that Americans were allowing the highs and lows of France's military campaigns to distract them from the broader importance of the revolution. "The mercury of republicanism in this city seems to rise and fall with the good or bad fortune of France," this person claimed, "and her measures are approved or condemned according to her victories or defeats."[64]

The "republicanism" to which this letter referred was the emerging Republican Party, of which the *National Gazette* was the most prominent mouthpiece. The Republicans were a coalition that aligned itself with revolutionary France and favored limitations on the national government. Though usually referred to at the time as "Republicans," some historians have called them the Democratic-Republican Party to avoid confusion with the Republican Party that has existed from the mid-nineteenth century to the present. Led by Thomas Jefferson and James Madison, the party had emerged in opposition to the Federalist faction that had coalesced around George Washington, Alexander Hamilton, John Adams, and others, which favored closer ties with Britain and a robust national government. According to the Spirit of 1776, the Republican Party's fortunes had become tied not only to the outcome of the French Revolution, but also to the day-to-day news about that revolution. News of French victories buoyed Philadelphia's Republican politics while news of French losses aided the Federalists. American politics had become deeply attached to information about France. Yet this entanglement was a problem because the news often seemed to arrive through channels that were prone to error and manipulation.

A similar letter appeared in the *Quebec Gazette* that same month. A person writing under the pseudonym "Scepticus" urged Canadians to "wait the course of events" and withhold "judgment 'till time shall have decided the experiments of that adventurous Nation."[65] Scepticus worried, like the Spirit of 1776, that people were allowing the ups and downs of France's military campaigns to distract them from the revolution's broader significance. In the United States, this kind of argument was not unusual. In fact, in the same issue in which the Spirit of 1776's essay appeared, the *National Gazette* published another letter echoing the worry that France's "military successes, or misfortunes are the thermometer of national regard in this country."[66] In Canada, though, such a claim was more anomalous. Shortly after Scepticus's letter appeared in the *Quebec Gazette*, printer John Neilson received a rebuttal mocking the idea that further information might show the revolution in a more positive light. According to this correspondent, all information pointed to the fact that the revolution had failed. If it had produced any "happy effects," then the revolution's "panegyrists would surely have pointed them out." If, on the other hand, the revolution had "on every occasion been subversive" of good effects, then this writer asked, "from what principles can it be favourably offered to the Public view from a British Press!"[67] According to this response, the lack of positive news from France was evidence of the revolution's corruption, which served, in turn, as a reason not to reprint any news from France. The circularity of this argument attracted no notice.

More than a year later, an anonymous essay published in the *Ottawa Times* took a different tack. This writer took for granted Canadian readers' reluctance to believe negative portrayals of revolutionary France. After describing the "anarchy and confusion" in France, they remarked, "What a deplorable picture! what a melancholy representation is this of a great and once florishing Kingdom. Is there such devastation in any land! Are such tragedies acted on the theatre of the Earth!" By posing these questions, the writer attempted to anticipate and disarm the suspicion that some still harbored toward antirevolutionary reports. They answered, "With pain and grief we Answer, Yes, it is but too true" and suggested that this conclusion was based on the word of "every authority in Europe." Without offering any evidence, the writer claimed that even the "Gazettes issued by the French" testified to these facts. But if these publications were "insufficient to impress upon the minds of Canadians a conviction that these tragic scenes have been acted in France," they also claimed to speak for "undoubted authorities" and "men of virtue and dignity" in Canada who had witnessed France's horrors. If Canadians did not believe these "incontrovertible testimonies" and "stuborn truths," then the "rest of the world will conclude" that they were "immersed in gross igno-rance."[68] This writer's plea targeted Canadians who doubted negative reports about France, a clear indication that such suspicions continued to linger after Canada's elites and its news media had turned firmly against revolutionary France.

Incredulous Canadians likely understood that the colony's printers faced pressure to minimize positive news from France. Some ordinary Canadians remained resistant to British narratives of revolutionary France as late as 1798. That year, a seigneurial elite, Le Compte de Colbert Maulevrier, com-plained that the small farmers of French descent, or *habitants*, refused to "be-lieve a word about the [French] revolution's horrors" and could not bring themselves to accept that "the French people are capable of the horrors that they committed." When the colony's priests "tried to speak to them about the revolution and the crimes that it occasioned," Maulevrier noted that the *ha-bitants* became suspicious of them. Some claimed, five years after the execu-tion of Louis XVI, that he had never actually died. If Louis was absent, it wasn't that he had been executed. He was only "hidden" because he "has the power to make himself invisible." Others argued that if the king had been ex-ecuted, he "must have been guilty."[69] The prorevolutionary narratives to which some Canadians continued to adhere may have been unfounded on evidence, but they were firm and could not easily be defeated by elites' intervention.

If prorevolutionary Canadians whispered about news from France, their counterparts in the United States screamed about it. With a wide range of news to choose from, America's emerging political coalitions became divided along a set of epistemological fault lines. Republicans favored news that ar-rived directly from France, especially printed sources, while Federalists were more inclined toward news from sea captains and Britain. Neither group, though, admitted to these criteria quite so clearly. Instead, they developed sophisticated ways of authenticating congenial news sources and scrutinizing other information. By the mid-1790s, disagreements about which sources were most authentic developed into separate Republican and Federalist systems of knowledge. Newspaper printers, who were growing increasingly partisan in this era, played a particularly important role in refracting other observers' views of the French Revolution.[70] Partisans' political preferences shaped how they approached the news, even as individuals' choices as news consumers contributed to the formation of their political identities. A mutually constitutive polarization process linked information with partisan politics.

Such disagreements about how to determine the authenticity of news sources were relatively new. In the early modern Atlantic world, observers had long been willing to trust the word of educated, elite white men.[71] In the late eighteenth century, though, new arguments about authority began to take shape. During the American Revolution, Patriot rebels had resisted the idea that British colonial officials should act as trusted intermediaries for news and boosted instead popular vehicles of information, such as newspapers, petitions, and pamphlets (see chapter 2). In the 1790s, this long-standing question of elite authority over information took on a new partisan dimension. Though fewer letters arrived in North America in the middle of the decade, Federalist printers drew more attention to what letters did arrive, especially from merchants and other familiar sources in British and French seaports. Printers were usually aware of the identity of a letter's author, even though they typically hid it from their readers. To cue their readers on the value of a letter, Federalist printers often introduced epistles by describing the author as a "respectable citizen," an "unquestionable authority," or a "high authority."[72] Republican mediators, on the other hand, were much less impressed by the social status of letter writers. For example, after some people asked about his correspondent, "whether he be a foreigner, or home born, or well-born . . . A man of property, or a no property man," Republican printer Philip Freneau instructed them to "*mind your own business.*"[73]

Just as they trusted letters from men of high status, Federalist printers went out of their way to emphasize the authenticity of oral reports from ship captains and merchants. Their papers printed information from captains whom they described as gentlemen of "reputation," "undoubted veracity," "great political information," and "a very respectable [mercantile] house."[74] Printers sometimes interviewed ship captains and judged their character for themselves. When Alexander Young and Thomas Minns, the Federalist editors of the Boston *Mercury*, sought Captain Bacon to learn about France's capture of the Spanish city of Bilbao in late 1794, they remarked that he was a "gentleman of veracity, and intelligence." Unfazed by the fact that he was "unacquainted with the language" in France, they passed along his vague secondhand news that Bilbao's capture had been "officially published in the papers" of his port of embarkation.[75]

Consulting with travelers was the best way for printers to contextualize published reports or find new details when two printed accounts diverged. For example, after "contradictory reports" in US newspapers about a naval battle reached Federalist printer Samuel Loudon in early 1795, he sought out news from a ship captain's "own mouth." After speaking to Captain Barnard, he resolved the matter to his satisfaction and pronounced Barnard to be a "man of respectable character and on whose testimony the fullest reliance may be placed." Tellingly, Loudon published the report under the heading "Who shall decide, when Printers disagree!"[76] For Loudon, a ship captain's singular assurances could provide an antidote to the messy business of reprinting.

Ship captains' networks of sociability, politics, and commerce often overlapped with Federalist circles. While sailors tended to participate in Republican politics, most merchants and ship captains gravitated toward Federalism.[77] Some Republican mediators were suspicious about the relationship between commerce and information flows. They often worried that merchants and ship captains held news back, or pushed false news, for their own financial gain.[78] When the ship *Charles* arrived in Newburyport in early 1795, for example, Republican printer Thomas Adams reported that it brought "no news." He complained that the response "all papers left behind" had lately become a "fashionable reply, when inquiry is made respecting the news from Europe." Suggesting that this might be a "commercial or political manoeuvre," Adams implied that the ship's captain, crewmen, and passengers were withholding information about French victories either to shape political opinion or to manipulate commodity prices for their own profit.[79] This latter accusation, which was part of an extensive debate in early US political discourse over the ethics of speculation, was probably false.[80] While Adams's *Independent Chronicle* received no news from the *Charles*, the Federalist *Impartial Herald* published a comprehensive report about French victories based on a conversation with the *Charles*'s captain, Joseph Perkins, whom the paper described as a "Gentleman of information and veracity." The *Impartial Herald*'s editors added a gloating postscript to their article, mocking Adams for charging Perkins with "bringing no news, when we have more authentic information by him, than we remember ever to have seen in all the antifederal [Republican] papers published in Boston."[81] In this case, the Federalist newspaper editor succeeded at getting oral news from Captain Perkins while the Republican editor had only sought newspapers for reprinting.

Republican mediators feared that Federalist-leaning ship captains were prone to providing anti-French narratives of events. For example, when a ship captain's report of a major victory for the English fleet over the French arrived in Boston in the summer of 1795, several Federalist newspapers reprinted it without comment.[82] Republican printer Benjamin Franklin Bache, in contrast, mocked the account's exaggerations, arguing that the English captain who had passed it along was "perfectly conscious that the late advantage gained on the coast of Brittany, wants some striking touches from the master hand of an ingenious painter, before it can be magnified into an important victory."[83] But when a prorevolutionary American captain brought news, Republican printers sometimes took note. In his *Independent Chronicle*, Republican printer Thomas Adams laid out the "oral testimony of Capt. Hallet, who is an inflexible republican, of varacity and information."[84] Perhaps because ship captains were known to lean toward Federalism, Adams felt the need to add this credential—which the Federalist *Salem Gazette* dropped when it shared Adams's report.[85]

Other Republican printers ultimately felt uncomfortable relying on ship captains at all, including those who sympathized with the French cause. Anthony Haswell of the Republican *Vermont Gazette* saw such observers as irrevocably embedded in their own perspectives: "There is very little need of logical argument to prove that men allow their prejudices to blind them." The arrival of a "hot democratical American captain" might bring news that "the current of events runs strong in favour of the republic," while the "arrival of a captain of different stamp" could suggest that "general distrust and deadly jealousies universally prevail, that every man suspects his neighbor; that the guillotine works as constant as a sawmill."[86] In this account, the archetypal ship captain was nothing like the "gentleman of veracity" that Federalist printers imagined. In Haswell's view, a ship captain, if not exactly deceptive, was prone to letting his partiality get the best of him. For Haswell and many other Republican printers, ship captains were not trustworthy authorities.

Because each layer of mediation could introduce falsehood or remove context, American observers had reason to prefer the most direct accounts from France. In August 1791, for example, printer Andrew Brown of the relatively apolitical *Federal Gazette* had noted a difference between the reports contained in English and French papers but concluded, "The most direct we hold as the most probable, and shall not trouble our readers with a perusal of those less to be depended on."[87] Republicans were generally more averse to heavily mediated news. Scholar Laura Mason has shown that the early French revolutionaries favored oral testimonies over written texts in part because they allowed for unmediated communication from the heart.[88] Their most ardent admirers in the United States were partial to printed accounts for the same reason: they seemed to promise the unfiltered voice of the French people.

As a result, while Federalists and Republicans cited British newspapers at roughly equal rates, Republican papers reprinted news from revolutionary France's presses at about twice the rate of their Federalist rivals from 1793 through 1796. During times of unusual division over information, these rates climbed. In April 1793, for example, when news of Louis XVI's death arrived in the United States, Republican papers cited French papers at three times the rate of Federalist newspapers. In January 1794, amid concern about Marie Antoinette's death, the seizure of Lyons, and the apparent capture of the Duke of York, Republican citations of French papers spiked to roughly five times the rate of Federalist newspapers.[89] During the middle of the decade, Republican printers often drew their readers' attention to news that came from France, employing headings such as "Direct from France" two and a half times as often as Federalist printers did. Likewise, they frequently cautioned their readers about news items that had originated in antirevolutionary British newspapers. Republican printers used headings with the term "ministerial," the most common pejorative tagging government-sponsored and ideologically antirevolutionary British newspapers, at more than three times the rate that Federalist newspapers did during the mid-1790s.[90]

When Federalists did publish news from French papers, it was sometimes done to undercut Republicans' persistent criticism of British sources. In 1793, for example, the arch-Federalist printer John Fenno wrote a letter to a friend about Maximilien Robespierre's leadership in Paris and the Reign of Terror, explaining, "I do not depend on english papers" for news about France. Though his newspaper contained numerous reprints from the British press about revolutionary France, the Paris papers were more damning than anything that could come from London: "I had a great number of paris papers for April & May their principal contents were the names of the victims executed daily."[91] Likewise, later in the decade, when Federalist printer Gottlob Jungman of the Reading, Pennsylvania, *Weekly Advertiser* passed along a Paris newspaper's report of a series of local executions, he could not refrain from adding a bracketed interruption: "[And yet a number of Americans have the audacity to tell us at large that all those published accounts of French cruelties, are fabricated lies, intended to make Frenchmen detestable in our eyes.]"[92] His point was similar to Fenno's argument. If British prints could not be trusted to provide a fair accounting of events in France, Parisian presses provided evidence enough of the revolution's violence and depravity.[93]

Republican observers and mediators cast doubt on British news whenever possible. A 1793 letter to the Republican *Independent Chronicle* complained about newspapers printing "every unfavourable occurrence" about the French "and seriously copying for truth every paragraph from the British papers. . . . it cannot but disgust every genuine American."[94] Many Republicans compared British newspapers' characterizations of the French to their accounts of the Patriots during the American Revolution. According to one Republican commentator, Federalist newspapers were falling for the same tricks that the British government had practiced decades earlier and had thereby made themselves the "echoes of British ministerial papers."[95] Anyone doubting that the British were fabricating news about France, according to one writer, needed "only look back at their former impositions during our own war with them."[96] Likewise, Republican Thomas Adams saw little difference between French émigré aristocrats who, he claimed, were working in London and the United States to spread falsehoods that would "excite the prejudice of the honest and unreflecting, against the French," and the actions of Loyalist and British propagandists during the American Revolution.[97]

If they wanted to avoid news from British sources or ship captains, Republican mediators needed to translate reports from French sources. British newspapers had long been the easiest news sources to gather, as New York printer Francis Childs noted, because they were written "in our own idiom."[98] As printers sought to expand their source base, they discovered that translation was a costly, time-consuming, and uncertain business. It took a considerable amount of effort or money to translate news. In 1795 Thomas Adams complained that the bulk of the Paris papers made it "almost impossible to give the translations at length."[99] One Federalist printer wrote that the difficulty of the task had prevented him from producing wholesale translations of French newspapers: "The editor has not been able to obtain but some short translations, for want of time, and the translator living at a considerable distance from the Office."[100] Moreover, as the number of newspapers printed in each major port city increased during the 1790s, French newspapers as material objects became scarcer. Printers described using "vigilance and exertion" and performing "the most unremitted exertions" to get hold of French newspapers.[101] One imagines a flock of printers meeting a ship at the docks, vying for its sustenance like a nest of baby birds.

Republican printers bore the burdens of translation more willingly than Federalists did. Their newspapers used words such as "translated" in headings describing news from French papers nearly twice as often as Federalist newspapers did from 1793 through 1795.[102] Moreover, partisan printers tended to rely on the translations of their ideological cohort. A news item translated for the Republican *Aurora General Advertiser* (whose editor, Benjamin Franklin Bache, was fluent in French) was unlikely to be reprinted in Federalist papers, while Republican newspapers ignored translations from the fiercely Federalist *Columbian Centinel*. Imagining that their rivals withheld or distorted information from French newspapers, printers distrusted each other's translations. In late 1794, for example, New York Republican printer Thomas Greenleaf wrote that his readers were "astonished" to hear the earliest reports of a French military victory in the Netherlands from "A MINISTERIAL PAPER," given that a ship from France had arrived earlier. But Greenleaf noted that those "Paris *papers* . . . fell into the hands of the Editor of the *Minerva*," his Federalist rival Noah Webster. Though Webster had printed three issues since receiving these papers, Greenleaf wrote, Webster "has not given a word that looks like victory." Greenleaf believed that Webster had chosen to ignore news of French successes for political purposes. He also accused Webster of infusing his translations "with *puerile* (low-cunning) interjections directed to American Jacobins, Democrats."[103]

Preferring direct, unmediated sources, Republican printers sometimes challenged the translation work of London newspapers. In March 1793, for example, several US newspapers reprinted a deputy's speech in the French National Assembly from late 1792, which had attacked religion in public education. The speech was taken from a supposed "exact Translation" provided by the London *Diary; or, Woodfall's Register*.[104] At the oration's sensational climax, the deputy had proclaimed, "I honestly avow to the Convention—*I am an Atheist!*" That, at least, is what readers of Philadelphia's leading Federalist newspaper, the *Gazette of the United States*, and several other Federalist papers would have read.[105] Readers of Philadelphia's *Dunlap's American Daily Advertiser*, a relatively nonpartisan paper, however, would have read the word "Deist" in place of "Atheist." This was a simple transcription error from the *Diary*, as John Dunlap admitted a few days later: "Errata in the speech of Mr. Duport, published in our Paper of Friday last—for 'deist,' read 'atheist.' "[106] Nevertheless, one Republican reader pointed out the discrepancy. "Some Philadelphia papers assert," noted a reader of the Republican *National Gazette*, "that Mr. Dupont had avowed himself a Deist, others, an Atheist." In the same issue, the *National Gazette's* printer, Philip Freneau, asserted, "In the French original M. Duport stiles himself a Deist."[107] Republicans such as Freneau recognized that the speech of a deist deputy threatened France's cause less than an atheist deputy did.

More worrying than mistranslations, though, were outright inventions. Partisans regularly accused their rivals of fabricating news about the French Revolution wholesale. Attempting to debunk news about French military victories, a Federalist using the name "A Friend to Truth" published evidence in 1794 to suggest that a letter "supposed to have been written in Bourdeaux," which had been the object of much discussion, had in fact "probably never crossed the sea." This writer signed off, "So much for the fabricated French news."[108] In 1795, Benjamin Franklin Bache, who was among the foremost Republican printers in the United States, accused his rival John Fenno of inventing an "electioneering lie" about the contents of the French newspapers.[109] For their part, Federalists regularly accused Bache of fabricating news from France for the benefit of the Republican Party. When a report about French military victories that Bache had published turned out to be a "string of lies," a Federalist commentator stormed that Bache was not fit to be a printer because he "betrays the confidence of his readers."[110] Federalists sometimes suggested that Republican papers were "in the pay of France," while Republicans alleged that the British had purchased their rivals.[111] Assigning malign and self-interested motives to rival mediators helped to account for the otherwise inexplicable sea of contradictions.

Indeed, some printers may have occasionally fabricated news from Europe for political purposes. Because newspaper sourcing was typically vague and anonymous, they could easily get away with this. Unless a printer identified a purported source and a date, it remains difficult for historians to detect such imposture. Partisan printers certainly faced pressure to produce politically potent news that could turn the political tides. For example, in a 1794 letter, a Federalist gentleman named Peter Van Schaack mocked the "distracted" state of France and encouraged Loring Andrews, editor of the Massachusetts *Western Star*, to "publish the accusation against Brissot, Roland [Jean-Marie Roland de la Platière], [Pierre-Victurnien] Vergniaud, etc." This request was perfectly ordinary in some ways. It was not unusual for readers to request that printers insert particular items in their papers, and the trial and execution of the Girondin leadership during the Reign of Terror was a matter of great interest. But Van Schaack was not motivated by curiosity or an interest in truth. He hoped to discredit the revolutionary government in France: "if these Articles [of accusation against the deputies] are true, the Government in France has not been so immaculate as their Friends suppo'd; if they are not true, & if Brissot etc were not culpable, what must those be, who have prosecuted & destroyed them?" Van Schaack was indifferent to whether or not the accusations were true, but he hoped to shape the public conversation surrounding revolutionary France by injecting it with information that would cast France's leadership in the worst possible light. A few years later, as the heat of partisan politics mounted, Peter's brother and Federalist ally Henry Van Schaack apparently lost patience with Andrews. Complaining of the "dulness" of recent issues of the *Western Star*, Henry forthrightly asked, "if you have no news from abroad why don't you fabricate some?"[112] Whether or not Andrews obliged, the casual nature of Henry Van Schaack's request (he quickly moved on to other complaints) suggests that partisans valued political outcomes more than truth. News was too important to be left to the uncertain tide of events.

As historians have long understood, US partisan politics took shape in large part through arguments about the French Revolution. That great event seemed to pose several questions for Americans. Would the United States follow France's example and embrace a more radically egalitarian worldview? Or should Americans heed the warning of French violence and disorder to restrain popular politics? Was the American Revolution more like, or more different from, the French Revolution? Would France succeed or fail with its experiment? These sorts of questions encouraged Americans to work out the unresolved conflict between the radical and traditionalist elements of the American Revolution.[113]

But American partisans were not only arguing about the meaning and implications of the French Revolution. They were spending much of their time disagreeing with each other about what the French Revolution was in the first place. In the mid-1790s, American partisans fought over nearly every significant piece of news about France and many more insignificant reports as well. As they tried to understand the revolution itself, they asked a different, more pragmatic set of questions. What had caused the revolution's excesses? How were France's various wars going? Was the violence in France genuine or had insidious mediators inflated it? Because distance allowed them to ask these sorts of questions, the ocean that separated American observers from the revolution in France was fundamental to their experience of it.

"Removed as we are from the scene of action, deprived therefore of an opportunity to examine official documents, to interrogate eye witnesses," a

Rhode Island essayist using the name "Brutus" commented in 1793 in response to news about the execution of King Louis XVI, "no one can determine on firm and satisfactory evidence, whether Louis was guilty or innocent." Americans only had information derived from "vague rumours" and newspapers "propagated by mercenary interested men." How would they make sense of these "mazes of conjecture"? Brutus concluded that perhaps when the "storm is blown over and history has deposited in her archives" sources about the French Revolution, humanity could "examine the controversy at our leisure, and decide with deliberation."[114] More than two centuries after the French Revolution, the storm has largely blown over. Yet despite decades of concerted investigation, historians are still arguing about what happened in France and its colonies during the 1790s. Certainty remains nearly as elusive for us as it was for contemporary observers. Thousands of miles separated observers such as Brutus from France, but hundreds of years now divide us.

If British news had continued to flood American ports and newspapers, as it did in Canada, US partisans might have had less to argue about. The French revolutionary wars had caused Franco-American commerce to expand, leading many observers in the United States to encounter prorevolutionary narratives alongside antirevolutionary accounts. Their realities seemed to fragment, entangling principles with perceptions, and ideologies with information. The partisan rancor that developed during the 1790s in the United States was not an inevitable consequence of the ideological fractures of the American Revolution. Rather, it owed much to the indirect and unexpected consequences of war in Europe. Though the United States attempted to remain neutral, in many ways the war had already come to North America.

CHAPTER EIGHT

Unmaking the Revolutionary Caribbean

Race, Commerce, and Communication in the Early Republic

In late 1794, a French painter named Jean-Louis Boquet presented to the public an illustration of the momentous destruction of Saint Domingue's port city of Cap-Français a year and a half earlier. Engravings of the landscape, titled *Vue de l'incendie de la ville du Cap Français*, were immediately sold to a mass audience in France. Set at night, the image depicts entwined columns of fire and smoke rising from the city's buildings like a swarm of red tornadoes. On the shoreline, tiny dark silhouettes dance in threatening postures. The blaze is doubled through its reflection in the harbor, from which Boquet's gaze emanates, and dozens of gawking ships gather around, their sails brightened orange by the flames. Boquet's image remains one of the most enduring representations of both the Haitian Revolution and the Age of Revolutions.[1]

There was more to the Haitian Revolution, however, than scenes of destruction. The revolution challenged a power structure that exploited and ignored thousands of enslaved people and French colonists in Saint Domingue. It was a revolution defined not just by violence and ruin but also by innovation and creation. In many ways, it was the most radical and transformative of the revolutions of the late eighteenth century.[2] But for nearly two centuries it was largely forgotten and robbed of its status as a revolution. The anthropologist and theorist Michel-Rolph Trouillot explained that a Black revolution was simply "unthinkable" for both contemporary white observers and subsequent historians. It was impossible for them to imagine that a movement led by people of color held any meaningful political content.[3] White North Americans usually separated Black radicalism, whether in Saint Domingue or elsewhere, from the revolutionary thought that characterized the American and

Jean-Louis Boquet, *Vue de l'incendie de la ville du Cap Français*, 1794. Bibliothèque nationale de France

French Revolutions. In some accounts, the violence of the Haitian Revolution seemed nearly apolitical, caused only by the viciousness that white racism ascribed to people of color.

Two centuries too late, the Haitian Revolution and its impact on the broader Atlantic world have finally won attention from historians and popular audiences. This long-overdue notice, though, can lead us to forget that it was not the only revolutionary event in the region at the time. More than a dozen revolts, conspiracies, and insurrections broke out in the broader Caribbean during the 1790s. Observers could not determine which, if any, of these uprisings would endure. Every burst of action in Grenada, Martinique, Saint Lucia, or Saint Vincent raised questions. Was this a revolution? Was it another Saint Domingue? Or was it a temporary convulsion that would recede in due course? The media available to North Americans limited their ability to answer inquiries like these. Most of the news that arrived in the continent addressed a different set of questions. How much property had been lost? Would a European army arrive soon? How will this affect me? The complex relationship between media and commerce narrowed observers' perspective on the revolutionary Caribbean.

Boquet's painting suggests a complementary explanation to Trouillot's thesis. The composition that Boquet chose, portraying the destruction of Cap-Français from across the harbor, provided perhaps the most dramatic view of the fires. It also captured the perspective of many observers from afar, who watched the Caribbean's revolutions erupt into flames. Like Boquet, white North Americans often viewed revolutionary events in the Caribbean from over the shoulders of commercial vessels. This vantage made it easy to learn about commodity prices, military movements, destruction, and trade—the sorts of things that one learns about in a harbor. It was challenging, or even impossible, though, for North Americans to see revolutionary politics, deliberation, and complex motives from the shoreline. As in Boquet's landscape, North Americans often needed to squint to see the actual people of the Caribbean, Black and white, enslaved and free. At moments of ferment, white Americans had little knowledge of the intentions of Caribbean revolutionaries, but instead saw only the consequences of their actions. News from Caribbean ship captains and letters usually portrayed only destruction, violence, and rebels without causes. If the revolutionary character of Black-led insurrections was "unthinkable," as Trouillot rightly observed, for white North America, it was also unknowable.[4]

Saint Domingue was the wealthiest and most valuable of France's overseas colonies in the eighteenth century. This wealth derived from dangerous and difficult labor unwillingly performed by enslaved and free people of color, primarily on sugar plantations. By the end of the eighteenth century, decades of slave importations, violence against enslaved people, and mistreatment of free people of color had bred a powerful discontent. During the early stages of the French Revolution, the colony's free people of color expressed their demands for equality with an insurgency in late 1790 and early 1791. Hearing rumors of the revolution in France, many enslaved people believed that France's government had emancipated them but that the planter class was hiding the news. They rose in a massive, coordinated revolt in the colony's northern province in the summer of 1791. Many of these rebels did not seek to leave the French empire but rather to participate in the French Revolution on more equal terms. Free people of color and enslaved people throughout Saint Domingue demanded their rights and their freedom.[5]

Alongside the events in Saint Domingue, France's Caribbean colonies Martinique and Guadeloupe enacted a different sort of revolutionary politics. Pre-existing tensions between wealthy white planters, who supported the French monarchy, and a class of revolutionary-minded merchants and working white people known as *petits blancs* boiled into civil war in Martinique by 1790. The island's free people of color, despised by the *petits blancs*, largely joined the royalist elites. A similar dynamic unfolded in Guadeloupe, where patriots aligned with revolutionary doctrines and counterrevolutionary royalists fought for control of the colony. In late 1792, angry with French laws allowing for greater racial equality for free people of color, the royalists on both islands rose up in a counterrevolution, but they were defeated by early 1793.[6]

North Americans learned about these early events from the usual mix of travelers' accounts, letters, and newspapers. While a few Lesser Antilles newspapers, including the *Gazette de Ste.-Lucie* and the *Gazette de la Martinique*, had been published before the 1790s, the revolutions in France and the Caribbean encouraged colonists to create new papers, including *L'ami de la liberté* and *Affiches litteraires* in Martinique. Printers arranged for the distribution of these papers across different islands, which allowed them to circulate throughout the Lesser Antilles. Likewise, newspapers thrived in Saint Domingue during the early 1790s. While only one newspaper, the semiofficial *Affiches americains*, had been published in Saint Domingue for much of the eighteenth century, a variety of new periodicals began to appear as revolutionary politics swept through the colony. From 1790 through 1793, Saint Dominguans started sixteen newspapers, primarily in the port cities of Cap-Français and Port-au-Prince.[7] The islands of the British Caribbean also developed more expansive print cultures in the late eighteenth century.[8]

Much as in Europe and North America, the Caribbean's newspapers occupied a wide ideological spectrum. A few, including the *Gazette de la Martinique* and the Port-au-Prince *L'ami de l'egalité*, aligned themselves with French radicalism, though they stopped short of supporting emancipation.[9] Others joined with local royalist factions supported by wealthy planters.[10] North Americans who followed the news from the revolutionary Caribbean likely recognized some of the distinctions between these papers. One piece from a Saint Domingue newspaper republished in Philadelphia, for example, blamed "our misfortunes" on the "inflammatory paragraphs in the *Courrier politique*," a short-lived Cap-Français publication. Close readers would have inferred from this comment that the *Courrier politique* supported revolutionary change. Some North Americans might have also questioned the reliability of the more heavily regulated Caribbean presses. In October 1790, for example, the provincial assembly for Saint Domingue's northern department barred printers from publishing accounts of the political ferment unfolding around them. As American readers later saw, the assembly decreed that "every citizen, journalist, printer, and bookseller of the Province, be, and is prohibited from composing, printing, selling, distributing, or publishing any writing whatsoever, on the insurrection of the people of colour and the causes thereof." That decree also restrained these groups from discussing the actions of either the French National Assembly or the colonial assemblies of Saint Domingue.[11]

In response, a defiant Saint Domingue printer named Jacques-Philippe-Daniel L'Honorey Dubuisson mocked and protested this order in his *Le gazette du jour*.[12] While the provincial assembly suppressed his paper for "containing false and calumnious facts," Dubuisson did not allow himself to be silenced.[13] Drawing on his connections in the United States, he distributed news of these events to several American printers, who took his side of the argument.[14] New York printer Archibald McLean, for example, provided readers with Dubuisson's account and accused the assembly of securing the "*slavery* of the *Blacks*" at the expense of the "*liberty* of the *Whites*." McLean asked Americans to consider: if maintaining slavery meant destroying the "liberties" of white people to speak and write freely, was slavery worth maintaining?[15] This was a remarkable comment, suggesting that protecting the liberties of white people like Dubuisson and his readers might require the emancipation of enslaved people.

Dubuisson's suppression reveals the extraordinary efforts that French Caribbean officials made to shape how their newspapers portrayed the revolutionary events around them. As historian Jeremy Popkin has noted, Saint Domingue newspapers were "extremely restrained" in their reports about the early stages of the Haitian Revolution. They may have feared that detailed accounts of violence or disorder could draw official ire, inspire further insurrection, or affect foreign merchants' interest in sending badly needed supplies to the island.[16] Newspapers in the Lesser Antilles also faced regulation from royalist authorities.[17] Such control probably made the early stages of the Caribbean revolutions seem relatively palatable to a white American audience. Other than the immediate reaction to the restraint of Dubuisson, there is little evidence that North Americans subjected French Caribbean newspaper accounts in the early 1790s to anything like the kind of scrutiny that they were applying to British prints' accounts of the French Revolution.

In the early years of the Haitian Revolution, commercial exchange between the French Caribbean and the United States was quite robust, allowing newspapers to circulate widely. With American independence, Britain had limited Americans' ability to trade with its Caribbean colonies whereas France opened its Caribbean ports to the United States. Focusing on monoculture sugar cultivation, these islands, especially Saint Domingue, depended on North America for lumber, flour, meat, and other commodities. By 1790, US merchants exported more goods to that colony than to the rest of the Caribbean combined.[18] Violence and revolution caused some French Caribbean islands to become more dependent than ever on American supplies. Acting on their own authority in December 1789, for example, Martinique planters opened their ports to more American trade.[19]

During the early 1790s, a robust stream of arrivals from Saint Domingue brought the colony's newspapers into the United States. Despite government regulation, they often contained accounts of the region's internal politics and revolutionary conflicts. This kind of detailed reporting was essential for North American observers. Anyone who wanted to understand why the French colonists and people of color had revolted needed more than the accounts of ship captains and letter writers, which tended to be terse and focused on commerce rather than politics. They needed detailed debates and declarations from those involved. Charleston printers John Markland and John McIver, for example, offered their readers extensive extracts "from the registers of the generall assembly" in Saint Domingue from 1790 and commented that these reports showed that "the revolutionists in the colonies are as busily employed as they are in the mother country, to frustrate the designs of the Tories, and to frame a new constitution."[20] The references to the "Tories" and the "mother country" suggest that Markland and McIver saw an affinity between the French, American, and Haitian Revolutions. Indeed, several American printers shared information from Haitian papers that allowed readers to make such connections. In an address to France's king shared in a Philadelphia paper, for example, the "Municipality of Port-au-Prince" declared that the "period of oppression is at an end for the Colonists of St. Domingo as well as for their brethren in Europe."[21]

To the east of Saint Domingue, newspapers in the Lesser Antilles likewise gave North Americans a window onto the region's internal politics. Martinique's radical *petits blancs* initially controlled the island's only newspaper, the *Gazette de la Martinique*. Consequently, it portrayed events there as an uprising against elite authority similar to the French Revolution.[22] McLean republished an account from the *Gazette de la Martinique*, for example, that concluded, "We have had here, as in France, an entire Revolution."[23] Likewise, Boston printer Benjamin Russell shared a widely republished abstract of news from the *Gazette de la Martinique* headed "Progress of the French Revolution," which described the "spirit of patriotism" fighting against the island's despotic enemies.[24] North Americans reading these materials had good reason to link the French Revolution with events in Martinique and Saint Domingue. Significantly, though, the earliest stages of the French Caribbean revolutions were often led by white colonists and free people of color, rather than by enslaved people. As historian James Dun has shown, this triggered fewer countervailing racist and anti-emancipationist impulses, allowing many Americans to think of these events as, according to one observer, "little else than the revolution in Old France in Miniature."[25]

Yet Americans' broadly prorevolutionary attitudes in the early 1790s also shaped how some of them viewed the region's slave revolts. In August 1789 in Martinique and April 1790 in Guadeloupe, hundreds of enslaved people rebelled against colonial rule, though in both cases they were quickly defeated.[26] Most early modern reports of slave revolts ignored both the violence of slavery and enslaved people's politics, as historian Ada Ferrer has shown, and instead began with the experiences of soldiers and others who sought to repulse the uprisings.[27] But the accounts of the revolts that emerged from Guadeloupe and Martinique were unusually willing to consider the oppressions and aims of enslaved people. Boston printers Thomas Adams and John Nourse noted how "remarkable" it was that the rebellion of enslaved people in Martinique "to recover their liberty" happened just as news of the French Revolution reached that island. Though they listed the gruesome details of a "horrid plot" that the enslaved people had supposedly planned to murder the island's whites, they concluded, "The time will probably come, when the blacks may injoy liberty by gentler means."[28] Instead of viewing the revolt of enslaved people as an expression of violent urges, these printers suggested that the uprising was a result of the example of the French Revolution. In this moment, mediators offered some space for the testimony of the region's Black inhabitants. A Philadelphia newspaper, for example, reprinted a description of the French Caribbean's uprisings that included a letter addressed to a French military officer, which was signed "All We Negroes," that commented, "We know that the King has made us free; we expect to be so."[29]

The ability to gather information from Caribbean newspapers allowed North Americans to remove potentially unreliable mediators from the news-gathering process. As with news that came from revolutionary France, ship captains arriving from the Caribbean earned special scrutiny from some observers. Philadelphia printer Benjamin Franklin Bache, an ally to global revolutionary movements who would go on to become one of the continent's most important mediators of information from the revolutionary Caribbean,

preferred accounts that originated in situ, whether in France or in the Caribbean. In July 1791, for example, news arrived in Philadelphia about the French
National Assembly's decision to extend political equality to free people of
color. Bache printed this news based on the word of a ship captain who had
recently arrived from Cap-Français.[30] But other ship captains quickly offered
different accounts. After two weeks of dispute, Bache grew frustrated and
complained that such news was unreliable because it had been "founded on
the reports of American Captains, from Cape-François, who generally not
speaking the language of the inhabitants, and being the greatest part of their
time on board their vessels, which, from the nature of the harbor, are an-
chored out at some distance from the town, have not many opportunities of
gathering information." He emphasized that "no papers, of a date late enough,
have been received, that could give certain information." Instead, he instructed his readers to rely on a recently published letter "written by a person
long established in the island."[31] Here, Bache effectively offered his readers a
hierarchy of news sources. Best of all would have been newspaper reports that
could provide certainty by printing the exact details of the new law. In the
absence of a printed report, a letter from a knowledgeable correspondent
could be valuable. Worst, for Bache, was the word of ship captains. Without
quite calling them liars, he distinguished news according to its point of origin. A letter from an insider who knew the colony and had good connections
was valuable because that author could provide more details and nuance than
an outsider who lacked context or even the language for inquiry.[32]

In the early 1790s, North American observers imbibed a healthy mix of
reprints from newspapers, oral accounts, and letters about the Caribbean revolutions. The fact that mediators such as Bache distinguished between them
demonstrated that observers could draw on multiple types of media during
that period. But compared to news from Europe, Caribbean sources tilted
heavily toward epistolary and oral media forms. In the influential Philadelphia *National Gazette*, for example, printer Philip Freneau published almost
a thousand news items relating to the French Revolution and about 116 regard-
ing the revolutionary Caribbean from 1791 through 1793. About seven-tenths
of his news about France came from European newspapers, whereas just over
a fifth of his Caribbean information came from newspapers. He published
letters from the Caribbean at about twice the rate of letters from revolutionary France. Only about 5 percent of his news about the French Revolution
came from oral reports, compared to more than one-third of his news about
the revolutionary Caribbean.[33] Like Bache, Freneau might have liked to draw

more of his news from the Caribbean's newspapers because, for all its limitations, print provided the most detailed accounts of revolutionary politics. Oral reports melted into rumor, and most letters were too short to provide the kind of particulars that newspapers offered. Only newspapers could offer a massive amount of detail to a potentially massive audience. Indeed, newspapers were essential to outsiders' ability to attribute meaning to events elsewhere. It was only by collecting newspapers printed abroad that observers could grasp the complex internal politics of revolutionary movements. Reading Caribbean newspapers allowed Americans in the early 1790s to experience, at least on occasion, revolutionaries' own accounts of their actions.

But this proved to be short-lived. By the mid-1790s, North Americans lost their steady access to Caribbean newspapers as the region erupted in a series of new revolts. Alongside ongoing disruptions in the French colonies of Saint Domingue, Guadeloupe, and Martinique, enslaved and free people of color, as well as some white colonists and Indigenous peoples, challenged local power structures around the greater Caribbean from 1794 through 1796. Revolts or thwarted conspiracies of various sorts occurred in the British colonies Dominica, Jamaica, Grenada, and Saint Vincent; the Dutch colonies Demerara and Curaçao; the French colony Saint Lucia; and the Spanish colonies Puerto Rico, Venezuela, Cuba, and Louisiana.[34] Each of these events was distinctive and resulted, at least in part, from local circumstances. Some were quite small, involving only a few people, while others were large enough to seize control of an island. One epicenter of conflict was in the Windward Islands in the Caribbean's southeast, where significant revolutionary events took place in Martinique, Saint Lucia, Saint Vincent, and Grenada.

In the mid-1790s, as this revolutionary activity escalated, mounting imperial conflict between Britain, France, and Spain finally reached the Caribbean. Beginning in 1794, French military forces led by Guadeloupe's governor, Victor Hugues, encouraged some colonists and enslaved people in enemy territories to revolt. They sometimes lent the rebels material support.[35] British military leaders also assisted rebels in enemy territories.[36] Additionally, Spanish and French legislation concerning the status of free people of color and enslaved people alienated colonial whites and fueled rumors among the free and enslaved populations. As in the early stages of the revolutions in Guadeloupe and Saint Domingue, many enslaved people believed that planters were hiding news of emancipation from them, and they revolted to claim that promise.[37] Rumors that France had emancipated its enslaved population proved to be true, which provided a powerful incentive for enslaved people in Spanish and British territories to ally with revolutionary France.

The same forces destabilizing the revolutionary Caribbean made these events more illegible to outsiders. Revolutionary and wartime violence blinked out of existence many of the Caribbean's newspapers from 1792 through 1794. In 1792 and 1793, six newspapers had been published in Saint Domingue. The destruction of Cap-Français in 1793, though, concluded the runs of the *Moniteur general* and the *Journal des revolutions de la partie française de Saint-Domingue*. The British military's capture of Port-au-Prince shuttered the radical *L'ami de l'egalité* and *Le republicain*. An insurgency of enslaved people in the south in 1792 hastened the end of *L'observateur colonial* in Les Cayes, while violence around Saint-Marc contributed to the demise of the *Chronique de Saint-Marc* in 1794. As a result, Saint Domingue was without newspapers during some of the most crucial stages of the Haitian Revolution.

Print culture in the French Lesser Antilles also ebbed at the same time. Grenada's *St. George's Chronicle* concluded in 1792, well before the massive rebellion that broke out there in 1795. The *Gazette de Ste.-Lucie* ended in 1794. Four French newspapers published in Martinique—the *Gazette de la Martinique*, *L'ami de la liberté*, *Affiches litteraires*, and the *Gazette nationale et politique*—ceased publication between 1791 and 1793, and Britain's occupation of Martinique beginning in 1794 made further prorevolutionary publications there impossible. Indeed, the only newspapers published in the Windward Islands during the mid-1790s came from British-held islands, where printers provided almost no information about revolutionaries' ideas and politics.[38] By the middle of the decade, North Americans encountered much less printed news from the Caribbean about the escalating Haitian Revolution and the revolutions in the Windward Islands. While these changes in Caribbean communications were under way, nearly an opposite set of developments was reshaping how Americans communicated with revolutionary France (see chapters 4 and 7). Even as fewer letters and more newspapers from metropolitan France were arriving in the United States, the composition of news from the revolutionary Caribbean included fewer newspapers, more letters, and more ship captains' reports.

This divergence is clearly visible in US newspapers from the mid-1790s. In Philadelphia, the continent's most significant port for gathering and distributing Caribbean news, printers often shared long extracts from European newspapers alongside shorter, less detailed letter extracts and travelers' accounts about the revolutionary Caribbean.[39] In a single issue from May 1795, for example, Bache published three and a half columns of news titled "From London Papers," reprints of Charleston, Baltimore, and New York papers concerning European news, and two extracts labeled "From a Paris Paper." These included details of military maneuvers in Europe, lengthy paragraphs from the French National Convention, and signals of bubbling political discontent in Dublin. Directly below the reprints from Paris, Bache printed a few scant paragraphs about the Caribbean. He provided a ship captain's account of a "bloody engagement" in Grenada and a paraphrase of a letter from Saint Domingue concerning a French general and the British navy.[40] These brief accounts said nothing of the Saint Dominguan or Grenadan rebels' motives or demands. As a thoroughgoing Republican who distrusted ship captains, Bache would have been, if anything, more attentive to Caribbean newspapers than were other news mediators. Yet in both column inches and detail, Bache's arrangement of news provided something like what Boquet's engraving offered: a commercial gaze toward a ruined, dehumanized Caribbean.

Another Philadelphia printer, Claude-Corentin Tanguy de la Boissière, was, unlike Bache, outwardly hostile to any revolutionary politics. A refugee who had fled the Haitian Revolution, Tanguy began an Anglophone and Francophone newspaper named the *American Star / L'étoile américaine*, which was devoted to sharing news about the revolutions in France and the Caribbean (which he disdained). Though his paper lasted only forty issues in early 1794, twenty-four of which have survived, Tanguy's obsession with collecting every bit of news from the Caribbean provides a useful window onto existing information flows. During his run, he published ten letters providing information about the Haitian Revolution and six oral reports, primarily from ship captains. Without any newspapers to draw on, he published no reprints from the Caribbean. In contrast, when he reported on the revolution in France, Tanguy relied far more on foreign newspapers: twenty-eight reprints from French, English, Dutch, and Spanish publications compared to only seven letters and four oral reports.

Such a small number of newspaper accounts narrowed Americans' perspective on one of the Caribbean's great revolutionary events, which took place in Grenada in 1795. Facing anti-Catholic persecution, a group of French colonists there rose against British rule under the leadership of a mixed-race plantation owner named Julien Fédon. Fédon and his allies had been secretly organizing against the British for months.[41] Fédon's Rebellion seized most of the island. The insurrectionists thought of themselves as revolutionaries following in the footsteps of the French people. They adopted symbols and language evoking revolutionary politics, donned liberty caps, and named their three camps Liberté, Fraternité, and Morte.[42]

Yet for American observers, this would always be a rebellion and never a revolution. In the three months following the uprising in Grenada, Bache and his partisan adversary in Philadelphia, John Fenno, published a combined fifty-four reports about it in their newspapers. Like most Federalist printers, Fenno published more news from ship captains than did Republicans like Bache. Of the twenty-five news items that Fenno printed about Fédon's Rebellion, twenty-one were derived from captains and three from letters. Bache's gleanings were more balanced. In his *Aurora General Advertiser*, he printed fifteen accounts from ship captains, whom he distrusted, two from travelers, and twelve from letters. Both Bache and Fenno also shared one piece of news from British Caribbean papers, compared to scores, perhaps hundreds, of extracts from European newspapers about the French Revolution during this period. Exactly none of this news of Fédon's Rebellion offered any explanation for the attackers' motives. Fenno and Bache's readers, as well as the readers of the many North American newspapers that relied on these seaport mediators to collect the freshest news, would have experienced the rebellion as a spasm of violence, rather than as a revolution.

Yet even when Americans received newspaper intelligence from the Caribbean, it could not always shed meaningful light on the region's revolutionary events. Newspapers published in British colonies often provided many details but almost never considered the intentions or aspirations of revolutionary actors. During what was known as the Second Carib War in Saint Vincent, for example, British newspapers concealed nearly as much as they revealed. Located south of Saint Lucia and north of Grenada, Saint Vincent had once been a French colony before its transfer to the British empire in the aftermath of the Seven Years' War in 1763. As a result, most of its white and Black settler population was Francophone, Catholic, and culturally French. These settlers lived alongside Native Caribs, many of whom had married Black people to produce a group known to settlers as the Black Caribs. In early 1795, Carib and Francophone peoples began to coordinate with French allies in nearby Saint Lucia, sending small canoes between the islands at night to evade British warships.[43] They revolted in March 1795, but were eventually repressed by British general Ralph Abercromby's forces in 1796.[44]

Several accounts of this insurrection from Saint Vincent's British newspaper circulated in US papers. Noah Webster of the New York *American*

Minerva, for example, published a lengthy report that described the Caribs deceiving British officials and embarking on an unprovoked campaign of brutality, destruction, and murder. The minute descriptions of military leaders' decision-making and movements suggest that they were the author's principal source of intelligence. After describing a battle between insurgents and imperial forces at length, the author stated that "a war of such unexampled barbarity" would seem "incredible to the world at large." Nevertheless, the writer insisted that it had been "commenced without provocation, and even without any pretext." The report failed to note that decades of imperialism and enslavement had in fact provoked the violence. There was no trace of an explanation for the revolutionaries' actions other than an aim of "extirpating a whole race of inhabitants."[45] Other accounts from Saint Vincent's newspaper were little different, largely reflecting the perspective of military officers.[46]

The most abundant source of Caribbean intelligence during the mid-1790s remained news from travelers, especially ship captains. Seaport printers had no trouble finding ship captains at the docks and in surrounding establishments. Some developed relationships with certain captains or learned about their reputations.[47] An observer could speak directly to a ship captain, ask follow-up questions, and judge his character as a way of determining the authenticity of his news. More than one observer remarked, as a Baltimore merchant did in 1795, that oral reports about the Windward Islands could be relied upon because "I conversed with the Captain, and he is a man of truth."[48] Captains' reports, though, rarely took observers past the shoreline.[49] When he landed in a port, a captain was busy unloading goods, selling them, buying and loading new goods, and leaving as quickly as possible. There was no profit in lingering. Captains inquired about local news and conditions, but they did not necessarily focus their attention beyond topics that helped them to make decisions about their business. When they stopped to converse, it would often be with other captains or merchants, perhaps at a tavern or coffee shop by the docks.[50]

In the United States, as a result, conversations between newspaper printers and ship captains usually focused on the impact of revolutionary events on Caribbean trade. During the early stages of Fédon's Rebellion, for example, Captain Kennard brought word to New Hampshire that "no business of any kind could be transacted" in Grenada.[51] For many, this kind of news could potentially be very valuable. It told merchants when and when not to dispatch a ship. Because they were the most consistent subscribers to North American newspapers, merchants' interests were also the interests of printers, which meant that newspapers carried a great deal of news about commodity prices, trade, and war. Printers Alexander Young and Thomas Minns of the Boston *Mercury*, for example, provided a detailed digest of news about the Windward Islands in May 1795, but prefaced it with the comment, "The situation of the West-Indies, being extremely interesting to Commerce, we are particularly careful in obtaining the truth."[52]

More detailed reports usually came not from ship captains but from those who had been residing in the Caribbean for some time. Indeed, the most extensive early account of Fédon's Rebellion to reach the United States was from a ship captain who had been forced by an embargo and injury to stay in port longer than usual.[53] Frequently, though, ship captains provided little more than news about the movements of ships and troops. One typical report, for example, read: "The ship Harmony arrived at Baltimore belonging to Messrs. Oliver and Thomson, merchants of Baltimore, left St. Marc the 5th of March, loaded with sugar, coffee, &c. The passengers report that the Cape was certainly in the possession of the Spaniards, together with the north part of the island, except Port de Paix."[54] To modern eyes, this is a rather dull dispatch. So are the scores of accounts that announced "the arrival of the fleet" or the result of a siege.[55] But those engaged in overseas trade read these reports differently. The arrival of a fleet might suggest that violence was imminent. A ship caught in an endangered city might be embargoed by local officials in case it was needed for an evacuation—a potential fiscal disaster. On the other hand, the capture of a city might suggest that it was pacified and therefore open to lucrative business opportunities. Understanding these cycles of violence allowed merchants to anticipate and exploit the tides of commerce.

Because they relied on commercially oriented news sources, many white newspaper readers, merchants, and travelers may have been more ignorant of the events in the revolutionary Caribbean than were North Americans of color. As historian Julius Scott has shown, people of color throughout the Caribbean widely spread news about the Haitian Revolution and other revolutionary events. Thousands of Black refugees, military deserters, and formerly enslaved people, many of them self-liberated, ran from their former lives by crossing to different islands or continents in the late eighteenth century. Some of them took up work as sailors, crisscrossing the region and carrying all kinds of news and rumors. Moreover, enslaved and free people of color in North America often worked in professions adjacent to maritime trade, putting them in a position to overhear news and ask questions while unloading cargo or outfitting ships. The so-called grapevine of enslaved and free people of color could be remarkably efficient, allowing news to spread at a rate that alarmed some white observers.[56] This communication stream was largely private and rarely appeared in venues such as newspapers. But it is difficult to imagine that Black mediators interpreted news of British abolitionism, Spanish reformism, Caribbean slave revolts, or the Haitian Revolution through the commercial lens of white mediators.

White leaders did their best to restrain the flow of news among enslaved and free people of color. In late 1792, the state government of Virginia renewed a long-dormant law entitled An Act against Divulgers of False News. It provided a fine for anyone who should "forge or divulge any such reports, tending to the trouble of the country."[57] While the law did not disclose its motivations, it was reaffirmed shortly after the onset of the rebellion of enslaved people in Saint Domingue. Even as white Virginians remained more intensely devoted than many other Americans to revolutionary France in the 1790s, they were deeply worried about slave revolts.[58] Likewise, in 1793 white citizens gathered in Charleston, South Carolina, to agree to prevent foreign news from reaching the region's Black observers by denying entrance in the city's harbor to people of color, who might spread "the example of the French Revolution or the insurrection on Santo Domingo."[59] In 1800, a conspiracy led by an enslaved man named Gabriel Prosser in Virginia caused some white Americans to seek even more restrictions on the flow of foreign news. Some evidence suggests that Prosser and his allies hoped to follow the examples of the Haitian and French Revolutions.[60] Whether or not that was truly the rebels' intention, several southern states passed laws in the aftermath of the uprising to expel people of color who had recently come from France or the French Caribbean.[61]

White North Americans often distrusted rumors and reports from Black mediators. A long tradition of "testimonial injustice," as philosopher Miranda Fricker has termed it, led white North Americans to subject information from people of color to greater scrutiny than accounts from white intermediaries.[62] In 1794, for example, Tanguy noted in his Philadelphia newspaper that a "trusty negro of Mr. Dacher, inhabitant of Du Bas de la Cote, who sailed from here in the month of October by order of his master," brought news, "which however wants confirmation, but which contains details so circumstantial that we cannot help placing some faith in them." A rabid antirevolutionary, Tanguy felt that this news, describing the defeat of an army led by André Rigaud that was aligned with the radical French commissioners, was so "favourable" that "we cannot resist the satisfaction of laying it before our readers."[63] Enslaved people, such as this unnamed "trusty negro," would have traveled often between the Caribbean and North America, carrying news with them. But racist distrust of people of color meant that their accounts were only recorded in newspapers on rare occasions. In this case, Tanguy found an account so compelling that he could not help publishing it, even while loading it with caveats. In most cases, Black news mediation was unthinkable for white observers.

White refugees also brought news to North America.[64] Because they were fleeing violence, refugees usually provided dramatic reports of extreme dissension or brutality. After the burning of Cap-Français in 1793, for example, thousands of refugees dispersed with dramatic accounts of the event.[65] The city's destruction had been brought on by a dispute between the newly arrived French governor, François-Thomas Galbaud du Fort, supported by a French fleet, and previously appointed commissioners supported by local people of color. This raised the politically charged question of blame. Many white refugees sided with Galbaud. But as they arrived in US ports by the shipload, their accounts differed so much that it was difficult for observers to develop a coherent picture of events. Bache provided an extensive report on the city's destruction, which he gathered "by conversing with several of the unfortunate colonists already arrived here, and comparing their accounts." Yet he did not accept their stories at face value. After recounting their contradictory narratives of events, Bache explained that "the naked truth" might come later "from less impassioned informants." His news, he pointed out, "at present is from one party."[66] John Dunlap, another Philadelphia printer, also struggled to make sense of the refugees' stories. He complained that it was "difficult, as yet, to arrange any thing like a connected account of this dreadful catastrophe," but he provided multiple reports from passengers and ship captains: "Some say . . . Others state . . . Some are of opinion that . . . It is not however easy to ascertain any real state of the affair until we receive further accounts." What all agreed on, however, was that the Black revolutionaries had committed "abominable cruelties" against their white victims.[67]

The arrival of so many refugees in North America no doubt stimulated exchanges of letters between those who fled and those remaining. Most letter authors were merchants, planters, refugees, or government officials whose interests led them often to focus on the destructive consequences of revolution. As a result, many letters reinforced the narratives collected from oral reports and British newspapers. Boston merchant Samuel Cary, for example, worked in Grenada during Fédon's Rebellion. In a long update written for his father,

Cary complained that "this insurrection . . . is likely to deprive almost every ~~man~~ proprietor in the island of half his fortune."[68] By striking out "man" and replacing it with "proprietor," Cary revealed his priority as a correspondent: business first. Cary was interested in the property of particular men rather than the rights of all men (let alone women). The next year, as the rebellion was repressed, he told his father that British authorities were "busy in closing accounts with those Frenchmen who have been so warm for the interest of the Republic in Grenada." An old neighbor's "account," he explained, had been closed "at the Gallows."[69] For Cary, news of the death of an old acquaintance was another tally in an account book.

Likewise, the financial ramifications of the rebellion most interested Cary's parents, Samuel Sr. and Sarah. "The moment I heard of the insurrection," the father wrote to his son, he inferred that it would hurt the family's finances, and so he "took your brother Charles from Boston and Lucius from the Academy" to reduce expenses and put them to work on the family farm.[70] Sarah shared her husband's concern about the rebellion's impact on the family's property in Grenada. In a letter to her son, she wrote at length on "the loss of negroes, the still more certain loss of mules, cattle, etc.; the destruction of the dwelling and negro houses, with the loss of the last crop."[71] In mid-September 1795, Samuel Sr. mentioned, "I see in the Newspaper a Letter is rec'd from Martinico," which claimed that "6000 troops would be there [Grenada] in a few days." He concluded that "a trade will open with your island" once the rebellion had been subdued.[72] While these parents expressed genuine love and concern about their son, their interest in the news of Fédon's Rebellion was clearly driven by financial considerations. Sarah and Samuel Sr. could not help but interpret revolutionary events as debits and credits, losses and profits.

Indeed, the contents of letters from the revolutionary Caribbean in the mid-1790s often read like a ledger sheet. Merchants' interests indelibly shaped what nonmerchants read and heard about the uprisings. Typical letters advised that it was "not very tempting to risk property" in Saint Lucia, Grenada, and Saint Vincent; that the sugar crop in Saint Vincent and Saint Lucia "is entirely ruined"; and that "produce is getting very high."[73] More bluntly, a letter from Tobago to a merchant in New Hampshire simply noted, "Property in the West-Indies is very unsafe at present."[74] Extracts from "a letter from a gentleman in St. Domingo, to a respectable [mercantile] house in this city" were fixtures of North American newspapers.[75]

Some letters aimed to encourage merchants to send aid. A 1793 letter from local leaders in Port-au-Prince, for example, exhorted American merchants to bring their products to Saint Domingue. This group dismissed stories about emancipation as an effort by counterrevolutionaries to "prevent that aid and subsistence which we should expect from the United States, & cause all kinds of shipments to this Island to cease."[76] Though this report was misleading (processes of emancipation were beginning in parts of the island), it must have seemed necessary to colonists seeking supplies from the United States. Indeed, early accounts of the revolutions in Saint Domingue and the greater Caribbean often played down the revolutions' dangers. One letter from Grenada after the outbreak of Fédon's Rebellion and more than a year before its end assured Bostonians that "every thing was again quiet there, and things going on in their usual manner."[77] Another received at about the same time falsely claimed that the rebels in Grenada had been "entirely defeated."[78] Such letters probably aimed to entice American merchants to gamble on a voyage that they would not have taken if they were given accurate information.

Additionally, many early reports about Caribbean insurrections mistakenly framed them as imperial military contests. The earliest letters and travelers' reports about the Windward revolutions, for example, falsely asserted that a French army had invaded.[79] One report from Norfolk, Virginia, claimed that "five accounts from different vessels" had confirmed that France had invaded Grenada.[80] Considering the context, though, this was a reasonable mistake. The French leader Hugues had been fighting British forces in the Lesser Antilles and had provided some material aid to the rebels. Moreover, some insurrectionists thought of themselves as fighting for France. It would have been easy for some eyewitnesses to mistakenly conclude that at least some of the insurgents were French invaders. The unprecedented number of uprisings across the Lesser Antilles in 1795 also seemed to suggest a coordinated series of invasions rather than separate rebellions. Yet however implausible to North American observers, most of those tearing down imperial institutions in the Caribbean were local inhabitants.

Other reports that circulated in North America focused on the French as provocateurs rather than invaders. A newspaper printer in Martinique, which had come under British occupation, explained that the "savage conduct" of the Caribs in Saint Vincent could "principally be ascribed to the instigations of" the French.[81] Boston printer Benjamin Russell attributed the insurrections in Grenada and the French colony of Saint Lucia, where a multiracial uprising had broken out to challenge British occupation, to the work of "French commissaries at Guadeloupe."[82] Two months into Fédon's Rebellion, Samuel Cary Jr. regarded the insurrection as being caused by Hugues, who had "so misrepresented things" to Grenada's free and enslaved people of color that they had "resolve[d] to take up arms against us."[83] That enslaved and free people of color had the capacity to gather such resolution on their own did not, apparently, seem likely to such writers.

Once reports clarified that the Caribbean revolutionaries were locals, mediators generally ignored them and instead focused on the consequences of their actions. Motives seemed irrelevant. Instead, observers drew on racist caricatures to blame violence on the inherent cruelty of people of African descent. A letter from Grenada, reprinted in Philadelphia from an Antigua newspaper, described the rebels of that island as "monsters" and called for them to be put "on that equality which their diabolical crimes and most horrid savage cruelties so loudly call for; their blood I hope will then fertilize the soil which they have desolated and laid waste."[84] Whereas reports in the early 1790s had compared the uprisings of enslaved people to the French Revolution's demands for equality, by the middle of the decade, this account suggested that the only equality they deserved was to be victimized in equal measure with their villainy. Reports from the Caribbean described a "system of terror," "scenes of carnage," "wanton" destruction, "barbarians," and "inhuman" murder.[85]

On the rare occasions when white mediators attempted to describe the insurrectionists' intentions or motives, they usually reinforced a cartoonish image of the rebels' villainy. In a report republished in Philadelphia, the British *Barbados Mercury* discussed Fédon's Rebellion in Grenada at length and claimed, "Fedon, the Republican General . . . wished he could exterminate the whole English nation."[86] A telling exception occurred in April 1795. That month, a ship called the *Nancy* arrived in Baltimore from Barbados with a copy of the British *Barbados Mercury*. The printers of the city's *Federal Intelligencer*, Leonard Yundt and Matthew Brown, explained that this paper "contains but little besides an account of the defeat of the Charaibs [in Saint Vincent], and the death of their chief, as before stated."[87] But the "mate of the Nancy" spoke to the printers of a different Baltimore paper and, unusually, described how in Saint Lucia "the negroes were every where ready to take up arms, and to sacrifice their lives in defence of liberty."[88] This statement, though quite limited, was one of the only serious efforts by Caribbean information mediators to explain the insurrectionists' aims in the mid-1790s. Significantly, this sailor's report did not stand on its own. It came accompanied with a British newspaper account focusing on the consequences of violence in Saint Vincent.

Only a few other sympathetic reports about the Windward revolutionaries surfaced in the American media. One came from Guadeloupe, where the French leader Victor Hugues had installed a printing press (though apparently not a newspaper) that published a decree headed "Liberty! Equality!" that North American printers shared. It characterized the insurrectionists as "Republicans," accused the English of "innumerable crimes," and sought to correct British publications that charged their allies, the Caribs, with "heinousness."[89] Another came from a speech by a member of the French National Convention, who praised the "valor" and "loyalty" of the inhabitants of Saint Lucia.[90] Tellingly, these two accounts were from French allies, rather than from the Caribbean revolutionaries themselves. Without direct information from the rebels, North Americans seldom read or heard about their politics. In fact, few North Americans applied the label "revolution" to events in the Windward Islands in the mid-1790s. One telling exception came from James Kirkaldie, printer of the Vermont *Rutland Herald*, who wrote in 1795 that "all the islands seem to be in a state of ferment, and verge to a Revolution."[91] But even this sympathetic account was merely prospective: a revolution seemed possible, but it had not yet occurred.

Although by 1796 a series of British invasions suppressed the political ferment of the Windward Islands, revolutionary conflicts continued in Saint Domingue until the colony gained independence as the nation of Haiti in 1804. In the late 1790s, as the revolutionary leader Toussaint Louverture consolidated power and temporarily restored stability to much of the colony, revolutionaries had begun to publish newspapers again in Saint Domingue. Between 1796 and 1802, nine newspapers were founded in the colony, although most were short-lived.[92] During this minor print renaissance, American trade with the French Caribbean began to wither because of increasing tensions and naval conflict between the two nations. Indeed, in response to French vessels' attacks on American shipping, the US government launched a trade embargo of the French empire in June 1798. A year later, Louverture and American leaders worked together to create an exception to the embargo, allowing American merchants to return to Saint Domingue. As they reopened trade, the US and British governments collaborated to guard against any "dissemination of dangerous principles" that may have occurred as a result of "intercourse with St. Domingo."[93] As much as possible, these governments wanted to place the colony under quarantine, permitting only money and goods to escape—and not the ideas, people, and information that usually accompanied commerce.

Beginning in the summer of 1799, as trade picked up, printed news began to flow once more between Saint Domingue and the United States. The political context had changed considerably from the early 1790s, when Americans had last been able to expect a regular stream of newspapers from the revolutionary Caribbean. In the United States, as chapter 9 documents, revolutionary politics were in disrepute following the nation's diplomatic rupture with France in 1798. At the same time, the balance of Saint Domingue's politics had shifted significantly with the emergence of two major figures.

Louverture was the dominant military leader in the colony, controlling its wealthy north. But his former ally Benoit Joseph André Rigaud, who commanded an army in the colony's south, became distrustful of Louverture's ambitions. Whereas Rigaud remained loyal to France, Louverture sought support from France's enemies Britain and the United States. Louverture limited privateering against American ships while Rigaud permitted it in ports that he controlled. The conflict between these two leaders, which devolved into outright warfare in mid-1799, became an object of political controversy in the United States. American Federalists, with support from the nation's merchants, generally trusted Louverture's leadership in Saint Domingue and pushed for closer commercial relations with the colony, hoping that this might encourage him to separate from France. Republicans, in contrast, supported France's rule over the colony and feared that the revolution's example might stir up violence in the slave states that formed their political base. They generally favored Rigaud.[94]

In effect, the contest between Rigaud and Louverture in the late 1790s served as a new front in American mediators' long-running information war over the French Revolution. Partisans condemned each other for spreading false news about the Saint Dominguan civil war. In July 1799, for example, a New York Federalist accused Republican mediators of spreading a false story that Louverture had died.[95] A few weeks later, as American trade with the northern part of the island (controlled by Louverture) opened up, Federalist printer Andrew Brown of the *Philadelphia Gazette* and printer William Duane of the Republican *Aurora General Advertiser* fell into an argument about whether Rigaud was allowing attacks on American ships in the southern part of the colony. Duane asserted that "during the whole administration of Rigaud in St. Domingo, there has been only one case of capture of an American vessel" and mocked Brown for asserting otherwise.[96] In response, Brown described the capture and sale of a ship called the *Amy* a few months earlier, and claimed that Rigaud had personally ordered the *Amy* destroyed because he believed that the captain had hidden money inside.[97] Duane retreated, acknowledging that it was "not improbable" that Rigaud's forces had attacked the ship, but he suggested that the account of Rigaud's personal involvement had a "touch of *Federal embellishment.*"[98]

Printed material from Saint Domingue reflected Louverture's ascension to control over the colony.[99] A 1799 piece of news originating in Cap-Français, which Brown reprinted, for example, began with the assurance that the city "begins to exhibit the happy effects of the measures which have been adopted by" Louverture.[100] Some mediators were suspicious of this material. A Baltimore printer noted with surprise in 1800 that the only information available about Louverture's ongoing conflict with Rigaud was a "proclamation of Toussaint's" published in the " 'official' Gazette of St. Domingo," presumably referring to the *Bulletin officiel de Saint-Domingue.*[101]

One of the high points of Saint Domingue's standing in the American news media came in the summer of 1801 when a new constitution framed by Louverture arrived in the United States. American printers extracted the constitution from copies of the *Bulletin officiel,* along with a lengthy speech from the president of the assembly that had created the document. The speech and the information about the constitution provided a brief but telling window onto a complex revolutionary political culture deeply concerned with balancing factionalism, "social order," and the rights of the people.[102] This was not a truly republican document since it installed Louverture in office for life and provided for the forced labor of citizens. But these elements did not concern Federalist observers, who praised its guards "against the introduction of popular *democratic* influence." The Federalist *Philadelphia Gazette* even suggested that the colony "has as strong a claim to the exercise of independent powers with regard to its internal government, as the American colonies had in '76."[103] After quoting Louverture describing the new constitution as a "support of the feeble against the enterprises of the powerful," Federalist printer Benjamin Russell added, "Amen, say we."[104]

That same year, however, Americans began to learn of renewed violence in Saint Domingue. In early 1801, Brown published rumors of "horrid scenes" in Saint Domingue: a "general massacre" of white colonists, who were "executed at the cannon's mouth." Many other Federalist printers shared this account. Though Federalists were generally supportive of Louverture's regime, reports of genocidal violence against white settlers overrode those commitments. Brown closed this account with the exhortation, "Tell these things in South-Carolina! Yea, let them be published in the State of Virginia!"[105] This taunt implied that US southerners would not circulate this rumor in order to avoid stirring up insurrection among the enslaved population.

In October 1801, a large-scale revolt in Saint Domingue's north created new worries about disorder, which Louverture aimed to combat with reassuring printed proclamations.[106] In 1802, Napoleon Bonaparte, who was now in power in France, sent a French force led by General Charles Leclerc to regain control of the colony. During this long campaign, the information flowing between Saint Domingue and the United States shifted decisively. Reports of the clash arrived not through buoyant newspaper reports, but once more primarily from ship captains and letters. After one of Louverture's generals set fire to Cap-Français in anticipation of a French landing in February 1802, for example, a ship captain arrived in Baltimore with a report about the "conflagration of the cape." He described the "horror and blood-shed" committed by the "black demons" in the colony and included some gruesome details.[107] Another captain reported only on "immense" property losses.[108]

Letters from Saint Domingue in 1802 focused heavily on military movements and violence.[109] Many of them renewed the discourse from the mid-1790s about the savagery and cruelty of Black people. A letter "from a Gentleman at the Cape" written to Robert Wilson, printer of the Federalist New York *Daily Advertiser*, described formerly enslaved people seeking to "murder their former masters" and committing gruesome attacks. Its author claimed to be writing from the "Ruins of Cape Francois."[110] The same author, whom Wilson now referred to as "our Correspondent at the Cape," also wrote a letter two months later that complained about Leclerc and the French invaders' conduct toward American sailors.[111] A few weeks later, the Republican printer William Duane alleged that the author of the "Ruins of Cape Francois" letters was an English merchant whose apparent care for the victimized Americans in Saint Domingue was belied by his reputation as a man with the "most sovereign contempt for every thing American!"[112]

By 1802, many of the island's newspapers had again been destroyed or shut down. Leclerc began to publish an official paper, which often made its way into the United States. Wilson's correspondent from the "Ruins of Cape Francois" had included with one of his letters a printed proclamation from Leclerc's government that accused an American merchant ship of smuggling in gunpowder to aid Louverture's forces. The letter writer called this an "infamous falshood."[113] Thereafter American newspapers regularly featured material from Leclerc's press, much of which attacked the "villain" Louverture.[114] Indeed, Leclerc's printers seem to have kept an eye on American newspapers, perhaps hoping to shape their coverage of the invasion. In July 1802, for example, Wilson promised readers an upcoming pamphlet detailing the crimes and tyranny of Leclerc, including his permitting depredations on American commerce.[115] In response, the official paper in Saint Domingue, perhaps at Leclerc's direction, refuted Wilson's "malignant paragraphs" with data about American ship arrivals.[116] Other than Leclerc's reports, relatively little printed information from Saint Domingue appeared in US newspapers in the first years of the nineteenth century.

Beginning with the US embargo of France in 1798 and continuing into the early 1800s, American trade with Saint Domingue began a long, slow decline. During the French invasion in 1802, dozens of American ships were embargoed in Haitian ports for weeks or months at a time, further discouraging trade. After Haiti declared its independence in 1804, some Republican leaders in the US Congress sought to regulate, or even end, trade with the new nation. In 1806, they succeeded in passing a bill prohibiting trade with Haiti.[117] Trade thus dropped rapidly over the first decade of the nineteenth century. After several years with little contact or news, Haiti faded from Americans' attention.[118]

Americans invented their own versions of the Caribbean revolutions of the 1790s largely based on the media that they received through commercially oriented sources. But they also evaluated this news according to racist ideas about Black people's ability to organize revolution, their capacity for brutality, and their untrustworthiness. The result was a familiarly American kind of willful ignorance.

About a year after news of the Saint Domingue Constitution of 1801 arrived in the United States, the Virginia provocateur James Callender, who had recently disclosed President Thomas Jefferson's sexual relationship with Sally Hemings in his Richmond newspaper, wrote a lengthy essay decrying other printers' choice to share the new constitution. Amid rumors of France landing "Frigates from St. Domingo" full of "Brigand Negros" in the United States, Callender feared that any news or printed material might excite rebellion among the US South's enslaved population. Indeed, he worried that newspapers "crammed with the glory, the constitution, and the victories of Toussaint" had already incited Gabriel Prosser's conspiracy. He scolded Washington, DC, printer Samuel H. Smith, who had paid for the 1801 constitution's translation for his *National Intelligencer*, "and all the rest of our typographical brethren" for printing this "piece of trash." While other mediators had shared the news, he promised to exclude this sort of material from his paper: "No stuff of that sort, none of your encomiums upon emancipation shall ever pollute a press of ours."[119] An inveterate self-promoter, Callender portrayed himself as the sole principled printer who was willing to resist his readers' curiosity and withhold dangerous information.

Even as he attacked others for sharing materials printed by Louverture and his allies, Callender had come to depend on Leclerc's press for his news about Saint Domingue. He mocked his rival printers for sharing what he considered to be exaggerated accounts of the French army's difficulties. American publishers, he wrote, "have since killed LeClerc's army with the yellow fever. They have excited a fresh insurrection in St. Domingo, of all which we do not believe much more than one single word." His language choices, attributing causal agency to the newspapers themselves as conjurers of yellow fever and insurrection, were deliberately provocative, but they also expressed the view that the actions of information mediators shaped the destiny of revolutions. Callender, of course, was wrong about the facts. Leclerc's invasion of Saint Domingue resulted in Louverture's capture and eventual death, but his successor, Jean-Jacques Dessalines, aided by epidemic disease, expelled the French forces and declared the independence of the nation of Haiti on January 1, 1804. Ultimately, though, Callender was indifferent to the truth. As for the latest uprising in Saint Domingue, he explained, "whether it is true, or false, all such newspapers should be cast into the fire."[120]

How many other printers or news mediators suppressed or ignored important information about the revolutionary Caribbean? This question is impossible to answer because, unlike Callender, most of them did not proudly announce their intention to hide news. White US mediators' desire to avoid provoking an internal rebellion and their related racist assumptions about the political capacities of Black people living in the Caribbean surely led them to sometimes filter out news that recognized the revolutionary nature of these events. Yet Callender's kind of intervention was atypical because mediators rarely got a chance to engage with accounts from the Caribbean revolutionaries. Changing patterns of commerce, war, and print opened only two brief windows, from roughly 1791 through 1792 and from 1799 through 1801, when Americans could have expected to receive detailed printed news from Caribbean sources sympathetic to local revolutionaries. In the cases of Fédon's Rebellion, the Second Carib War, and revolutionary politics in Saint Lucia, Martinique, Guadeloupe, and other islands in the mid-1790s, Americans practically never encountered mediators supportive of the Caribbean's radical politics.

The difference between a meaningful revolution and a senseless revolt is largely a matter of narrative. Rebels committed acts of heinous violence during the American and French Revolutions, but they earned the label "revolutionaries" because they told a story of themselves that began in oppression, proceeded with resistance against the powerful, and ended in liberation. This narrative legitimized violence and disorder. Revolutionaries across the Caribbean could only rarely use print to record their ideas and politics and thereby shape the stories that outside observers used to understand them. Instead, for most of the 1790s and early 1800s, Americans examined Caribbean events only from an outsider's vantage. Because the travels and letters of merchants and sea captains provided the main sources in the United States about the revolutionary Caribbean, Americans learned more about consequences than causes. As in Jean-Louis Boquet's painting, they saw more violence and destruction than ideas and politics. In consequence, the revolutionary character of these events was unknowable to many white American observers, reinforced by and reinforcing the racist attitudes that made a Black revolution "unthinkable."

The Fruits of Revolution

False News and the Eclipse of the Federalists

In late 1798, the American ambassador in London, Rufus King, dispatched an urgent coded letter to the American secretary of state, Timothy Pickering. He had heard from a consul that "Matthew Salmon, a Mulatto, formerly a St. Domingo Representative in the Convention" would soon leave Hamburg with his wife and two accomplices. They were headed to Charleston, South Carolina, aboard a vessel called the *Minerva* with "Dispatches from the French Directoire concealed in tubs (cases) with false bottoms."[1] After he received this account, Pickering passed it on to Governor Edward Rutledge of South Carolina, who let it slip to the press. The *Minerva* was soon hotly expected in Charleston harbor. When the ship docked after a long passage, port officials arrested the conspirators, broke open their tubs, and discovered the papers. One newspaper described how the "horrors of guilt were depicted strongly on the countenances of the guilty wretches, and their bodies shook with fear and trembling."[2] Another paper announced that the conspirators had hoped to bring about "the conflagration of the city of Charleston, and an insurrection among the Blacks."[3]

Franco-American relations had become increasingly hostile in recent years, and an undeclared naval war and diplomatic ruptures had led many Americans to conclude that the French were practicing a campaign of deception. Here, it seemed, was confirmation that France was aiming to bring its bloody revolution to the United States. The smuggled papers were surely meant, as one observer put it, to "sow more sedition in this country."[4] If not for the vigilance of the government, one letter writer commented, "Throats might have been cut; Carnage and Devastation roaming thro' our Land, and our fair

City one Pile of Ruins."[5] Another worried that French agents sought to carry the "fate of St. Domingo" into America. Throughout this affair, public focus remained on the documents contained in the tubs' false bottoms. Were they dispatches from the French Directory to its agents in the United States? Were they pamphlets or broadsides intended to incite violence? Were they signs of France's "fraudulent arts"?[6]

How disappointing, then, when the tub tale washed out. Though the officials in charge did not publicize it, they quickly learned that the hidden papers were no threat. Sources disagreed about the contents of the letters, whether they were about love or commerce or family matters.[7] Privately, Pickering conceded that "instead of being agents of the Directory," the travelers "probably consider the French government as hostile to the interest of the people of colour and the blacks of St. Domingo."[8] There was reason to believe that the travelers' aim was not to create a revolution in Charleston but instead to join in the revolution already under way in Saint Domingue.

This story appeared around the same time as two other lurid false stories about French aggression. The first account concerned an American ship called the *Ocean*, which reportedly was seized by the French, who massacred its passengers. This story must have been quite a surprise to the *Ocean*'s sailors when they arrived unharmed in Baltimore. A second conspiracy theory, the "Tailor Plot," held that a busy tailor shop in Philadelphia was sewing uniforms for a French invasion force. In fact, the tailors were working under a commission for Toussaint Louverture's army in Saint Domingue.[9] These false accounts spread according to observers' political preferences. To the Federalists, the French wolf was howling at the door. For Republicans, though, their rivals were "cry[ing] wolves so often . . . they will not be believed when danger is really at hand."[10]

During their imperial crisis and revolutionary war, American colonists had also worried about false news and misperceptions. In response to the apparent deception of British mediators, Patriot leaders pushed for more democratic and public forms of information exchange. The result of this was an increasingly plural marketplace of information, plump with contradictions and falsehoods. Louis XVI was dead—and he was alive. A Prussian army had ended the Dutch Patriot Revolt—and the Dutch had defeated them. The tub was a Trojan horse—and it was a well-flogged dead horse. Who had spread such lies? Although some of them were probably harmless errors—mistaken rumors or misinterpreted details—North Americans usually assumed that false news was the product of deception. Contradiction required villains.

While the crisis of false news in the 1760s and 1770s seemed to reveal the limitations of monarchical and imperial rule, the crises of the 1790s led many Americans to question the foundations of more democratic notions of truth and, indeed, the epistemic foundations of the US republic more generally. Truth seemed to be endangered. To protect it, Federalist leaders embarked on a campaign to regulate falsehood. Identifying error with French artifice, they sought to exclude news arriving from Saint Domingue and France. While observers had once sought news from France as an alternative to prejudiced British accounts, over the course of the 1790s, many Americans came to view French news as a threat to US sovereignty. They sought out deceivers everywhere: in the streets, in printing offices, and in town assemblies. But the most well-known measures to restrain falsehoods occurred at the national level, where Federalist leaders passed the infamous Alien and Sedition Acts in 1798.

In popular memory as well as in many scholarly accounts, the Alien and Sedition Acts appear to be little more than a power grab by Federalist elites seeking to limit criticism and suppress dangerous ideas.[11] This narrative, though, forgets an important element of the broader context surrounding this legislation. Like their counterparts in the governments of Canada and Louisiana, Federalists believed that truth was vulnerable to an unrestrained flow of foreign news and that falsehoods were corrosive to the integrity and stability of government (see chapter 6). For Congressman James Otis, it seemed that the "press is the engine which is probably destined to overturn the Government of this country."[12] The only way to protect the nation from itself, or so it seemed, was to lay a heavy hand on the mediation of information.

As the Federalists' critics understood, whoever controlled the news set the boundaries of politics. A government regulating truth, then, would inevitably enforce a reality consistent with the perpetuation of its own power. According to Republicans, popular government therefore required an open, disputatious politics of information. In response to the Sedition Act, they argued for a legal order that prevented any restraint of information exchange. With few exceptions, they triumphed—and they were rewarded with decades of dispute. This clash between proper and promiscuous speech, between restrained and free information, has never been resolved. Who, after all, can be trusted to regulate truth? This remains an open question. Americans today, in some ways, are still living through the backlash to the Sedition Act.

In 1793, President George Washington had declared that the United States would remain neutral in the wars between revolutionary France and most of

Europe. Yet that was never really an option. Both Britain and France seized US ships carrying commodities that might have fed their enemies, forcing Americans to either join the war or negotiate a solution. The Jay Treaty, signed in late 1794 and effective in early 1796, ended both British depredations of American commerce and French hopes for an American ally. The treaty controversially brought the United States closer to Britain while alienating France. By 1797, France's leadership had become hostile toward the United States. With this diplomatic fissure, some Americans now feared that French information sources had been corrupted. "It is well known that the presses in France are under the immediate controul of the *Directory*, and its Ministers," charged one Federalist printer.[13] For a New York preacher, commercial intercourse between the two nations seemed to be bringing "evil communication" to American shores.[14]

To avoid further conflict, the president sent Charles Cotesworth Pinckney to Paris to find a solution. Just as tensions escalated, however, Washington relinquished the office to John Adams, who soon learned that France had refused to acknowledge Pinckney as ambassador. One of Adams's first actions as president was to send Elbridge Gerry and John Marshall to join Pinckney to resolve the crisis.[15] Talks dragged on for some time, but in March 1798 Adams received a series of dispatches from the envoys narrating the negotiations with several representatives of the French Directory. Speaking for French foreign minister Charles Maurice de Talleyrand-Périgord, a person named Pierre Bellamy had demanded that the Americans provide a sizable bribe as well as a loan for France. When the envoys protested, Bellamy haughtily explained that it was the best offer they could get. If they didn't take it, he claimed, France would wield its influence in the United States to blame the Federalists for the breakdown in relations: "you ought to know that the diplomatic skill of France and the means she possesses in your country, are sufficient to enable her, with the French party in America, to throw the blame which will attend the rupture of the negociations on the Federalists."[16] The envoys gave up and composed their account to the president. After some debate, Adams sent the dispatches to Congress with the names of the French diplomats redacted. They were labeled "X," "Y," and "Z."

It was unclear at first if the dispatches would have much of an impact. France and the United States had weathered several recent diplomatic disasters: Edmond-Charles Genêt's tumultuous tenure as ambassador from France in 1793, the embargo of American ships in Bordeaux from September 1793 through March 1794, an explosive intercepted letter of French minister Jean

Antoine Joseph Fauchet that became public in late 1794, and ambassador Pierre-Auguste Adet's efforts to tamper with the election of 1796. Each of these incidents had provoked outrage, but each had also failed to fundamentally change Americans' beliefs about revolutionary France. For many, it seemed that the XYZ affair would follow the same path of dimming outrage. "The information from our Commissioners is unpleasant, but not alarming," Republican printer Thomas Adams claimed. "All that we know now, we knew before."[17] Some Republicans simply dismissed the "trivial and uninteresting" dispatches.[18] The *Farmers' Register*, a Republican paper in rural Pennsylvania, declined to reprint the entirety of the dispatches, citing their "unnecessary formality and repetition" and fearing that to give so much space to them might "be a mean of excluding other important articles."[19] Republican printer Benjamin Franklin Bache shared this opinion. When he abstracted the dispatches for his readers, he asserted that they merely related to "informal conferences held by unofficial agents of the department of foreign affairs with our commissioners."[20] As a result, they could not offer any insight into the intentions of the French Directory. Republican leader Thomas Jefferson privately concurred that "the XYZ dish cooked up by Marshall" had allowed a group of "swindlers" to "appear as the French government." As a result of the Federalists' "art and industry," he complained, the people "have been astonished more than they have understood it."[21]

In a debate about the number of copies that the House of Representatives should print of the dispatches, arch-Republican Matthew Lyon suggested a high number because he felt that the papers were "so trifling and unimportant, that no printer would risk the printing of them in a pamphlet." Massachusetts Federalist Harrison Gray Otis was so taken aback by this comment that he halted debate to ask Lyon to repeat it.[22] But a few weeks earlier, Otis had privately expressed some reservations about the dispatches' impact on the public: they might "electrise the whole American people" or they could "demonstrate such an utter prostration of national spirit & honor as would shew all hopes of resistance to be vain."[23]

Since contemporaries did not agree that a backlash to the XYZ dispatches was inevitable, the dramatic impact of the incident requires some explanation. It owed much to the dispatches' form. While the regular stream of oral, printed, and handwritten news left room for controversy, private details about a secret negotiation seemed singularly persuasive. Fatigued by years of uncertain accounts, many readers experienced the dispatches as a "light of truth" breaking "from the thick clouds in which party has involved it as clear as the sun."[24] For one writer, they established "strong FACTS . . . which none can deny!"[25] Federalist printer William Cobbett rejoiced in the incontrovertibility of the information, which left his rivals "no hole to creep out."[26] Mediators expected that the dispatches would convert the "honest man who has been mislead by false information" and would silence the "uninformed and unreasonably impassioned."[27] Republicans who attempted to discredit the dispatches had little success. A writer in the Republican *Time Piece* charged that the dispatches had been "fabricated by Porcupine [Cobbett] and his gang."[28] There was no evidence for this, except the redaction of the French diplomats' names. Most agreed that the idea "that the dispatches are fabricated, is too silly to gain the least credit."[29]

When Republicans offered summaries or abstracts, Federalists accused their enemies of playing tricks to mislead readers "by omitting many material parts of the dispatches, and giving other parts a false coloring."[30] Fearful of partial accounts, Federalist mediators recommended that observers read the dispatches for themselves.[31] One printer dramatically encouraged readers to "never lose, nor for a moment mislay, these papers. Meditate on them through the labours of the day, and let them be the first thing that revisit your mind when you awake from your nightly slumbers."[32] Some Federalist printers filled their columns with the dispatches, suspending other news and even advertisements.[33] For those who lived outside the cities where observers encountered print most easily, one commentator proposed that preachers read the dispatches from their pulpits.[34]

While mediators could cloud most reports from Europe with alternative accounts, the dispatches seemed to stand alone. Republicans who were accustomed to a plural information landscape expected to quickly hear a rebuttal to the reports. Republican printer Thomas Adams, for example, counseled his readers to "wait for Mr. Talleyrand's reply" to the US commissioners before deciding what was true.[35] In the contradiction-fueled politics of the 1790s, this was a sensible suggestion. But the idea of seeking out a French perspective had come to seem treasonous to Adams's fierce local rival Benjamin Russell, who predicted that Adams's comments "will not much longer be borne; the eyes of the people are opening—instead of viewing such writers as composing a discontented faction . . . they must, e're long be known as traitors— since they openly side with those who are now the avowed enemies of their country."[36] For Russell, the act of seeking information directly from France was disloyal, a betrayal of the United States.

Yet as Adams hoped, Talleyrand had written a reply. It took too long to arrive in the United States, though, to effectively dampen the backlash to the dispatches. The first American newspaper to publish it was Bache's Republican *Aurora General Advertiser*.[37] In the firestorm of Federalist censure that followed, Russell's warning seemed prophetic. Among many others, Federalist representative George Thatcher accused Bache of being a French agent who had published Talleyrand's response "by order of the Executive Directory."[38] Others emphasized that Bache was not only a servant of France but also a traitor to the United States for printing Talleyrand's rebuttal.[39] Several claimed that Talleyrand had not realized that the envoys had already sent their dispatches and intended his account not as a response, but as a way to "get the start" on them.[40] In the Federalist *Gazette of the United States*, "Junius" deduced that Talleyrand sought to "surprise the people and government of the United States . . . long before a reply could be furnished." This would be a poison to "divide the people and weaken their opposition to French aggressions" without the "antidote of our Envoy's reply." This author believed that luck had thwarted this scheme because the ship carrying Talleyrand's letter had taken a "providential long passage" across the Atlantic while the ship carrying the envoys' message had zipped across the ocean.[41] Another commentator likewise suggested that Talleyrand had sent a translated version of his letter to Bache "in order to circulate the poison without its antidote."[42] Poisons and antidotes had become common tropes in Federalists' rhetoric as they came to see information flowing from France as not only false but harmful.[43]

To Federalists and other suspicious observers, Bache's publication of Talleyrand's letter suggested that the French Directory was employing Republican newspaper printers to hide their evil intentions. Some claimed that Talleyrand had sent his letter directly to Bache, and a number of travelers testified that they had seen a letter for Bache with Talleyrand's seal aboard a ship.[44] Bache protested his innocence and asserted that the US government had received Talleyrand's letter but had suppressed it.[45] He insisted that a "gentleman of this city" had provided him with his copy and that he had received no such letter directly from France and certainly none with the French minister's seal. But if a letter meeting that description had been sent, he suspected that it would have come from an acquaintance of his, a "Citizen Pechon," who worked in France's office of foreign affairs. Bache went to great lengths to prove his innocence by printing statements from the man who had taken the letter with Talleyrand's seal from the ship to the post office and from his letter carrier. He even made a sworn statement before the city's mayor.[46]

Eventually, though, Bache did receive a belated letter with Talleyrand's seal and opened it in front of witnesses to find an unrelated pamphlet authored by Pechon.[47] Bache collected evidence of his innocence into a pamphlet titled *Truth Will Out!* to clear his name.[48] Federalists remained unconvinced, of course, and their most reliable provocateur, William Cobbett, responded with a handbill titled *The Detection of Bache*. In it, he quoted one of the letter's carriers who, probably eager to settle questions of his own innocence, suggested that Bache was Talleyrand's tool.[49] In an echo of the 1770s, Federalists insisted that their rivals were tools of a European power.

Talleyrand's letter was just the sort of information that Republicans would have hoped for. He described the Directory's "conciliatory dispositions" while painting the envoys' account of events as "partial and incorrect." After listing France's grievances, he claimed to be "ready to discuss them in the most amicable manner" and charged that the envoys had been unwilling to bring this about.[50] This letter muddied the waters and raised questions about the reliability of the envoys' account. In years past, Republicans had often shared the French perspective whenever possible, usually as a point of contrast with distrusted British news sources. Yet during the XYZ affair, Talleyrand's letter was pitted not against a narrative spun by the despised British ministry, but against the account of a bipartisan group of three well-known American gentlemen.

The dispatches also sparked indignation in part because they spoke to existing concerns about falsehood and foreign news. Though it was not explicitly stated, many observers interpreted Bellamy's reference to France's "diplomatic skill" and the "French party" to mean that France was engaged in a campaign of deception in the United States. Bellamy probably did not intend to suggest that France controlled or even directed a "French party" in the United States. Indeed, he followed this point by referring to the Federalists as "the British party, as France terms you," suggesting that he was employing the adjectives "French" and "British" to refer to the parties' sympathies, as Americans had long done, rather than revealing French state secrets about their origin.[51] Nevertheless, many observers inferred that Bellamy was admitting that France was determining what information Americans received.[52] Federalist congressman John Allen, for example, claimed on the floor of the House of Representatives that Bache's newspaper was "the fruits of 'the diplomatic skill of France'—these are the effects of her 'means'—these are the efforts of 'her party in this country.' "[53]

A stream of reports from abroad indicated that deception was one of the essential weapons in France's expansionist arsenal. France's military successes against the First Coalition of European powers brought new territorial gains in the late 1790s as the French Directory installed friendly governments in the Netherlands and Switzerland. Some viewed these events as evidence of a nation bent on "universal domination."[54] They believed that France had "seduced, oppressed, and destroyed" these nations by sowing division and discord in order to ease their absorption into the French empire.[55] According to a Charleston writer, these countries had tasted the "bitter fruits of Jacobinical seeds, which were sowed by democrats and demagogues."[56] The French seemed to consistently precede their invasions with propaganda campaigns to soften opposition and bolster allies' positions. Since the "grossest falsehoods, the blackest deceptions, the most artful persuasions, the most alluring promises" had been used to "seduce" the Swiss to France's cause, orator Zechariah Lewis asked, "Shall we blindly credit the sincerity of their professions?"[57] That other nations had fallen to French invasions after imbibing French lies offered a powerful warning for Americans. Accounts from France were not simply news but rather the vanguard of an invading force, the spear tip of a "Reign of Terror and Seduction."[58]

Inflamed Federalist fears of French infidelity had an immediate impact on the Boston preacher and cartographer Jedidiah Morse. In earlier years, Morse had distinguished himself as an apologist for revolutionary France. When the French nation took a more radical and violent course beginning in 1793, Morse repeatedly assured his congregants that the cause remained "unquestionably good" despite some "errors and irregularities." Whatever violence was taking place in France was no more than Americans had practiced "at the height of our revolution."[59] Even in private correspondence, where Morse had no need to appease an audience of parishioners, he displayed genuine trust in the French Revolution.[60] By 1796, as several New England preachers began to turn against the revolution, Morse complained in a letter that "very few of the clergy in the circle of my acquaintance seem disposed to pray for the success of the French."[61]

This all changed for Morse in April 1798. He happened to be traveling through Philadelphia when the XYZ dispatches were released to the public, and he witnessed the uproar that they caused firsthand. By coincidence, in the middle of that month, Philadelphia printer Thomas Dobson published the first American edition of Scottish academic John Robison's book *Proofs of a Conspiracy*.[62] Hearing "men of judgment" speak of the work, Morse brought a copy home with him to Boston.[63] Morse had heard rumors about a secret society called the Illuminati a year earlier, but Robison's book described this conspiracy in great detail.[64] It claimed, among other things, that the godless Illuminati had plotted the French Revolution and aimed to transform the press to serve its nefarious purposes.[65] Though written in an entirely different context, Robison's account of the secret society suited the mood of Federalists in the spring of 1798 as their suspicions escalated about apparently corrupt mediators such as Bache.

On May 9, Morse mounted his pulpit and shared Robison's fantastic account of this antireligious group. He also added some of his own flourishes, contending that the Illuminati had begun to spread the "bitter fruit" of their conspiracy into the United States.[66] By extending Robison's account, he incited what historians have called the "New England Illuminati scare."[67] This panic drew on the anxiety about information flows that the XYZ dispatches had provoked. Indeed, Morse admitted that his claims would have likely been dismissed if not for the publication of the dispatches.[68] Morse and his acolytes argued that the Illuminati had plotted the violent, radical, and irreligious French Revolution and had practiced "concealing or disguising the truth, and propagating falsehoods."[69]

The idea of an international secret society conspiring against the truth proved irresistible to observers, such as Morse, who had formerly been keen supporters of revolutionary France. The conspiracy absolved them of any guilt for failing to see the revolution's shortcomings years earlier and, in Morse's case, for going well out of his way to extenuate unpleasant reports about the French. Now confident of revolutionary France's deceptiveness, antiradical activists read this back into earlier stages of the revolution. "Judging from the fruits of the French revolution," Morse argued, "it must have had an impure origin."[70] His logic was simple: pure seeds did not beget foul fruit, and a genuinely republican revolution could not have created a government that would extort US envoys, seize neutral ships, and use hidden agents to deceive the American public. To say otherwise was to indict the republican revolution that Americans thought of themselves as having inherited. Critics claimed that sympathetic news about France's republicanism in the early 1790s must have been lies carefully orchestrated by deceptive conspirators. As a preacher, Morse's choice of the word "fruits" reflected his concern with deception. The often-quoted verses of Matthew 7:15–16 instruct Christians to guard against "false prophets" and wolves in sheep's clothing: "By their fruits shall ye know them."

Though some scholars have dismissed the Illuminati scare as delusional or irrational, it was in many ways consistent with the broader context of US information politics.[71] The Illuminati conspiracy gave a name and face to the otherwise ill-defined fear about deception that the XYZ dispatches had inaugurated. Morse's sermon invoked the dispatches on several occasions as evidence of a conspiracy to confuse and divide the American people.[72] Those who believed his charges imagined that the Illuminati controlled important streams of communication. Ten days after Morse's speech, Cobbett claimed that the Illuminati and the Jacobins were responsible for slowing down his newspapers in transit to readers across the continent.[73] Others alleged that the Illuminati had targeted American "printers, journalists, and booksellers," hoping to shape the media that readers consumed.[74]

It was clear to many observers that the Illuminati had succeeded in duping Americans for years. In a 1799 oration, for example, William Brown described how Americans had long labored under the "fatal delusion" that the French Revolution's violence was simply a necessary by-product of a struggle against despotism. Now they saw this delusion as the will of the Illuminati, who had used the "weapons of sophistry" to put "truth . . . to flight." But finally the "dark mist" of deception by the "industrious votaries of anarchy and confusion" had been "dissipated by the light of historic truth."[75] Other observers regarded the Illuminati in theological terms. Elijah Parish, for example, saw them as a fulfillment of the Book of Revelation—the "spontaneous fruit" of Satan, who would fight God "by intrigue, by deceit," and in an echo of the dispatches, "by 'skill.' "[76]

In response to these provocations, hundreds of town assemblies in the United States drafted loyalty addresses to President Adams and gathered signatures to support them. These statements generally claimed that their citizens had been deceived into supporting France. An address in Dedham, for example, commented that France had "practiced amongst us a successful imposture" by pretending to be seekers of liberty, which had provoked a general "delusion." It seemed extraordinary in retrospect that this "political misinformation" had led many of their community to "have believed, that France" had "enjoyed liberty" under the revolutionary regime. An assembly of citizens in Newark, New Jersey, told Adams, "The delusions and misrepresentations, which have misled so many citizens, are very serious evils" and recommended that the falsehoods be "discountenanced by authority, as well as by the citizens at large, or they will soon produce all kinds of calamities in this country." A contingent of Vermont petitioners blamed "the exertions of dangerous and misleading men" for "misleading the understandings of our well-meaning citizens." Many blamed the deception on "factious and designing men," "foreign intrigue," and the "deceptive arts" of France's allies. They also accepted that falsehoods traveled both ways. When William Austin printed a collection of hundreds of these popular addresses in 1798, he sarcastically dedicated the volume to the French Directory. Addressing the Directory, Austin explained that the volume would "undeceive them" of the "clouds of error" about the United States that they had encountered through the "false insinuations of your agents."[77]

Most addresses explained that their towns had come to see the error of their ways and now rejected such falsehoods.[78] An assembly in Cambridge, Massachusetts, described how the XYZ dispatches had awakened the "public mind" from "partial and erroneous conceptions," which had led the people to "an honest, but misguided attachment to the French nation." Providence residents noted that while many Americans had been lulled into the "dangerous mistake" of attaching themselves to France, "the scales have now fallen from their eyes."[79] If misinformation had caused political dissent, the petitioners asserted, the XYZ dispatches had put an end to such false news and allowed for the creation of a consensus. Yet such pretensions to harmony masked a significant amount of continued dissent.[80] Some refused to endorse the addresses. One Republican, for example, complained about the "tricks which were used to *co-erce* the citizens" into signing the petitions. He described how one Federalist threatened to add the names of those who refused to sign to an undefined "black list."[81]

The XYZ disclosures, the Talleyrand letter, and the Illuminati conspiracy theory had stoked popular outrage against French deception. Even if these addresses only truly represented a portion of the public, they led sympathetic leaders to conclude that the people at large had risen to reject falsehoods. The next step would be government action. The prominent jurist Alexander Addison urged Americans to "silence slanderers, and set our faces against them. We have seen the sad effects, and the gross misrepresentations of those lying newspapers, lying pamphlets, lying letters, and lying conversations, with which the country has been filled."[82] Deception even seemed to threaten the continued existence of governments. Federalist Stephen Higginson wrote to Secretary of State Timothy Pickering that the "Seditions, conspiracies, seductions, and all the Arts which the french use to fraternise and overturn nations, must be guarded against by strong and specific Acts of Congress."[83] In response to an address from the people of Harrisburg, Pennsylvania, President Adams likewise expressed hope that the United States would "have the glory of arresting this torrent of error," and he promised to confront the information flows that had produced so much misperception.[84]

In the summer of 1798, the US Congress responded to this outcry by creating a series of bills known as the Alien and Sedition Acts. The Sedition Act was crafted according to English common-law principles that empowered the government to define what was truthful and to punish falsehood. It also drew on colonial precedents. In the seventeenth century, Maryland, Virginia, South Carolina, Massachusetts, Pennsylvania, and New York had defined false news as a punishable form of seditious speech.[85] While these laws largely fell out of force during the eighteenth century, the principles behind them remained uncontroversial. Even with the passage of the First Amendment to the US Constitution, which guaranteed no abridgment of free speech or the free press, few imagined that a geyser of falsehoods should go unplugged. It was not unusual for American elites to propose, as Thomas Jefferson did in 1783, that presses should have "no other restraint than liableness to legal prosecution for false facts printed and published."[86]

As Congress crafted it, the sedition law provided fines and imprisonment for those who would "write, print, utter or publish" any "false, scandalous and malicious writing or writings against the government of the United States."[87] Aiming to extirpate pernicious falsehoods, it provided that defendants under this law could be acquitted if they could prove to a jury that their statements were true. The act's supporters targeted, among other forms of speech, foreign news that cast the US government in a poor light. During the congressional debate, one of the law's most vocal proponents, Federalist congressman John Allen, gave a fiery speech that included excerpts from Bache's *Aurora*, which he claimed were intended to convince Americans that the French desired peace and prosperity in their diplomacy with the United States. A sedition law was necessary, he argued, because a group of conspirators sought to persuade the public of "certain facts" that Congress, whose members had read the XYZ dispatches, "kn[e]w to be unfounded." At the speech's climax, he thundered, "God deliver us from such liberty, the liberty of vomiting on the public floods of falsehood."[88]

The Federalists believed that those who perpetuated falsehoods that could destabilize the government must be punished. While the US republic had escaped the need for such regulation for a few years, French duplicity made it immediately necessary. Congressman Robert Goodloe Harper commented that every day he saw more evidence of this conspiracy of deception and "stronger indications of its systematic exertion."[89] Truth, as Federalists understood it, was the foundation of all order. But truth was also weak and easily destroyed. At the sedition trial of Pennsylvania printer Thomas Cooper, the prosecutor argued that falsehoods led people to be "less informed," which could lead the "peace of the country" to "be endangered." Unchecked falsehoods could bring an end to government: "Error leads to discontent, discontent to a fancied idea of oppression, and that to insurrection."[90] Whether it was an insult to John Adams or a letter from France, a statement of opinion or a statement of fact, anything false that sapped the strength of the political order was seditious.

Republican leaders, by contrast, pointed out that political speech was not always falsifiable. The Republicans' leader in the House of Representatives, Albert Gallatin, believed that by defining uncongenial opinions as falsehoods, the Federalists would "suffer the people at large to hear only partial accounts, and but one side of the question; to delude and deceive them by partial information, and, through those means, to perpetuate themselves in power." If the bill passed, Gallatin feared, the Federalist authorities would "punish printers who may publish against them, whilst their opponents will remain alone . . . exposed to the abuse of Ministerial prints."[91] Employing the decades-old trope of "Ministerial prints," Gallatin evoked a long-standing fear of government-aligned newspapers.

On July 14, 1798, the ninth anniversary of the revolutionary seizure of the Bastille, President John Adams signed the Sedition Act into law. Government officials brought forward seventeen indictments before the act's expiration two years later. Many of these focused simply on dissent against the Adams administration in print, in private letters, and even in drunken conversation.[92] As Gallatin understood, there was a thin line between falsehoods and unpopular opinions. Several of the prosecutions, however, focused on restraining the flow of false news. The member of the executive branch who was most involved in prosecutions was Secretary of State Pickering. He was an uncompromising enforcer, the sort of person who, as one biographer described, was insulted by the idea that "there are two sides to every question. . . . There was right and wrong, and the eternal battle between them; there could be nothing else."[93] Pickering set to work closing off American information sources from what he viewed as deceptive foreign interference.

In response to the Sedition Act, Federalist news mediators were careful to only share information from French sources as evidence of "French Art, Impudence, and Villainy."[94] When Boston Federalist printer Benjamin Russell received a collection of French newspapers in August 1798, for example, he urged his readers to remember that because "all the newspapers are under the immediate controul of the Directory's minions, their contents must be considered as most favorable to the views of those Tyrants of mankind." The "present 'gag state' of the papers" in France meant that any printed news originating from there was suspect. He even placed a paragraph that claimed President John Adams had recalled the US envoy in Paris under the heading "A French Lie."[95] A few weeks later, Russell alleged that the French papers had not published the XYZ dispatches, which seemed to be "no small evidence of guilt," though it was unsurprising given that the French presses "are under the immediate controul of the *Directory*."[96]

The most obvious target of the Sedition Act was Benjamin Franklin Bache. His decision to publish Talleyrand's letter just as Congress was considering the new legislation galvanized support for the law. Indeed, Federalist authorities were so eager to use the law against him that they arrested him on common-law charges of sedition before the act officially went into effect. Bache died of yellow fever in prison before he could be tried in court, so it is uncertain what charges he might have faced. Yet because he was arrested only ten days after publishing the Talleyrand letter, it is fair to assume that prosecutors planned to punish him for sharing information from France.[97]

The Irish-born Vermont congressman and printer Matthew Lyon was among the first to be prosecuted under the new sedition law. Lyon's indictment charged him with publishing a "letter from an American diplomatic character in France" in September 1798.[98] This letter, written from Paris by American expatriate Joel Barlow just after the US envoys had been rejected by the French Directory, argued that the diplomatic rupture between the two nations was as much the fault of the Americans as the Directory. Like Talleyrand's missive, the letter from Barlow summarized France's perspective on the diplomatic fallout of early 1798.[99] Though Barlow's letter was focused primarily on providing information about France's attitudes toward the United States, a Vermont jury deemed it to be seditious because it cast the executive of the United States in a negative light.

Federalists believed that Lyon and his allies were coordinating with the French to sow sedition and lies. Toward the end of 1798, an advertisement for a "Runaway" appeared in the Vermont *Rutland Herald*. While notices that sought to recapture self-emancipated people were a fixture of many states' newspapers, Vermont had never had a substantial population of enslaved people and had begun to emancipate its small enslaved population more than twenty years earlier. Advertisements for self-emancipated enslaved people were therefore unusual in the Vermont press. But the mystery of this novelty would have been revealed to readers when they reached the name of this "runaway": the "citizen servant" Nathan Durkee, an ally to Lyon. In one of the many political tussles that seemed vivid and essential in their moment but have been subsequently forgotten, Federalists had accused Durkee of spreading falsehoods about Lyon's opponents and about an affair of honor in which Lyon was involved.[100] According to the runaway advertisement, Durkee had last been seen wearing a "French Cap of liberty" and leading a horse "loaded with pamphlets replete with electioneering lies." The reward for his return? A "commission from the Directory of the terrible Republic to burn his neighbor's barn" or "cut down his apple Trees." The satirical notice's punchline was the name of the advertiser: "TALLEYRAND."[101] This advertisement suggested that Talleyrand was using Lyon and his allies to spread untruths to benefit the Republican Party. If this piece of satire was funny to its audience, it was probably because of the implication that Durkee and Lyon belonged to Talleyrand and the French government as totally as a servant belonged to his employer.

Like Lyon, Boston printers and brothers Thomas Adams and Abijah Adams, who published the Republican *Independent Chronicle*, faced sedition charges for sharing foreign news that Federalist authorities deemed untrue. In addition to two counts for criticizing the John Adams administration, Thomas Adams faced prosecution for refuting the Federalist narrative of the XYZ affair. He contended that the US envoys had been dealing with British and Dutch officials. Using common-law precedents rather than the Sedition Act, the state of Massachusetts also indicted both Abijah and Thomas Adams for essays that they had published criticizing the Alien and Sedition Acts. Thomas Adams died before these trials could be held, but Abijah Adams was convicted, fined, and imprisoned for thirty days.[102]

A few years later, when Congress debated renewing the Sedition Act, Republican representative Joseph Nicholson of Maryland made a veiled reference to Thomas Adams, a "printer, who died in prison, where he lay convicted under that law." Federalist John Rutledge of South Carolina (the governor's brother) attempted to correct Nicholson, pointing out that Adams had faced charges from the state of Massachusetts under the common law rather than under the terms of the Sedition Act. He further contended that the printer was still alive, though he was thinking of Abijah rather than Thomas Adams. The next day, Massachusetts Federalist Harrison Gray Otis clarified the matter by distinguishing between the brothers and their cases. He argued, however, that the confusion was instructive: "What plainer evidence can you have to prove that these outrageous falsehoods do not merely waste their force upon the desert air?" If "men in important public stations" like themselves were confused about a printer's prosecution when "all the avenues of intelligence are open," then what could be expected from the "gaping and promiscuous crowd"?[103] The lawmakers' errors became further evidence of the law's necessity.

Along with the Sedition Act, the US Congress had passed two laws regulating the movement of "aliens" into and within the nation. Targeting the numerous Republican printers who had been born abroad, these laws allowed the president to expel foreigners whom he had "reasonable grounds to suspect are concerned in any treasonable or secret machinations against the government."[104] The acts also required that ship captains disclose any aliens they were bringing into an American port. But they were hardly enforced. Their most significant impact was in pushing radical and prorevolutionary immigrants from Ireland and France to leave of their own accord rather than risk prosecution and deportation.[105]

The Federalists' campaign against falsehoods and French news resembled in many ways the efforts by the imperial governments of Louisiana and Canada to control foreign information streams. As chapter 6 shows, Canadians similarly formed popular associations to reject French lies, and the government passed laws to crack down on sedition and "alien" residents. Likewise, the Louisiana government intrusively policed oral communication and deported foreigners. While there is no evidence that the leaders of the United States took inspiration from their continental counterparts, they relied on a remarkably similar set of tactics. Indeed, across North America, governments and elite leaders had come to accept that ordinary people could not be trusted to discern truth on their own.

While Americans had once accepted that truth inevitably emerged from the contest among all kinds of information, some now worried that deception was more powerful than honesty. In the 1801 debate over the renewal of the Sedition Act, Delaware Federalist James Bayard rebutted those who believed that the "good sense of the people" allowed them to detect "false publications." Even "the most intelligent," he pointed out, "are deceived" by unfounded information.[106] This attitude resembled that held by British colonial leaders in the 1760s, who believed that the people could not be trusted to mediate foreign news. The information politics of recent years, which had been both chaotic and democratic, seemed to prove that.

Whether or not this position was correct, it proved to be very unpopular. Anticipating the outbreak of violence with France at any moment, many Federalists had imagined the Alien and Sedition Acts to be wartime measures. But the conflict never came. While Americans might have accepted an abridgment of liberties during wartime, in peacetime such measures looked more like an "insidious artifice" to protect Federalist power.[107] The state legislatures of Virginia and Kentucky passed resolutions declaring the laws null and void within their borders. The backlash against the Sedition Act was centered around a new "libertarian" view of speech and falsehood, which insisted that with few exceptions, governments should simply stay out of the business of determining what sorts of news were true and leave it to participants in civil society and the public sphere.[108] According to these critics, it was impossible to restrain the "licentiousness" of the press without also abridging the liberty of the press.

One of the most important articulators of these ideas was New York Republican politician and lawyer Tunis Wortman. In his 1800 work, *A Treatise concerning Political Enquiry, and the Liberty of the Press*, Wortman mocked Federalists as "advocates of mystery" who believed that it was the "eternal destiny of the human species to be governed by the delusion of their senses, and not by the conviction of their understanding." To Wortman, the Federalists' language resembled that of the despots who cared more for their own power than for the "improvement of society." He believed, though, that "opposite opinions" had led Americans to collect and distribute facts that led them toward "many invaluable pages of the important volume of truth." Why then should the government restrain popular participation in the production of knowledge? Why should there be a "forbidden tree of knowledge, the fruit of which it is sacrilegious to touch?"[109]

Wortman's book echoed the information script, suggesting that the ultimate cause of arbitrary and despotic government was "ignorance and the imposture which it nourishes." The obvious "antidote" to ignorance was the "progress of information." A sentence later, though, Wortman switched nouns, arguing that "Knowledge is therefore a more powerful corrective than coercion." This linguistic slippage between information and knowledge, treating them as synonyms, was at the heart of libertarian critique. Libertarians argued that ordinary people could transform information into knowledge, whereas Federalists believed that an abundance of contradictory information inhibited the production of meaningful knowledge. Wortman optimistically suggested that disputed inquiry "corrects our errors, removes our prejudices, and strengthens our perceptions; it compels us to seek for the evidences of our knowledge, and habituates us to a frequent revisal of our sentiments." Like the proponents of an open press decades earlier, libertarians believed that the "energies of Truth" would inevitably overcome falsehood.[110]

Wortman was not alone. Writers John Thomson and George Hay, among others, wrote similar tracts at about the same time.[111] According to the emerging libertarian consensus, there could be no harm in any kind of publication. If someone shared claims that were true, then "their circulation will be beneficial: if they are false, it will be the means of destroying them."[112] If only.

While libertarians agreed with the information script's essential premise that information defeated despotism, they rejected the notion that truth led to revolution. In fact, Wortman insisted that a free flow of information actually forestalled revolution by preventing the evils of misgovernment.[113] Libertarian Thomas Cooper argued that an open exchange of ideas and information had not caused the French Revolution, but rather would have prevented it if such a condition had existed in prerevolutionary France.[114] The despotism that the libertarians imagined was not so much that of centuries-old absolute rulers but rather that of creeping authoritarianism within popular government.

Although these writers aimed to prevent revolution, they arguably contributed to one. Popular opposition to the Sedition Act combined with the rising tide of libertarian sentiment helped to carry the Republican opposition into national power for the first time. The election of 1800, or the "Revolution of 1800" as it is sometimes known, marked the ascendance of libertarian thought. While the administration of President Thomas Jefferson occasionally prosecuted its enemies for seditious libel, by the beginning of the nineteenth century, Americans' expectations about truth and regulation had begun to change decisively.[115] With the exception of imminently dangerous speech, especially during wartime, Americans have generally taken an expansive view of their rights to free speech and held a tolerant attitude toward falsehood. This outlook has long been premised on the optimistic—some would say naïve—view that truth is resilient while falsehood is weak and harmless. Modern discourse has updated libertarian views with the neoliberal idiom of a "marketplace" of information whose invisible hand pushes errors to the margins and raises truth to the fore.

Yet with the benefit of hindsight, these hopes have proven to be largely delusive. The outcome of truth's contest with falsehood has never been inevitable. Although it mostly has excluded the government from the process of regulating truthfulness, the libertarian approach to speech has allowed powerful institutions, elites, corporations, and social groups to define dangerous speech, promote information that serves their ends, and decide which accounts of the world are true. Assuming that unfettered communication would lead always toward truth, the early libertarians believed that government could do nothing to improve public discourse.[116] Again, they were incorrect. Public investments in research, education, communications infrastructure, archives, science, and libraries have proven essential for promoting truthful communication. Truth can only flourish when supported by robust institutions committed to the production of knowledge. Truth does not simply happen; it must be nurtured.

Tanguy's Faithful Mirror

In the 1794 prospectus for his Philadelphia newspaper, the *American Star*, the embittered Saint Domingue printer and refugee planter Claude-Corentin Tanguy de la Boissière promised his readers that he would "shew things such as they really are" by offering a "faithful mirror" of the world's news.[1] This was a typical promise for a newspaper printer in the early US republic. It relied on the commonsensical notion that an honest mediator would spread truth. Yet after fleeing the Haitian Revolution and arriving in Philadelphia alongside thousands of other émigrés, Tanguy was unprepared for the chaotic and uncertain flow of information in North America. As a result, he gave up on his editorial pretensions about two weeks after the prospectus was published. In the *American Star*'s fifth issue, he questioned the very possibility of precise journalism that a "faithful mirror" represented. Explaining his decision not to share rumors that other "American papers" had reported, Tanguy tossed aside his visual metaphor: "A Journal is an echo . . . but it should, as much as possible, be an echo of truths." This new comparison reflected his frustrations with the information available to him. Publishing on a Tuesday, he noted that a piece of news about the defeat of a French squadron that arrived on Saturday "was doubtful on Monday, on Wednesday it will, it is supposed, be shewn to be fictitious."[2]

An echo, like the news, is easily distorted by the medium through which it travels. From his vantage in Philadelphia, Tanguy could count on a daily relay of information from all around the world. But even this massive volume of raw information, he came to accept, could only offer an echo of the events unfolding globally. Tanguy's rapid shift from an optimistic visual metaphor to a cautious aural one was a response to the contingency of facts in the revolutionary Atlantic world. Flawed media systems, the politicization of news, and Americans' dependence on commerce for news all contributed to dysfunctional information exchange. It was impossible for Tanguy to hold up a faithful mirror of events under these circumstances.

Journalism scholar Michael Schudson closed his influential 1978 history of objectivity in the American news media with a similar anecdote from the prospectus of a nineteenth-century Boston penny paper, which promised to provide readers with an exact image, a "daguerreotype," of the news. Schudson pondered, "What kind of prospectus could one write for a newspaper today?"[3] His query is a difficult one. Whatever answers that Schudson or his readers could have provided to that question in the 1970s would undoubtedly be quite different than any answer available to twenty-first-century readers. Few today would consider updating the technological idioms of the preceding centuries to promise a crisp selfie or a faithful retweet of the news. The rapid rise of digital media in the twenty-first century has introduced enormous challenges for those who hope to gather truthful accounts of the world. It has also provoked the development of more cynical cultures of information, within which mediators' claims to impartiality or objectivity, mirrors and daguerreotypes, ring hollow.

I have written this study of media, politics, and falsehood in revolutionary America during an era of information polarization, "fake news," and epistemic skepticism. This context has inevitably guided the kinds of questions I have pursued in this book. Historical inquiry benefits from new questions generated by the concerns of the present. One of those questions must surely be whether or not the information wars of the twenty-first century represent something substantially new or whether they are merely the latest example of a longer disordered relationship between information and politics.

Many writers and theorists have identified a steady decline of truth in Western society. The twentieth-century postmodernist philosopher Jean Baudrillard, for example, drew attention to the ways that modern society's representations of itself were becoming untethered from reality.[4] Media theorist Neil Postman argued in the 1980s that when US society turned from print to electronic media, it became fixated on triviality instead of truth.[5] More recently, a toxic brew of internet media, anti-intellectualism, and political ferment have led many to invoke the concepts of a "post-truth" society and the "death of truth" to describe their collective experience of a world losing its shared standards of evidence and its ability to discern falsehood.[6] Each of these diagnoses contains an implicit historical declension narrative, in which faithful mirrors give way to mere echoes. If pressed, many Americans would articulate a historical arc from a golden age in the early to mid-twentieth century, when honest journalists such as Walter Cronkite relayed trustworthy information to a broad audience, to the chaos of contemporary social media, where every faction makes its own truth, and misinformation defines political behavior.

It is a tempting narrative. And indeed, it was during the early twentieth century that some members of the American news media developed an ethic of "objectivity." Journalists began to acknowledge and minimize uncertainty by using several sources, checking facts, presenting multiple possibilities, and actively investigating formidable individuals and institutions. Yet while these techniques were an improvement on the partisan and sensationalistic journalism of previous decades, objectivity always remained an aspiration rather than a reality. Those who did not belong to the most powerful groups in society often saw nothing objective about the narratives emanating from their newspapers, radios, and televisions. Even this fuzzy mirror was short-lived. In the long history of news in the United States, information mediators who were devoted to truthfulness have been more aberrant than typical. If we begin this story in the seventeenth and eighteenth centuries, rather than in the twentieth century, it becomes clear that there has been no simple, linear declension of truth in US history.

How, then, should we respond to Schudson's query? What happens when we hold Tanguy's mirror up to ourselves? History is an uncertain guide. But as Tanguy discovered long ago, the work of producing and consuming knowledge about the world has always been difficult. It is not a novel problem introduced by digital communications. Social media have created challenges, but they are not unprecedented; print, too, was once new. It took more than two centuries for American society to develop norms to restrain falsehoods in print media. Perhaps the questions to be asking, then, are more about news cultures than about information technologies.

In July 1775, a few months after the start of the American revolutionary war and a year before the Continental Congress declared American independence, an unusual essay appeared in James Rivington's Loyalist newspaper, the *New-York Gazetteer*. Like Tanguy, Rivington was not known for conciliatory rhetoric. Yet this essay made the case for embracing epistemological humility. Its authorship is unclear. It appeared above the New York heading, where Rivington and other printers sometimes shared their own words. But it was not signed pseudonymously nor formally addressed to Rivington, as were most political essays appearing in his pages. Instead, it began with a quotation from the English poet John Dryden's translation of the *Aeneid*: "Embrace again, my sons, be foes no more."[7] The essay sought reconciliation between Loyalists and Patriots, but through mutual self-reflection rather than disarmament.

The unnamed writer observed that when public disputes reach a crisis, partisans aim to "contradict, vilify and supplant each other" rather than "arrive at truth and promote the interests of society." "Pride and a latent belief of the infallibility of our own judgments" naturally led people to "suspect every man of ignorance, hypocrisy, or dishonesty, who is so unfortunate, or so presumptuous, as to differ from us in sentiment." In his view, Americans refused to consider the possibility of "ourselves being in an error" or that others might be mistaken rather than intentionally deceptive: "We do not consider the delicate texture of human understanding, and how liable it is to be warped, by prejudice and passion; but intoxicated, as we are, with fond notions of our own sagacity and penetration; and, perhaps, at the same time, conscious of the integrity and goodness of our own intentions, we cannot forbear wondering how any can be so blind and stupid, as not to discern the reality of those truths, which to us appear incontestable."[8] Those who happened to possess superior information, as this writer understood, nevertheless often shared the same cognitive weaknesses that led others into misperception. In a world of "prejudice and passion," in which truth was politicized and few news mediators could be trusted, it was remarkable, really, that anyone knew anything that occurred beyond their own personal experience. Attaining a truthful measure of the world, this author recognized, was quite difficult.

It was an unusual statement for its time. As I researched this book, what most surprised me was how seldom I encountered observers and mediators reflecting on the limitations of their own ability to discern truth. But neither revolutions nor news thrive in doubt. News that acknowledges its limitations and therefore seeks out verification or offers competing possibilities is always vulnerable to those who claim to dispense unalloyed truth. As the internet has democratized the news media, scrupulous journalists now compete with hubristic hucksters—who are frequently untruthful but seldom uncertain. Certainty earns attention because it provides clear explanations, often within a linear narrative populated with heroes, victims, and villains. Conspiracy theories, racist mythologies, and violent extremism thrive in information ecosystems that disincentivize doubt and reflection. Responsible news-gathering is difficult in environments that itch for entertainment, conflict, and narrative. When truth becomes a commodity to be bought and sold, observers become an audience, and an audience expects to be entertained.

Yet the world is rarely as exciting as the headlines suggest. What Tanguy indicated in shifting his metaphor from a mirror to an echo was the sort of humility that observers and mediators must rediscover today. Because our immediate perceptions often deceive us, we should be suspicious of certainty. Only once we interrogate and thereby strengthen those perceptions—something that rarely happened in revolutionary America—can our politics proceed from shared premises. Observers and mediators today would benefit from building cultures that valorize uncertainty and reward the unglamorous, plodding processes of verification that so often ruin a good story. A fact-checking revolution may seem unlikely in our moment of misinformation, but so did all revolutions until they became inevitable.

A Note on Data Sources

When I started this project, I faced a problem that my historical subjects would have sympathized with. I had too much news. Hundreds of newspapers had published four pages one or more times a week across a century, which produced an unmanageable volume of text. There was far more evidence to examine and far more stories to tell than any single researcher or writer could handle.

The quantity of the material made it necessary to rely on text searches of newspaper databases along with targeted analyses of a few significant newspapers. Keyword searches, though, too often show us what we want to see rather than what we need to see.* I therefore decided to systematically build a data set that would guide my inquiry about the complex relationships among information flows, politics, commerce, war, and diplomacy. I have only sparingly cited this data set throughout this book, which understates its importance because this data set guided the questions that I asked as well as the conclusions I reached.

Using Readex's America's Historical Newspapers, which provides a nearly complete archive of surviving eighteenth-century American newspaper issues, I gathered direct citations of other newspapers that appeared in eighteenth-century American newspapers. The greatest challenge in working on older digitized newspapers is the limitations of optical character recognition (OCR). Even the most advanced OCR software cannot reliably interpret the smudgy words printed by well-worn eighteenth-century presses. Luckily, however, when Readex built its database, it generated metadata for individual news items, including the relevant heading or headline. This was executed imperfectly, but it allows eighteenth-

---

* Lara Putnam's extraordinary essay on this topic pushed me to avoid cherry-picking sources and instead work through the material as systematically as possible. Putnam, "The Transnational and the Text-Searchable: Digitized Sources and the Shadows They Cast," *American Historical Review* 121 (April 2016): 377–402.

century American newspapers' headings to be reliably searched and, more important for my purposes, to be aggregated.

The method for assembling my data set was straightforward. I initially searched within the database's headings for the phrase "from the," which appeared in many citational headings, while excluding North American place names, such as "New-York" or "Charleston." In a spreadsheet, I generated a list of foreign newspapers that American printers cited with the phrase "from the." I then searched for headings that featured each of these individual newspaper names (while excluding confounding North American place names, such as the *New-London Gazette*, which appeared in searches for the *London Gazette*) and noted the citing newspaper alongside the date. Altogether, I collected more than 40,000 citations in American newspapers to non-American papers. I also collected citations from Canadian newspapers through a much slower process of paging through microfilm copies.

Collecting and analyzing these data required months of tedious spreadsheet work. It is important to note that these data do not encompass the entirety of all relevant citational headings. In addition to the small number of papers that Readex does not include, some printers placed bracketed citations at the end of a news item, where they remain hidden from Readex's metadata collection. Moreover, explicitly cited news was unusual in eighteenth-century newspapers. I estimate that only around one-fifth of news reports included a citational heading. Because of these limitations, my data set provides an incomplete but useful specimen of news reprints. Based on complementary issue-by-issue analyses of several early newspapers, I am confident that these data are a highly representative sample.

Introduction

1. *Federal Mirror* (Concord, NH), Nov. 1, 8, 1796.

2. Jonathan Senchyne, *The Intimacy of Paper in Early and Nineteenth-Century American Literature* (Amherst, MA, 2019).

3. Will Slauter, "The Paragraph as Information Technology: How News Traveled in the Eighteenth-Century Atlantic World," *Annales* 67 (Apr.–June 2012): 253–78.

4. [Benjamin Franklin], *The Yearly Verses of the Printer's Lad, Who Carrieth about the Pennsylvania Gazette, to the Customers Thereof* (Philadelphia, 1739).

5. *Amherst Journal*, Mar. 20, 27, 1795.

6. *National Gazette* (Philadelphia), Mar. 13, 1793.

7. Samuel Miller, *A Brief Retrospect of the Eighteenth Century* (New York, 1803), 2:251; Isaiah Thomas, *The History of Printing in America* (1810; rpt., New York, 1970), 13–21.

8. On "passive," see Joseph M. Adelman and Victoria E. M. Gardner, "News in the Age of Revolution," in *Making News: The Political Economy of Journalism in Britain and America from the Glorious Revolution to the Internet*, ed. Richard R. John and Jonathan Silberstein-Loeb (Oxford, 2015), 52. On "regurgitated journalism," see Adrian Johns, *Piracy: The Intellectual Property Wars from Gutenberg to Gates* (Chicago, 2009), 181. See also Thomas C. Leonard, *The Power of the Press: The Birth of American Political Reporting* (New York, 1986), 14–15.

9. "Dublin, Jan. 25," *Boston News-Letter*, Apr. 10, 1735.

10. "From the Dublin Journal, Jan. 25," *Boston News-Letter*, Apr. 23, 1752.

11. "Latest London Accounts," *Aurora General Advertiser* (Philadelphia), Jan. 7, 1795.

12. Early Americans read newspapers almost as pedantically as do academics who read notes like this one.

13. *Connecticut Courant* (Hartford), Aug. 12, 1776; *Eastern Herald* (Portland, MA), July 27, 1795.

14. The first instance of this poem appears to be in *Farmer's Weekly Museum* (Walpole, NH), Apr. 8, 1799.

15. In this book, I aim to help bring together what Johann N. Neem has called the new "neoliberal" field of early American history, focused on exchange and pluralism, with the older, nation-centered version of the field. Neem, "From Polity to Exchange: The Fate of Democracy in the Changing Fields of Early American Historiography," *Modern Intellectual History* 17, no. 3 (2020): 867–88.

16. Richard D. Brown, *The Strength of a People: The Idea of an Informed Citizenry in America, 1650–1870* (Chapel Hill, NC, 1996); Sophia Rosenfeld, *Democracy and Truth: A Short History* (Philadelphia, 2019).

17. Stephen Botein, "'Meer Mechanics' and an Open Press: The Business and Political Strategies of Colonial American Printers," *Perspectives in American History* 9 (1975): 127–228.

18. Gordon S. Wood, "Conspiracy and the Paranoid Style: Causality and Deceit in the Eighteenth Century," *William and Mary Quarterly* 39 (July 1982): 401–41.

19. Will Slauter, "Forward-Looking Statements: News and Speculation in the Age of the American Revolution," *Journal of Modern History* 81 (Dec. 2009): 759–92.

20. John C. Miller, *Samuel Adams, Pioneer in Propaganda* (Boston, 1936); Philip Davidson, *Propaganda and the American Revolution, 1763–1783* (Chapel Hill, NC, 1941); Arthur M. Schlesinger, *Prelude to Independence: The Newspaper War on Britain, 1764–1776* (1958; rpt., Boston, 1980). On the historiography of this problem, see Gordon S. Wood, "Rhetoric and Reality in the American Revolution," *William and Mary Quarterly* 23 (Jan. 1966): 3–32.

21. Wood, "Conspiracy and the Paranoid Style"; Bernard Bailyn, *The Ideological Origins of the American Revolution* (Cambridge, MA, 1967); Richard Hofstadter, *The Paranoid Style in American Politics* (1952; rpt., Cambridge, MA 1996); Pauline Maier, *From Resistance to Revolution: Colonial Radicals and the Development of American Opposition to Britain, 1765–1776* (New York, 1972), xix–xx.

22. My focus on the flow of misinformation departs from twenty-first-century scholarship that often focuses on the intentional production of disinformation. Russ Castronovo, *Propaganda 1776: Secrets, Leaks, and Revolutionary Communications in Early America* (Oxford, 2014), 4–9; Robert G. Parkinson, *Thirteen Clocks: How Race United the Colonies and Made the Declaration of Independence* (Chapel Hill, NC, 2021), ch. 1; Gregory Evans Dowd, *Groundless: Rumors, Legends, and Hoaxes on the Early American Frontier* (Baltimore, 2015).

23. John Adams to Benjamin Waterhouse, Oct. 29, 1805, Founders Online, National Archives, https://founders.archives.gov/documents/Adams/99-02-02-5107.

24. Jürgen Habermas, *The Structural Transformation of the Public Sphere: An Inquiry into a Category of Bourgeois Society*, trans. Thomas Burger (1962; rpt., Cambridge, MA, 1995).

25. For examples of scholars relying on Habermas's model of the public sphere, see Michael Warner, *The Letters of the Republic: Publication and the Public Sphere in Eighteenth-Century America* (Cambridge, MA, 1990); David Waldstreicher, *In the Midst of Perpetual Fetes* (Chapel Hill, NC, 1997); Simon P. Newman, *Parades and the Politics of the Street: Festive Culture in the Early American Republic* (Philadelphia, 1997); Catherine O'Donnell Kaplan, *Men of Letters in the Early Republic: Cultivating Forms of Citizenship* (Chapel Hill, NC, 2008); John L. Brooke, *Columbia Rising: Civil Life on the Upper Hudson from the Revolution to the Age of Jackson* (Chapel Hill, NC, 2010); Michael Eamon, *Imprinting Britain: Newspapers, Sociability, and the Shaping of British North America* (Montreal, 2015), 11.

26. Bernard Bailyn, ed., *Pamphlets of the American Revolution, 1750–1776* (Cambridge, MA, 1965); Bailyn, *Ideological Origins of the American Revolution*; Gordon S. Wood, *The Radicalism of the American Revolution* (New York, 1991); J. G. A. Pocock, *The Machiavellian Moment: Florentine Political Thought and the Atlantic Republican Tradition* (Princeton, NJ, 1975); Jonathan Israel, *A Revolution of the Mind: Radical Enlightenment and the Intellectual Origins of Modern Democracy* (Princeton, NJ, 2010).

27. Bernard Bailyn, *The Origins of American Politics* (New York, 1968), 53.

28. Thomas Paine, *Rights of Man: Being an Answer to Mr. Burke's Attack on the French Revolution* (Philadelphia, 1791), 105.

Chapter 1 · *Foreign Advices and False Friends*

1. Walter Benjamin, *Illuminations: Essays and Reflections*, trans. Harry Zohn (New York, 1968), 88.

2. *Green Mountain Patriot* (Peacham, VT), Feb. 23, 1798.

3. Charles E. Clark, *The Public Prints: The Newspaper in Anglo-American Culture, 1665–1740* (New York, 1994), 216.

4. New York heading, *Hudson Gazette* (New York), July 23, 1799.

5. Philadelphia heading, *Independent Gazetteer* (Philadelphia), Nov. 5, 1782.

6. Scholarship on early modern Atlantic communications generally focuses on the era before the Age of Revolutions: Ian K. Steele, *The English Atlantic, 1675–1740: An Exploration of Communication and Community* (New York, 1986); Kenneth J. Banks, *Chasing Empire across the Sea: Communications and the State in the French Atlantic, 1713–1763* (Montreal, 2002). Scholarship on late eighteenth-century American newspapers generally focuses on domestic matters: Joseph M. Adelman, *Revolutionary Networks: The Business and Politics of Printing the News, 1763–1789* (Baltimore, 2019); Robert G. Parkinson, *The Common Cause: Creating Race and Nation in the American Revolution* (Chapel Hill, NC, 2016).

7. "Just Imported from London . . . ," *New Hampshire Gazette* (Portsmouth), May 28, 1773.

8. Andrew Jackson O'Shaughnessy, *An Empire Divided: The American Revolution and the British Caribbean* (Philadelphia, 2000), xi; Banks, *Chasing Empire across the Sea*, 8; Michael J. Seymour, *The Transformation of the North Atlantic World, 1492–1763* (Westport, CT, 2004), 194; Jack P. Greene and Philip D. Morgan, *Atlantic History: A Critical Appraisal* (Oxford, 2009), 11; Karen Ordahl Kupperman, *The Atlantic in World History* (Oxford, 2012), 98.

9. David S. Shields, *Civil Tongues and Polite Letters in British America* (Chapel Hill, NC, 1997), 60; Peter Thompson, *Rum Punch and Revolution: Taverngoing and Public Life in Eighteenth-Century Philadelphia* (Philadelphia, 2010), 90–91, 106.

10. David Cressy, *Coming Over: Migration and Communication between England and New England in the Seventeenth Century* (New York, 1987), ch. 10.

11. William Byrd to Daniel Horsmanden, Aug. 8, 1690, in *Virginia Magazine of History and Biography* 26 (1918): 392.

12. John Pynchon to John Winthrop Jr., Apr. 5, 1669, in *The Pynchon Papers*, ed. Carl Bridenbaugh (Boston, 1982), 1:83.

13. Jane Kamensky, *Governing the Tongue: The Politics of Speech in Early New England* (New York, 1997), 19–22.

14. Jason T. Sharples, *The World That Fear Made: Slave Revolts and Conspiracy Scares in Early America* (Philadelphia, 2020).

15. Larry D. Eldridge, "Before Zenger: Truth and Seditious Speech in Colonial America, 1607–1700," *American Journal of Legal History* 39 (July 1995): 345, 352.

16. *Acts of Assembly, Passed in the Colony of Virginia, from 1662 to 1715* (London, 1727), 1:36; William S. Powell, *North Carolina through Four Centuries* (Chapel Hill, NC, 2010), 80; William Henry Whitmore, *The Colonial Laws of Massachusetts Reprinted from the Edition of 1672 with the Supplements through 1686* (Boston, 1890), 91–92; *Minutes of the Provincial Council of Pennsylvania* (Philadelphia, 1852), 1:40; *Acts and Laws of His Majesties Colony of Connecticut in New-England* (Boston, 1702), 67.

17. Eldridge, "Before Zenger," 352–55.

18. Kamensky, *Governing the Tongue*, 46–48.

19. Edward Rawson, *The Revolution in New-England Justified* (Boston, 1773), 11–12.

20. Owen Stanwood, *The Empire Reformed: English America in the Age of the Glorious Revolution* (Philadelphia, 2011), ch. 3.

21. Daniel R. Headrick, *When Information Came of Age: Technologies of Knowledge in the Age of Reason and Revolution, 1700–1850* (Oxford, 2000).

22. Steele, *English Atlantic*, chs. 7–9.

23. Konstantin Dierks, *In My Power: Letter Writing and Communications in Early America* (Philadelphia, 2009), 25.

24. Dierks, *In My Power*, 42–43, 46–47, 49. On packet ships, see Brad A. Jones, *Resisting Independence: Popular Loyalism in the Revolutionary British Atlantic* (Ithaca, NY, 2021), 19–20.

25. Susan Whyman, *The Pen and the People: English Letter Writers, 1660–1800* (Oxford, 2009), ch. 2.

26. Steele, *English Atlantic*, 134–36; Clark, *Public Prints*, 70.

27. Andrew Pettegree, *The Invention of News: How the World Came to Know about Itself* (New Haven, CT, 2014), 370.

28. Harry B. Weiss, *A Graphic Summary of the Growth of Newspapers in New York and Other States, 1704–1820* (New York, 1948), 5.

29. "Port of Philadelphia," *Gazette of the United States* (Philadelphia), May 15, 1795.

30. *Pennsylvania Gazette* (Philadelphia), Jan. 22, 1745.

31. New York heading, *Aurora General Advertiser* (Philadelphia), July 23, 1795.

32. New York heading, *Daily Advertiser* (New York), Oct. 1, 1792; *Star* (London), Aug. 15, 16, 1792.

33. New York heading, *Daily Advertiser* (New York), Oct. 13, 1792.

34. London heading, *Boston News-Letter*, Oct. 30, 1755.

35. *Montreal Gazette*, Dec. 3, 1789.

36. See, for example, Matthew Ridley to William Lux, Jan. 24 and June 16, 1777, both in Letterbook, 1776–1778, box 6, Matthew Ridley Papers II, Massachusetts Historical Society, Boston.

37. Samuel Cary to unknown correspondent, Oct. 6, 1790, folder: Cary Family 1789–1790, box 1, Cary Family Papers, 1789–1883, Massachusetts Historical Society, Boston.

38. Cressy, *Coming Over*, 237.

39. R. R. Logan to John Dickinson, Jan. 7, 1775, folder 7, box 1, John Dickinson Papers, 1676–1885, Library Company of Pennsylvania, Philadelphia.

40. J. Forbes and R. B. Forbes to James Perkins and Thomas Perkins, Jan. 12, 1801, folder 8, box 1, Thomas H. Perkins Papers, Massachusetts Historical Society, Boston.

41. Steele, *English Atlantic*, 235–36.

42. Jones, *Resisting Independence*, ch. 1.

43. *Publick Occurrences* (Boston), Sept. 25, 1690; Clark, *Public Prints*, 72–73.

44. Advertisement, *Boston News-Letter*, Apr. 9, 1705.

45. Clark, *Public Prints*, 85.

46. Clyde Augustus Duniway, *The Development of Freedom of the Press in Massachusetts* (Cambridge, MA, 1906), 99.

47. Harold L. Nelson, "Seditious Libel in Colonial America," *American Journal of Legal History* 3 (Apr. 1959): 160–72.

48. Jeffery A. Smith, *Printers and Press Freedom: The Ideology of Early American Journalism* (New York, 1988), 8.

49. Hannah Barker, *Newspapers, Politics, and Public Opinion in Late Eighteenth-Century England* (Oxford, 1998), 97, 127–28, 136–37.

50. Clark, *Public Prints*, 222.

51. P. M. Handover, *A History of the London Gazette, 1665–1965* (London, 1965), 42, 47.

52. Dierks, *In My Power*, 107.

53. W. Jeffrey Bolster, *Black Jacks: African American Seamen in the Age of Sail* (Cambridge, MA 1997); Leona M. Hudak, *Early American Women Printers and Publishers, 1639–1820* (Metuchen, NJ, 1978).

54. George D. Terry, "South Carolina's First Negro Seaman's Acts, 1793–1803," *Proceedings of the South Carolina Historical Association* (1980): 78–93.

55. Julius S. Scott, *The Common Wind: Afro-American Currents in the Age of the Haitian Revolution* (London, 2018).

56. Jonathan Senchyne, "Under Pressure: Reading Material Textuality in the Recovery of Early African American Print Work," *Arizona Quarterly* 75 (Fall 2019): 114–15.

57. E. S. Thomas, *Reminiscences of the Last Sixty-Five Years, Commencing with the Battle of Lexington* (Hartford, CT, 1840), 1:77–78.

58. Charles G. Steffen, "Newspapers for Free: The Economies of Newspaper Circulation in the Early Republic," *Journal of the Early Republic* 23 (Autumn 2003): 396.

59. Phillip Troutman, "Grapevine in the Slave Market: African American Geopolitical Literacy and the 1841 Creole Revolt," in *The Chattel Principle*, ed. Walter Johnson (New Haven, CT, 2004).

60. Kate Carté Engel, "Connecting Protestants in Britain's Eighteenth-Century Atlantic Empire," *William and Mary Quarterly* 75 (Jan. 2018): 39

61. Levi Beardsley, *Reminiscences* (New York, 1852), 69.

62. "Mr. Fleet," *Boston Evening-Post*, Nov. 23, 1747.

63. Dierks, *In My Power*, xvii; Steele, *English Atlantic*, 127.

64. *To the Patrons of Relf's Philadelphia Gazette, on the Commencement of the Year 1808* (Philadelphia, 1807).

65. Susanna Dillwyn to William Dillwyn, Nov. 10, 1794, folder 3, box 3, Dillwyn and Emlen Family Correspondence, Library Company of Philadelphia.

66. Susanna Dillwyn to William Dillwyn, Apr. 6, 1791, folder 2, box 2, Dillwyn and Emlen Family Correspondence, Library Company of Philadelphia.

67. Susanna Dillwyn to William Dillwyn, Dec. 23, 1792, folder 7, box 2, Dillwyn and Emlen Family Correspondence, Library Company of Philadelphia.

68. "Population: 1790 to 1990," US Census Bureau, https://www.census.gov/population /censusdata/table-4.pdf.

69. Beardsley, *Reminiscences*, 67.

70. John L. Brooke, *Columbia Rising: Civil Life on the Upper Hudson from the Revolution to the Age of Jackson* (Chapel Hill, NC, 2010); Richard D. Brown, *Knowledge Is Power: The Diffusion of Information in Early America, 1700–1865* (Oxford, 1989), ch. 3; William J. Gilmore, *Reading Becomes a Necessity of Life: Material and Cultural Life in Rural New England, 1780–1835* (Knoxville, TN, 1989), 194.

71. Milton W. Hamilton, *The Country Printer: New York State, 1785–1830* (Port Washington, NY, 1936).

72. James Cowan, *To the Public: It Is of Infinite Importance . . .* (Annapolis, MD, 1789).

73. *Quebec Gazette*, Oct. 6, 8, 1791.

74. *Boston News-Letter*, Nov. 12, 1705; Clark, *Public Prints*, 92.

75. Stephen Botein, "'Meer Mechanics' and an Open Press: The Business and Political Strategies of Colonial American Printers," *Perspectives in American History* 9 (1975): 127–228; Robert W. T. Martin, *The Free and Open Press: The Founding of American Democratic Press Liberty, 1640–1800* (New York, 2001).

76. "Apology for Printers," June 10, 1731, Founders Online, National Archives, http:// founders.archives.gov/documents/Franklin/01-01-02-0061.

77. Clark, *Public Prints*, 97.

78. Advertisement, *Boston News-Letter*, Apr. 30, 1705.

79. Advertisement, *Boston News-Letter*, Apr. 9, 1705.

80. "Charlestown, April 2," *South Carolina Gazette* (Charleston), Apr. 2, 1737.

81. "Mr. De Foreest," *New-York Evening Post*, Nov. 16, 1747.

82. *New-York Weekly Journal*, June 2, 1740. See also *New-York Gazette*, Nov. 28, 1757; New York heading, *Boston Gazette*, Aug. 2, 1762.

83. Philadelphia heading, *General Advertiser* (Philadelphia), July 26, 1793.

84. Henry Kendall to Mathew Carey, June 12, 1795, folder 2, box 9, Lea and Febiger Records, Historical Society of Pennsylvania, Philadelphia.

85. Portsmouth heading, *Oracle of the Day* (Portsmouth, NH), Sept. 28, 1793.

86. *Pittsburgh Gazette*, July 28, 1786.

87. John Hunt to Matthew Ridley, Dec. 16, 1776, folder: Matthew Ridley: 1775–Aug. 1776, Business Correspondence, box 3, Matthew Ridley Papers, Massachusetts Historical Society, Boston.

Chapter 2 · *Taxation with Misrepresentation*

1. *The Representations of Governor Hutchinson and Others, Contained in Certain Letters Transmitted to England* (Boston, 1773), 10–11.

2. Boston heading, *Boston Gazette*, Jan. 16, 1769.

3. Bernard Bailyn, *The Ordeal of Thomas Hutchinson* (Cambridge, MA 1974), chs. 2, 7; *Representations of Governor Hutchinson and Others*, 10–11. See also Thomas C. Leonard, "News for a Revolution: The Expose in America, 1768–1773," *Journal of American History* 67 (June 1980): 37.

4. "Copy of Letters Sent to Great Britain," Annotated Newspapers of Harbottle Dorr Jr., 4:1151–52, Massachusetts Historical Society, http://www.masshist.org/dorr/volume/4/sequence /1240.

5. *Massachusetts Spy* (Boston), July 1, 1773; *Boston News-Letter*, July 15, 29, 1773; *Boston Gazette*, July 19, Aug. 2, 1773; *Boston Post-Boy*, Aug. 2, 1773; *Lloyd's Evening Post* (London), Sept. 3, 1773.

6. Sergio Serulnikov, *Revolution in the Andes: The Age of Túpac Amaru* (Durham, NC, 2013), 38; Charles F. Walker, *The Tupac Amaru Rebellion* (Cambridge, MA, 2014), 34–35.

7. Julius S. Scott, *The Common Wind: Afro-American Currents in the Age of the Haitian Revolution* (London, 2018), 13.

8. Laurent Dubois, *Avengers of the New World: The Story of the Haitian Revolution* (Cambridge, MA, 2004), 98.

9. Wim Klooster, "Slave Revolts, Royal Justice, and a Ubiquitous Rumor in the Age of Revolutions," *William and Mary Quarterly* 71 (July 2014): 401–24.

10. Edmund S. Morgan, *Inventing the People: The Rise of Popular Sovereignty in England and America* (New York, 1988), 30–31; Pauline Maier, *From Resistance to Revolution: Colonial Radicals and the Development of American Opposition to Britain, 1765–1776* (New York, 1972), 45. See also Michael D. Hattem, *Past and Prologue: Politics and Memory in the American Revolution* (New Haven, CT, 2020), esp. ch. 2.

11. Morgan, *Inventing the People*, 19.

12. *Boston Gazette*, Apr. 24, 1769.

13. Edmund S. Morgan and Helen M. Morgan, *The Stamp Act Crisis: Prologue to Revolution* (Chapel Hill, NC, 1953), 73.

14. Maier, *From Resistance to Revolution*, 149–57.

15. *The Correspondence of Colonial Governors of Rhode Island, 1723–1775* (Boston, 1903), 2:372; Ian K. Steele, *The English Atlantic, 1675–1740: An Exploration of Communication and Community* (New York, 1986), ch. 12, esp. 236–37, 241.

16. Michael G. Kammen, *A Rope of Sand: The Colonial Agents, British Politics, and the American Revolution* (Ithaca, NY, 1968).

17. Steele, *English Atlantic*, ch. 12, esp. 235–38.

18. Jared Ingersoll to Thomas Fitch, Feb. 11, 1765, in *The Fitch Papers: Correspondence and Documents during Thomas Fitch's Governorship of the Colony of Connecticut, 1754–1766*, vol. 2: *January 1759–May 1766* (Hartford, CT, 1920), 320.

19. Ingersoll to Fitch, Feb. 11, 1765, in *Fitch Papers*, 320–33.

20. See P. D. G. Thomas, ed., "Parliamentary Diaries of Nathaniel Ryder, 1764–7," in *Camden Miscellany*, ser. 4 (London, 1967), 23:260.

21. Jared Ingersoll, *Mr. Ingersoll's Letters Relating to the Stamp-Act* (New-Haven, CT, 1766); *Providence Gazette*, Apr. 13, 1765; Martha Joanna Lamb, *History of the City of New York: Its Origin, Rise, and Progress* (New York, 1877), 1:716.

22. *Boston News-Letter*, Sept. 19, 1765.

23. John Phillip Reid, *The Concept of Representation in the Age of the American Revolution* (Chicago, 1989), 12.

24. See, for example, "Messieurs Edes & Gill," *Boston Gazette*, Nov. 26, 1770.

25. Mark Knights, *Representation and Misrepresentation in Later Stuart Britain: Partisanship and Political Culture* (Oxford, 2005), 31.

26. J. R. Pole, *The Gift of Government: Political Responsibility from the English Restoration to American Independence* (Athens, GA, 1983), 90; Reid, *Concept of Representation*, chs. 6–8.

27. Morgan and Morgan, *Stamp Act Crisis*, 81.

28. Joseph M. Adelman, *Revolutionary Networks: The Business and Politics of Printing the News, 1763–1789* (Baltimore, 2019), ch. 2.

29. *Copy of Letters Sent to Great-Britain by His Excellency Thomas Hutchinson, the Hon. Andrew Oliver, and Several Other Persons* (Boston, 1773), 5.

30. *Letters to the Ministry from Governor Bernard, General Gage, and Commodore Hood* (Boston, 1769), 4–5. See also *The American Gazette, Being a Collection of All the Authentic Addresses, Memorials, Petitions, and Other Papers . . .* (London, 1770), 6.

31. *Letters to the Ministry*, 19.

32. "To the Printers," *Boston Gazette*, Nov. 5, 1770. See also Boston heading, *New-York Journal*, Dec. 22, 1768.

33. *Maryland Gazette* (Annapolis), May 4, 1769.

34. *New-York Journal*, Apr. 21, 1774.

35. "The Following Is Said to Be an Exact Copy of a Letter from an Officer of Rank, then at Boston, to a Noble Lord," *Virginia Gazette* (Williamsburg), Feb. 4, 1775.

36. Charles Lee to Edmund Burke, Dec. 16, 1774, in *Collections of the New-York Historical Society for the Year 1871* (New York, 1872), 145–46. See also Charles Lee to Earl Percy, ca. early 1775, in *Collections of the New-York Historical Society for the Year 1871*, 170–72.

37. Mark G. Schmeller, *Invisible Sovereign: Imagining Public Opinion from the Revolution to Reconstruction* (Baltimore, 2016), 9.

38. Gary B. Nash, *The Urban Crucible: Social Change, Political Consciousness, and the Origins of the American Revolution* (Cambridge, MA, 1979), chs. 9–11.

39. *Letters to the Ministry*, 32, 15.

40. John Phillip Reid, *In a Rebellious Spirit: The Argument of Facts, the Liberty Riot, and the Coming of the American Revolution* (University Park, PA, 1979), 11–19.

41. G. G. Wolkins, "Daniel Malcom and Writs of Assistance," *Proceedings of the Massachusetts Historical Society*, ser. 3, 58 (1925): 20, 16.

42. *A Report of the Record Commissioners of the City of Boston, Containing the Boston Town Records*, vol. 16: *1758 to 1769* (Boston, 1886), 193–94.

43. Shelburne's letter is in *Boston Evening-Post*, Mar. 7, 1768.

44. *Boston Gazette*, Feb. 22, May 2, 1768.

45. *American Gazette*, 4–5, 8.

46. Francis G. Walett, "Governor Bernard's Undoing: An Early Hutchinson Letters Affair," *New England Quarterly* 38 (June 1965): 218. See also Dennys De Berdt to Richard Cary, ca. Dec. 1768, in *Transactions of the Colonial Society of Massachusetts*, ed. Henry Lefavour et al. (Boston, 1912), 13:348.

47. Oliver Morton Dickerson, ed., *Boston under Military Rule, 1768–1769* (Boston, 1936), 13, 30.

48. Diary of John Adams [1768–1770], Founders Online, National Archives, http://founders.archives.gov/documents/Adams/01-03-02-0016-0015.

49. Walett, "Governor Bernard's Undoing," 217–26, esp. 220.

50. *Letters to the Ministry*, 107.

51. Walett, "Governor Bernard's Undoing," 225.

52. On the epistemological standards of early modern British elites, see Steven Shapin, *A Social History of Truth: Civility and Science in Seventeenth-Century England* (Chicago, 1994).

53. *Letters to the Ministry*, 53.

54. [Samuel Adams], *An Appeal to the World; or, A Vindication of the Town of Boston* . . . (Boston, 1770), 28, 5, 7, 40.

55. *A Short Narrative of the Horrid Massacre in Boston, Perpetrated in the Evening of the Fifth Day of March, 1770* (Boston, 1770), 3–5, 7, 8.

56. Bailyn, *Ordeal of Thomas Hutchinson*, 250.

57. *Representations of Governor Hutchinson and Others*, 37.

58. For the earliest publication of this account, see *London Evening-Post*, May 29, 1775.

59. David Hackett Fischer, *Paul Revere's Ride* (New York, 1994), 275.

60. *London Gazette*, May 31, 1775.

61. London heading, *Newport Mercury*, Apr. 3, 1775. See also a letter from London in *Pennsylvania Journal* (Philadelphia), Oct. 12, 1774; London heading, *Boston Post-Boy*, Apr. 10, 1775; "Extracts of a Speech of a Virginia Gentleman at the Temple," *Virginia Gazette* (Williamsburg), Mar. 23, 1776.

62. Troy Bickham, *Making Headlines: The American Revolution as Seen through the British Press* (DeKalb, IL, 2009), 11, 72, 97.

63. William Strahan to David Hall, July 13, 1771, folder 31, box 1, William Strahan Letters, Historical Society of Pennsylvania, Philadelphia.

64. *Newport Herald*, May 9, 1774.

65. Reprinted in *Connecticut Gazette* (New London), May 12, 1775.

66. *Massachusetts Spy* (Boston), May 6, 1773; *The Votes and Proceedings of the Freeholders and Other Inhabitants of the Town of Boston, in Town Meeting Assembled, According to Law, the 5th and 18th Days of November, 1773* (Boston, 1773).

67. Philip Grant, *Propaganda and the American Revolution, 1763–1783* (Chapel Hill, NC, 1941); Arthur M. Schlesinger, *Prelude to Independence: The Newspaper War on Britain, 1764–1776* (1958; rpt., Boston, 1980), esp. ch. 2; Russ Castronovo, *Propaganda 1776: Secrets, Leaks, and Revolutionary Communications in Early America* (Oxford, 2014); Robert G. Parkinson, *The Common Cause: Creating Race and Nation in the American Revolution* (Chapel Hill, NC, 2016), esp. 17–18.

68. Ian R. Christie, *Wilkes, Wyvill and Reform: The Parliamentary Reform Movement in British Politics, 1760–1785* (London, 1962), 65.

69. *Massachusetts Spy* (Worcester), Nov. 10, 1774.

70. "To the King's Most Excellent Majesty," *New-York Gazette and Weekly Mercury*, Dec. 25, 1775.

71. "From the London Chronicle, April 9, 1767," *New-York Journal*, June 18, 1767.

72. *Boston Evening-Post*, Oct. 6, 1766; *Pennsylvania Chronicle and Universal Advertiser* (Philadelphia), Aug. 1, 1768; Dan Benezet et al., "Letter from a Committee of Merchants in Philadelphia to the Committee of Merchants in London," *Pennsylvania Magazine of History and Biography* 27, no. 1 (1903): 85; letter from Charleston printed in *Essex Gazette* (Salem, MA), Aug. 16, 1768.

73. *Pennsylvania Journal* (Philadelphia), Sept. 4, 11, 1766.

74. *Virginia Gazette* (Williamsburg), June 29, 1776.

75. *The Parliamentary Register* (London, 1802), 1:90.

76. *Journals of the House of Burgesses of Virginia: 1773–1776*, ed. John Pendleton Kennedy (Richmond, VA, 1905), 254–55.

77. *Journals of the House of Burgesses of Virginia*, 256, 254. See also "Frederick County Committee," *Virginia Gazette* (Williamsburg), July 7, 1775.

78. *Pennsylvania Journal* (Philadelphia), Oct. 11, 1775.

79. *Pennsylvania Packet* (Philadelphia), Oct. 24, 1774; *New-York Gazette and Weekly Mercury*, Sept. 5, 1774.

80. *Connecticut Journal* (New Haven), Nov. 11, 1774, May 31, 1775.

81. [Samuel Peters], *A General History of Connecticut, from Its First Settlement under George Fenwick, Esq. to Its Latest Period of Amity with Great Britain* (London, 1782), viii. On Peters, see Wayne N. Metz, "A Connecticut Yankee in King George III's Court: A Loyalist Anglican Clergyman in England, 1774–1804," *Historical Magazine of the Protestant Episcopal Church* 52 (Mar. 1983): 29–41.

82. *Virginia Gazette* (Williamsburg), Feb. 9, 1775.

83. Letter signed "Censor," *Virginia Gazette* (Williamsburg), July 22, 1775.

84. Bailyn, *Ordeal of Thomas Hutchinson*, ch. 7.

85. Katlyn Marie Carter, "Denouncing Secrecy and Defining Democracy in the Early American Republic," *Journal of the Early Republic* 40 (Fall 2020): 410.

86. Castronovo, *Propaganda 1776*, 46.

87. William Franklin to William Strahan, Feb. 18, 1765, in *Letters from William Franklin to William Strahan*, ed. Charles Henry Hart (Philadelphia, 1911), 26.

88. *Journal and Letters of the Late Samuel Curwen, Judge of Admiralty, etc., an American Refugee in England from 1775–1784*, ed. George Atkinson Ward (New York, 1842), 41.

89. *Short Narrative of the Horrid Massacre in Boston.*

90. *Letters to the Ministry*, 39.

91. See discusson in Alan Taylor, *American Revolutions: A Continental History, 1750–1804* (New York, 2016), 212, 544n5.

92. Maier, *From Resistance to Revolution*, 203–13.

93. *Boston Post-Boy*, Oct. 10, 1768.

94. "Messrs Fleets," *Boston Evening-Post*, July 24, 1769.

95. *Journals of the American Congress: From 1774 to 1788*, vol. 1: *From September 5, 1774, to December 31, 1776, Inclusive* (Washington, DC, 1823), 48. See also letter to Benjamin Edes and John Gill, *Boston Gazette*, Nov. 26, 1770.

96. *Journals of the Continental Congress, 1774–1789*, ed. Worthington C. Ford et al. (Washington, DC, 1904–1937), 2:159.

97. James E. Bradley, *Popular Politics and the American Revolution in England: Petitions, the Crown, and Public Opinion* (Macon, GA, 1986), chs. 1–2.

98. *Essex Gazette* (Salem, MA), Nov. 1, 1768.

99. *Pennsylvania Chronicle and Universal Advertiser* (Philadelphia), Aug. 1, 1768. See also *Boston Gazette*, Sept. 26, 1768.

100. *A Report of the Record Commissioners of the City of Boston, Containing the Boston Town Records*, vol. 18: *1770 through 1777* (Boston, 1887), 124.

101. *Essex Gazette* (Salem, MA), May 23, 1769.

102. William Samuel Johnson to Jonathan Trumbull, Oct. 16, 1769, in *Collections of the Massachusetts Historical Society*, ser. 5, 9 (1885): 375.

103. De Berdt to Thomas Cushing, Dec. 7, 1768, and De Berdt to James Otis, July 2, 1766, in Lefavour et al., *Transactions of the Colonial Society of Massachusetts*, 13:317, 352.

104. Joseph Sherwood to Governor [Stephen] Hopkins, Aug. 7, 1767, in *The Correspondence of the Colonial Governors of Rhode Island, 1723–1775* (Boston, 1903), 2:397.

105. William Samuel Johnson to William Pitkin, Feb. 9, 1769, in *Collections of the Connecticut Historical Society* (Hartford, CT, 1921), 19:321.

106. Dennys De Berdt to Lord Dartmouth, Aug. 6, 1765, in *Letters of Dennys De Berdt, 1757–1770*, ed. Albert Matthews (Cambridge, MA 1911), 433–34. Ironically, Dartmouth was initially more sympathetic to popular forms of communications than were some of his predecessors. See Maier, *From Resistance to Revolution*, 230.

107. William Samuel Johnson to William Pitkin, Apr. 11, 1767, in *Collections of the Massachusetts Historical Society*, ser. 5, 9 (1885): 228; William Samuel Johnson to Joseph Trumbull, Apr. 15, 1769, in *Collections of the Massachusetts Historical Society*, ser. 5, 9 (1885): 333. See also *Collections of the Massachusetts Historical Society*, ser. 5, 9 (1885): 448; Kammen, *Rope of Sand*, 184–89.

108. Benjamin Franklin to Noble Wimberly Jones, Apr. 3–21, 1769, Founders Online, National Archives, https://founders.archives.gov/documents/Franklin/01-16-02-0046.

109. "The Rise and Present State of Our Misunderstanding," Founders Online, National Archives, http://founders.archives.gov/documents/Franklin/01-17-02-0163.

110. *Boston Gazette*, May 2, 1768. See also *Connecticut Gazette* (New London), Nov. 11, 1774; *Connecticut Journal* (New Haven), Oct. 14, 1774.

111. Jasper Yeates, "Draft of an Intended Address to the People, on the Meeting at Lancaster July 9, 1774 in Order to Send a Committee to Philad[elphi]a," folder 8, box 7, Jasper Yeates Papers, Historical Society of Pennsylvania, Philadelphia.

112. Julie M. Flavell, "Government Interception of Letters from America and the Quest for Colonial Opinion in 1775," *William and Mary Quarterly* 58 (Apr. 2001), 403–40.

113. *Massachusetts Spy* (Worcester), Dec. 16, 1774.

114. Thomas Paine, *Common Sense* (Philadelphia, 1776), 9, 25, 38.

Chapter 3 · *The Lying Gazettes*

1. Hugh Palliser to Lord Edgmont, Mar. 31, 1766, CO 194/27, 178–79, Records of the Colonial Office, National Archives, Kew, England.

2. Hugh Palliser to Francis Bernard, in *The Papers of Francis Bernard: Governor of Colonial Massachusetts, 1760–69*, vol. 3: *1766–1767*, ed. Colin Nicholson (Boston, 2013), 197. Nicholson notes, "No reply has been found in the Library and Archives of Canada, Ottawa."

3. "By Order of His Excellency the Governor," *Massachusetts Gazette and Boston News-Letter*, Jan. 8, 1767.

4. *Journals of the House of Representatives of Massachusetts* (Boston, 1974), 43:pt. 2:257–58.

5. *Massachusetts Gazette and Boston News-Letter*, Jan. 8, 1767; *Journals of the House of Representatives of Massachusetts*, 43:pt. 2:xi–xii, 256–57, 360–61.

6. Samuel Adams to John Adams, Nov. 25, 1790, Founders Online, National Archives, http://founders.archives.gov/documents/Adams/99-02-02-1087.

7. On the politicization of everyday life, see Eric Slauter, "Revolutions in the Meaning and Study of Politics," *Early American Literature* 45, no. 2 (2010): 301–18; Joanne B. Freeman, *Affairs of Honor: National Politics in the New Republic* (New Haven, CT, 2001), ch. 1; T. H. Breen, *The Marketplace of Revolution: How Consumer Politics Shaped American Independence* (Oxford, 2004), ch. 7; Kate Haulman, *The Politics of Fashion in Eighteenth-Century America* (Chapel Hill, NC, 2011). On the politicization of newspapers, see Arthur M. Schlesinger, *Prelude to Independence: The Newspaper War on Britain, 1764–1776* (1958; rpt., Boston, 1980); Thomas C. Leonard, *The Power of the Press: The Birth of American Political Reporting* (New York, 1986); Carol Sue Humphrey, *"This Popular Engine": New England Newspapers during the American Revolution, 1775–1789* (Newark, NJ, 1992), ch. 9; Jeffrey L. Pasley, *"The Tyranny of Printers": Newspaper Politics in the Early American Republic* (Charlottesville, VA, 2001), ch. 2, appendix 1, 403–5.

8. "London, Sept. 19," *Boston Chronicle*, Dec. 21, 1767.

9. "Messieurs Edes & Gill," *Boston Gazette*, Jan. 18, 1768.

10. "From the Massachusetts Gazette of Thursday Last," *Boston Gazette*, Jan. 25, 1768.

11. Schlesinger, *Prelude to Independence*, 104.

12. Freeman, *Affairs of Honor*, esp. 128, 172.

13. *Newport Mercury*, Aug. 1, 1774. See Bernard Bailyn, *The Ideological Origins of the American Revolution* (Cambridge, MA, 1967), ch. 4; Gordon S. Wood, *The Creation of the American Republic, 1776–1787* (Chapel Hill, NC, 1969), 39; Pauline Maier, *From Resistance to Revolution: Colonial Radicals and the Development of American Opposition to Britain, 1765–1776* (New York, 1972), ch. 6.

14. Arthur Aspinall, *Politics and the Press, c. 1780–1850* (London, 1949), 66–69; Lucyle Werkmeister, *The London Daily Press, 1772–1792* (Lincoln, NE, 1963), 4; Jeremy Black, *The English Press in the Eighteenth Century* (Philadelphia, 1987), ch. 6. Others suggest that profits, rather than political subsidies, guided British newspapers' decision-making. See Hannah Barker, *Newspapers, Politics, and Public Opinion in Late Eighteenth-Century England* (Oxford, 1998), 46–49; Troy Bickham, *Making Headlines: The American Revolution as Seen through the British Press* (DeKalb, IL, 2009), 11, 23–25, 44–45, 58.

15. Solomon Lutnick, *American Revolution and the British Press, 1775–1783* (Columbia, SC, 1967), 20–21.

16. "Copy of Letters Sent to Great Britain," Annotated Newspapers of Harbottle Dorr Jr., 3:363, Massachusetts Historical Society. See also Richard Henry Lee, *Life of Arthur Lee, LL.D.* (Boston, 1829), 2:307; *The New-Year's Verses of Those Who Carry the Pennsylvania Journal to the Customers* (Philadelphia, 1775).

17. Extract from *Public Ledger*, in *Boston Gazette*, Oct. 4, 1773.

18. See *Massachusetts Spy* (Boston), Feb. 18, 1773; petition in *Boston Post-Boy*, June 14, 1773.

19. *Dunlap's Pennsylvania Packet* (Philadelphia), Apr. 25, 1774.

20. *Morning Post* (London), Sept. 5, 1776. See also "To the Printer," *New-York Journal*, May 12, 1774.

21. "London, March 10, 1774," *New-York Journal*, May 12, 1774.

22. New York heading, *Boston Post-Boy*, May 16, 1774.

23. Trenton heading, *Pennsylvania Packet* (Philadelphia), July 14, 1781.

24. *Massachusetts Spy* (Worcester), May 24, 1775; London heading, *Pennsylvania Evening Post* (Philadelphia), Sept. 14, 1775; letter from London, Newport heading, *Boston Gazette*, Oct. 9, 1775.

25. *Boston Evening-Post*, Feb. 6, 1775. See also letter from London, *New-York Journal*, Sept. 29, 1774.

26. *Norwich Packet*, Nov. 17, 1774.

27. *Newport Mercury*, Sept. 26, 1774; *Massachusetts Spy* (Worcester), Dec. 16, 1774.

28. Philadelphia heading, *Connecticut Journal* (New Haven), Sept. 23, 1774.

29. *Continental Journal* (Boston), Mar. 13, 1777.

30. *New-York Journal*, Feb. 9, 1775.

31. Robert G. Parkinson, *The Common Cause: Creating Race and Nation in the American Revolution* (Chapel Hill, NC, 2016), 53.

32. "A New Catechism," *Boston Gazette*, Mar. 31, 1777.

33. Boston heading, *Independent Chronicle* (Boston), Apr. 6, 1780.

34. Thomas Paine, *The American Crisis, Number II: By the Author of Common Sense* (Philadelphia, 1777), 23.

35. *Journals of the Continental Congress, 1774–1789*, ed. Worthington C. Ford et al. (Washington, DC, 1904–1937), 4:20.

36. *Journals of the Continental Congress*, 8:402, 9:1045.

37. *The Public Acts of the General Assembly of North Carolina* (New Bern, NC, 1804), 1:229.

38. Kenneth Scott, comp., *Rivington's New York Newspaper: Excerpts from a Loyalist Press, 1773–1783* (Binghamton, NY, 1973), 4–5; Robert W. S. Martin, "The 'Free and Open Press': The Foundation of Modern American Democratic Press Liberty," PhD diss., University of Minnesota, 1997, 176.

39. James Rivington, *To the Public* (New York, 1775), n.p.

40. *New-York Gazetteer*, Feb. 16, 1775.

41. *Boston News-Letter*, Apr. 12, 1770, Aug. 5, 1773.

42. *Quebec Gazette*, Oct. 9, 1777, June 17, 1779, July 6, 1780, June 26, 1783, Oct. 8, 1778.

43. *Quebec Gazette*, Jan. 29, 1778.

44. See also Ruma Chopra, "Printer Hugh Gaine Crosses and Re-Crosses the Hudson," *New York History* 90 (Fall 2009): 272.

45. *New-York Journal*, May 24, 1770. Low would later become a Loyalist.

46. *New-York Journal*, Apr. 26, 1770, Jan. 5, 1775.

47. *Pennsylvania Journal* (Philadelphia), Aug. 17, 1774.

48. From 1770 through 1774, Patriot papers cited opposition and radical newspapers 20.5 percent of the time, while Loyalist papers cited them only 8.1 percent of the time (see appendix).

49. From 1775 to 1779, the *London Gazette* made up 22.3 percent of Patriot citations abroad and 54.3 percent of Loyalist citations abroad. From 1780 to 1784, the *London Gazette* provided 33.5 percent of Patriot citations and 48.6 percent of Loyalist citations (see appendix).

50. Lutnick, *American Revolution and the British Press*, 20–22. From 1775 to 1779, opposition prints made up 22.5 percent of Patriot citations and 10.9 percent of Loyalist citations. From 1780 to 1784, they made up 24.4 percent of Patriot citations abroad and only 7.4 percent of Loyalist citations (see appendix).

51. From 1775 to 1779, radical opposition prints made up 47.1 percent of Patriot citations and 15.2 percent of Loyalist citations. From 1780 to 1784, they constituted 19.5 percent of Patriot citations and 5.3 percent of Loyalist citations (see appendix).

52. *Maryland Journal* (Baltimore), Feb. 29, 1780.

53. *Pennsylvania Packet* (Philadelphia), Aug. 5, 1776. See similar headings in *Connecticut Journal* (New Haven), Sept. 13, 1775; *Massachusetts Spy* (Worcester), Dec. 24, 1778. On the term's use in London, see Lutnick, *American Revolution and the British Press*, 22.

54. *Massachusetts Spy* (Worcester), Jan. 23, 1783. See also *London Courant*, Sept. 28, 1782.

55. *Boston Gazette*, June 15, 1778. For other examples of the term's use against Loyalist presses, see *Massachusetts Spy* (Worcester), Feb. 16, 1775; "Boston, June 9," *Connecticut Gazette* (New London), June 13, 1777; *New-Jersey Gazette* (Trenton), June 24, 1778; *Continental Journal* (Boston), Nov. 5, 1778, Sept. 14, 1780.

56. *Pennsylvania Evening Post* (Philadelphia), July 13, 1776; *Virginia Gazette* (Williamsburg), July 27, 1776; *Connecticut Courant* (Hartford), July 29, 1776; *Constitutional Gazette* (New York), July 10, 1776; *New-York Gazette and Weekly Mercury*, July 15, 1776. Other efforts to debunk this rumor appeared in "Debates in the British House of Lords," *Providence Gazette*, Aug. 3, 1776; "From the Leyden Gazette of April 12, 1776," *Pennsylvania Journal* (Philadelphia), Aug. 21, 1776; "Extract of a Letter from Portsmouth, May 22," *New-York Journal*, Aug. 29, 1776.

57. New York heading, *Newport Gazette*, July 10, 1776.

58. "For the Public Ledger," *Boston Gazette*, July 9, 1770; Lutnick, *American Revolution and the British Press*, 63–65.

59. Bailyn, *Ideological Origins of the American Revolution*, 134, 145.

60. *Journal and Letters of the Late Samuel Curwen, Judge of Admiralty, etc., an American Refugee in England from 1775–1784*, ed. George Atkinson Ward (New York, 1842), 218, 226.

61. *Rivington's New-York Gazetteer*, Aug. 11, 1774.

62. *New-York Journal*, Aug. 18, Sept. 1, Aug. 25, 1774.

63. "New York, Jan. 25, 1775," *New-York Journal*, Feb. 9, 1775.

64. Philadelphia heading, *Rivington's New-York Gazetteer*, Jan. 19, 1775. Rivington likely saw the full letters in the *Pennsylvania Journal* (Philadelphia), Jan. 11, 1775.

65. *Rivington's New York Gazetteer*, Feb. 16, 1775.

66. *New-York Journal*, Mar. 2, 1775.

67. *Boston News-Letter*, Feb. 16, 1775.

68. *New-York Journal*, Aug. 11, 1774.

69. *Rivington's New-York Gazette*, Aug. 11, 1774.

70. Boston heading, *Boston Gazette*, Jan. 16, 1775.

71. *Boston Gazette*, Feb. 6, 1775.

72. *Evening Post* (London), Jan. 29, 1774; *Boston Gazette*, Apr. 25, 1774; "From the London Evening Post, of March 5," *Norwich Packet*, June 24, 1776.

73. *Connecticut Gazette* (New London), Nov. 11, 1774; *Connecticut Courant* (Hartford), Oct. 3, 1774; *Connecticut Journal* (New Haven), Oct. 14, 1774. See also letter from London, *New-York Journal*, June 9, 1774.

74. "To Massachusettensis," *Boston Post-Boy*, Dec. 26, 1774.

75. "To the Author of a Piece Signed a Son of New-England," *Boston Post-Boy*, Jan. 16, 1775.

76. *St. James's Chronicle* (London), Apr. 4, 1776.

77. James E. Bradley, *Popular Politics and the American Revolution in England: Petitions, the Crown, and Public Opinion* (Macon, GA, 1986), 5; John Sainsbury, *Disaffected Patriots: London Supporters of Revolutionary America, 1769–1782* (Montreal, QC, 1987), 30.

78. Sainsbury, *Disaffected Patriots*, chs. 3 and 4, esp. 57; Eliga H. Gould, *The Persistence of Empire: British Political Culture in the Age of the American Revolution* (Chapel Hill, NC, 2000), chs. 2 and 5, esp. 177; W. M. Elofson, *The Rockingham Connection and the Second Founding of the Whig Party* (Montreal, 1996), 167. Bradley, *Popular Politics and the American Revolution in England*, dissents from the consensus by suggesting that there was considerable public opposition in Britain to coercive measures against the Americans. Even if this objection were granted, it remains that this support was much more limited than Patriots hoped.

79. New York heading, *Massachusetts Gazette; and Boston Post-Boy and Advertiser*, May 16, 1774.

80. Lutnick, *American Revolution and the British Press*, 65–69.

81. London heading, *New-York Gazette and Weekly Mercury*, May 13, 1771; *Essex Journal* (Newburyport, MA), Mar. 22, 1775; London heading, *Pennsylvania Evening Post* (Philadelphia), Sept. 14, Nov. 2, 1775; "From the Public Advertiser," *Dunlap's Pennsylvania Packet* (Philadelphia), Oct. 9, 1775.

82. *Pennsylvania Gazette* (Philadelphia), May 30, 1771.

83. *New-York Gazette and Weekly Mercury*, May 13, 1771. See also *Pennsylvania Gazette* (Philadelphia), July 26, 1770.

84. Paul Langford, "The British Business Community and the Later Nonimportation Movements, 1768–1776," in *Resistance, Politics, and the American Struggle for Independence, 1765–1775*, ed. Walter H. Conser Jr. et al. (Boulder, CO, 1986), 278–79.

85. "From the Public Advertiser," *Pennsylvania Journal* (Philadelphia), Nov. 11, 1772.

86. Boston heading, *Essex Journal* (Newburyport, MA), Oct. 26, 1774; *Newport Mercury*, Aug. 22, 1774. See also *Boston Gazette*, May 9, 1774.

87. *Boston Gazette*, Dec. 5, 1774.

88. "From the Public Advertiser," *Virginia Gazette* (Williamsburg), June 22, 1775; "From the Public Ledger," *Providence Gazette*, Feb. 18, 1775; "From the Public Ledger," *Virginia Gazette* (Williamsburg), May 27, 1775; *Newport Mercury*, June 12, 1775.

89. *Massachusetts Spy* (Worcester), Dec. 1, 1774.

90. Sainsbury, *Disaffected Patriots*, 98.

91. Langford, "British Business Community," 282–85; Breen, *Marketplace of Revolution*, 224–25; Sainsbury, *Disaffected Patriots*, 41, 69–82.

92. *Connecticut Courant* (Hartford), Aug. 16, 1774.

93. Letter from London, *Boston Post-Boy*, Jan. 18, 1773.

94. "A Friend to Liberty," *Virginia Gazette* (Williamsburg), Apr. 26, 1770.

95. William Strahan to David Hall, July 13, 1771, Nov. 4, Dec. 2, 1772, Jan. 16, Aug. 8, 1776, Aug. 24, 1770, folder 31, box 1, William Strahan Letters, Historical Society of Pennsylvania, Philadelphia.

96. *Boston News-Letter*, Feb. 16, 1775.

97. Charleston heading, *Boston Evening-Post*, Apr. 9, 1770.

98. *Massachusetts Spy* (Worcester), Dec. 10, 1774. See also *Essex Journal* (Newburyport, MA), Oct. 26, 1774.

99. *A Proclamation for Suppressing Rebellion and Sedition* (London, 1775).

100. New York heading, *New-York Gazette and Weekly Mercury*, Oct. 16, 1775, reprinted in New York heading, *Story and Humphrey's Pennsylvania Mercury* (Philadelphia), Oct. 20, 1775, quoted in Paul Langford, "British Correspondence in the Colonial Press, 1763–1775: A Study in Anglo-American Misunderstanding before the American Revolution," in *The Press and the American Revolution*, ed. Bernard Bailyn and John B. Hench (Boston, 1981), 309.

101. Bailyn, *Ideological Origins of the American Revolution*, 144–59; James H. Hutson, "The American Revolution: Triumph of a Delusion?," in *New Wine in Old Skins*, ed. Erich Angermann, Marie-Luise Frings, and Hermann Wellenreuther (Stuttgart, 1976), 179; Gordon S. Wood, "Conspiracy and the Paranoid Style: Causality and Deceit in the Eighteenth Century," *William and Mary Quarterly* 39 (July 1982): 405–6.

102. Bailyn, *Ideological Origins of the American Revolution*, ch. 2.

103. Langford, "British Correspondence in the Colonial Press," 302–11.

104. Schlesinger, *Prelude to Independence*; Carol Sue Humphrey, *The American Revolution and the Press: The Promise of Independence* (Evanston, IL, 2013); Parkinson, *Common Cause*.

Chapter 4 · An Ocean of News

1. *Pennsylvania Evening Herald* (Philadelphia), Sept. 28, 1785.

2. New York heading, *Daily Advertiser* (New York), Aug. 16, 1786.

3. Boston heading, *Independent Chronicle* (Boston), Apr. 26, 1792.

4. *Massachusetts Gazette* (Springfield), Jan. 13, 1784.

5. *The News-Carrier's Address to His Customers, Hartford, January 1, 1784* (Hartford, CT, 1784), n.p.

6. *The News-Carrier's Address to His Customers, Hartford, January 1, 1785* (Hartford, CT, 1785), n.p.

7. Portsmouth heading, *New-Hampshire Spy* (Portsmouth), Nov. 1, 1788.

8. *Federal Gazette* (Philadelphia), Oct. 5, 1790.

9. *Massachusetts Spy* (Worcester), Nov. 15, 1787.

10. *Proposal of Hall and Macclintock, for Publishing the Times; or, the Evening Entertainer* (Boston, 1794), 3.

11. Kariann Akemi Yokota, *Unbecoming British: How Revolutionary America Became a Postcolonial Nation* (New York, 2011); Sam W. Haynes, *Unfinished Revolution: The Early American Republic in a British World* (Charlottesville, VA, 2010); P. J. Marshall, *Remaking the British Atlantic: The United States and the British Empire after American Independence* (Oxford, 2012).

12. *Gazette of the United States* (New York), Oct. 9, 1790.

13. *Daily Advertiser* (New York), Sept. 30, 1790.

14. Philip S. Foner, ed., *The Democratic-Republican Societies, 1790–1800: A Documentary Sourcebook of Constitutions, Declarations, Addresses, Resolutions, and Toasts* (Westport, CT, 1976), 109.

15. Poughkeepsie heading, *Poughkeepsie Journal* (New York), May 8, 1793.

16. "Communications: The French," *Independent Chronicle* (Boston), Apr. 19, 1793.

17. *Pennsylvania Packet* (Philadelphia), Oct. 14, 1785.

18. Walter Lippmann, *Public Opinion* (New York, 1922), 329.

19. *Massachusetts Centinel* (Boston), Apr. 17, 1784; *Hampshire Chronicle*, May 8, 1787.

20. New York heading, *Daily Advertiser* (New York), Aug. 16, 1786.

21. Richard B. Morris, *The Forging of the Union, 1781–1789* (New York, 1987), 14. See, for example, *Massachusetts Centinel* (Boston), Jan. 3, 1789; *South-Carolina Gazette and General Advertiser* (Charleston), Nov. 15, 1783; "To the Public," *Independent Gazetteer* (Philadelphia), Dec. 20, 1783; Philadelphia heading, *Pennsylvania Evening Herald* (Philadelphia), Aug. 30, 1786; *Pennsylvania Journal* (Philadelphia), June 12, 1784.

22. *New Hampshire Gazette* (Portsmouth), Feb. 25, 1786.

23. Philadelphia heading, *Gazette of the United States* (New York), Aug. 25, 1790.

24. Portland heading, *Herald of Freedom* (Boston), Aug. 7, 1789.

25. *New-Jersey Journal* (Elizabethtown), May 7, 1788. See also "Abridgement of the State of Politics this Week," *Pennsylvania Journal* (Philadelphia), Aug. 16, 1783.

26. *State Gazette of South-Carolina* (Charleston), Dec. 22, 1785.

27. *Independent Chronicle* (Boston), Apr. 20, 1780.

28. Baltimore heading, *Independent Gazetteer* (Philadelphia), Feb. 12, 1788. See also "Extract of a Letter from a Gentleman in New-York, to His Friend in This City," *Independent Gazetteer* (Philadelphia), Aug. 2, 1787.

29. London heading, *New-Hampshire Spy* (Portsmouth), Sept. 25, 1787.

30. *New-York Journal*, Sept. 20, 1787.

31. Boston heading, *Massachusetts Centinel* (Boston), Oct. 3, 1787.

32. *Massachusetts Centinel* (Boston), Nov. 17, 1787.

33. *Gazette of the United States* (New York), Dec. 30, 1789. See also "Extract of a Letter from an American Gentleman in Paris, to His Friend in This City, Dated Aug. 31," *Litchfield Monitor*, Dec. 1, 1789.

34. New York heading, *Daily Advertiser* (New York), May 27, 1791. For other examples, see *Oracle of the Day* (Portsmouth, NH), Sept. 13, 1794; *Aurora General Advertiser* (Philadelphia), Oct. 6, 1795.

35. *Courier de Boston: Affiches, nouvelles, & avis. Prospectus* (Boston, 1789), 6.

36. My data set on letters was generated by searching America's Historical Newspapers for headings with the signal phrase "letter from" in proximity to a mix of geographic place names (regions, cities, and nations) that were common in eighteenth-century newspapers. The proportion of letters from the British empire published in British American papers compared to all letters was as follows: 1720s: 40.8 percent; 1730s: 16.7 percent; 1740s: 28.7 percent; 1750s: 27.4 percent; 1760s: 55.4 percent; 1770s: 48.3 percent; 1780s: 35.7 percent; 1790s: 39.9 percent.

37. Jill Lepore, *Book of Ages: The Life and Opinions of Jane Franklin* (New York, 2013), 193–94.

38. Jane Mecom to Benjamin Franklin, Jan. 4, 1779, Founders Online, National Archives, https://founders.archives.gov/documents/Franklin/01-28-02-0279.

39. This analysis is based on examining the search results for "letter from London" and several variants in the America's Historical Newspapers database. I focused on the following

long-running and accessible newspapers: *Boston Gazette, Connecticut Courant, New Hampshire Gazette, New-York Journal and Weekly Mercury, Pennsylvania Gazette, Pennsylvania Journal, Providence Gazette,* and *Rivington's New-York Gazette* (and other titles published by Rivington).

40. Bradford Perkins, *The First Rapprochement* (Berkeley, CA, 1967), 35.

41. Peter P. Hill, "Prologue to the Quasi-War: Stresses in Franco-American Commercial Relations, 1793–96," *Journal of Modern History* 49 (Mar. 1977): D1039–69.

42. Silvia Marzagalli, "Establishing Transatlantic Trade Networks in Time of War: Bordeaux and the United States, 1793–1815," *Business History Review* 79 (Winter 2005): 825.

43. On sailors' use of paper documents to establish their identity, see Nathan Perl-Rosenthal, *Citizen Sailors: Becoming American in the Age of Revolution* (Cambridge, MA, 2015).

44. Perkins, *First Rapprochement*, 35.

45. *American Mercury* (Hartford, CT), Mar. 3, 1794; *Aurora General Advertiser* (Philadelphia), Aug. 13, 1795; *Philadelphia Gazette*, Feb. 28, 1794. Freneau warned captains that "when the British privateers board our vessels, they take full liberty of opening any letters they please which they can find aboard." *National Gazette* (Philadelphia), July 27, 1793.

46. *American Minerva* (New York), Mar. 5, 1794.

47. Perkins, *First Rapprochement*, 35.

48. Samuel Cary Sr. to David Barry, Aug. 30, 1795, folder: Cary Family 1795, box 1, Cary Family Papers, 1789–1883, Massachusetts Historical Society, Boston.

49. Samuel Cary Sr. to Samuel Cary Jr., Sept. 14, 1795, folder: Cary Family 1795, box 1, Cary Family Papers, 1789–1883, Massachusetts Historical Society, Boston.

50. Samuel Cary Sr. to Samuel Cary Jr., June 10, 1800, folder: Cary Family 1800–May 1801, box 2, Massachusetts Historical Society, Boston.

51. Samuel Cary Sr. to Sarah Cary, Mar. 15, 1797, folder: March 1797–December 1798, box 2, Cary Family Papers III, 1769–1919, Massachusetts Historical Society, Boston.

52. Henry Corbieres to James Perkins and Thomas Perkins, Oct. 27, 1798, folder 6, box 1, Thomas Handasyd Perkins Papers, 1783–1892, Massachusetts Historical Society, Boston.

53. *Daily Advertiser* (New York), Apr. 25, 1793; *Impartial Herald* (Newburyport, MA), Dec. 11, 1795; *Massachusetts Mercury* (Boston), Dec. 25, 1795.

54. As mentioned above, this analysis is based on examining results from the America's Historical Newspapers database using searches for "letter from London," "letter from Paris," and several widely used variants. I focused on the following newspapers: *City Gazette* (Charleston, SC), *Columbian Centinel* (Boston), *Connecticut Courant* (Hartford), *Daily Advertiser* (New York), *Gazette of the United States* (Philadelphia), *New Hampshire Gazette* (Portsmouth), *New-Jersey Journal* (Elizabethtown), *Newport Mercury,* and *Vermont Gazette.*

55. *National Gazette* (Philadelphia), Oct. 31, 1791.

56. Andrew Pettegree, *The Invention of News: How the World Came to Know about Itself* (New Haven, CT, 2014).

57. *National Gazette* (Philadelphia), Oct. 31, 1791.

58. Harry B. Weiss, *A Graphic Summary of the Growth of Newspapers in New York and Other States, 1704–1820* (New York, 1948).

59. Stephen Conway, *The British Isles and the War of American Independence* (Oxford, 2000); Jeffrey L. Pasley, *"The Tyranny of Printers": Newspaper Politics in the Early American Republic* (Charlottesville, VA, 2001), 33; Charles G. Steffen, "Newspapers for Free: The Economies of Newspaper Circulation in the Early Republic," *Journal of the Early Republic* 23 (Autumn 2003): 419; David Copeland, "America, 1750–1820," in *Press, Politics and the Public Sphere in Europe and North America, 1760–1820,* ed. Hannah Barker and Simon Burrows (Cambridge, 2002), 149.

60. Other scholars have correctly pointed out that the expansion of the periodical press in the late eighteenth century also depended on the coalescence of several long-term structural changes, including changing legal norms, the growth of postal operations and packet ships, and rising literacy. See, for example, William B. Warner, "Truth and Trust and the Eighteenth-Century Anglophone Newspaper," in *Travelling Chronicles: News and Newspapers from the Early Modern Period to the Eighteenth Century,* ed. Siv Gøril Brandtzæg, Paul Goring, and Christine Watson (Leiden, 2018), 31.

61. John A. Lent, "Oldest Existing Commonwealth Caribbean Newspapers," *Caribbean Quarterly* 22 (Dec. 1976): 90–106; Howard S. Pactor, *Colonial British Caribbean Newspapers: A Bibliography and Directory* (Westport, CT, 1990).

62. Mrinal Kanti Chanda, *History of the English Press in Bengal* (Calcutta, 1987), 5.

63. Boston heading, *Massachusetts Centinel* (Boston), Apr. 18, 1789.

64. Hugh Gough, *The Newspaper Press in the French Revolution* (London, 1988), ch. 1.

65. Marie-Antoinette Menier and Gabriel Debien, "Journaux de Saint-Domingue," *Revue d'histoire des colonies* 36, nos. 127–28 (1949): 424–75.

66. Jeremy D. Popkin, "A Colonial Media Revolution: The Press in Saint-Domingue, 1789–1793," *Americas* 75 (Jan. 2018): 4.

67. Will Slauter, "Periodicals and the Commercialization of Information in the Early Modern Era," in *Information: A Historical Companion,* ed. Ann Blair, Paul Duguid, Anja-Silvia Boeing, and Anthony Grafton (Princeton, NJ, 2021), 146–47.

68. *Massachusetts Centinel* (Boston), July 31, 1784.

69. [Philip Freneau], *New Year's Verses, for 1786: Addressed to the Customers of the Columbian Herald, by the Printers Lads Who Carry It* (Charleston, SC, 1786).

70. Paul Cheney, "A False Dawn for Enlightenment Cosmopolitanism? Franco-American Trade during the American War of Independence," *William and Mary Quarterly* 63 (July 2006): 463–88; Edmond Buron, "Statistics on Franco-American Trade, 1778–1806," *Journal of Economic and Business History* 4 (May 1932): 580; Marzagalli, "Establishing Transatlantic Trade Networks," 813; Douglas A. Irwin, *Clashing over Commerce: A History of U.S. Trade Policy* (Chicago, IL, 2017), 50.

71. Marshall, *Remaking the British Atlantic,* ch. 5.

72. William Gray Jr. to William Ward, Aug. 9, 1792, folder: Thomas Wren Ward, box 1, Ward Family Correspondence, Massachusetts Historical Society, Boston.

73. Brooke Hunter, "Wheat, War, and the American Economy during the Age of Revolution," *William and Mary Quarterly* 62 (July 2005): 505–26, esp. 506; Timothy Pitkin, *A Statistical View of the Commerce of the United States of America* (Hartford, CT, 1816), 185; Buron, "Statistics on Franco-American Trade," 578–80.

74. *Pennsylvania Gazette* (Philadelphia), Apr. 5, 12, 1764.

75. *General Advertiser* (Philadelphia), Mar. 5, 1794; "Extract of a Letter from Bourdeaux 1st Dec. 1794," *General Advertiser* (Philadelphia), Mar. 1, 1794; "Just Imported in the Ship Richmond," *Philadelphia Gazette,* Mar. 14, 1794; *Gazette of the United States* (Philadelphia), Mar. 7, 1794; Philadelphia heading, *Boston Gazette,* Mar. 10, 1794; *Philadelphia Gazette,* Mar. 6, 1794.

76. Sam A. Mustafa, *Merchants and Migrations: Germans and Americans in Connection, 1776–1835* (Abingdon, England, 2001), ch. 5; Slauter, "Periodicals and the Commercialization of Information," 146.

77. *North-Carolina Journal* (Halifax), Nov. 27, 1793.

78. Thomas M. Truxes, *Irish-American Trade, 1660–1783* (Cambridge, 1988), 249.

79. Jeremy D. Popkin, *News and Politics in the Age of Revolution: Jean Luzac's "Gazette de Leyde"* (Ithaca, NY, 1989).

80. *Gazette of the United States* (New York), May 1, 1790; *Maryland Journal* (Baltimore), Mar. 25, 1791; *Newhampshire Gazetteer* (Exeter), Apr. 16, 1791.

81. John Sevier diary, June 8, 1790, in John H. DeWitt, "Journal of John Sevier," *Tennessee Historical Magazine* 5 (Oct. 1919): 161.

82. Sevier diary, Jan. 14, 1794, in DeWitt, "Journal of John Sevier," 167–68.

Chapter 5 · The Genius of Information

1. *Montreal Gazette*, Mar. 1, 1792.

2. Mason Wade, "Quebec and the French Revolution of 1789: The Missions of Henri Mezière," *Canadian Historical Review* 31 (1950): 351.

3. This was one of several scripts circulating around the revolutionary Atlantic. See Keith Michael Baker and Dan Edelstein, eds., *Scripting Revolution: A Historical Approach to the Comparative Study of Revolutions* (Stanford, CA, 2015).

4. *National Gazette* (Philadelphia), Apr. 24, 1793.

5. George Blake, *An Oration* (Boston, 1795), 24.

6. On the connections between revolutions, see, for example, Suzanne Desan, "Internationalizing the French Revolution," *French Politics, Culture and Society* 29 (2011): 137–60; Suzanne Desan, Lynn Hunt, and William Max Nelson, eds., *The French Revolution in Global Perspective* (Ithaca, NY, 2013); Janet Polasky, *Revolutions without Borders: The Call to Liberty in the Atlantic World* (Cambridge, MA, 2015).

7. *Independent Gazetteer* (Philadelphia), Sept. 11, 1790.

8. *Independent Gazetteer* (Philadelphia), Apr. 10, 1790.

9. Boston heading, *Pennsylvania Packet* (Philadelphia), Feb. 26, 1782.

10. Joseph Lathrop, *National Happiness, Illustrated in a Sermon, Delivered at West-Springfield* (Springfield, MA, 1795), 17.

11. Thomas Fessenden, *A Sermon, Preached at Walpole* (Walpole, MA, 1795), 16.

12. *Massachusetts Spy* (Worcester), July 11, 1793.

13. *National Gazette* (Philadelphia), Nov. 28, 1792.

14. Phinehas Hedges, *An Oration, Delivered before the Republican Society of Ulster County, and Other Citizens* (Goshen, NY, 1795), 3.

15. *Western Star* (Stockbridge, MA), Aug. 2, 1791.

16. Joel Barlow, *Advice to the Privileged Orders, in the Several States of Europe* (New York, 1792), 95, 10.

17. Philadelphia heading, *Pennsylvania Evening Herald* (Philadelphia), June 16, 1787.

18. John Lathrop, *An Oration, Written at the Request of the Officers of the Boston Regiment* (Boston, 1795), 13. See also *Independent Gazetteer* (Philadelphia), July 9, 1791.

19. Thomas Paine, *Rights of Man: Being an Answer to Mr. Burke's Attack on the French Revolution* (Philadelphia, 1791), 79.

20. *Gazette of the United States* (Philadelphia), Dec. 22, 1792.

21. "For the Massachusetts Spy," *Massachusetts Spy* (Worcester), Sept. 18, 1783.

22. *Dunlap's American Daily Advertiser* (Philadelphia), Jan. 2, 1792.

23. Richard D. Brown, *The Strength of a People: The Idea of an Informed Citizenry in America, 1650–1870* (Chapel Hill, NC, 1996), esp. ch. 2.

24. Keith Michael Baker, "Revolutionizing Revolution," in Baker and Edelstein, *Scripting Revolution*, 32–33.

25. I have found only one use of the indefinite article with the phrase. See *Daily Advertiser* (New York), Jan. 2, 1788.

26. Philadelphia heading, *Independent Gazetteer* (Philadelphia), Nov. 22, 1783.

27. Chandler Robbins, *Mr. Robbins's Address, Delivered at Plymouth, on the 24th Day of January, 1793, to Celebrate the Victories of the French Republic* (Boston, 1793), 17.

28. New York heading, *Gazette of the United States* (New York), Feb. 24, 1790.

29. Northampton heading, *Hampshire Gazette* (Northampton, MA), Nov. 18, 1789.

30. Lathrop, *Oration*, 13.

31. James Kelly, "Patriot Politics, 1750–91," in *The Oxford Handbook of Modern Irish History*, ed. Alvin Jackson (Oxford, 2014), 479–96.

32. Thomas Bartlett, *Ireland: A History* (Cambridge, 2011), 179–82; Kelly, "Patriot Politics," 488–89.

33. John Adams to President of Congress, Mar. 24, 1780, in *The Revolutionary Diplomatic Correspondence of the United States*, ed. Francis Wharton (Washington, DC, 1889), 3:570–71. See also Adams to President of Congress, Apr. 4, 1780, Founders Online, National Archives, http://founders.archives.gov/documents/Adams/06-09-02-0080.

34. Boston heading, *Independent Chronicle* (Boston), Nov. 18, 1779.

35. John Adams, "Memorial to the States General," Apr. 19, 1781, Founders Online, National Archives, http://founders.archives.gov/documents/Adams/06-11-02-0204.

36. Boston heading, *Independent Chronicle* (Boston), Apr. 20, 1780.

37. Boston heading, *Massachusetts Spy* (Worcester), June 1, 1780.

38. Philadelphia heading, *Pennsylvania Journal* (Philadelphia), May 10, 1783.

39. "From the Belfast Mercury, Dated May 4, 1784," *South-Carolina Gazette and General Advertiser* (Charleston), Aug. 10, 1784.

40. Boston heading, *Continental Journal* (Boston), July 18, 1782; Philadelphia heading, *Pennsylvania Gazette* (Philadelphia), June 23, 1784.

41. Albany heading, *Vermont Gazette* (Bennington), Dec. 11, 1783.

42. New York heading, *Daily Advertiser* (New York), Oct. 28, 1785.

43. New-Haven heading, *New-Haven Gazette*, July 1, 1784.

44. Boston heading, *United States Chronicle* (Providence, RI), Oct. 13, 1784.

45. *Boston Gazette*, Oct. 13, 1783.

46. New York heading, *Pennsylvania Packet* (Philadelphia), July 20, 1784.

47. Albany heading, *Vermont Gazette* (Bennington), Dec. 11, 1783.

48. Vincent Morley, *Irish Opinion and the American Revolution, 1760–1783* (Cambridge, 2002), 331. See also James Kelly, "Mathew Carey's Irish Apprenticeship: Editing the Volunteers Journal, 1783–84," *Éire-Ireland* 49 (Fall–Winter 2014): 238; Jonathan Israel, *The Expanding Blaze: How the American Revolution Ignited the World, 1775–1848* (Princeton, NJ, 2017), ch. 12, esp. 297.

49. Dublin heading, *New-York Journal*, June 24, 1784.

50. "From a Late Irish Paper," *South Carolina Gazette* (Charleston), Aug. 10, 1784.

51. "From the Dublin Evening Post," *Freeman's Journal* (Philadelphia), July 2, 1783.

52. Boston heading, *Massachusetts Centinel* (Boston), Dec. 4, 1784.

53. Philadelphia heading, *Freeman's Journal* (Philadelphia), June 23, 1784.

54. "On the Volunteers of Ireland," *Freeman's Journal* (Philadelphia), Feb. 2, 1785.

55. *Pennsylvania Evening Herald* (Philadelphia), Feb. 5, 1785.

56. Kelly, "Patriot Politics," 490.

57. For US newspapers sharing reports about the crackdown on print in Ireland, see *New-Haven Gazette*, July 1, 1784; London heading, *New-York Journal*, July 28, 1785; *Independent Chronicle* (Boston), July 1, 1784; Baltimore heading, *Vermont Journal* (Windsor), Aug. 25, 1784.

58. James Kelly, "Regulating Print: The State and the Control of Print in Eighteenth-Century Ireland," *Eighteenth-Century Ireland / Iris an dá chultúr* 23 (2008): 167.

59. New York heading, *Pennsylvania Packet* (Philadelphia), July 20, 1784.

60. Kelly, "Mathew Carey's Irish Apprenticeship," 224–25, 240.

61. William Cobbett to Mathew Carey, May 24, 1785, folder 12, box 5, Lea and Febiger Records, 1785–1982, Historical Society of Pennsylvania, Philadelphia.

62. Wayne P. Te Brake, "Popular Politics and the Dutch Patriot Revolution," *Theory and Society* 14 (Mar. 1985): 204.

63. See, for example, a lengthy debate from the *Morning Chronicle* (London), reprinted in the *Independent Journal* (New York), Oct. 6, 10, 20, 1787.

64. "More Intelligence from Europe," *Massachusetts Centinel* (Boston), Nov. 28, 1787.

65. Sinclair Thomson, *We Alone Will Rule: Native Andean Politics in the Age of Insurgency* (Madison, WI, 2002); Sergio Serulnikov, *Revolution in the Andes: The Age of Túpac Amaru* (Durham, NC, 2013).

66. New York heading, *Connecticut Journal* (New Haven), Oct. 5, 1780. I have been unable to identify the original New York newspaper account, which the *Journal* cited as being published on September 15, but only Loyalist papers were printed in the city at that time.

67. "From the Royal South Carolina Gazette, Dated January 3d, 1782," *Royal Gazette* (New York), Feb. 23, 1782.

68. "By the Ship Ruby, Capt. Morrison, in 12 Weeks from Glasgow," *New-York Gazette and Weekly Mercury*, Dec. 10, 1781.

69. Charleston heading, *South-Carolina Gazette and General Advertiser* (Charleston), Dec. 27, 1783.

70. "Spain," *Salem Gazette*, Feb. 28, 1782. See also Boston heading, *Independent Ledger* (Boston), Oct. 7, 1782; "Extract of a Letter from the Archbishop of Lima . . . ," *Pennsylvania Packet* (Philadelphia), Oct. 26, 1782.

71. *New-York Journal and Patriotic Register*, Jan. 12, 1793.

72. María DeGuzmán, *Spain's Long Shadow: The Black Legend, Off-Whiteness, and Anglo-American Empire* (Minneapolis, 2005).

73. *New-York Morning Post*, July 4, 1785.

74. *New York Packet*, Aug. 30, 1784.

75. *Massachusetts Centinel* (Boston), May 8, 1784.

76. "Liberty in Spain," *Cumberland Gazette* (Portland, MA), Jan. 18, 1789.

77. *Diary; or, Loudon's Register* (New York), Oct. 20, 1792. See also *Gazette of the United States* (Philadelphia), Aug. 29, 1792; "Extract of a Letter from Perpignam," *Daily Gazette* (New York), Mar. 4, 1790.

78. *Pennsylvania Packet* (Philadelphia), Mar. 23, 1784.

79. *Carlisle Gazette* (PA), July 9, 1788.

80. Levi Frisbie, *An Oration, Delivered at Ipswich, at the Request of a Number of the Inhabitants* (Boston, 1783), 16.

81. James Madison to Edmund Pendleton, Feb. 21, 1788, Founders Online, National Archives, https://founders.archives.gov/documents/Madison/01-10-02-0306. On the relationship between the Dutch uprising of 1787 and the US Constitution, see Robert W. Smith, "The Dutch Crisis of 1787, American Foreign Policy, and the Constitution," *Journal of the Early Republic* 40 (Summer 2020): 267–95.

82. *Daily Advertiser* (New York), Dec. 11, 1787.

83. Max Farrand, *The Records of the Federal Convention of 1787* (New Haven, CT, 1911), 2:362.

84. Merrill Jensen, ed., *The Documentary History of the Ratification of the Constitution: Ratification of the Constitution by the States*, vol. 9: *Virginia*, no. 2 (Madison, WI, 1976), 1071.

85. Elias Lee, *The Dissolution of Earthly Monarchies* (Danbury, CT, 1794), 16.

86. Richard Price, *A Discourse on the Love of Our Country* (Boston, 1790), 40.

87. Benjamin Wadsworth, *Mr. Wadsworth's Thanksgiving Sermon, February 19, 1795* (Salem, MA, 1795), 25.

88. See, for example, "From the New-York Journal," *State Gazette of South-Carolina* (Charleston), July 17, 1793; Elisha Lee, *An Oration, Delivered at Lenox* (Stockbridge, MA, 1793), 12; George Richards, *An Oration on the Independence of the United States of Federate America*

(Portsmouth, NH, 1795), 6; Samuel Kendal, *A Sermon, Delivered on the Day of National Thanksgiving* (Boston, 1795), 15.

89. Barlow, *Advice to the Privileged Orders*, 14–15.

90. New-Haven heading, *Connecticut Journal* (New Haven), Dec. 9, 1789.

91. Jerzy Lukowski and Hubert Zawadzki, *Concise History of Poland* (Cambridge, 2001), 100; Daniel Stone, *The Polish-Lithuanian State, 1386–1795* (Seattle, 2001), 279–81.

92. Philadelphia heading, *Gazette of the United States* (Philadelphia), July 23, 1791.

93. Philadelphia heading, *General Advertiser* (Philadelphia), July 27, 1791.

94. Philadelphia heading, *Mail; or, Claypoole's Daily Advertiser* (Philadelphia), Aug. 11, 1791.

95. *Amherst Village Messenger*, Nov. 29, 1796; Lathrop, *Oration*, 13; Richards, *An Oration*, 31.

Chapter 6 · The American Constellation

1. "For the Columbian Herald, &c.," *Columbian Herald* (Charleston, SC), Dec. 24, 1793.

2. "For the Columbian Herald, &c."

3. Michael L. Kennedy, "A French Jacobin Club in Charleston, South Carolina, 1792–1795," *South Carolina Historical Magazine* 91 (1990): 15–17; Rachel N. Klein, *Unification of a Slave State: The Rise of the Planter Class in the South Carolina Backcountry, 1760–1808* (Chapel Hill, NC, 1990), ch. 7; Robert J. Alderson Jr., *This Bright Era of Happy Revolutions: French Consul Michel-Ange-Bernard Mangourit and International Republicanism in Charleston, 1792–1794* (Charleston, SC, 2008), esp. 33–34.

4. On Canada, see Howard A. Vernon, "The Impact of the French Revolution on Lower Canada, 1789–1795," PhD diss., University of Chicago, 1951; Mason Wade, "Quebec and the French Revolution of 1789: The Missions of Henri Meziere," *Canadian Historical Review* 31 (1950); F. Murray Greenwood, *Legacies of Fear: Law and Politics in Quebec in the Era of the French Revolution* (Toronto, 1993); Michel Ducharme, *The Idea of Liberty in Canada during the Age of Atlantic Revolutions, 1776–1838*, trans. Peter Feldstein (Montreal, 2014). On Louisiana, see Frederick J. Turner, "Documents on the Relations of France to Louisiana, 1792–1795," *American Historical Review* 3 (Apr. 1898): 508; Ernest R. Liljegren, "Jacobinism in Spanish Louisiana, 1792–1797," *Louisiana Historical Quarterly* 22 (Jan. 1939): 48; Kimberly Hanger, "Conflicting Loyalties: The French Revolution and Free People of Color in Spanish New Orleans," *Louisiana History* 34 (Winter 1993): 5–33; Gilbert C. Din, "Carondelet, the Cabildo, and Slaves: Louisiana in 1795," *Louisiana History* 38 (Winter 1997): 5–28.

5. Ruth Bloch, *Visionary Republic: Millennial Themes in American Thought, 1756–1800* (Cambridge, 1985).

6. Julius S. Scott, *The Common Wind: Afro-American Currents in the Age of the Haitian Revolution* (London, 2018), 265.

7. Eliga H. Gould, *Among the Powers of the Earth: The American Revolution and the Making of a New World Empire* (Cambridge, MA 2012), ch. 4; Drew R. McCoy, *The Elusive Republic: Political Economy in Jeffersonian America* (Chapel Hill, NC, 1980), ch. 5.

8. Liljegren, "Jacobinism in Spanish Louisiana," 48.

9. Kingston heading, *Connecticut Courant* (Hartford), Oct. 7, 1783.

10. Massachusetts heading, *American Recorder* (Boston), May 19, 1786.

11. Jonathan Israel, *The Expanding Blaze: How the American Revolution Ignited the World, 1775–1848* (Princeton, NJ, 2017), 200–203.

12. Frederick Haldimand to George Clinton, Mar. 5, 1782, Haldimand Papers, Canadiana Héritage, http://heritage.canadiana.ca/view/oocihm.lac_reel_h1649/1088?r=0&s=4.

13. London heading, *Pennsylvania Packet* (Philadelphia), Mar. 30, 1784. See also Providence heading, *United States Chronicle* (Providence, RI), July 27, 1785.

14. Boston heading, *Massachusetts Centinel* (Boston), June 12, 1784.

15. "Of France," *New-York Daily Gazette*, Dec. 27, 1790.

16. Charles Gayarré, *History of Louisiana: The Spanish Domination* (New York, 1854), 327; Liljegren, "Jacobinism in Spanish Louisiana," 48, 51.

17. Morgan John Rhees, *An Oration Delivered at Greenville* (Philadelphia, 1795), 6.

18. Thomas Paine, *Rights of Man, Part the Second* (Philadelphia, 1792), 9.

19. *New-York Journal and Patriotic Register*, Dec. 17, 1791.

20. Israel, *Expanding Blaze*, 203.

21. François Furstenberg, *When the United States Spoke French: Five Refugees Who Shaped a Nation* (New York, 2014), 249–52.

22. Joel Barlow, *Advice to the Privileged Orders, in the Several States of Europe* (New York, 1792).

23. Joel Barlow, *A Letter Addressed to the People of Piedmont, on the Advantages of the French Revolution, and the Necessity of Adopting Its Principles in Italy* (1792; trans., New York, 1795), 13–14.

24. Jacques-Pierre Brissot, *New Travels in the United States of America* (1791; rpt., New York, 1792), 262–63.

25. Wesley J. Campbell, "The French Intrigue of James Cole Mountflorence," *William and Mary Quarterly* 65 (Oct. 2008): 795.

26. Turner, "Documents on the Relations of France to Louisiana," 508.

27. Robert Durden, "Joel Barlow in the French Revolution," *William and Mary Quarterly* 8 (July 1951): 348–50; Campbell, "French Intrigue of James Cole Mountflorence," 780.

28. Eran Shalev, "'A Republic amidst the Stars': Political Astronomy and the Intellectual Origins of the Stars and Stripes," *Journal of the Early Republic* 31 (Spring 2011): 53.

29. Linda S. Frey and Marsha L. Frey, *The French Revolution* (Westport, CT, 2004), 151–53.

30. Furstenberg, *When the United States Spoke French*, 304–6.

31. Alderson, *This Bright Era of Happy Revolutions*, 22.

32. Michel Brunet, "La revolution française sur les rives du Saint-Laurent," *Revue d'histoire de l'Amérique française* 11, no. 2 (1957): 157; Wade, "Quebec and the French Revolution of 1789," 357, 349.

33. For Genêt's news abstracts, see reels 35–38, Edmond Charles Genet Papers, Library of Congress, Washington, DC.

34. Wade, "Quebec and the French Revolution of 1789," 350–52.

35. Bernard Andrès, *La conquête des lettres au Québec (1759–1799): Anthologie* (Quebec, 2007), 532, 535.

36. It was not unusual for Girondin emissaries to print pamphlets along these lines. William S. Cormack, *Patriots, Royalists, and Terrorists in the West Indies: The French Revolution in Martinique and Guadeloupe, 1789–1802* (Toronto, 2019), 146.

37. Edmond-Charles Genêt, *Les français libres à leurs frères les canadiens* (N.p., 1793), 1–2, 6.

38. "Correspondence of French Ministers to the United States, 1791–1797," in *Annual Report of the American Historical Association for the Year 1903*, ed. Frederick J. Turner (Washington, DC, 1904), 2:265–68.

39. James Monk to Lord Dorchester, June 18, 1794, Colonial Office 42, C-11909, Q69-1:55, Canadiana Héritage, http://heritage.canadiana.ca/view/oocihm.lac_reel_c11909/1629?r=0&s=3.

40. Greenwood, *Legacies of Fear*, 78, 96.

41. Wade, "Quebec and the French Revolution of 1789," 355.

42. Thomas Paine, *Rights of Man: Being an Answer to Mr. Burke's Attack on the French Revolution* (Philadelphia, 1791), 40.

43. Samuel Miller, *A Sermon, Preached in New-York, July 4th 1793* (New York, 1793), 30, 29, 34.

44. Louis Didier, "Le citoyen Genêt," *Revue des questions historiques* 92 (July 1912): 358.

45. Jeremy D. Popkin, *You Are All Free: The Haitian Revolution and the Abolition of Slavery* (Cambridge, 2010).

46. Wade, "Quebec and the French Revolution of 1789," 358–61.

47. Wade, "Quebec and the French Revolution of 1789," 360.

48. Annie Jourdan, "A Tale of Three Patriots in a Revolutionary World: Théophile Casenove, Jacques-Pierre Brissot, and Joel Barlow (1788–1811)," *Early American Studies* 10 (Spring 2012): 367n25.

49. R. R. Palmer, *Twelve Who Ruled: The Year of the Terror in the French Revolution* (Princeton, NJ, 1941), ch. 5.

50. Frank Maloy Anderson, *The Constitutions and Other Select Documents Illustrative of the History of France, 1789–1907* (Minneapolis, 1904), 133.

51. Durden, "Joel Barlow in the French Revolution," 350–51.

52. "Editorial Note: The Recall of Edmond Charles Genet," Jefferson Papers, Founders Online, National Archives, https://founders.archives.gov/documents/Jefferson/01-26-02-0629-0001.

53. T. S. Webster, "A New York Revolutionary in the Era of the French Revolution: Stephen Thorn, Conspirator for a Canadian Revolution," *New-York Historical Society Quarterly* 53 (July 1969): 252–53.

54. Greenwood, *Legacies of Fear*, 81–82.

55. Albany heading, *Albany Gazette*, July 28, 1794.

56. Newburyport heading, *Morning Star* (Newburyport, MA), Oct. 21, 1794.

57. Turner, *Annual Report of the American Historical Association*, 2:288–89; Greenwood, *Legacies of Fear*, 83.

58. Jeanne A. Ojala, "Ira Allen and the French Directory, 1796: Plans for the Creation of the Republic of United Columbia," *William and Mary Quarterly* 36 (July 1979): 436–48.

59. Webster, "New York Revolutionary," 252–45; J. Kevin Graffagnino, "'Twenty Thousand Muskets!!!': Ira Allen and the Olive Branch Affair, 1796–1800," *William and Mary Quarterly* 48 (July 1991): 409.

60. Webster, "New York Revolutionary," 261.

61. Pierre-Auguste Adet to Minister of Foreign Relations, Feb. 9, 1796, in "Correspondence of French Ministers to the United States," in Turner, *Annual Report of the American Historical Association*, 2:826.

62. For an overview of Adet's tenure as ambassador, see Michael F. Conlin, "The American Mission of Citizen Pierre-Auguste Adet: Revolutionary Chemistry and Diplomacy in the Early Republic," *Pennsylvania Magazine of History and Biography* 124 (Oct. 2000): 489–520.

63. Greenwood, *Legacies of Fear*, 83. In late 1796 Britain's minister to the United States suspected that this was France's plan. Robert Liston to Major General Robert Prescott, Nov. 28, 1796, Colonial Office 42, C-11911, Q78:208, Canadiana Héritage, http://heritage.canadiana.ca/view/oocihm.lac_reel_c11911/1732?r=0&s=3.

64. Greenwood, *Legacies of Fear*, ch. 7; Executive Council meeting minutes, Oct. 30, 1796, Colonial Office 42, C-11911, Q78:97–98, Canadiana Héritage, http://heritage.canadiana.ca/view/oocihm.lac_reel_c11911/1621?r=0&s=3.

65. William Kingsford, *The History of Canada*, vol. 7: *1779–1807* (London, 1894), 453.

66. Major General Robert Prescott to the Duke of Portland, Colonial Office 42, C-11911, Q78:209, Canadiana Héritage, http://heritage.canadiana.ca/view/oocihm.lac_reel_c11911/1734?r=0&s=3.

67. Lawrence Kinnaird, ed., *Annual Report of the American Historical Association for the Year 1945: Spain in the Mississippi Valley, 1765–1794*, vol. 4: *Problems of Frontier Defense, 1792–1794* (Washington, DC, 1949), 255–56.

68. Genêt, *Français libres à leurs frères les canadiens*, 1–2, 6.

69. Hanger, "Conflicting Loyalties," 6–7.

70. Manuel Gayoso de Lemos, "Political Condition of the Province of Louisiana," July 5, 1792, in *Louisiana under the Rule of Spain, France, and the United States, 1785–1807*, ed. James Alexander Robertson (Cleveland, OH, 1911), 1:288.

71. Thomas Marc Fiehrer, "The Baron de Carondelet as Agent of Bourbon Reform: A Study of Spanish Colonial Administration in the Years of the French Revolution," PhD diss., Tulane University, 1977, 474.

72. Liljegren, "Jacobinism in Spanish Louisiana," 58.

73. Gwendolyn Midlo Hall, "The 1795 Slave Conspiracy in Pointe Coupée: Impact of the French Revolution," *Proceedings of the Meeting of the French Colonial Historical Society* 15 (1992): 131, 137, 140; Jack D. L. Holmes, "The Abortive Slave Revolt at Pointe Coupée, Louisiana, 1795," *Louisiana History* 11 (Autumn 1970): 341–62.

74. Liljegren, "Jacobinism in Spanish Louisiana," 58. See also Hanger, "Conflicting Loyalties," 9. Perhaps because of its tiny circulation, *Le moniteur de la Louisiane* has not been well preserved. Jack D. L. Holmes, "Louisiana in 1795: The Earliest Extant Issue of the 'Moniteur de la Louisiane,'" *Louisiana History* 7 (Spring 1966): 133–51.

75. James A. Padgett, ed., "A Decree for Louisiana, Issued by the Baron of Carondelet, June 1, 1795," *Louisiana Historical Quarterly* 20 (July 1937): 595–96, 598.

76. Holmes, "Abortive Slave Revolt," 357.

77. Ada Ferrer, *Freedom's Mirror: Cuba and Haiti in the Age of Revolution* (New York, 2014), 61–62.

78. Hall, "1795 Slave Conspiracy in Pointe Coupée," 130.

79. Fiehrer, "Baron de Carondelet as Agent of Bourbon Reform," 469.

80. Kinnaird, *Annual Report of the American Historical Association*, 137.

81. Hanger, "Conflicting Loyalties," 20.

82. Kinnaird, *Annual Report of the American Historical Association*, 137–38.

83. Kinnaird, *Annual Report of the American Historical Association*, 139.

84. Padgett, "Decree for Louisiana," 590–605.

85. James Monk to Lord Dorchester, June 18, 1794, Colonial Office 42, C-11909, Q69-1:54–55, Canadiana Héritage, http://heritage.canadiana.ca/view/oocihm.lac_reel_c11909/1629?r=0&s=3.

86. James Monk to Lord Dorchester, May 29, 1794, image 1575, Colonial Office: Canada, Formerly British North America, Original Correspondence, Colonial Office 42, C-11909, Canadiana Héritage, http://heritage.canadiana.ca/view/oocihm.lac_reel_c11909/. On the riots, see Greenwood, *Legacies of Fear*, 80–83.

87. Lord Dorchester to Henry Dundas, June 21, 1794, image 1623, Colonial Office: Canada, Formerly British North America, Original Correspondence, Colonial Office 42, Canadiana Héritage, https://heritage.canadiana.ca/view/oocihm.lac_reel_c11909/1623?r=0&s=1.

88. On British loyal associations, see Gregory Claeys, *The French Revolution Debate in Britain: The Origins of Modern Politics* (Houndmills, UK, 2007), 92.

89. *Liberty and Property Preserved against the Republicans and Levellers: A Collection of Tracts Recommended to Perusal at the Present Crisis* (London, 1793).

90. *London Chronicle*, Dec. 6, 1792; *Liberty and Property Preserved*, 13.

91. Vernon, "Impact of the French Revolution on Lower Canada," 150.

92. *Quebec Gazette*, July 3, 10, 17, 23, Aug. 7, 21, 28, Sept. 18, 1794.

93. "Committee of Association William Henry," July 9, 1794, image 253, vol. 58, Civil

Secretary's Correspondence, "S" ser., Quebec and Lower Canada, C-3009, Canadiana Héritage, http://heritage.canadiana.ca/view/oocihm.lac_reel_c3009/.

94. Charles Thomas to Thomas Dunn, July 4, 1794, image 242, vol. 58, Civil Secretary's Correspondence, "S" ser., Quebec and Lower Canada, C-3009, Canadiana Héritage, http://heritage.canadiana.ca/view/oocihm.lac_reel_c3009/.

95. George Allsop to Thomas Dunn, July 12, 1794, image 274, "S" ser., Quebec and Lower Canada, C-3009, Canadiana Héritage, http://heritage.canadiana.ca/view/oocihm.lac_reel_c3009/.

96. Hugh Munro to Thomas Dunn, Sept. 16, 1794, image 659, "S" ser., Quebec and Lower Canada, C-3009, Canadiana Héritage, http://heritage.canadiana.ca/view/oocihm.lac_reel_c3009/.

97. *Ottawa Times*, June 25, 1794.

98. Greenwood, *Legacies of Fear*, 110.

99. Vernon, "Impact of the French Revolution on Lower Canada," 103.

100. A. G. Bradley, *Lord Dorchester* (Toronto, 1911), 278.

101. Larry Eldridge, *A Distant Heritage: The Growth of Free Speech in Early America* (New York, 1994), 30; William Blackstone, *Commentaries on the Laws of England* (Oxford, 1770), 4:149.

102. *Quebec Gazette*, Aug. 9, 1792, Nov. 28, 1793.

103. *The Provincial Statutes of Lower-Canada* (Quebec, 1795), 1:75.

104. Premiere declaration de J. B. Vocel Belhumeur, image 1593, Colonial Office: Canada, Formerly British North America, Original Correspondence, Colonial Office 42, C-11909, Canadiana Héritage, http://heritage.canadiana.ca/view/oocihm.lac_reel_c11909/.

105. Greenwood, *Legacies of Fear*, 79.

106. Declaration of John Neilson, May 30, 1795, Lower Canada, Declarations of Aliens, image 314, Canadiana Héritage, http://heritage.canadiana.ca/view/oocihm.lac_reel_h1154.

107. Brian Tobin, *The Upper Canada Gazette and Its Printers, 1793–1849* (Toronto, 1993), 9.

108. Greenwood, *Legacies of Fear*, ch. 6, esp. 116.

109. "Circulaire, a messieurs les curés à l'occasion des rumeurs de guerre," in *Mandements, lettres pastorals et circulaires des évêques de Québec*, ed. Henri Têtu (Quebec, 1888), 2:471–73.

110. Robert Lee, "Accounting for Conquest: The Price of the Louisiana Purchase of Indian Country," *Journal of American History* 103 (Mar. 2017): 921–42.

111. Levi Beardsley, *Reminiscences* (New York, 1852), 18–19.

Chapter 7 · Bentalou's Wager

1. Carroll D. Wright, *Comparative Wages, Prices, and Cost of Living* (Boston, 1889), 53.

2. *Baltimore Daily Repository*, Sept. 9, 27, 28, 1793.

3. *Baltimore Daily Repository*, Sept. 28, 1793.

4. Baltimore Town, Baltimore, Maryland, 1790 census, http://www.ancestry.com.

5. The Baltimore Republican Society, a prorevolutionary and pro-French organization, listed Bentalou among its officers. See Baltimore heading, *Baltimore Daily Intelligencer*, June 9, 1794.

6. *Baltimore Daily Repository*, Oct. 2, 1793.

7. Tucker had sent this response to the *Repository*, but its printer apparently declined to publish it, leading him to send it to a Virginia paper. *Virginia Chronicle and Norfolk and Portsmouth General Advertiser* (Norfolk), Nov. 9, 1793.

8. Baltimore heading, *Baltimore Daily Repository*, Oct. 2, 1793.

9. New York heading, *New-York Journal*, Nov. 29, 1790.

10. Ruth Bloch, *Visionary Republic: Millennial Themes in American Thought, 1756–1800* (Cambridge, 1985), chs. 7–9.

11. London heading, *Montreal Gazette*, Oct. 3, Nov. 7, 1793.

12. Mason Wade, "Quebec and the French Revolution of 1789: The Missions of Henri Meziere," *Canadian Historical Review* 31 (1950): 362.

13. Some scholars of Canada interpret the French Revolution's impact as part of the process of imperial integration that commenced with the Seven Years' War. They attribute Canadians' quick hostility to the French Revolution to the colony's particular class tensions, government regulations, and ideological currents. Michel Brunet, "La revolution française sur les rives du Saint-Laurent," *Revue d'historie de l'Amérique française* 11, no. 2 (1957): 155–62; Claude Galarneau, *La France devant l'opinion canadienne (1760–1815)* (Paris, 1970); Jean-Pierre Wallot, "La revolution française, le Canada et les Droits de l'homme (1789–1840)," *Etudes canadiennes / Canadian Studies* 28 (1990): 7–18; F. Murray Greenwood, *Legacies of Fear: Law and Politics in Quebec in the Era of the French Revolution* (Toronto, 1993). Historians of the United States, likewise, set the story of the French Revolution within a national context of postrevolutionary ideological and political polarization. For many historians, the contest over the French Revolution in the United States functioned as a proxy war in a broader conflict among various social, cultural, and political forces. Gary Nash, "The American Clergy and the French Revolution," *William and Mary Quarterly* 22 (1965): 399; Rachel N. Klein, *Unification of a Slave State: The Rise of the Planter Class in the South Carolina Backcountry, 1760–1808* (Chapel Hill, NC, 1990), ch. 7; David Waldstreicher, *In the Midst of Perpetual Fetes* (Chapel Hill, NC, 1997); Susan Branson, *These Fiery Frenchified Dames: Women and Political Culture in Early National Philadelphia* (Philadelphia, 2001), ch. 2; Matthew Rainbow Hale, " 'Neither Britons nor Frenchmen': The French Revolution and American National Identity," PhD diss., Brandeis University, 2002; Rachel Hope Cleves, *The Reign of Terror in America: Visions of Violence from Anti-Jacobinism to Antislavery* (Cambridge, 2009); Seth Cotlar, *Tom Paine's America: The Rise and Fall of Transatlantic Radicalism in the Early Republic* (Charlottesville, VA, 2011).

14. Beatrice F. Hyslop, "The American Press and the French Revolution of 1789," *Proceedings of the American Philosophical Society* 104 (Feb. 1960): 67–68; *Quebec Gazette*, Oct. 1, 1789.

15. "Mr. Fenno," *Gazette of the United States* (New York), Dec. 30, 1789.

16. *Massachusetts Mercury* (Boston), Feb. 28, 1793. See also *Columbian Centinel* (Boston), Dec. 25, 1790; *National Gazette* (Philadelphia), Apr. 20, 1793.

17. *Montreal Gazette*, July 1, 1790.

18. *Montreal Gazette*, Oct. 28, 1790.

19. Wade, "Quebec and the French Revolution of 1789," 362.

20. *Columbian Centinel* (Boston), Apr. 13, 1791.

21. *Montreal Gazette*, Jan. 28, 1790.

22. *Gazette of the United States* (Philadelphia), Mar. 16, 1791.

23. *National Gazette* (Philadelphia), June 18, 1792.

24. Jeremy D. Popkin, *Revolutionary News: The Press in France, 1789–1799* (Durham, NC, 1990), 222, 241–42.

25. *National Gazette* (Philadelphia), July 24, 1793.

26. Gary Kates, *The Cercle Social, the Girondins, and the French Revolution* (Princeton, NJ, 1985), 177.

27. Hugh Gough, *The Newspaper Press in the French Revolution* (London, 1988), chs. 3 and 4, esp. 83, 98, 103.

28. Popkin, *Revolutionary News*, 110; Gough, *Newspaper Press*, 127.

29. See criticisms of growing "abuse" and factionalism in French print culture in *American Minerva* (New York), June 15, 1795; *Aurora General Advertiser* (Philadelphia), Dec. 31, 1795.

30. Clive Emsley, *Britain and the French Revolution* (New York, 2000), 18.

31. *Morning Chronicle* (London), Nov. 1, 1793; Gregory Claeys, *The French Revolution Debate in Britain: The Origins of Modern Politics* (Houndmills, UK, 2007), 9.

32. Greenwood, *Legacies of Fear*, 68.

33. *Quebec Gazette*, May 9, 1793.

34. Jane E. Harrison, "The Intercourse of Letters: Transatlantic Correspondence in Early Canada, 1640–1812," PhD diss., University of Toronto, 2000, 205. For an example of non-British news arriving in Canada through the United States, see New York heading, *Quebec Gazette*, Nov. 14, 1799.

35. *Quebec Gazette*, Apr. 3, 1794.

36. *National Gazette* (Philadelphia), Sept. 15, 1792. See also Mar. 6, 1793.

37. Boston heading, *Independent Chronicle* (Boston), Apr. 19, 1793.

38. "To the Editor of the National Gazette," *National Gazette* (Philadelphia), May 11, 1793.

39. Samuel Miller, *A Sermon, Preached in New-York, July 4th, 1793* (New York, 1793), 30–33; James Malcolmson, *A Sermon, Preached on the 14th of July, 1794* (Charleston, SC, 1795), 27.

40. "Domestic Miscellany," *Independent Chronicle* (Boston), Oct. 21, 1793.

41. *Dunlap's American Daily Advertiser* (Philadelphia), Aug. 8, 1792.

42. *General Advertiser* (Philadelphia), Aug. 30, 1792.

43. *Dunlap's American Daily Advertiser* (Philadelphia), Aug. 20, 1792; *General Advertiser* (Philadelphia), Aug. 30, 1792.

44. Portsmouth heading, *Oracle of the Day* (Portsmouth, NH), Oct. 28, 1793.

45. See the following newspapers for January 1794: *Columbian Centinel* (Boston), *Baltimore Daily Intelligencer, City Gazette* (Charleston, SC), *Columbian Gazetteer* (New York), *Gazette of the United States* (Philadelphia), *General Advertiser* (Philadelphia).

46. Lucyle Thomas Werkmeister, *A Newspaper History of England, 1792–1793* (Lincoln, NE, 1967), 412. See also Linda Colley, *Britons: Forging the Nation, 1707–1837* (New Haven, CT, 1992), 255.

47. *Daily Advertiser* (New York), Jan. 9, 1794. See also *American Minerva* (New York), Jan. 9, 1794.

48. *Dunlap's American Daily Advertiser* (Philadelphia), Jan. 10, 1794.

49. *Columbian Centinel* (Boston), Jan. 18, 1794.

50. "Important Intelligence! Direct from France," *Massachusetts Mercury* (Boston), Jan. 10, 1794.

51. *Independent Chronicle* (Boston), Jan. 13, 1794.

52. *American Minerva* (New York), Jan. 22, 1794.

53. *American Minerva* (New York), Jan. 17, 16, 1794.

54. *Greenleaf's New York Journal*, Jan. 18, 1794.

55. *Columbian Gazetteer* (New York), Jan. 20, 1794.

56. *Greenleaf's New York Journal*, Jan. 18, 1794.

57. *General Advertiser* (Philadelphia), Jan. 15, 17, 1794; *Daily Gazette* (New York), Jan. 17, 1794; *Vermont Gazette* (Bennington), Jan. 17, 1794; *American Minerva* (New York), Jan. 18, 1794.

58. *Greenleaf's New York Journal*, Jan. 22, 1794.

59. *Massachusetts Mercury* (Boston), Jan. 10, 1794.

60. *Western Star* (Stockbridge, MA), Feb. 18, 1794.

61. *Quebec Gazette*, Feb. 6, 1794.

62. *Montreal Gazette*, Feb. 6, 1794; *Albany Register*, Jan. 13, 1794.

63. Montreal heading, *Montreal Gazette*, Feb. 13, 1794.

64. *National Gazette* (Philadelphia), Apr. 20, 1793.

65. *Quebec Gazette*, Apr. 4, 1793. While historian Matthew Hale has argued that US Federalists sought to slow down Americans' response to the French Revolution, in my observa-

tion all sorts of political coalitions adopted this posture when it was convenient. Matthew Rainbow Hale, "On Their Tiptoes: Political Time and Newspapers during the Advent of the Radicalized French Revolution, circa 1792–1793," *Journal of the Early Republic* 29 (Summer 2009): 204.

66. *National Gazette* (Philadelphia), Apr. 20, 1793.

67. *Quebec Gazette*, May 9, 1793.

68. *Ottawa Times*, June 25, 1794.

69. Le Compte de Colbert Maulevrier, *Voyage dans l'intérieur des États-Unis et au Canada*, ed. Gilbert Chinard (1798; rpt., Baltimore, 1935), 66.

70. Donald H. Stewart, *The Opposition Press of the Federalist Period* (Albany, NY, 1969); Jeffrey L. Pasley, *"The Tyranny of Printers": Newspaper Politics in the Early American Republic* (Charlottesville, VA, 2001), chs. 3–5.

71. Steven Shapin, *A Social History of Truth: Civility and Science in Seventeenth-Century England* (Chicago, 1994), ch. 3.

72. *Gazette of the United States* (New York), Aug. 25, 1790; *Columbian Centinel* (Boston), May 2, 1795; *Columbian Herald* (Charleston, SC), Nov. 9, 1793. See also *Columbian Centinel* (Boston), Apr. 6, 1793; *American Apollo* (Boston), Apr. 5, 1793.

73. *National Gazette* (Philadelphia), June 18, 1792.

74. *Catskill Packet*, May 20, 1793; *Columbian Centinel* (Boston), Jan. 29, 1794; *Oracle of the Day* (Portsmouth, NH), July 15, 1794; *Daily Advertiser* (New York), May 7, 1793.

75. *Mercury* (Boston), Dec. 16, 1794.

76. See reprint in the *American Minerva* (New York), Mar. 17, 1795. See also *Philadelphia Gazette*, Mar. 2, 1795.

77. Paul Gilje, "On the Waterfront: Maritime Workers in New York City in the Early Republic, 1800–1850," *New York History* 77 (Oct. 1996): 418–19.

78. Will Slauter, "Forward-Looking Statements: News and Speculation in the Age of the American Revolution," *Journal of Modern History* 81 (Dec. 2009): 759–92.

79. This would have likely appeared in the *Independent Chronicle* (Boston) on or around February 5, 1795. See reprint in *New-Hampshire Gazette*, Feb. 10, 1795.

80. Stewart, *Opposition Press of the Federalist Period*, ch. 2.

81. *Impartial Herald* (Newburyport, MA), Feb. 6, 1795.

82. *Columbian Centinel* (Boston), Aug. 15, 1795; *New-York Gazette*, Aug. 18, 1795; *Oracle of the Day* (Portsmouth, NH), Aug. 15, 1795; *American Minerva* (New York), Aug. 19, 1795; *Daily Advertiser* (New York), Aug. 19, 1795.

83. *Aurora General Advertiser* (Philadelphia), Aug. 25, 1795.

84. See reprint of *Independent Chronicle* (Boston), Jan. 13, 1794, in *Hartford Gazette*, Jan. 16, 1794.

85. *Salem Gazette*, Jan. 14, 1794.

86. *Vermont Gazette* (Bennington), Feb. 7, 1794.

87. *Federal Gazette* (Philadelphia), Aug. 12, 1791.

88. Laura Mason, "The 'Bosom of Proof': Criminal Justice and the Renewal of Oral Culture during the French Revolution," *Journal of Modern History* 76 (Mar. 2004): 29–61.

89. In April 1793, six citations of French papers appeared in 190 issues of Federalist papers, while twelve appeared in 128 Republican newspaper issues. In January 1794, seven citations of French newspapers appeared in 130 Republican issues. Only four appeared in 352 Federalist issues.

90. These conclusions are based on an analysis of nine Republican newspapers and twenty-one Federalist newspapers published regularly over the period from 1793 to 1795, which are preserved in the America's Historical Newspapers database. It is adjusted for the number of issues each paper published during this period.

91. John B. Hench, ed., "Letters of John Fenno and John Ward Fenno, 1779–1800: Part 2: 1792–1800," *Proceedings of the American Antiquarian Society* 90, no. 1 (1980): 198–99.

92. *Weekly Advertiser of Reading*, Aug. 12, 1797.

93. See also "Characteristics of Opposition to Government," *Gazette of the United States* (Philadelphia), Apr. 4, 1797.

94. *Independent Chronicle* (Boston), Sept. 2, 1793.

95. "From the Virginia Chronicle, of May 11," *National Gazette* (Philadelphia), May 22, 1793. See also Boston heading, *Independent Chronicle* (Boston), Apr. 19, 1793.

96. Poughkeepsie heading, *Poughkeepsie Journal*, May 8, 1793.

97. Boston heading, *Independent Chronicle* (Boston), June 20, 1793.

98. New York heading, *Daily Advertiser* (New York), Aug. 16, 1786.

99. Boston heading, *New Hampshire Gazette* (Portsmouth), Feb. 10, 1795.

100. *Medley; or, Newbedford Marine Journal*, Oct. 31, 1794.

101. *Massachusetts Mercury* (Boston), Nov. 15, 1793; *Philadelphia Gazette*, Dec. 8, 1794.

102. The word "translated" and variants appears in the headings of 330 relevant news items from 1793 through 1795 in the America's Historical Newspapers database: 188 appear in 10,704 Federalist newspaper issues, and 142 in 4,465 Republican newspaper issues. Republican papers noted translations at approximately 1.81 times the rate of Federalist newspapers.

103. *New-York Journal*, Nov. 29, 1794.

104. *Diary; or, Woodfall's Register* (London), Jan. 4, 1793.

105. *Gazette of the United States* (Philadelphia), Mar. 13, 1793; *Providence Gazette*, Mar. 23, 1793; *Columbian Centinel* (Boston), Mar. 23, 1793; *Western Star* (Stockbridge, MA), Mar. 26, 1793; *Massachusetts Spy* (Worcester), Mar. 28, 1793.

106. *Dunlap's American Daily Advertiser* (Philadelphia), Mar. 8, 11, 1793.

107. *National Gazette* (Philadelphia), Mar. 27, 1793.

108. New-York heading, *New-York Daily Gazette*, July 16, 1794.

109. "Another Electioneering Lie Detected," *Aurora General Advertiser* (Philadelphia), Oct. 12, 1795.

110. "April 25," *Columbian Centinel* (Boston), May 3, 1794.

111. "Communication," *Western Star* (Stockbridge, MA), May 29, 1797.

112. Peter Van Schaack to Loring Andrews, Feb. 5, 1794; Henry Van Schaack to Loring Andrews, ca. Mar. 1799, both in folder 1, box 1, Henry Van Schaack Letters, 1793–1799, Massachusetts Historical Society, Boston.

113. See Stanley M. Elkins and Eric McKitrick, *The Age of Federalism* (New York, 1993), ch. 9; Gordon S. Wood, *Empire of Liberty: A History of the Early Republic* (New York, 2009), ch. 5.

114. "For the United States Chronicle," *United States Chronicle* (Providence, RI), Aug. 15, 1793.

Chapter 8 · Unmaking the Revolutionary Caribbean

1. For historical background on the painting, see Laurence Brown, "Visions of Violence in the Haitian Revolution," *Atlantic Studies* 13, no. 1 (2016): 146.

2. Robin Blackburn, "Haiti, Slavery, and the Age of the Democratic Revolution," *William and Mary Quarterly* 63 (2006): 643–74; Nick Nesbitt, *Universal Emancipation: The Haitian Revolution and the Radical Enlightenment* (Charlottesville, VA, 2008).

3. Michel-Rolph Trouillot, *Silencing the Past: Power and the Production of History* (Boston, 1995), ch. 4.

4. In his perceptive study of the Haitian Revolution and Philadelphia, James Dun, drawing on Trouillot, emphasized the complex relationship between narrative-making and commercially driven information. He focused on Philadelphians' knowledge of events in Saint

Domingue, rather than absences in information flows. Yet, I argue, compared to contemporaneous news about the French Revolution, news from the revolutionary Caribbean was flattened and scant. James Alexander Dun, *Dangerous Neighbors: Making the Haitian Revolution in Early America* (Philadelphia, 2016).

5. Laurent Dubois, *Avengers of the New World: The Story of the Haitian Revolution* (Cambridge, MA, 2004), chs. 4–5.

6. William S. Cormack, *Patriots, Royalists, and Terrorists in the West Indies: The French Revolution in Martinique and Guadeloupe, 1789–1802* (Toronto, 2019), chs. 3–5.

7. Marie-Antoinette Menier and Gabriel Debien, "Journaux de Saint-Domingue," *Revue d'histoire des colonies* 36, nos. 127–28 (1949): 424–75.

8. John A. Lent, "Oldest Existing Commonwealth Caribbean Newspapers," *Caribbean Quarterly* 22 (Dec. 1976): 90–106; Howard S. Pactor, *Colonial British Caribbean Newspapers: A Bibliography and Directory* (Westport, CT, 1990).

9. Jeremy D. Popkin, "A Colonial Media Revolution: The Press in Saint-Domingue, 1789–1793," *Americas* 75 (Jan. 2018): 6.

10. Julius S. Scott, *The Common Wind: Afro-American Currents in the Age of the Haitian Revolution* (London, 2018), 129.

11. "From a Late St. Domingo Paper," *Dunlap's American Daily Advertiser* (Philadelphia), Aug. 4, 1791.

12. "From Le Gazette du Jour," *Daily Gazette* (New York), Dec. 27, 1790.

13. "Extracts from La Gazette du Jour," *Pennsylvania Mercury* (Philadelphia), Jan. 4, 1791.

14. Dubuisson had some connections with Philadelphia's print culture. A footnote in an account of the provincial assembly's decree, apparently inserted by New York *Daily Gazette* printer Archibald McLean, noted that Dubuisson printed his paper "with American types" and that it was staffed with "American workmen, which the Editor engaged some time ago at Philadelphia." "From Le Gazette du Jour," *Daily Gazette* (New York), Dec. 27, 1790. Indeed, an ad in August 1790 placed in a Philadelphia newspaper asked for five or six journeymen printers who could speak French and directed readers to "J. Dubuisson." *Federal Gazette* (Philadelphia), Aug. 14, 1790.

15. "Cape Francois, 3d November," *Daily Gazette* (New York), Dec. 27, 1790.

16. Popkin, "Colonial Media Revolution," 7.

17. Cormack, *Patriots, Royalists, and Terrorists*, 105, 116.

18. John H. Coatsworth, "American Trade with European Colonies in the Caribbean and South America, 1790–1812," *William and Mary Quarterly* 24 (Apr. 1967): 245–46.

19. Cormack, *Patriots, Royalists, and Terrorists*, 66–67.

20. Charleston heading, *City Gazette* (Charleston, SC), Dec. 3, 1790.

21. Philadelphia heading, *General Advertiser* (Philadelphia), May 20, 1791.

22. Cormack, *Patriots, Royalists, and Terrorists*, 67, 71.

23. Martinique heading, *New-York Daily Gazette*, Apr. 30, 1790.

24. Boston heading, *Massachusetts Centinel* (Boston), Apr. 14, 1790. See also Thomas Cushing's description of the Martinique patriots as peaceful, committed, and generous. Salem heading, *Salem Gazette*, Nov. 23, 1790.

25. Dun, *Dangerous Neighbors*, 37.

26. Cormack, *Patriots, Royalists, and Terrorists*, 43–45, 81.

27. Ada Ferrer, *Freedom's Mirror: Cuba and Haiti in the Age of Revolution* (New York, 2014), 46.

28. Boston heading, *Independent Chronicle* (Boston), Nov. 27, 1789.

29. Paris heading, *Pennsylvania Packet* (Philadelphia), Mar. 2, 1790.

30. Philadelphia heading, *General Advertiser* (Philadelphia), July 20, 1791.

31. Philadelphia heading, *General Advertiser* (Philadelphia), Aug. 4, 1791. He appears to have been referring to a letter published in the *General Advertiser*, July 30, 1791.

32. Dun, *Dangerous Neighbors*, 27–29.

33. The exact figures for the Haitian Revolution are 116 total news items, including 25 foreign newspaper reprints, 44 letters, and 42 oral reports. For revolutionary France, there were 978 total news items, including 691 foreign newspaper accounts, 172 letters, and 51 oral reports. Some material on both topics was taken from other North American newspapers. Those reprints are not included in these tabulations because their origin is sometimes obscure.

34. David Barry Gaspar and David Geggus, eds., *A Turbulent Time: The French Revolution and the Greater Caribbean* (Bloomington, IN, 1997), 47–48.

35. Beverley A. Steele, *Grenada: A History of Its People* (Oxford, 2003), 109–10, 120–21.

36. Gaspar and Geggus, *Turbulent Time*, 21.

37. David Patrick Geggus, "Slave Resistance in the Spanish Caribbean in the Mid-1790s," in Gaspar and Geggus, *Turbulent Time*, 7–10, 135–36; Laurent Dubois, *A Colony of Citizens: Revolution and Emancipation in the French Caribbean* (Chapel Hill, NC, 2004), ch. 3.

38. In Martinique, the British published the *Martinico Gazette* by 1795, though it is unclear how long this newspaper lasted during their eight-year occupation of the island. See reprint in "From the Martinico Gazette of March 18," *American Minerva* (New York), Apr. 10, 1795. By the middle of the decade, the only other newspapers published in the Windward Islands were the resolutely pro-British *Barbados Mercury* and another (name unknown) briefly published by the British in Saint Vincent. Gaspar and Geggus, *Turbulent Time*, 24.

39. On Philadelphia's role in continental news distribution, see Dun, *Dangerous Neighbors*, 11–12.

40. *Aurora General Advertiser* (Philadelphia), May 13, 1795.

41. George Brizan, *Grenada, Island of Conflict: From Amerindians to People's Revolution, 1498–1979* (London, 1984), 49–52.

42. Kit Candlin, *The Last Caribbean Frontier, 1795–1815* (New York, 2012), 15–17.

43. Michael Duffy, *Soldiers, Sugar, and Seapower: The British Expeditions to the West Indies and the War against Revolutionary France* (Oxford, 1987), 145.

44. Paul Friedland, "Every Island Is Not Haiti: The French Revolution in the Windward Islands," in *Rethinking the Age of Revolutions: France and the Birth of the Modern World*, ed. David A. Bell and Yair Mintzker (New York, 2018), 67–69.

45. "From a Paper Printed at St. Vincent, the 30th of March," *American Minerva* (New York), July 17, 1795. It is unclear in what newspaper this report originated. Bibliographers have not noted the existence of a British paper in Saint Vincent in 1795. Lent dates the earliest paper there to 1817. Lent, "Oldest Existing Commonwealth Caribbean Newspapers," 105.

46. "St. George's (Grenada), February 5," *Georgia Gazette* (Savannah), Mar. 17, 1796; Portland heading, *Eastern Herald* (Portland, MA), June 6, 1796.

47. See Tanguy's reference to the "well known character" of Captain Trusdel. Philadelphia heading, *American Star* (Philadelphia), Mar. 13, 1794.

48. "Extract of a Letter from a Merchant in Baltimore to His Friend in This City, Dated April 4," *Aurora General Advertiser* (Philadelphia), Apr. 10, 1795.

49. Julius Scott has offered a different interpretation, emphasizing the "vivid and detailed reports" from ship captains. Scott, *Common Wind*, 139.

50. For an example of intelligence deriving from a coffee shop, see "Grenada Taken," *Gazette of the United States* (Philadelphia), Apr. 2, 1795. For a ship captain relying on a merchant's news, see *Windham Herald*, Apr. 4, 1795.

51. Portsmouth heading, "Grenada," *Courier of New Hampshire* (Concord), May 9, 1795.

52. Boston heading, "The West-Indies," *Mercury* (Boston), May 5, 1795.

53. Boston heading, "From Grenada, April 14," *Mercury* (Boston), May 8, 1795.

54. *American Star* (Philadelphia), Apr. 1, 1794.

55. "The Courier Francois of This Morning Contains the Following Intelligence," *Gazette of the United States* (Philadelphia), July 16, 1796.

56. Scott, *Common Wind*, 64–75, 77, 195–98.

57. *The Revised Code of the Laws of Virginia: Being a Collection of All Such Acts of the General Assembly, of a Public and Permanent Nature, as Are Now in Force, with a General Index* (Richmond, VA, 1819), 1:555.

58. Alan Taylor, *The Internal Enemy: Slavery and War in Virginia, 1772–1832* (New York, 2013).

59. George D. Terry, "South Carolina's First Negro Seaman's Acts, 1793–1803," *Proceedings of the South Carolina Historical Association* (1980): 83.

60. Douglas R. Egerton, *Gabriel's Rebellion: The Virginia Slave Conspiracies of 1800 and 1802* (Chapel Hill, NC, 1993).

61. Scott, *Common Wind*, 200.

62. Miranda Fricker, *Epistemic Injustice: Power and the Ethics of Knowing* (Oxford, 2007), ch. 1.

63. "Fresh News from St. Domingo," *American Star* (Philadelphia), Feb. 4, 1794.

64. Ashli White, *Encountering Revolution: Haiti and the Making of the Early Republic* (Baltimore, 2010).

65. Scott, *Common Wind*, 162.

66. Philadelphia heading, "Conflagration of Cape-Francois," *General Advertiser* (Philadelphia), July 9, 1793.

67. Philadelphia heading, *Dunlap's American Daily Advertiser* (Philadelphia), July 8, 1793.

68. Samuel Cary Jr. to Samuel Cary Sr., Nov. 18, 1795, folder: Cary Family 1795, box 1, Cary Family Papers, 1789–1883, Massachusetts Historical Society, Boston.

69. Samuel Cary Jr. to Samuel Cary Sr., May 2, 1796, folder: Cary Family 1796, box 1, Cary Family Papers, 1789–1883, Massachusetts Historical Society, Boston.

70. Samuel Cary Sr. to Samuel Cary Jr., July 1, 1795, folder: Cary Family 1795, Cary Family Papers, 1789–1883, Massachusetts Historical Society, Boston.

71. Sarah Cary to Samuel Cary Jr., Nov. 13, 1795, folder: 1795–1796, box 2, Cary Family Papers III, 1769–1919, Massachusetts Historical Society, Boston.

72. Samuel Cary Sr. to Samuel Cary Jr., Sept. 14, 1795, folder: Cary Family 1795, box 1, Cary Family Papers, 1789–1883, Massachusetts Historical Society, Boston.

73. Philadelphia heading, "Extract of a Letter Received per Captain Green," *Aurora General Advertiser* (Philadelphia), Apr. 20, 1795; "Extract of a Letter from Martinico," *Herald* (New York), Apr. 11, 1795.

74. Portsmouth heading, *New Hampshire Gazette* (Portsmouth), Apr. 14, 1795.

75. *Dunlap and Claypoole's American Daily Advertiser* (Philadelphia), June 17, 1794.

76. "St. Domingo: Interesting Information to the Mercantile Interest," *General Advertiser* (Philadelphia), July 30, 1793.

77. *Mercury* (Boston), Apr. 24, 1795.

78. Newfield heading, *American Telegraphe* (Bridgeport, CT), Apr. 29, 1795. See also "Extract from the New-London Marine List," *Windham Herald*, May 2, 1795.

79. "Extract of a Letter from Antigua Dated 11th of March to a Gentleman in This City," *American Minerva* (New York), Mar. 31, 1795; "French Attack on Grenada," *Daily Advertiser* (New York), Mar. 31, 1795; *Federal Intelligencer* (Baltimore), Mar. 31, 1795; "Charleston," *City Gazette* (Charleston, SC), Apr. 2, 1795; "New-London," *Connecticut Gazette* (New London), Apr. 2, 1795.

80. "Norfolk, April 8, Island of Grenada," *Daily Advertiser* (New York), Apr. 18, 1795.

81. "From the *Martinico Gazette*, of March 18," *Aurora General Advertiser* (Philadelphia), Apr. 14, 1795.

82. Boston heading, "Saint Lucia," *Columbian Centinel* (Boston), Apr. 8, 1795.

83. Untitled document, May 30, 1795, folder: Cary Family, box 1, Cary Family Papers, 1789–1883, Massachusetts Historical Society, Boston.

84. "Extract of a Letter from Grenada," *Aurora General Advertiser* (Philadelphia), June 10, 1796.

85. Boston heading, *Columbian Centinel* (Boston), Apr. 15, 1795; "Post News, Halifax, April 21," *Columbian Centinel* (Boston), May 13, 1795; "Extract of a Letter to a Merchant in This City, Dated St. Pierre, Martinico, 6th April, 1795," *Herald* (New York), May 13, 1795; Alexandria heading, "From Bermuda, Nov. 7," *Aurora General Advertiser* (Philadelphia), Dec. 7, 1795.

86. "From the Barbados Mercury Received by the Schooner Betsey Arrived at the Fort Yesterday from Barbados," *Gazette of the United States* (Philadelphia), July 22, 1795.

87. Baltimore heading, *Federal Intelligencer* (Baltimore), Apr. 23, 1795.

88. Baltimore heading, *Aurora General Advertiser* (Philadelphia), Apr. 27, 1795.

89. "A Merchant of This City Has Favoured the Editor of the Philadelphia Gazette with the Following Decree," *Philadelphia Gazette*, May 26, 1795.

90. "From French Papers, Translated for the Aurora," *Aurora General Advertiser* (Philadelphia), Nov. 11, 1795.

91. Rutland heading, *Rutland Herald*, May 4, 1795.

92. Menier and Debien, "Journaux de Saint-Domingue," 470–73.

93. Gordon S. Brown, *Toussaint's Clause: The Founding Fathers and the Haitian Revolution* (Jackson, MS, 2005), ch. 8, quote on 99.

94. Brown, *Toussaint's Clause*, ch. 7; Dun, *Dangerous Neighbors*, ch. 5.

95. New York heading, *New-Hampshire Sentinel* (Keene), July 13, 1799.

96. Philadelphia heading, *Aurora General Advertiser* (Philadelphia), Aug. 8, 1799.

97. Philadelphia heading, *Philadelphia Gazette*, Aug. 8, 1799.

98. Philadelphia heading, *Aurora General Advertiser* (Philadelphia), Aug. 9, 1799; Philadelphia heading, *Philadelphia Gazette*, Aug. 7, 1799.

99. See, for example, "The Telegraph," *Telegraphe and Daily Advertiser* (Baltimore), Aug. 14, 1800; New York heading, *New-York Gazette*, Oct. 24, 1800; "The Philadelphia Gazette," *Philadelphia Gazette*, Aug. 13, 1801.

100. "Cape Francois," *Philadelphia Gazette*, Sept. 7, 1799. See also Philadelphia heading, *Philadelphia Gazette*, Mar. 13, 1801.

101. Baltimore heading, *Constitutional Diary* (Philadelphia), Jan. 25, 1800.

102. *National Intelligencer* (Washington, DC), Aug. 10, 1801.

103. "St. Domingo," *Philadelphia Gazette*, Aug. 17, 1801.

104. Boston heading, *Columbian Centinel* (Boston), Nov. 4, 1801. On Federalist responses, see Dun, *Dangerous Neighbors*, 185–86.

105. "St. Domingo," *Philadelphia Gazette*, Jan. 16, 1801. See also "Insurrections," *Columbian Centinel* (Boston), Jan. 24, 1801; Philadelphia heading, *Massachusetts Spy* (Worcester), Jan. 28, 1801.

106. Dun, *Dangerous Neighbors*, 180.

107. Baltimore heading, "Conflagration of the Cape!," *Commercial Advertiser* (New York), Mar. 8, 1802.

108. "From Poulson's Daily Advertiser," *Commercial Advertiser* (New York), Mar. 18, 1802.

109. "Extract of a Letter, Received by the Lydia . . . ," *Daily Advertiser* (New York), Mar. 19, 1802.

110. *Daily Advertiser* (New York), Mar. 26, 1802.

111. New York heading, *Daily Advertiser* (New York), May 21, 1802.

112. Philadelphia heading, *Aurora General Advertiser* (Philadelphia), June 9, 1802; Dun, *Dangerous Neighbors*, 187, 193.

113. New York heading, *Daily Advertiser* (New York), May 21, 1802.

114. "From Cape-Francois," *Commercial Advertiser* (New York), Mar. 22, 1802. See also "From the Gazette Officielle of St. Domingo, 25th August, 1802," *New-York Evening Post*, Sept. 18, 1802; "Translated for the American," *Federal Gazette* (Baltimore), July 20, 1802; *National Intelligencer* (Washington, DC), Oct. 20, 1802.

115. New York heading, *Daily Advertiser* (New York), July 23, 1802.

116. New York heading, *Daily Advertiser* (New York), Sept. 30, 1802.

117. Tim Mathewson, "Jefferson and the Nonrecognition of Haiti," *Proceedings of the American Philosophical Society* 140 (Mar. 1996): 31–32.

118. Dun, *Dangerous Neighbors*, 231.

119. "Free Negroes," *Recorder* (Richmond, VA), Nov. 10, 1802.

120. "Free Negroes."

Chapter 9 · The Fruits of Revolution

1. Rufus King to Timothy Pickering, Nov. 5, 1798, in *The Life and Correspondence of Rufus King*, ed. Charles R. King (New York, 1895), 2:457.

2. "Read This," *South-Carolina State-Gazette* (Charleston), Feb. 22, 1799.

3. Dedham heading, *Columbian Minerva* (Dedham, MA), Mar. 21, 1799.

4. "Another Account of the Tubs," *Commercial Advertiser* (New York), Mar. 16, 1799.

5. "Extract of a Letter from Charleston, South-Carolina, Dated February 22," *Newport Mercury*, Mar. 26, 1799.

6. Richmond heading, *City Gazette* (Charleston, SC), Mar. 23, 1799.

7. Donald H. Stewart, *The Opposition Press of the Federalist Period* (Albany, NY, 1969), 269; John C. Miller, *Crisis in Freedom: The Alien and Sedition Acts* (Boston, 1951), 149.

8. Timothy Pickering to John Adams, Mar. 19, 1799, Founders Online, National Archives, https://founders.archives.gov/documents/Adams/99-02-02-3384.

9. Stewart, *Opposition Press of the Federalist Period*, 326–27.

10. *Independent Chronicle* (Boston), May 2, 1799.

11. On the Federalists using the Alien and Sedition Acts as a partisan tool, see Leonard W. Levy, *Emergence of a Free Press* (New York, 1985), 280; Terri Diane Halperin, *The Alien and Sedition Acts of 1798: Testing the Constitution* (Baltimore, 2016), 69. On the Alien and Sedition Acts as attacks on dangerous ideas, see Miller, *Crisis in Freedom*, 74; Seth Cotlar, "The Federalists' Transatlantic Cultural Offensive of 1798 and the Moderation of American Democratic Discourse," in *Beyond the Founders: New Approaches to the Political History of the Early American Republic*, ed. Jeffrey L. Pasley, Andrew W. Robertson, and David W. Waldstreicher (Chapel Hill, NC, 2004), 277. See also a discussion of the historiography in Douglas Bradburn, "A Clamor in the Public Mind: Opposition to the Alien and Sedition Acts," *William and Mary Quarterly* 65 (July 2008): 595–600.

12. *Annals of Congress*, 6th Cong., 2nd sess., 956.

13. *Columbian Centinel* (Boston), Aug. 25, 1798.

14. William Linn, *A Discourse on National Sins* (New York, 1798), 23.

15. Alexander DeConde, *The Quasi-War: The Politics and Diplomacy of the Undeclared War with France, 1797–1801* (New York, 1966); Albert Hall Bowman, *The Struggle for Neutrality: Franco-American Diplomacy during the Federalist Era* (Knoxville, TN, 1974), ch. 13.

16. *Message of the President of the United States to Both Houses of Congress* (Philadelphia, 1798), 45.

17. *Independent Chronicle* (Boston), Apr. 16, 1798.

18. *Bee* (New London, CT), Apr. 18, 1798. See also *Independent Chronicle* (Boston), Apr. 16, 1798; *Farmers' Register* (Chambersburg, PA), Apr. 25, 1798; *Aurora General Advertiser* (Philadelphia), Apr. 9, 16, 20, 1798.

19. *Farmers' Register* (Chambersburg, PA), Apr. 25, 1798.

20. *Aurora General Advertiser* (Philadelphia), Apr. 9, 1798. See also Apr. 16, 20, 1798.

21. Thomas Jefferson to Edmund Pendleton, Jan. 29, 1799, Founders Online, National Archives. http://founders.archives.gov/documents/Jefferson/01-30-02-0458.

22. *Annals of Congress*, 5th Cong., 2nd sess., 1379.

23. Samuel Eliot Morison, *The Life and Letters of Harrison Gray Otis, Federalist, 1765–1848* (Boston, 1913), 1:89.

24. *Minerva* (New York), Apr. 19, 1798.

25. *Albany Centinel*, Mar. 16, 1798.

26. *Porcupine's Gazette* (Philadelphia), June 6, 1798.

27. Edward St. Loe Livermore, *An Oration, in Commemoration of the Dissolution of the Political Union between the United States of America and France* (Portsmouth, NH, 1799), 25; [William Austin], *A Selection of the Patriotic Addresses, to the President, of the United States, Together with the President's Answers* (Boston, 1798), 74.

28. *Time Piece* (New York), Apr. 18, 1798.

29. *Oriental Trumpet* (Portland, MA), Apr. 19, 1798.

30. *Spectator* (New York), Apr. 18, 1798.

31. *Commercial Advertiser* (New York), Apr. 14, 1798; *Eastern Herald* (Portland, MA), Apr. 30, 1798; *Springer's Weekly Oracle* (New London, CT), Apr. 21, 1798.

32. *Springer's Weekly Oracle* (New London, CT), Apr. 21, 1798.

33. *Alexandria Advertiser*, Apr. 20, 1798; *Western Star* (Stockbridge, MA), Apr. 23, 1798; *Eastern Herald* (Portland, MA), Apr. 23, 1798.

34. *Newburyport Herald and Country Gazette*, May 1, 1798.

35. *Independent Chronicle* (Boston), Apr. 16, 1798.

36. *Columbian Centinel* (Boston), Apr. 18, 1798. On the rivalry between the two newspapers, see John Bixler Hench, "The Newspaper in a Republic: Boston's 'Centinel' and 'Chronicle,' 1784–1801," PhD diss., Clark University, 1979.

37. *Aurora General Advertiser* (Philadelphia), June 16, 1798.

38. *Annals of Congress*, 5th Cong., 2nd sess., 1972.

39. *Spectator* (New York), June 23, 1798.

40. *Gazette* (Portland, MA), June 25, 1798.

41. *Gazette of the United States* (Philadelphia), June 19, 1798. See also "An American," *Gazette of the United States* (Philadelphia), June 16, 1798. The movement of Talleyrand's letters and the dispatches is confirmed by the *Federal Gazette* (Baltimore), June 20, 1798.

42. *Massachusetts Mercury* (Boston), June 22, 1798.

43. See Stephen Higginson to Timothy Pickering, Feb. 13, 1798, in "Letters of Stephen Higginson, 1783–1804," in *Annual Report of the American Historical Association for the Year 1896*, ed. J. Franklin Jameson (Washington, DC, 1897), 1:800.

44. *Porcupine's Gazette* (Philadelphia), June 22, 1798; *Federal Gazette* (Baltimore), June 21, 1798.

45. *Greenleaf's New York Journal*, June 23, 1798.

46. *Aurora General Advertiser* (Philadelphia), June 21, 1798; *Greenleaf's New York Journal*, June 23, 1798.

47. *Gazette of the United States* (Philadelphia), June 25, 1798.

48. Benjamin Franklin Bache, *Truth Will Out! The Foul Charges of the Tories against the Editor of the Aurora Repelled by Positive Proof and Plain Truth and His Base Calumniators Put to Shame* (Philadelphia, 1798).

49. William Cobbett, *The Detection of Bache* (Philadelphia, 1798).

50. *Aurora General Advertiser* (Philadelphia), June 16, 1798.

51. *Message of the President of the United States to Both Houses of Congress*, 45.

52. Augustus Pettibone, *An Oration, Pronounced at Norfolk, on the Anniversary of American Independence, Fourth of July, 1798* (Litchfield, CT, 1798), 11; *Annals of Congress*, 5th Cong., 2nd sess., 1482; Cobbett, *Detection of Bache*; *Gazette of the United States* (Philadelphia), Apr. 17, 1798; *Animadversions on James Holland's Strictures on Joseph Dicksons' Circular Letter, of the First of May 1800* (Lincolnton, NC, 1800), 13; *An Address to the Voters of Anne-Arundel and Prince-George's Counties, and City of Annapolis* (Annapolis, MD, 1798), 9.

53. *Annals of Congress*, 5th Cong., 2nd sess., 1485.

54. On "universal domination" or "universal dominion," see Livermore, *Oration*, 9; Alexander Addison, *An Infallible Cure for Political Blindness* (Richmond, VA, 1798), 18; Thomas Stearns Sparhawk, *An Oration, Delivered at Buckston* (Boston, 1798), 14; Josiah Crocker Shaw, *An Oration, Delivered July 4th, 1798* (Newport, RI, 1798), 17; Henry William De Saussure, *An Oration, Prepared, to Be Delivered in St. Phillip's Church* (Charleston, SC, 1798), 41; James Gould, *An Oration, Pronounced at Litchfield* (Litchfield, CT, 1798), 24; John Thayer, *A Discourse, Delivered, at the Roman Catholic Church in Boston* (Boston, 1798), 23; Jonathan Freeman, *A Sermon Delivered at New-Windsor and Bethlehem* (New Windsor, CT, 1799), 21.

55. Zechariah Lewis, *An Oration, on the Apparent, and the Real Political Situation of the United States* (New Haven, CT, 1799), 26.

56. Charleston heading, *Federal Gazette* (Baltimore), Oct. 15, 1798.

57. Lewis, *Oration*, 10–12. See also *Massachusetts Mercury* (Boston), June 22, 1798.

58. [Austin], *Selection of the Patriotic Addresses*, 148.

59. Jedidiah Morse, *The Present Situation of Other Nations of the World, Contrasted with Our Own* (Boston, 1795), 15.

60. Jedidiah Morse Jr. to Jedidiah Morse Sr., Oct. 11, 1792, folder: 1792 Oct., box 1; Jedidiah Morse to C. D. Ebeling, May 27, 1794, folder: 1794 Apr.–July; Harry Channing to Jedidiah Morse, Apr. 8, 1795, folder: 1795 Apr., box 2; Noah Webster to Jedidiah Morse, July 24, 1797, folder: 1797 July–Aug. 12, all in Morse Family Papers, Yale University Archives, New Haven, CT.

61. Gary Nash, "The American Clergy and the French Revolution," *William and Mary Quarterly* 22 (1965): 399.

62. John Robison, *Proofs of a Conspiracy against All the Religions and Governments of Europe* (Philadelphia, 1798).

63. *Independent Chronicle* (Boston), June 18, 1798.

64. A letter from John Erskine in early 1797 referenced "a society . . . created first under the name of the Illuminati" in a discussion about the religious state of Europe. John Erskine to Jedidiah Morse, Jan. 27, 1797, folder: 1797 Jan., box 2, Morse Family Papers, Yale University Archives, New Haven, CT.

65. Robison, *Proofs of a Conspiracy*, 237.

66. Jedidiah Morse, *A Sermon, Delivered at the New North Church in Boston* (Boston, 1798), 21, 13.

67. The only monograph on the Illuminati scare remains Vernon Stauffer, *New England and the Bavarian Illuminati* (1918; rpt., Woodbridge, NJ, 2005). Notably, this panic spread outside New England; see Jacob Mountain, *A Sermon, Preached at Quebec, on Thursday, January 10th, 1799* (Quebec, 1799), 14–15, 22–23.

68. Jedidiah Morse to Oliver Wolcott, May 21, 1798, quoted in Stauffer, *New England and the Bavarian Illuminati*, 207.

69. Jedidiah Morse, *A Sermon, Exhibiting the Present Dangers, and Consequent Duties of the Citizens of the United States of America* (Boston, 1799), 17.

70. Jedidiah Morse, *A Sermon, Preached at Charlestown, November 29, 1798* (Boston, 1798), 32. See also John Cotton Smith, *Oration, Pronounced at Sharon, on the Anniversary of American Independence* (Litchfield, CT, 1798); Livermore, *Oration*, 5–6, 8, 26.

71. On Morse, the Illuminati, and information politics, see Jordan E. Taylor, "The Literati and the Illuminati: Atlantic Knowledge Networks and Augustin Barruel's Conspiracy Theories in the United States, 1794–1800," *Mémoires du livre / Studies in Book Culture* 11 (Autumn 2019), https://www.erudit.org/en/journals/memoires/2019-v11-n1-memoires05099/1066939ar/. On the Illuminati scare as irrational, see Richard Hofstadter, *The Paranoid Style in American Politics and Other Essays* (1952; rpt., Cambridge, 1996), 10–14.

72. Morse, *A Sermon, Preached at Charlestown*, 12, 14.

73. *Porcupine's Gazette* (Philadelphia), May 18, 1798.

74. Smith, *Oration, Pronounced at Sharon*, 9. See also *Cicero; or, A Discovery of a Clan of Conspirators against All Religions and Governments in the Whole World* (Baltimore, 1799), 23.

75. William Brown, *An Oration, Spoken at Hartford in the State of Connecticut* (Hartford, CT, 1799), 5–6, 8.

76. Elijah Parish, *An Oration Delivered at Byfield* (Newburyport, MA, 1799), 7.

77. [Austin], *Selection of the Patriotic Addresses*, 66–67, 169, 9–10, 46, 73, 107, 148, iii–iv.

78. Thomas M. Ray, "'Not One Cent for Tribute': The Public Addresses and American Popular Reaction to the XYZ Affair, 1798–1799," *Journal of the Early Republic* 3 (Winter 1983): 393–99.

79. [Austin], *Selection of the Patriotic Addresses*, 59–60, 115.

80. Cotlar, *Tom Paine's America*, 107–8; Bradburn, "Clamor in the Public Mind," 566.

81. "For the Aurora," *Aurora General Advertiser* (Philadelphia), May 8, 1798.

82. Addison, *Infallible Cure for Political Blindness*, 31.

83. Stephen Higginson to Timothy Pickering, June 9, 1798, in "Letters of Stephen Higginson 1783–1804," 808.

84. [Austin], *Selection of the Patriotic Addresses*, 224.

85. Larry Eldridge, *A Distant Heritage: The Growth of Free Speech in Early America* (New York, 1994), 30–33.

86. "Jefferson's Draft of a Constitution for Virginia," Founders Online, National Archives, http://founders.archives.gov/documents/Jefferson/01-06-02-0255-0004.

87. An Act for the Punishment of Certain Crimes against the United States, 1 Stat. 596.

88. *Annals of Congress*, 5th Cong., 2nd sess., 2094, 2098.

89. *Annals of Congress*, 5th Cong., 2nd sess., 2165.

90. Francis Wharton, *State Trials of the United States and Administrations of Washington and Adams with Historical and Professional and Preliminary Notes on the Politics of the Times* (Philadelphia, 1849), 663–66.

91. *Annals of Congress*, 5th Cong., 2nd sess., 2162.

92. James Morton Smith, *Freedom's Fetters: The Alien and Sedition Laws and American Civil Liberties* (Ithaca, NY, 1956), 185.

93. Henry Cabot Lodge, *Studies in History* (Boston, 1884), 201.

94. "French Art, Impudence, and Villainy," *Salem Gazette*, Aug. 28, 1798. See also "Quellque Chose," *Massachusetts Mercury* (Boston), Aug. 31, 1798.

95. "Foreign Intelligence," *Columbian Centinel* (Boston), Aug. 1, 1798.

96. Boston heading, *Columbian Centinel* (Boston), Aug. 25, 1798.

97. James Tagg, *Benjamin Franklin Bache and the Philadelphia "Aurora"* (Philadelphia, 1991), 387–89.

98. Wharton, *State Trials of the United States*, 333–34.

99. Joel Barlow, *Copy of a Letter from an American Diplomatic Character in France, to a Member of Congress in Philadelphia* (Fairhaven, MA, 1798).

100. "Hampton, Sept. 7, 1798," *Rutland Herald*, Sept. 17, 1798; Albany heading, *Times and District of Columbia Daily Advertiser*, Oct. 8, 1798.

101. "Advertisement Extra," *Rutland Herald*, Dec. 3, 1798.

102. Wendell Bird, *Criminal Dissent: Prosecutions under the Alien and Sedition Acts of 1798* (Cambridge, MA, 2020), 114, 117.

103. *Annals of Congress*, 6th Cong., 2nd sess., 922, 929–30, 955–56.

104. Michael Durey, *Transatlantic Radicals and the Early American Republic* (Lawrence, KS, 1997), 250–51; *Annals of Congress*, 5th Cong., 2nd sess., 571.

105. Smith, *Freedom's Fetters*, ch. 9.

106. *Annals of Congress*, 6th Cong., 2nd sess., 946–47.

107. John Thomson, *The Letters of Curtius* (Richmond, VA, 1798), 18.

108. Levy, *Emergence of a Free Press*, 269–72.

109. Tunis Wortman, *A Treatise concerning Political Enquiry, and the Liberty of the Press* (New York, 1800), 16–18.

110. Wortman, *Treatise concerning Political Enquiry*, 26, 123, 149.

111. John Thomson, *An Enquiry, concerning the Liberty, and Licentiousness of the Press* (New York, 1801); George Hay, *An Essay on the Liberty of the Press* (Philadelphia, 1799).

112. Wortman, *Treatise concerning Political Enquiry*, 142. See also Thomson, *Enquiry*, 59.

113. Wortman, *Treatise concerning Political Enquiry*, ch. 14.

114. Richard Buel Jr., "Freedom of the Press in Revolutionary America," in *The Press and the American Revolution*, ed. Bernard Bailyn and John B. Hench (Worcester, MA, 1980), 91–92. See also Thomson, *Enquiry*, ch. 8.

115. Leonard W. Levy, "Liberty and the First Amendment: 1790–1800," *American Historical Review* 68 (Oct. 1971): 30–31; Levy, *Emergence of a Free Press*, 269–72.

116. Wortman, *Treatise concerning Political Enquiry*, 130.

Epilogue

1. *American Star* (Philadelphia), Jan. 30, 1794.

2. *American Star* (Philadelphia), Feb. 11, 1794.

3. Michael Schudson, *Discovering the News: A Social History of American Newspapers* (New York, 1978), 194.

4. Jean Baudrillard, *Simulacra and Simulation*, trans. Sheila Faria Glaser (Ann Arbor, MI, 1994).

5. Neil Postman, *Amusing Ourselves to Death: Public Discourse in the Age of Show Business* (New York, 1985).

6. "Word of the Year 2016," Oxford Dictionaries, https://languages.oup.com/word-of-the-year/2016/; Michiko Kakutani, *The Death of Truth: Notes on Falsehood in the Age of Trump* (New York, 2018); Jennifer Schuessler, "Jill Lepore's New Podcast Is a Murder Mystery: Who Killed Truth?," *New York Times*, May 13, 2020, https://www.nytimes.com/2020/05/13/arts/podcast-jill-lepore-last-archive.html.

7. *Rivington's New-York Gazetteer*, July 13, 1775.

8. *Rivington's New-York Gazetteer*, July 13, 1775.